STYLISTS ON STYLE

Pieter Brueghel, *Self-Portrait,* "The Painter and the Connoisseur" (Photo courtesy of the Fonds Albertina from the archives of the Austrian National Library)

Stylists on Style

A Handbook with Selections for Analysis

LOUIS T. MILIC The Cleveland State University

Charles Scribner's Sons · NEW YORK

A–10.69[V]

Printed in the United States of America
Library of Congress Catalog Card Number 76-84982

ACKNOWLEDGMENTS

On this and pages v and vi, which constitute an extension of the copyright page, acknowledgment is gratefully made to those publishers, agents, and individuals who have permitted the use of the following materials in copyright:

From *The ABC of Reading* by Ezra Pound. All Rights Reserved. Reprinted by permission of New Directions Publishing Corporation and Faber and Faber Ltd.

From *Against the American Grain* by Dwight MacDonald. © Copyright 1958 by Dwight MacDonald. Reprinted by permission of Random House, Inc. and Victor Gollancz, Ltd.

From *The American Language: Fourth Edition* by H. L. Mencken. Copyright 1936 and renewed 1963 by Alfred A. Knopf, Inc. Reprinted by permission.

From *Contemporaries* by Alfred Kazin. Copyright 1924, 1946, 1952, 1955, ©, 1956, 1957, 1958, 1959, 1960, 1961, 1962 by Alfred Kazin. Reprinted by permission of Atlantic-Little, Brown and Co.

From *Death in the Afternoon* by Ernest Hemingway. Copyright 1932 Charles Scribner's Sons; renewal copyright © 1960 Ernest Hemingway. Reprinted with the permission of Charles Scribner's Sons, Jonathan Cape Ltd, and The Executors of the Ernest Hemingway Estate.

From *The Elements of Style* by William Strunk, Jr., and E. B. White. © The Macmillan Company 1959. Reprinted with permission of The Macmillan Company.

From *Enemies of Promise* by Cyril Connolly. Copyright 1939 by Cyril Connolly. Reprinted by permission.

From *Essays, Speeches and Public Letters by William Faulkner,* edited by James B. Meriwether. Copyright 1953 by Estelle Faulkner and Jill Faulkner Summers. Reprinted by permission of Random House, Inc., Chatto and Windus Ltd, and the Author's Literary Estate.

"Essentials of Spontaneous Prose" by Jack Kerouac. Copyright © 1958 by Jack Kerouac. Reprinted by permission of The Sterling Lord Agency.

From *Explorations in Communication,* edited by Edmund Carpenter and Marshall McLuhan. Copyright © 1960 by the Beacon Press. Reprinted by permission of The Beacon Press.

From *From Virgil to Milton,* by C. M. Bowra. Reprinted by permission of St. Martin's Press, Inc., Macmillan & Co., Ltd.

From Lionel Trilling's Introduction to *The Adventures of Huckleberry Finn* by Mark Twain, Rinehart Edition. Introduction copyright 1948 by Lionel Trilling. Reprinted by permission of Holt, Rinehart and Winston, Inc., Publisher.

From *Lectures in America* by Gertrude Stein. Copyright 1935 and renewed 1962 by Alice B. Toklas. Reprinted by permission of Random House, Inc., David Higham Associates, Ltd., and the Executors of the Gertrude Stein Estate.

From "Cooper's Prose Style" in *Letters from the Earth* by Mark Twain, edited by Bernard DeVoto. Copyright 1946 by The Mark Twain Company. Originally published under the title "Fenimore Cooper's Further Literary Offenses." Reprinted by permission of Harper & Row, Publishers.

From "Lost in the Whichy Thicket: II" by Tom Wolfe. Copyright © 1965 World Journal Tribune, Inc. Reprinted by permission of Tom Wolfe, c/o Marvin Josephson Associates, Inc.

From *On the Contrary* by Mary McCarthy. Copyright © by Mary McCarthy. Reprinted with the permission of Farrar, Straus & Giroux, Inc. and William Heinemann Ltd. of London.

From *Oxford Addresses on Poetry* by Robert Graves. Copyright © 1962 by Robert Graves. Reprinted by permission of Collins-Knowlton-Wing, Inc., Robert Graves and Cassell & Co. Ltd.

From *The Peace of the Augustans* by George Saintsbury, published by Oxford University Press. Reprinted by permission of Oxford University Press, London.

From *Portraits from Life* by Ford Madox Ford. Reprinted by permission of Houghton Mifflin Company, publisher, and Janice Biala.

From *A Preface to Paradise Lost* by C. S. Lewis, published by Oxford University Press. Reprinted by permission of Oxford University Press, London.

From "The Sentimental Journey" in *The Second Common Reader* by Virginia Woolf, copyright, 1932 by Harcourt, Brace & World, Inc.; renewed, 1960 by Leonard Woolf. Reprinted by permission of Harcourt, Brace & World, Inc., Leonard Woolf, and the Hogarth Press Limited.

From "'Rhetoric' and Poetic Drama" in *Selected Essays* by T. S. Eliot, copyright 1932, by Harcourt, Brace & World, Inc.; copyright, 1960, by T. S. Eliot. Reprinted by permission of Harcourt, Brace & World, Inc. and Faber and Faber Ltd. publishers.

FOR PAMELA AND MY OTHER STUDENTS

. . . *ne pueros coram populo Medea trucidet*

TABLE OF CONTENTS

BRITISH AUTHORS—Synchronic Selections

AMERICAN AUTHORS

ANNOTATIONS

STYLISTS ON STYLE

INTRODUCTORY ESSAY

This book is an attempt to construct a handbook of stylistics, something that will provide between two covers what is needed to pursue the study of English prose style: theory, method, and practice. The book is based on the belief that there is such an entity as style despite the doubts that have sometimes been cast on its existence and the difficulty of defining it precisely.

The word *style* has meant many things during its history in English, which begins around the fourteenth century. It has meant variously a pointed stick or writing implement, writing or manner of writing and at last a manner of doing anything in general, which opens the door to almost any application (the style of a printed page, of a dog, or of an athlete). In literary contexts, the word is often used to mean the presence or absence of desirable qualities: "his writing has no style," "the substance of the novel is weak but it has style." Such absolute uses do not tell us much because the entity *style* is never defined. But even when the term is used to refer to the manner of writing rather than as a measure of quality, the uses are generally vague and slipshod. Such expressions as "Swift's style is lucid, sinewy and terse," "Milton's style reminds one of a mountain range," and "Gibbon's prose evokes the tread of the Roman legions" are merely impressionistic and bypass the realities of the writer's language. Unless *style* is applied to the accurate description of the details of language, its usefulness as a critical term will disappear.

Style might be described as that aspect of a piece of writing that we *perceive* but do not *observe,* what we respond to in writing without being aware of it. We observe the meaning, for that is the way our minds work, but we are hardly aware of the linguistic instrument unless we have misunderstood and gone back or unless we are rereading. If we concentrated our attention on the details of the form of a work, we would fail to take in the meaning. As writers or speakers, we cannot concern ourselves primarily with the details of the grammar or we find that we lose track of the ideas we intended to set forth. As readers, we operate in the same way. But as students of style we are required to give our main attention not to what is being said but to how it is conveyed.

This simple distinction between the *what* and the *how* is a thumbnail definition of style and it is one that every user of language acts on in practice. It is not, however, altogether satisfactory and it has more than once been challenged by aestheticians. Their argument is based on the claim that every form has its own particular meaning. This implies that there cannot be two ways of saying the same thing because each way says something different. Essentially, this would mean that there could not be any synonymous statements. The consequence of this reasoning is that two such entities as style and substance cannot exist and that the study of style is unnecessary and useless. Let us examine this claim.

It often happens to most writers or speakers that after they have formulated a thought in a certain set of words they do not find the formulation satisfactory and proceed to reword. In so doing, they believe that they are saying the same thing in different words. A number of phrases attest to this: "in other words," "to put it another way," "let me say it this way. . . ." According to the proponents of an organic (or unitary) theory of content and form, these are not rewordings but different meanings. An illustration may clarify these distinctions.

The first sentence from the Ezra POUND selection (No. 87) reads: "Literature does not exist in a vacuum." Superficially, this seems to be easy enough to understand. Actually, it is not literally clear inasmuch as literature is not a thing and the vacuum is only figurative. We may suppose that Pound meant that literature is not written without some concern with things outside of literature. He might then have said something like "Literature must be concerned with things outside itself." But he chose not to do so. Instead, he went on to explain the meaning of the first sentence by beginning the next one as follows: "Writers as such have a definite social function. . . ." This sequence suggests that he might have saved himself the extra labor by saying right off "Literature has a social function." That he selected the rather hackneyed metaphor of the vacuum probably means, not that he wished to say something different, but that he preferred the effect of one over the other. Like Robert GRAVES (No. 1), whose first sentence begins "Dedicated poets cannot exist in a vacuum," he seemed to feel that the vacuum made the thought more expressive. Graves also found it necessary to explain the vacuum image, by adding "discarding all tradition, all knowledge, rejecting society."

Clearly, these suggested alternatives are not all identical, but they would be accepted by most readers of English as roughly synonymous, as reasonable paraphrases of each other. The difference among them is not in the content but in the effect on the reader. If it is conceded that these stylistic changes are really changes of meaning, it then becomes necessary to distinguish between two kinds of meaning: *referential* or *cognitive* meaning, which denotes the substance of what is being said (the difference between "Literature cannot exist in a vacuum" and "People cannot exist in a vacuum"); and *affective* or *expressive* meaning, which refers to the means for producing different effects on the reader (the difference between "Literature cannot exist in a vacuum" and "Writers must be concerned with society"). In effect, the distinction between these two kinds of meaning reaffirms the separation of substance from style.

Theoretically, of course, the complete dichotomy between these two entities should not be insisted on. After all, we know too little about how the mind works with verbal images to be able to claim a theoretical understanding of the relation between thing, idea and word. But for practical purposes, the claim that style and substance are separate entities which can be kept apart for the purpose of analysis seems fully consistent with intuition and experience.

Since style is form and form in writing depends on language, it seems appropriate to consider in what respect the nature of language can help to clarify some of the problems of style. Much has been learned in recent years, especially during the decades since the war, about the complexity of natural language (i.e., English, as opposed to Esperanto and other synthetic languages), partly as a result of the work of the generative grammarians, partly from the efforts of the linguists who tried to make a reality of the concept of translation by the use of computers. Curiously enough, the most interesting discoveries have come from an unexpected source. Electrical engineers searching for ways to make communication channels more efficient were constrained to examine language from a new angle, as basically a code with certain characteristics which could be expressed quantitatively. The consequence of their findings has been to provide a new perspective on language and, by implication, on certain uses of language in the domain of rhetoric and style.

To begin with, in information theory (as the work of these engineers is called), the meaning of a message is inconsequential. A message is simply an arrangement of symbols which differs from every other possible arrangement. Thus a code of maximal efficiency would contain the number of messages which represented the largest possible variety of arrangements of its constituent symbols. Assume a set of two symbols (A,B) arranged in groups of three. The number of possible messages in this code would be eight (2x2x2): AAA, AAB, ABA, ABB, BAA, BAB, BBA, BBB. It is immaterial whether a message represents a numeral, a name, a word, a phrase, a sentence, or a paragraph. The potential message content of the code is eight.

The difficulty with such an efficient code is obvious. If one digit of the message is mis-sent, garbled in transmission or mis-read at the receiving end, the message received is different from the one intended. An error of this kind might have annoying consequences if one sent AAA, which meant "Come at once," and AAB was received, which meant "Arriving tomorrow." Such errors are rare in natural languages because a change of a single digit seldom does more than cause a typographical error. If English were built on the model of the code just described, the number of possible three-letter words would be 17,576 (26x26x26 or 26^3). But the actual number is not nearly so great. It is easier to think of three-letter combinations which do not form English words: CHQ, AVX, ZAK, APD, BGH, AKN, LMW. . . . One factor which works to reduce the number of actual possibilities in English is the requirement that at least one letter be a vowel, of which there are only five (or six). Then, certain letters do not combine with others (KQ, LJ, GD . . .), others are seldom found in initial position (X) or in final position (Q). These limitations, however they came about, make English spelling somewhat easier than it might be if English were a highly efficient code.

The efficient code is paradoxically more subject to error than the inefficient one because each digit carries more *information* than is true in a natural language. *Information* in this sense is a measure of the predictability of any single digit: the more unpredictable, the more information. In English, only the first letter of a word is totally unpredictable and therefore carries maximum information. Let us suppose the letter P. The second letter of the word is governed by the incompatibility of P with about half of the letters in the alphabet when it is in initial position (B, C, D, F, G, J, K, M, Q, V, W, X, Z). This process continues with increasing restriction as letters are added. By the time we have read half the letters in a word like *pandemonium,* we recognize the word, and the remaining letters provide us with little additional information. They merely confirm our estimate. We could make English more efficient by shortening such words to the necessary minimum for recognition. In fact, such a process exists for frequently-used long words: *hypo* (dermic), *exam* (ination), *log* (arithm). . . .

Let us apply these characteristics of English spelling to the three-digit code. By reducing the information conveyed by any single digit, we can protect the message against garbling caused by encoding, decoding, or transmission errors. Instead of forming the messages in the way previously described, let us increase the safety factor by modifying the structure of the message. Each message will now consist of A or B repeated three times. Thus the messages will be either AAA or BBB. The major consequence of this change is to reduce the possible number of messages from eight to two. In that sense, the code will have lost three-quarters of its efficiency since the same two messages could be conveyed by a single binary digit (A/B). The safety factor, however, will have been greatly increased. The message would still be meaningful even if one of the digits were incorrectly transmitted or received. If AAB or BBA were received, it could be interpreted as "meaning" AAA or BBB with a high probability of correctness. These forms could be considered as merely variant forms of the correct messages.

Reducing the number of possible messages from eight to two means reducing the information carried by each digit. The second and third digits merely repeat the information provided by the first. The significance of this modification in the direction of inefficiency is that it protects the message against loss. The protection is provided by making the message *redundant*: repeating the significant symbol. Redundancy in this context has nothing to do with the rhetorical vice of redundancy, which simply refers to an excess of words perhaps better called "prolixity." *Redundancy,* as it is used here, is the name of the process by which significant elements of the message are repeated. A redundant code contains fewer messages, carries less information, but it safeguards these messages and opens the door to the possibility of choice of expression, which is the basis of style in natural language. That is, the redundancy of a natural language means that not every change of form produces a different meaning. These differences make the choice of message and the choice of the form of the message different activities. The latter choice is the one associated with the concept of style, as we shall see if we make a further modification in our binary code.

Let us now suppose that the area in which the messages are used has two sections, say East and West. The East uses the AAA/BBB form, but the machines in the West cannot produce three identical digits in a row. Therefore, the Western code is modified to AAB/BBA. This variant, incidentally, serves to identify the origin of the sender as either in the East or West. But the amount of information in the two variant forms is the same. After a time, with changes in machines, both areas are capable of sending either message and the two sets of forms come to be used indifferently. *Cognitively,* the two variants are identical. *Affectively,* they differ because each will continue to retain some association with the place of its origin. Careful stylists in that limited language would use AAA if they wanted Eastern flavor and AAB if they wanted to seem Western.

As we have seen, the three-digit code actually carries only two messages, each of which has two variant forms. AAA is synonymous with AAB and BBA is synonymous with BBB. The difference between the two variants is not substantive but stylistic. Whether AAA is chosen or BBB depends on which message one wants to send. But whether AAA or AAB is sent is a choice based on form, the varying forms of two identical messages. The option is made possible by the high redundancy of the code achieved at the sacrifice of information. Despite its simplicity, this model parallels the structure of a natural language like English, which is highly redundant and consequently offers a variety of stylistic options to the user.

Although there is naturally a very considerable difference between a three-digit code containing two messages and a natural language like English, which contains a boundless number, the basic principle of their information structure is the same. Like the code, our language has a set of protective devices to prevent the loss or garbling of the message owing to transmission failures, inattention, fatigue, impediments of speech, typographical errors and the many other interferences which affect communication. The redundancy of English can be readily detected in the tendency of the words in any utterance to be predictable. Thus, anyone can easily foretell the last word in the following incomplete sentence: "I said hello and we shook—." In this particular case, the predictability (the measure of redundancy) is due most obviously to the association certain words have with each other. Such *collocations* are very common: *shake* and *hands* is one instance. When we find one of these words in an utterance, we know that there is a certain probability of finding the other. The two items are sometimes combined into a single unit (*handshake*) and one may even be left out because of its high predictability, as in "Let's shake on it," where the absence of the word *hands* causes no difficulty in understanding.

Collocation (the tendency of certain words to stick together) is not, however, the main instrument of redundancy in English. The grammatical system (syntax, inflection, parts of speech) is a complex network of redundant interrelationships. Each word and phrase dictates (or predicts) a number of later events in each sentence, so that the chance of a misreading becomes very low. Native speakers of a language are not usually aware how sophisticated and conservative the grammar is, in the sense that the grammar is a system of overlapping signals which preserves the message. Consider, for instance, the simple utterance, "John sees Jim." We decode the sentence by deciding that the subject is *John* and the object is *Jim* because the order of the words in English is normally subject-verb-object. This much we require or we would not be able to interpret the sentence correctly. If the order of the words is changed to "Jim sees John," we have a different sentence. In the absence of other clues, word order is a primary signalling-system in English.

Suppose, however, that the sentence had been "John sees the animals." In interpreting this sentence, we could acquire full understanding by relying on word order. But we have additional clues. *John* is singular and the verb form ending in *-s* can only agree with a singular subject; it cannot agree with the object, *the animals*. Thus, even if the word order were reversed, so that the sentence read "The animals sees John," we could still decode it properly. There are two means of analyzing this sentence: word order and inflection, only one of which is really necessary. The other is redundant. But this is not the limit of redundancy. We could rewrite the sentence in this way to incorporate yet another component of predictability, another signalling-system: "John talks to the animals." Not only the word order and the agreement between subject and verb, but the lexical compatibility between *John* and *talks* help us to interpret this sentence. Normally the verb *talk* requires a human subject (like *John* and unlike *the animals*). Therefore, even a thorough scrambling like "John the animals talks to," which destroys the word order system, would not destroy the message because of the remaining signals (inflection, lexical compatibility).

Even more extensive guidance is provided to the user of language by the *situational context,* the circumstance that in certain social frameworks some kinds of statements are more likely to be made than others. If you are introduced to someone at a very noisy party and the other person extends his hand and says something beginning with "How" but you do not hear the rest, the context indicates that he said "How do you do?" or "How are you?" or something similar. Under those circumstances no sane person would be likely to say "How do you feel about Brahms?" Akin to the situational context is the literary context, if we are interpreting a written message. The interpretation of a sentence like "Oft on the dappled turf at ease I sit, and play with similes" will depend on whether we take it to be part of a poem or some other literary form. We are accustomed to statements of this kind from poets but not from other writers. The narrowed range of interpretation provided by a knowledge of the literary context is also part of the signalling-system of the language. It should be evident from this sketch of the structure of the language that speaking or writing is not a random or free process but one which is governed by stringent limitations which work to keep language intelligible.

The language of an individual is also restricted. When a native speaker learns to use his own language, he does not actually learn the whole language. For instance, he never commands its entire vocabulary but only the part which is associated with his daily activity and his special interests, and which has developed from his reading and his education. Similarly, though he is generally able to interpret the entire range of syntactic patterns that the language affords, for some reason he seems to depend for his expressive needs on merely a selection from the available total. Most readers can understand Santayana's sentence, "How find happiness in peace, if we love danger," because of their latent mastery of English grammar. But only a very few writers have such a structure in their active repertories. Doubtless the fraction of the total syntax that an individual controls varies considerably between the poles of illiteracy and literary sophistication. Nonetheless, it is certain that to every single user of a language pertains his own *idiolect,* his peculiar and unique combination of vocabulary and syntax, which differs slightly or greatly from that of every other user. This unique combination of linguistic resources in the individual is the foundation of what we call his *style*.

A style is not necessarily a praiseworthy thing, in the sense of the expression "His writing has style." This laudatory sense of the term could profitably be abandoned because of its power to confuse. The style of a piece of writing is merely one of its properties. Every piece of writing has a style, the style of the writer. This may be pleasing or it may not be, but it is nonetheless his style.

Most writers have some ideal of style to which they try to conform. But the ideal is always a certain distance away from the real. And many a writer consequently struggles against the way that he cannot help writing. Critics have often been misled into confusing a writer's stated ideal of style with his actual performance, which may not match it at all. ORWELL, for example, commits some of the errors he censures in his essay (No. 3), and it is certain that he did not do so deliberately. How does it happen that the writer has such uncertain control over his medium?

The answer, to the extent that it is known, has to do with the process of language acquisition and of expression. The child learning his native language is exposed to a variety of linguistic stimuli (his parents, his playmates, his siblings, radio, television, records, books . . .) which form a uniquely different combination, separating him ever so slightly even from a brother or sister. Varying educational and social levels, amounts of exposure to language, different dialect areas, and other variables impose greater variation of idiolect. It is not surprising that people speak and write differently. It is more surprising that they have so much in common.

The child acquires language in uneven increments. He learns a great deal during the third year and again when he first goes to school. Later, there are other stages that mark considerable leaps in his control of language. In general, however, the curve of language learning describes a downward trend. The more he has learned about his language, the less he is able to change. The longer he speaks or writes, the more fixed become the patterns in his active repertory. The older he gets, in short, the less he can modify his style. The implications of this conclusion are of obvious importance for both students and teachers of composition. This progressive hardening or "set" of the style also helps to explain why the writer seems so much at the mercy of his medium.

A speaker of English in rapid conversation has scarcely any conscious control of the syntactic choices that he makes. He may consciously select certain significant lexical items and he may even pause in order to make a choice between syntactic alternatives if the matter is important to him or the conversion from idea to word especially difficult. But for the most part, the ready flow of conversation is dependent on the suppression of conscious thought about linguistic form. A transcript of an actual conversation reveals how greatly recorded speech or conversation differs from writing. Speech has indistinct sentence boundaries, patterns are begun but not completed; it is highly repetitive, with a great deal of structural framework and many asides. But the most striking aspect of speech is the meager range of syntactic variety. The same few patterns predominate. Whole strings of sentences begin with "But," "The point really is," "Don't you see," "Actually, one of the most important . . ." and similar openings. It is probable that a different, much more limited, part of the syntactic idiolect is drawn on in speaking than in writing.

The writer is subject to the same necessity as the speaker, that of keeping his attention on the substance. But the process of writing is about ten times slower, a factor which allows the writer to give more of his attention to the form of the composition. As a result, he can draw more effectively on his idiolect, use more of his resources than the speaker. Indeed, he can slow up the process to any rate he wishes. Some writers have claimed that they compose one word at a time and others that they frame a sentence completely in their minds before setting pen to paper. Still, these are anomalies which do not alter the fact that writing, like speaking, is a process which has a considerable degree of unconsciousness about it.

In one respect, the writer has a real advantage over the speaker: he can revise until he is satisfied with the form. Study of the manuscripts of novelists reveals successive layers of modification which often effect considerable alteration in the original draft, though some writers' alterations are self-cancelling in that they return to their original formulation after experimenting with alternatives. Revision in general offers the writer the opportunity to edit out unwanted repetitions, correct grammatical errors, substitute one word for another and improve syntax and logic. In addition, rhetorical features can be introduced into the composition or existing ones can be brightened, emphasized, made consistent, and otherwise realized.

These conditions of the writing process certainly do much to fortify the writer's hand and to make the written word a more satisfactory medium for the preservation of serious messages than the spoken word. The writer's greater range and his ability to revise his work do not, however, alter the essentially unconscious and therefore idiosyncratic nature of the processes of expression. The writer can only draw on his own idiolect, and he does so largely without thinking about it.

Style, as shown in the example of the three-digit code, is made possible by the availability of variant forms with synonymous content and is realized by a choice among these variant forms. But the concept of style as resulting from a conscious choice among clear-cut alternatives of expression must be qualified. The writer's choice is not really free. As we have seen, his stylistic options are limited by the resources of his idiolect (his active repertory of lexicon and syntax) and by the way this idiolect functions below the surface of his consciousness. Thus, though a writer may state his stylistic preferences, cultivate rhetorical choices he considers effective, or even pattern his style upon models, the essence of his expression, that which is inescapably unique to him, is governed by factors over which he has little control.

The stylistic uniqueness of certain famous writers has inspired the idea of a relationship between the writer's personality and his style best summed up in Buffon's aphorism "The style is the man." This is usually interpreted to mean that a writer's personality is somehow reflected in his style and that a careful examination of the style will uncover the man. Such attempts as have been made, following this reasoning, have not been very convincing. The conclusions reached are usually either circular or too general to be meaningful. Critics who do this sort of analysis usually begin with a knowledge of the author's biography and a hypothesis about his personality and then attempt to find evidence for their hypothesis in the writing. Such a procedure is scientifically worthless since the critic can usually manage to find the evidence he needs and can conveniently ignore what does not happen to fit. Even when the reasoning is not circular, the conclusions are expressed in terms so vague and general as to convey nothing specific. The novelist W. Somerset Maugham discussing the style of Matthew Arnold says that "it seems to express very clearly his character, slightly feminine, pettish, a little magisterial, cold, but redeemed by a wonderful grace, agility of thought and unfailing elegance." This is unsatisfactory both as a description of style and a description of personality, and it really tells us nothing about their relation. Yet it is quite typical of this kind of criticism.

If some formula existed by means of which we could equate certain stylistic traits with certain personality traits, it would be possible to feel some confidence in the connection between personality and style. If long sentences, for example, always meant undisciplined thinking, short ones arrogance, or complex ones subtlety, we would have something solid on which to base our estimates of the author's personality. But no such equation is possible because people who are not arrogant may write short sentences for a variety of reasons. They may have been exposed to English teachers who were fanatics about short sentences. Or they may simply articulate their thought in short units. The connection between personality and style may indeed be there but it awaits confirmation. At present, all we can really say is that a writer's style has certain characteristics; we cannot look beyond them to see into his soul.

To say that style is choice is merely to say that a writer decides what to say and how to say it. But it might be pointed out that when the writer exercises his stylistic options something else happens. As we have seen, every writer's style differs from everyone else's by virtue of the uniqueness of his idiolect. The idiolect, however, is merely a selection from the total language, as a given piece of writing or a person's conversational style is merely a selection from his idiolect. The idiolect is conveniently classified as a selection from the total language, but it might equally well be called a deviation from the norm. That is, assuming that there were a standard form of expression, any individual writer's particular mode of expression would deviate from this norm in the ways made possible by the resources of his idiolect. Of course, no one by definition uses this norm, since everyone deviates from it. Nonetheless, our recognition that someone's style is individual is an admission that it deviates from some expected norm. The stylistic options made available by the redundancy of the language to the writer deviating from the hypothetical norm are very extensive. Although they cannot be completely inventoried, they can be classified and illustrated.

A given sentence—for the present sketch is confined to that level—can be subjected to four kinds of changes. We may suppose, if we like, that the sentence in question is a norm and that the changes effected in it are deviations. Or we may simply think of it as a sentence that a writer has written and is now revising. In either case, there are only four possible options. He can *add, omit, transpose,* or *substitute.*

1. *Addition:* a word, phrase or clause is added ("The poem is complex" = "The poem is, I think, complex").

2. *Omission:* a word, phrase or clause is omitted ("The poem is very complex" = "The poem is complex").

3. *Transposition:* the elements are rearranged in different order ("On first reading, the poem is complex" = "The poem is complex on first reading").

4. *Substitution:* an element is replaced by another ("The poem is complex" = "The poem is complicated").

The *addition* option takes in a considerable stylistic territory. It covers such modifications as the insertion of adjectives before nouns, intensifiers before adjectives and adverbs (*very, quite, somewhat*), the doubling of items called **pleonasm** (*suppose and assume, give and devise, hale and hearty*), parenthetical asides like "I think" and "I guess." Addition also describes a number of the standard rhetorical figures, such as **polysyndeton** (repetition of the connective: "Ye observe days, and months, and times, and years"), and **anaphora** (repetition of the same word(s) at the beginning of successive clauses: "The voice of the Lord is powerful: the voice of the Lord is full of majesty: the voice of the

Lord shaketh the wilderness"). **Parallelism,** of which anaphora is one kind, is a general term describing almost any sort of repetition of syntactic or structural elements in a sentence. It is part of many rhetorical figures in which it normally acts to increase the number of words used. Similarly, the tendency to provide lists of illustrations (**seriation**) rather than individual instances could be included. There are many other ways to expand, augment, inflate, to add words, in short, but those described are representative.

Omission is clearly less important than *addition,* partly because added elements are more emphatic than deleted ones. For this reason, omission is involved in few rhetorical figures, though there are some, like **asyndeton** (omission of the connective: "I came, I saw, I conquered"). **Ellipsis** (leaving out duplicated parts of the structure) is a figure of omission. Transitional words (like *however, therefore, then*) can be omitted and so can intensifiers, qualifiers and modifying adjectives and adverbs.

With *transposition,* the stylistic opportunities are greater. Adjectives (and some adverbs) may occasionally be placed before or after the words they modify: "enough money," "money enough"; "beautiful house," "house beautiful." Adverbial phrases and clauses may often be placed initially or finally, sometimes even medially: "On first acquaintance, his writing seems charming and light," "His writing, on first acquaintance, seems charming and light," "His writing seems charming and light on first acquaintance." Sentence adverbs (*however, therefore*) may be placed almost anywhere in a sentence. Word order inversion is a major type of transposition. Placing the object before the subject ("This page he liked") or the subject after the verb for emphasis ("This epic wrote Milton") are permissible kinds of inversion. The most drastic kind of inversion is the periodic sentence, in which the grammatical structure of the sentence cannot be certainly identified until the end: "That he was not altogether free from literary hypocrisy, and that he sometimes spoke one thing and wrote another, cannot be denied."

Substitution, of course, provides the greatest range and number of options, to the extent that these options should be further subdivided into lexical, morphological, syntactic, and figurative (or rhetorical) classes. Lexical substitutions are the most familiar of all the stylistic options. Whether to say *stay* or *remain* (popular/learned), *paternal* or *fatherly* (Romance/Saxon), *chauffeur* or *driver* (foreign/native), *charming* or *cute* (standard/informal) involves the type of decision that writers are most aware of. Not only single words but expressions, idioms and even the use of clichés may be involved at the lexical level. This is the most obvious place to begin a stylistic investigation, because the phenomena are most visible and results are easy to achieve. But it is perhaps the least rewarding because generalizations about individual words, to be accurate, require a large word-mass and a great deal of tedious effort. Intuitions based on casual samples are likely to be misleading. This is due to the context-bound nature of vocabulary and to the statistical characteristics governing the frequency of lexical items. Morphological substitutions, on the other hand, are comparatively rare. They are limited to alternative forms of inflected words, such as *lit/lighted, dove/dived, has/hath, thou/you, loaded/laden.*

Syntactical substitutions are of many kinds and are probably central to the understanding of an author's stylistic personality. This is in part the result of their lack of visibility and of the essential insensitivity of both readers and writers to the formal aspects of the text, as opposed to the vocabulary which appears to be the substantive part of any communication. Such alternatives as active/passive ("He greeted me" = "I was greeted by him"), nominal/verbal ("After his arrival" = "After he arrived"), attributive/phrasal modifiers ("Ruskin's style" = "The style of Ruskin"), participle/finite verb ("After arriving, he spoke" = "After he arrived, he spoke"), participle/infinitive ("He liked reading the paper" = "He liked to read the paper"), and *that/which* typify some simple kinds of syntactical decisions. More complicated ones occur, for example, in connection with verb forms and large-scale sentence constructions.

Finally, the most difficult stylistic options to deal with are the figurative, especially those employing imagery. Simple figurative examples are negativization or **litotes** ("This is a good painting" = "This is not a bad painting"), **simile** ("The sun is gold-colored" = "The sun is like gold"), **personification** ("Great men smile with disdain" = "Grandeur smiles with disdain"), **hyperbole** ("There are many mistakes" = "There are a million mistakes").

More complicated figures, such as **metonymy** and **metaphor** involve substitution of more than one unit of the sentence and produce changes which verge on the substantive. For example, such metonymies as "he has a good arm" for "he throws well" and "he has a good ear" for "he reproduces speech accurately in writing" introduce the question of the extent to which the literal and the figurative statements say the "same thing." This is even more true of metaphors, even of such a relatively plain one as "my library was dukedom large enough." Such a statement can be reduced to a more literal level thus, "my library was a territory large enough," but that still has figurative elements in it. A more explicit rendering might be "I was satisfied to devote myself to study rather than to military or political conquest," yet even this does not include such additional information as the fact that the speaker is (or was) a duke. If the information were added in an introductory clause ("Though I am a duke . . ."), the rendering would be even that much longer than the original metaphor. This condensing quality of metaphors is one of the most puzzling features for the student of style bent on unravelling the complex of decisions which go to make it up. Another difficulty lies in their ambiguity, which is of course another means of condensing meaning. There is also the tendency of metaphors to mix with one another and to intertwine with the literal level. Despite these difficulties, the student of style is obligated to consider metaphoric substitutions as genuinely involved in the process of style.

The selection of stylistic options made by the writer is an internal process largely determined, as we have seen, by forces below consciousness. There is, nevertheless, a part of the process of composition which allows for conscious decision. If the unconscious component is called "stylistic option," this one might be named "rhetorical choice." It is this conscious use of the artifices of effective communication which is covered by the term *rhetoric*. Although the number of conscious choices is exceeded by the decisions which are determined by the writer's unconscious preferences, this rhetorical component is not a minor one. It is the realm in which the writer openly struggles with the problems of effectiveness and where he exerts his art.

In availing himself of the devices of rhetoric, the writer brings into play what he can command of objectivity about his work. He tries, as much as he can, to assess his writing as it will appear to someone else. He plays reader and critic to himself. The process continues to be dominated by habitual and unconscious preferences, but it is subject now to an awareness of the need to write effectively. Effectiveness in writing may be achieved in a number of ways but the most significant results depend on placing the proper emphasis on the significant parts of the message. *Rhetoric* might be defined as the use of proper means to secure needed emphasis. *Emphasis* is the key term and it stands in an illuminating relationship to the principles of information theory described earlier.

Information has been defined as roughly equivalent to unpredictability. The greater the number of possible items from which the second unit in a sequence is selected, whether the unit is a letter, syllable, word, phrase, or other combination, the lower the probability of our predicting its identity correctly and the greater the information it carries. That is a quantitative condition of codes. The human response to this characteristic of codes is another matter, less easily quantified, but nonetheless consistent and describable. The effect on the human nervous system, or on the mind, of dealing with redundant codes has probably been to establish certain patterns of expectation which govern our perceptions when we listen or read. We are conditioned to expect a certain norm or system of redundancy and to interpret messages at that level without extra efforts of attention. When the patterns of expectation built on that redundant norm are violated, when, that is, more information is conveyed to us than we expect, we respond by increased attention and interpret the additional information as added emphasis.

Consider the simple signalling-device used to arrange the members of a grammatical series (say nouns). Each item is usually followed by a comma and the last two items are joined by a conjunction (usually *and,* sometimes *or,* occasionally *but*) : e.g., "books, magazines, journals, and newspapers." As we read, we expect the series to continue until we reach the conjunction, which is a signal that the series is about to end. That is the normal procedure. There are two variations of it, both of which are more emphatic because they violate our normal expectations. If the writer omits the conjunction (a rhetorical device called **asyndeton**), the series seems to go on but ends abruptly, before we have received any signal that it is going to: "books, magazines, journals, newspapers." Because we expect the *and,* such a series has the effect of seeming to continue beyond its last member; it seems longer than it is and implies further items left unsaid. The other possibility is to insert the conjunction after every item but the last, thus: "books and magazines and journals and newspapers." In this case (**polysyndeton**), the violation of our expectations takes a different form. We are led to expect the series to end after the second item and when it does not we are at a loss. We simply continue to take in the items as they come along. Unlike the asyndetic series, however, which suggests an endless number of items, the polysyndetic series calls attention to the items themselves. Both of these violations of normal order and expectation operate by reducing the redundancy of the signalling system and, however simple the mechanism employed, they significantly increase emphasis. The same formulation adequately describes more complicated means of achieving emphasis: **anaphora, anacoluthon, syllepsis, parallelism, antithesis, irony**—the whole list of hard words borrowed from classical rhetoric.

Unfortunately the matter immediately becomes more complicated if, not a single sentence or device, but a whole discourse is examined. The human mind, it seems, quickly adjusts its expectations, or adapts its conditioning, to different norms. If a reader begins reading a work in which the writer makes emphatic use of short sentences, as Macaulay and Hemingway have done, he responds at first to these short sentences as disappointments of his expectation, that is to say., as means of emphasis. But after a short while of reading, scarcely predictable because it varies from person to person, he adjusts his norm so as to expect short sentences. Instead of remaining emphatic, they become part of the context and lose their rhetorical value. Short sentences then become part of the norm.

Any reader of Gibbon who has had his attention drawn to the periodic sentences, the nominal constructions, the balance and the parallels knows how quickly he becomes accustomed to them, indeed comes to expect them. Readers of Henry James have the same experience with the involuted syntax, the extensive asides, appositives and parentheses. The same is true of the shock value of certain four-letter vulgarisms freely used by some modern novelists. The shock fades as the vulgarity becomes part of the context. The characteristics of the style lose their prominence when they are neutralized by familiarity. This is true whether these characteristics are unconscious habits or conscious artifice. Not infrequently, of course, the artifice becomes a habit. The rhetorical choice becomes a stylistic option.

The writer intent on effectiveness must overcome this tendency toward the entropy of his style by recourse to conscious means which will disappoint his reader's new expectations. Having established a new norm for the reader, the writer must find ways to achieve emphasis by departing from his norm. If he has a certain range of variation in his sentence-length, for example, he must, when he wants something to be specially noticeable, introduce a series of short sentences, perhaps even fragments. If his vocabulary has been steadily casual, he can use some formal or learned terms. He must strive to remain to some extent unpredictable. If there is a secret of good writing, perhaps that is it. Because there is a limit to inventiveness, in a long work, repetition of emphasis eventually occurs and even the most startling deviations become assimilated into the norm. Perhaps that is why very long works of great merit are in short supply. It may be that the short piece (essay, short story, sermon) is the ideal. It does not tire us stylistically. This may also be why reading the complete works of any author in succession is seldom a good notion.

Ultimately, the student interested in style comes to the point where he wishes to try his hand and eye on an actual piece of prose. Let us assume that he is serious and sensible and not satisfied with the woolly generalities which make up much of the criticism of style, past or present. If he has been reading Dickens, he is not tempted to say that the prose is "hard, compact and unsparing." If he has been admiring Dryden's critical prose, he will not be satisfied with comparing it to "a cheerful English river." And if he has been impressed with Swift's command of English, he will not feel that he has contributed anything to the criticism of Swift's style by saying that it is *simple* or *masculine* or *lucid* or *muscular* or *clear*. Let us suppose that he is determined to provide a verifiable description and conclusions both justified and useful. How should he proceed?

If he has read a representative range of commentaries on style, he has noticed that they seldom provide much evidence for their conclusions. Some few selected examples usually preface extensive claims. In order to correct this imbalance it may occur to him to try a quantitative approach, that is, to count certain units in the author's language. This might not be a mistake, but such an approach must be carefully pursued because it is subject to a number of pitfalls which will be mentioned in their place.

In approaching style quantitatively, the student must first decide what to count. There are two paths he may follow. One, which derives from the work of the eminent European philologist Leo Spitzer, consists of reading the text to be analyzed until some recurrent stylistic features are observed. A count is then made of these. The alternative is to count any or all from a list of standard characteristics of style, some of which have been found of importance in describing certain writers. These include sentence-length, sentence construction, word-length distribution (in letters or syllables), parts of speech distribution, types and frequency of connectives or verb forms, and a number of other linguistic features. Possibly, even some likely measures may be devised to test complexity-simplicity, phrasal or clausal modification, nominal-verbal preference, etc. . . . Whatever is selected, some elementary precautions must be taken.

Quantitative results, to be worthwhile, must fulfill certain statistical requirements. The sample (the selection in which the count is made) must be large enough to be representative of the "population" (the writer's work). It must also be drawn so as to be typical, without bias. Assuming that the unit to be counted is sentence-length, as measured by number of words, it is obvious that a sample containing only a few sentences might not be at all representative. One scholar (see Sherman, Bibliography No. 21) found that 300 consecutive sentences would adequately represent a writer's corpus in the measurement of sentence-length. Possibly a smaller sample would be equally trustworthy, but it would have to be selected in such a way as to exclude bias. Selecting a sample so as to prove a particular point tends to produce bias. One way to avoid bias is to select pages from the numbers on a random number table. Another is to take a "stratified" sample: the first, or second or last sentence on every third or tenth page, for instance.

Aside from proper sampling, the student must have a standard of reference. If Writer A has a sentence-length of 20.5, this information is useless unless we know that his contemporaries had an average of 30 and Writer B of 25.5, let us say. Numerical values are meaningless except by comparison. This implies that any quantitative study must be made of several authors at once or against a background of available data. The comparison of values with each other is not simply a matter of deciding that one is bigger than another and therefore different. Figures that look the same may do so as the result of chance; figures that look different may merely be the product of random variation. The only security in deciding whether differences are meaningful lies in the application of tests of statistical significance. Such tests are conveniently described in any statistics primer (e.g., M. J. Moroney, *Facts from Figures,* Penguin Books, 1951).

Because all statements about style are essentially quantitative, in that they state that a given writer's style is marked by much, little, or no use of a particular device, an understanding of this approach is important in stylistics. For the beginner, however, counting is likely to be excessively laborious, unless he is also a computer programmer. Moreover, though he may find counting to be the simplest kind of stylistic activity, the results may not be as rewarding as if he occupied himself with something more directly connected with the stylistic process.

Better than the purely quantitative approach for the novice is a method of analysis which permits him to grasp immediately the choices that the writer has made, so that he may concern himself with the overall pattern of the writer's style, the reasons behind his conscious decisions, and their effectiveness. To be able to do this, ideally it would be necessary to know what the writer had intended to say and then to compare this with what he actually said, noting the stylistic options and the rhetorical choices he made. Naturally, there is no way to know what he intended to say or had in mind and we do not know what sort of medium such an intention would be in, whether words, images, ideas, or electrochemical traces. The closest we can come is to create an artificial and simplified form of each sentence and compare it with the actual sentence. This process is here called Propositional Reduction and will now be described.

Propositional Reduction consists of taking each Text Sentence and reducing it to a Proposition. The Proposition is the basic minimum form of the Text Sentence, stripped of all its recognizable stylistic adornment. Of course, this cannot be literally performed, since every sentence bears the style of its author. But certainly the more visible rhetorical features can be stripped away. The Proposition can be described as the cognitive content of the Text Sentence with the affective aspect deleted. The Proposition is seen then as the raw material from which Text Sentences are produced. Every Proposition can generate a limitless number of such sentences or stylistic variants. And the Proposition is itself one form of these possible variants.

The instructions for Propositional Reduction are simply stated.

1. Each sentence yields one proposition. No sentence is left out and none subdivided.
2. Word order is restored to normal if inversion occurs.
3. All connective links are omitted and all pronouns and similar words which refer to items in other sentences are replaced by their referents.
4. Subordinate ideas and non-essential modifiers are deleted.

5. Figurative language is replaced by literal equivalents.
6. The diction is made neutral and commonplace.
7. Normal ellipsis is used: repetition within a given proposition should be avoided.
8. Quotations are omitted or preserved but not paraphrased.
9. Statements disguised as questions are reworded as declaratives.

When this process is concluded, the Proposition is often found to be shorter, more direct and easier to understand than the Text Sentence. If the Text Sentence contains a number of pronouns and other substitution words, the Proposition may be longer. Naturally, certain kinds of decisions, such as those involving the subordination of one idea to another and the interpretation of subtle and complex utterances, carry a certain risk that the Proposition will not cognitively match the Text Sentence. Nonetheless, the process is recommended to the student of style. It forces him to deal in the details of the style and to become aware of the thought behind the statement. At the same time, it permits him to form a sense for the kinds of options that a writer prefers, with the consequence that a stylistic personality emerges from the writing.

To illustrate the process, let us reduce a paragraph from Ezra POUND (No. 87) to propositions. Here is the paragraph:

> [1.] Good writers are those who keep the language efficient. [2.] That is to say, keep it accurate, keep it clear. [3.] It doesn't matter whether the good writer wants to be useful, or whether the bad writer wants to do harm.

According to the instructions given earlier, we should end with three propositions, even though some writers would have punctuated sentences 1 and 2 as a single sentence.

Examining the first sentence, we find no connectives, no pronouns with external reference, no inversion of the word order. The diction is plain and there is no figurative language. It looks as if there is not much that requires change here in the direction of simplification, with the exception of the construction which creates an unnecessary clause by erecting a dummy predicate noun (*those*) and then attaching a relative clause to it ("who keep . . ."). This can be deleted to produce the reduced proposition: "1. Good writers keep the language efficient."

The second sentence is grammatically defective, as neither of the verbs has a subject. The subject, of course, is in the previous sentence (*good writers/ those*). Here the task is easier because the subject must be supplied and the connective ("that is to say") deleted. Also, there is no need to repeat the verb. The form suggests itself: "2. Good writers keep the language accurate and clear." That this version is an unsatisfactory reduction is made plain by the obvious function of the connective, which serves to connect the two adjectives (*accurate, clear*) with *efficient* in the first sentence. This relationship can be indicated by putting *efficient* somehow in the subject of the second sentence, as follows:

"2. Efficiency in language is accuracy and clarity."

The third sentence is even more elusive, as it does not state its topic but merely exemplifies by contrasted examples. The net result of the contrast between *good* and *bad* writer is to suggest any writer. "To be useful" contrasts with "to do harm." Together with the verb *wants,* they equal "social intention." "It doesn't matter" is a casual way of saying that something is irrelevant. The sum of these equations permits us to produce the following reduction: "3. The social intentions of a writer are irrelevant."

The sentences of Pound's paragraph have been reduced to these three propositions:

1. Good writers keep the language efficient.
2. Efficiency in language is accuracy and clarity.
3. The social intentions of a writer are irrelevant.

It may be assumed that the 39 words of the original are adequately expressed in the 21 words of the reduction. Thus, some 18 words represent the affective aspect of the paragraph, as opposed to the cognitive. This measure should not be taken literally, because some highly stylized passages might well be "reduced" to a greater length than the original sentences. In this particular instance, however, one aspect of Pound's conversion of thought into word might be described as expansion. This is syntactic in the first sentence (the addition of a non-essential clause) and rhetorical in the second and third (anaphoric repetition in the second, antithetic illustration in the third). Other aspects of the style that emerge from this comparison are the plainness of the diction and a certain casualness about forms (incomplete sentence 2, "doesn't" in 3). Finally, there is a certain dogmatism about the polarity between *good* and *bad* writers. These conclusions are, to be sure, far from final. They serve merely as hypotheses in the light of which other paragraphs can be analyzed. Possibly, some are in error and must be discarded and others reinterpreted in the face of new evidence. For instance, there is a contradiction between the formal nature of anaphora and antithesis and a casualness about forms. More information about such a paradoxical stylistic procedure is indispensable for a fair evaluation of Pound's style. Still, tentative as the results of this preliminary analysis may be, they can serve as a basis for what is to follow. The value of the reductive procedure is the necessity it puts the analyst of style under to observe the actual detailed mechanism of the style at work.

Apart from what takes place within sentence boundaries, the analyst of style (the rhetorician) is interested in the manner in which the sentences are combined with each other, in their logical structure. This logic is not the same as formal logic. In fact, good formal logic may be ineffective rhetorically, and fallacious logic, it has often been seen, may be rhetorically persuasive. The logic here referred to is merely the nature of the relationship between one sentence (or proposition) and the next. Some rhetoricians have classified such relations into as many as forty categories. A simpler system can usefully cover the same ground. The procedure suggested here results in a scheme called the Logical Diagram, which gives a graphic summary of the internal logic of the relationship between sentences.

Although it is not always completely adequate, a system of eight relations covers the vast majority of sentences. A sentence is defined as one of the following types, if it is in the relationship described with one of the sentences which precede it. These are the types, together with the symbols which are used in the Logical Diagram:

( ) *Initial,* the first sentence of a paragraph.
(+) *Additive,* a proposition which has no organic relation with its predecessor (and).
(–) *Adversative,* a proposition which changes the direction of the argument (but).
(o) *Alternative,* a proposition which may be substituted for the previous one (or).
(=) *Explanatory,* a restatement, definition or expansion of the previous proposition (that is).
(×) *Illustrative,* an instance or illustration (for example).
(:) *Illative,* a conclusion (therefore).
(!) *Causal,* the cause for a preceding conclusion (for).

It should be noted that the connectives shown in parentheses are prototypic and may not always be those used by the writers themselves. Writers often use logical connectives rhetorically, to suggest connections which may not really be implicit in the argument itself. Others may use them decoratively or habitually. That is one reason why the propositions are shorn of their connectives: so that their rhetorical value may not influence the logical interpretation of the propositions in which they appear.

In making a Logical Diagram, four columns are set up with the number corresponding to the propositions at the left and a symbol corresponding to the logical value of the sentence placed opposite each number. The columns are not integral to the system; they merely space the symbols for easier visualization. It has been found convenient to put *Initials* in Column A, *Explanatories* in B, *Illustratives* in C, and *Illatives* in D. The other four types appear in whatever column is appropriate to describe the relation with the previous sentence. To show the workings of the Diagram, let us apply it to the Pound paragraph.

	A	B	C	D
1.	( )			
2.		(=)		
3.	(–)			

The first sentence of the paragraph is by definition an Initial. The second is an Explanatory, marked, as it happens, by the connective "that is to say." It is placed in Column B. The third sentence is an Adversative, showing a deviation from the line of argument proposed in the first sentence. This is shown by placing the symbol in Column A. Although the paragraph is too short to give much information about the logical structure of Pound's thought, it reveals a pattern which is probably typical of Pound. The progress from statement to conclusion (A to D) is surprisingly consistent in most writers. The application of this technique to several paragraphs of an author will usually yield a typical pattern which is a component of his style.

The selections in this Handbook are intended to provide the raw material for the kind of analysis that has just been described. They are arranged in three parts, of which the first two consist of British writings and the third of American. The first part includes writers between Caxton and Robert Graves, who span almost five centuries of English prose. Between them will be found most of the important stylists at intervals of roughly a decade (usually based on date of publication). The third (American) part is similarly arranged between Cotton Mather and Tom Wolfe, though the intervals are less regular. The selections in both these parts are arranged in reverse chronological order to permit the student to proceed from the familiar language of his own time to the gradually more unfamiliar language of earlier eras.

The second part has been provided in an attempt to make the student realize that changes in the state of the language or in rhetorical fashion must be kept distinct from individual differences between writers (their styles). This part therefore consists of three sets of five selections representing the language at these fixed points: 1700, 1800, 1900. By comparing the performance of contemporaries, the student will be able to distinguish what is individual in these writers from what is typical of their time. It should be noticed, however, that writers do not always publish their works as soon as they finish them, so that two contemporary books may have been written a decade or two apart. More important, even two books written and published at the same time may not be truly contemporary in the sense that one writer may be older than the other, sufficiently so sometimes to give his work the old-fashioned feeling of an earlier state of the language or of disused rhetorical practices.

Every effort has been made to give the reader the actual words of each writer represented in the Handbook. To this end, the most authoritative texts (often the original editions) have been used and every vagary of punctuation, spelling, typography and word choice has been preserved. The sources have been indicated in every case.

To minimize the possible tendency of writers to write variously about different subjects, all the writings were selected from more or less the same subject: language and style. Apart from making the selections more easily comparable, this policy has the advantage of providing the reader with an anthology of significant readings on the subject matter of his study. Many of these selections repay careful reading for that reason alone.

The notes are intended to aid the student in interpreting the stylistic and rhetorical significance of the selections. They contain a wide variety of information which bears on the style of the author: definitions of obsolete or unusual words, explanations of rhetorical devices, displays of interesting or emphatic arrangements of syntax, historical and biographical facts, contrasts with other writers (sometimes enriched with quotations), comments of critics and scholars, and linguistic data. Two-thirds of the selections are covered by annotations that might be called essential: anything is annotated which might mislead or confuse. Some fifteen selections have been fully annotated: everything that might possibly raise a question has been discussed and much relevant information has been added. In addition, Propositional Reductions and Logical Diagrams have been provided. These full-scale annotations contain the material for essays on the styles of these writers. Another fifteen selections have been left unannotated, so that the student, under the guidance of his teacher, might attempt the analysis of style altogether on his own.

The Bibliography contains titles of general theoretical and methodological interest as well as studies of individual writers.

. . . . .

Like most books, this one leaves a trail of obligations behind it. I am happy to acknowledge these, beginning first with the students in my courses in Stylistics at Columbia University, at Teachers College and in two Esso Institutes for English Teachers, a New York State Institute and one supported by

N.D.E.A., where these materials were variously tested. I am glad to give particular acknowledgment to Mrs. Elizabeth MacAndrew and Mrs. Mary Hiatt, one my former, one my present student, for their unsparing criticism. Among my colleagues, I am glad to mention Professor Robert L. Allen, whose interest in this work has always been gratifying to me. My publishers, Charles Scribner's Sons, deserve more than the usual acknowledgment. Working with them has given me an understanding of how complete the partnership between author and publisher can be. My further thanks go to Mrs. Dorothy Doyle, who typed the final version of the Introduction and helped to compile the index, and to Mrs. Helene E. Milic, who typed all the drafts of the entire manuscript, not letting the hard words and strange names defeat them.

SELECTIONS

BRITISH AUTHORS

BRITISH AUTHORS—SYNCHRONIC SELECTIONS

AMERICAN AUTHORS

Note

[After the author's name and dates, at the head of each selection, occurs the abbreviation *aet.,* followed by a number. This signifies the year in the author's life when the work containing the selection was published (or, occasionally, written). The date in parentheses at the end of the selection is the date of first publication or of writing. This date may differ from that given in the source note which specifies the particular edition from which the selection was taken.]

1. Robert GRAVES (*b. 1895*) æt. *66*

Dedicated poets cannot exist in a vacuum, discarding all tradition, all knowledge, rejecting society.[1] They must be at least as well grounded as was Shakespeare, whose Petty School *A.B.C. with the Catechism,* his *Primer and Catechism,* his *Book of Common Prayer* and *Psalter,*[2] assisted him later to a self-education in more readable works. But Shakespeare was a special case; and so was John Clare,[3] who had an equally limited schooling. I believe that every poet should read our English Classics, master the main grammatic[4] rules before daring to bend or break them; should travel abroad, be at ease among all sorts and conditions of men, and experience not only the horrors of thwarted passion but, if he is fortunate, the tranquil love of an honest woman.[5] The supreme gift bestowed on him by the Muse is that of poetic humour: a grasp of the identity of opposites, the wearing of Welshman's hose.[6] Sometimes, in fact, when a poem has been assiduously refined and refined[7] under the white blaze of inspiration, its final draft becomes so perfect in its ambivalence as to make the poet humorously doubt whether the insertion of a simple 'not' will perhaps improve it.[8]

Good manners demand that visitors should respect the laws of whatever society has courteously entertained them—court, university, public house, or gipsy camp;[9] and poets, by their nature, are perpetual visitors. Skelton, like Naaman,[10] bowed in the House of Rimmon, his fingers humorously[11] crossed. I piously[12] follow his example; and look with disgust on the so-called beatnik[13] poets whose boast is that they conduct themselves with equal bad manners in all societies.

(*1961*)

Robert Graves, *Oxford Addresses on Poetry* (London, 1962), pp. 22–23.

2. Bertrand RUSSELL (*b. 1872*) æt. *84*

I cannot pretend to know [1] how writing ought to be done, or what a wise critic would advise me to do with a view to improving my own writing. The most that I can do is to relate some things about my own attempts.

Until I was twenty-one, I wished to write more or less in the style of John Stuart Mill. I liked the structure of his sentences and his manner of developing a subject. I had, however, already a different ideal, derived, I suppose, from mathematics. I wished to say everything in the smallest number of words [2] in which it could be said clearly. Perhaps, I thought, one should imitate Baedeker rather than any more literary model. I would spend hours trying to find the shortest way of saying something without ambiguity, and to this aim I was willing to sacrifice all attempts at aesthetic excellence.

At the age of twenty-one, however, I came under a new influence, that of my future brother-in-law, Logan Pearsall Smith.[3] He was at that time exclusively interested in style as opposed to matter. His gods were Flaubert and Walter Pater,[4] and I was quite ready to believe that the way to learn how to write was to copy their technique. He gave me various simple rules, of which I remember only two: "Put a comma every four words," and "never use 'and' except at the beginning of a sentence." His most emphatic advice was that one must always rewrite. I conscientiously tried this, but found that my first draft was almost always better than my second. This discovery has saved me an immense amount of time. I do not, of course, apply it to the substance, but only to the form. When I discover an error of an important kind, I rewrite the whole. What I do not find is that I can improve a sentence when I am satisfied with what it means.

Bertrand Russell, "How I Write," *Portraits from Memory* (New York, 1965), pp. 210–213.

Very gradually I have discovered ways of writing with a minimum of worry and anxiety. When I was young each fresh piece of serious work used to seem to me for a time—perhaps a long time—to be beyond my powers. I would fret myself into a nervous state from fear that it was never going to come right. I would make one unsatisfying attempt after another, and in the end have to discard them all. At last I found that such fumbling attempts were a waste of time. It appeared that after first contemplating a book on some subject, and after giving serious preliminary attention to it, I needed a period of subconscious incubation which could not be hurried and was if anything impeded by deliberate thinking. Sometimes I would find, after a time, that I had made a mistake, and that I could not write the book I had had in mind. But often I was more fortunate. Having,[5] by a time of very intense concentration, planted the problem in my subconsciousness, it would germinate underground until, suddenly, the solution emerged with blinding clarity, so that it only remained to write down what had appeared as if in a revelation.

The most curious example of this process, and the one which led me subsequently to rely upon it, occurred at the beginning of 1914. I had undertaken to give the Lowell Lectures at Boston, and had chosen as my subject "Our Knowledge of the External World." Throughout 1913 I thought about this topic. In term time in my rooms at Cambridge, in vacations in a quiet inn on the upper reaches of the Thames, I concentrated with such intensity that I sometimes forgot to breathe and emerged panting as from a trance. But all to no avail. To every theory that I could think of I could perceive fatal objections. At last, in despair, I went off to Rome for Christmas, hoping that a holiday would revive my flagging energy. I got back to Cambridge on the last day of 1913, and although my difficulties were still completely unresolved I arranged, because the remaining time was short, to dictate as best as I could to a stenographer. Next morning, as she came in at the door, I suddenly saw exactly what I had to say, and proceeded to dictate the whole book without a moment's hesitation.

I do not want to convey an exaggerated impression. The book

was very imperfect, and I now think that it contains serious errors. But it was the best that I could have done at that time, and a more leisurely method (within the time at my disposal) would almost certainly have produced something worse. Whatever may be true of other people, this is the right method for me. Flaubert and Pater, I have found, are best forgotten so far as I am concerned.

Although what I now think about how to write is not so very different from what I thought at the age of eighteen, my development has not been by any means rectilinear. There was a time, in the first years of this century, when I had more florid and rhetorical ambitions. This was the time when I wrote *A Free Man's Worship,* a work of which I do not now think well. At that time I was steeped in Milton's prose, and his rolling periods reverberated through the caverns of my mind. I cannot say that I no longer admire them, but for me to imitate them involves a certain insincerity. In fact, all imitation is dangerous. Nothing could be better in style than the Prayer Book and the Authorized Version of the Bible, but they express a way of thinking and feeling which is different from that of our time.[6] A style is not good unless it is an intimate and almost involuntary expression of the personality of the writer, and then only if the writer's personality is worth expressing. But although direct imitation is always to be deprecated, there is much to be gained by familiarity with good prose, especially in cultivating a sense for prose rhythm.

(1956)

3. George ORWELL [pseud. of Eric Blair] (*1903–1950*) æt. *43*

But if thought corrupts language, language can also corrupt thought. A bad usage can spread by tradition and imitation, even among people who should and do know better. The debased language that I have been discussing is in some ways very convenient. Phrases like *a not unjustifiable assumption, leaves much to be desired, would serve no good purpose, a consideration which we should do well to bear in mind,* are a continuous temptation, a packet of aspirins always at one's elbow. Look back through this essay, and for certain you will find that I have again and again committed the very faults I am protesting against.[1] By this morning's post I have received a pamphlet dealing with conditions in Germany. The author tells me that he 'felt impelled' to write it. I open it at random, and here is almost the first sentence that I see: '(The Allies) have an opportunity not only of achieving a radical transformation of Germany's social and political structure in such a way as to avoid a nationalistic reaction in Germany itself, but at the same time of laying the foundations of a co-operative and unified Europe.' You see, he 'feels impelled' to write—feels, presumably, that he has something new to say—and yet his words, like cavalry horses answering the bugle, group themselves automatically into the familiar dreary pattern. This invasion of one's mind by ready-made phrases (*lay the foundations, achieve a radical transformation*) can only be prevented if one is constantly on guard against them, and every such phrase anaesthetizes a portion of one's brain.

I said earlier that the decadence of our language is probably curable. Those who deny this would argue, if they produced an

George Orwell, "Politics and the English Language," *Shooting an Elephant* (New York, 1950), pp. 155–156.

argument at all, that language merely reflects existing social conditions, and that we cannot influence its development by any direct tinkering with words and constructions. So far as the general tone or spirit of a language goes, this may be true, but it is not true in detail. Silly words and expressions have often disappeared, not through any evolutionary process but owing to the conscious action of a minority. Two recent examples were *explore every avenue* and *leave no stone unturned*, which were killed by the jeers of a few journalists.[2] There is a long list of flyblown metaphors[3] which could similarly be got rid of if enough people would interest themselves in the job; and it should also be possible to laugh the *not un-* formation out of existence, to reduce the amount of Latin and Greek in the average sentence, to drive out foreign phrases and strayed scientific words, and, in general, to make pretentiousness unfashionable. But all these are minor points. The defence of the English language implies more than this, and perhaps it is best to start by saying what it *does not* imply.

To begin with it has nothing to do with archaism, with the salvaging of obsolete words and turns of speech, or with the setting up of a 'standard English' which must never be departed from. On the contrary, it is especially concerned with the scrapping of every word or idiom which has outworn its usefulness. It has nothing to do with correct grammar and syntax,[4] which are of no importance so long as one makes one's meaning clear, or with the avoidance of Americanisms, or with having what is called a 'good prose style'. On the other hand it is not concerned with fake simplicity and the attempt to make written English colloquial. Nor does it even imply in every case preferring the Saxon word to the Latin one, though it does imply using the fewest and shortest words that will cover one's meaning. What is above all needed is to let the meaning choose the word, and not the other way about. In prose, the worst thing one can do with words is to surrender to them. When you think of a concrete object, you think wordlessly, and then, if you want to describe the thing you have been visualizing you probably hunt about till you find the exact words that seem to fit it.[5] When you think of something abstract you are more inclined to use words from the start, and unless you make a conscious effort to prevent it, the existing dialect will come rushing in and do the job for you, at the expense of blurring or even changing your meaning. Probably it is better to put off using words as long as possible and get one's meaning as clear as one can through pictures or sensations. Afterwards one can choose—not simply *accept*—the phrases that will best cover the meaning, and then switch round and decide what impression one's words are likely to make on another person. This last effort of the mind cuts out all stale or mixed images, all prefabricated phrases, needless repetitions, and humbug and vagueness generally.[6]

(1946)

4. C. M. BOWRA (*b. 1898*) æt. *47*

Between Homer's oral and Virgil's written art there is an enormous difference. The poet who writes for readers operates less with phrases and formulas than with single words. He fashions his sentences carefully and individually; he takes care to avoid omissions and contradictions, to harmonise the details of his plot, to secure an interwoven unity for his whole design. Even when he follows Homer in using the oral device of repetition, Virgil goes his own way and makes variations on a given form. For him the artifices of oral poetry are valuable for their archaic elegance; their beauty is no longer functional. Virgil is seldom wholehearted in his attempts at repetition. He prefers to vary the words and to show in how many different ways he can describe such familiar matters as the coming of dawn or of evening. Even when his characters speak to each other, they do so not with Homer's regular forms of address but with elaborate variations, no two of which are quite alike. The old formulas were of no real use to Virgil and were even a hindrance; for his aim was to compose a poem which could be read with exact and appreciative care, and for that reason he gains more by variation than by repetition.

Virgil's art is in fact akin to other modern poetry. Its aim is to pack each line with as much significance as possible, to make each word do its utmost work and to secure that careful attention which the reader, unlike the listener, can give. If the oral epic triumphs through its simplicity and strength and straightforwardness, through the unhesitating sweep of its narrative and a brilliant clarity in its main effects, the written epic appeals by its poetical texture, by its exquisite or apt or impressive choice of words, by the rich significance of phrases and lines and paragraphs. Homer sweeps us away by the irresistible movement of

C. M. Bowra, *From Virgil to Milton* (New York, 1945), pp. 4–5.

lines through a whole passage to a splendid climax. What counts is the singleness of his effect, the unbroken maintenance of a heroic or tragic mood, the concentration on some action vividly imagined and clearly portrayed without irrelevance or second thoughts or even those hints that lure into bypaths of fancy and suggest that there is more in the words than is obvious at first sight. But in Virgil, great though the paragraphs are, compelling though the climax is when it is reached, we are more concerned with the details, with each small effect and each deftly placed word, than with the whole. We linger over the richness of single phrases, over the "pathetic half-lines", over the precision or potency with which a word illuminates a sentence or a happy sequence of sounds imparts an inexplicable charm to something that might otherwise have been trivial. Of course Homer has his magical phrases and Virgil his bold effects, but the distinction stands. It is a matter of composition, of art, and it marks the real difference between the two kinds of epic, which are not so much "authentic" and "literary" as oral and written.

(1945)

5. C. S. LEWIS (*1898–1963*) æt. *44*

The style of Virgil and Milton arises as the solution of a very definite problem. The Secondary epic aims at an even higher solemnity than the Primary; but it has lost all those external aids to solemnity which the Primary enjoyed. There is no robed and garlanded *aoidos*, no altar, not even a feast in a hall—only a private person reading a book in an armchair. Yet somehow or other, that private person must be made to feel that he is assisting at an august ritual, for if he does not, he will not be receptive of the true epic exhilaration. The sheer writing of the poem, therefore, must now do, of itself, what the whole occasion helped to do for Homer. The Virgilian and Miltonic style is there to compensate for—to counteract—the privacy and informality of silent reading in a man's own study. Every judgment on it which does not realize this will be inept. To blame it for being ritualistic or incantatory, for lacking intimacy or the speaking voice, is to blame it for being just what it intends to be and ought to be. It is like damning an opera or an oratorio because the personages sing instead of speaking.

In a general and obvious sense this effect is achieved by what is called the 'grandeur' or 'elevation' of the style. As far as Milton is concerned (for I am not scholar enough to analyse Virgil) this grandeur is produced mainly by three things. (1) The use of slightly unfamiliar words and constructions, including archaisms. (2) The use of proper names, not solely nor chiefly for their sound, but because they are the names of splendid, remote, terrible, voluptuous, or celebrated things. They are there to encourage a sweep of the reader's eye over the richness and variety of the world—to supply that *largier aether* which we breathe as long as the poem lasts. (3) Continued allusion to all the sources of heightened interest in our sense experience (light,

C. S. Lewis, *A Preface to Paradise Lost* (London, 1942), pp. 39–40.

darkness, storm, flowers, jewels, sexual love, and the like), but all over-topped and "managed" with an air of magnanimous austerity. Hence comes the feeling of sensual excitement *without* surrender or relaxation, the extremely tonic, yet also extremely rich, quality of our experience while we read. But all this you might have in great poems which were not epic. What I chiefly want to point out is something else—the poet's unremitting *manipulation* of his readers—how he sweeps us along as though we were attending an actual recitation and nowhere allows us to settle down and luxuriate on any one line or paragraph. It is common to speak of Milton's style as organ music. It might be more helpful to regard the reader as the organ and Milton as the organist. It is on us he plays, if we will let him.

(*1942*)

6. Cyril CONNOLLY (*b. 1903*) æt. *35*

From the realists, the puritans, the colloquial writers and talkie-novelists there is also much that he will take and much that he will leave. The cursive style, the agreeable manners, the precise and poetical impact of Forster's diction, the lucidity of Maugham, last of the great professional writers, the timing of Hemingway, the smooth cutting edge of Isherwood, the indignation of Lawrence, the honesty of Orwell, these will be necessary and the touch of those few journalists who give to every word in their limited vocabulary its current topical value. But above all it is construction that can be learnt from the realists, that discipline in the conception and execution of a book, that planning which gives simply-written things the power to endure, the pruning [1] without which the imagination reverts to the wilderness.[2]

He will not borrow from the realists, or from their imitators, the flatness of style, the homogeneity of outlook, the fear of eccentricity, the reporter's horror of distinction, the distrust of beauty, the cult of a violence and starkness that is masochistic. Nor will he adopt the victory mentality of those left-wing writers who imagine themselves already to be the idols of a conquering proletariat and who give their laws in simple matter-of-fact hard-hitting English to a non-existent congregation. That time is not yet; the artist today is in the position of a patient Mahomet towards whom the great art-hating mountain of the British public must eventually come.[3]

This would seem the state of our literature. The battle between the schools I think has been proved to exist, but as with all civil wars, there are places where and moments when the fight rages with greater violence than at others. I have concentrated on those writers in the forefront of that battle, and any criticism I have made of them is intended only to relate them to

Cyril Connolly, *Enemies of Promise* (Boston, 1939), pp. 107–109.

it. Thus to call Proust a bad influence is not to deny that he is a great writer, but rather to consider his work in terms of what can be learnt from it today. It is the privilege of living in the twentieth century that one can take both sides in controversies.[4]

What I claim is that there is action[5] and reaction between these styles, and that necessary as it was[6] and victorious though it seems,[7] the colloquial style of the last few years is doomed and dying. Style, as I have tried to show, is a relationship between a writer's mastery of form and his intellectual or emotional content. Mastery of form has lately been held, with some reason, to conceal a poverty of content but this is not inevitable[8] and for too long writers have had to prove their sincerity by going before the public in sackcloth and ashes or rather in a fifty-shilling suit and a celluloid collar. Now the moment has come[9] when the penance is complete and when they may return to their old habit. It is not a question of taking sides about one way of writing or another,[10] but a question of timing, for the you-man writing of he-men authors is going out and the form must be enriched again. Our language is a sulky and inconstant beauty and it is important to know at any given moment[11] what liberties she will permit. Now all seems favourable. Experiment and adventure is indicated,[12] the boom of the twenties has been paid for by the slump of the thirties; let us try and break[13] the vicious circle by returning to a controlled expenditure, a balanced literary budget, a reasoned extravagance.

(1938)

7. W. Somerset MAUGHAM
(*1874–1965*) æt. *64*

I do not know whether it was a subconscious feeling that this sort of writing was contrary to my bent or a naturally methodical cast of mind that led me then to turn my attention to the writers of the Augustan Period. The prose of Swift enchanted me. I made up my mind that this was the perfect way to write and I started to work on him in the same way as I had done with Jeremy Taylor.[1] I chose *The Tale of a Tub*.[2] It is said that when the Dean re-read it in his old age he cried: 'What genius I had then!' To my mind his genius was better shown in other works. It is a tiresome allegory and the irony is facile. But the style is admirable. I cannot imagine that English can be better written. Here are no flowery periods, fantastic turns of phrase or high-flown images. It is a civilized prose, natural, discreet and pointed. There is no attempt to surprise by an extravagant vocabulary. It looks as though Swift made do with the first word that came to hand, but since he had an acute and logical brain it was always the right one, and he put it in the right place.[3] The strength and balance of his sentences are due to an exquisite taste. As I had done before I copied passages and then tried to write them out again from memory. I tried altering words or the order in which they were set. I found that the only possible words were those Swift had used and that the order in which he had placed them was the only possible order. It is an impeccable prose.[4]

But perfection has one grave defect: it is apt to be dull. Swift's prose is like a French canal, bordered with poplars, that runs through a gracious and undulating country.[5] Its tranquil charm fills you with satisfaction, but it neither excites the emotions nor stimulates the imagination. You go on and on and

W. Somerset Maugham, *The Summing-Up* (Garden City, 1938), pp. 26–30.

presently you are a trifle bored.[6] So, much as you may admire Swift's wonderful lucidity, his terseness, his naturalness, his lack of affectation,[7] you find your attention wandering after a while unless his matter peculiarly interests you. I think if I had my time over again I would give to the prose of Dryden the close study I gave to that of Swift. I did not come across it till I had lost the inclination to take so much pains. The prose of Dryden is delicious. It has not the perfection of Swift nor the easy elegance of Addison,[8] but it has a springtime gaiety, a conversational ease, a blithe spontaneousness that are enchanting. Dryden was a very good poet, but it is not the general opinion that he had a lyrical quality; it is strange that it is just this that sings in his softly sparkling prose. Prose had never been written in England [9] like that before; it has seldom been written like that since. Dryden flourished at a happy moment. He had in his bones the sonorous periods and the baroque massiveness of Jacobean language and under the influence of the nimble and well-bred felicity that he learnt from the French [10] he turned it into an instrument that was fit not only for solemn themes but also to express the light thought of the passing moment. He was the first of the rococo artists. If Swift reminds you of a French canal Dryden recalls an English river winding its cheerful way round hills, through quietly busy towns and by nestling villages, pausing now in a noble reach and then running powerfully through a woodland country. It is alive, varied, windswept; and it has the pleasant open-air smell of England.[11]

The work I did was certainly very good for me. I began to write better; I did not write well. I wrote stiffly and self-consciously. I tried to get a pattern into my sentences, but did not see that the pattern was evident.[12] I took care how I placed my words, but did not reflect that an order that was natural at the beginning of the eighteenth century was most unnatural at the beginning of ours. My attempt to write in the manner of Swift made it impossible for me to achieve the effect of inevitable rightness that was just what I so much admired in him. I then wrote a number of plays and ceased to occupy myself with anything but dialogue. It was not till five years had passed that

I set out again to write a novel. By then I no longer had any ambition to be a stylist; I put aside all thought of fine writing. I wanted to write without any frills of language, in as bare and unaffected a manner as I could. I had so much to say that I could afford to waste no words. I wanted merely to set down the facts.[13] I began with the impossible aim of using no adjectives at all. I thought that if you could find the exact term a qualifying epithet could be dispensed with. As I saw it in my mind's eye my book would have the appearance of an immensely long telegram in which for economy's sake you had left out every word that was not necessary to make the sense clear. I have not read it since I corrected the proofs and do not know how near I came to doing what I tried. My impression is that it is written at least more naturally [14] than anything I had written before; but I am sure that it is often slipshod and I daresay there are in it a good many mistakes in grammar.

Since then I have written many other books; and though ceasing my methodical study of the old masters (for though the spirit is willing, the flesh is weak), I have continued with increasing assiduity to try to write better. I discovered my limitations and it seemed to me that the only sensible thing was to aim at what excellence I could within them. I knew that I had no lyrical quality. I had a small vocabulary and no efforts that I could make to enlarge it much availed me. I had little gift of metaphor; the original and striking simile seldom occurred to me. Poetic flights and the great imaginative sweep were beyond my powers. I could admire them in others as I could admire their farfetched tropes and the unusual but suggestive language in which they clothed their thoughts, but my own invention never presented me with such embellishments; [15] and I was tired of trying to do what did not come easily to me. On the other hand, I had an acute power of observation and it seemed to me that I could see a great many things that other people missed. I could put down in clear terms what I saw. I had a logical sense, and if no great feeling for the richness and strangeness of words, at all events a lively appreciation of their sound. I knew that I should never write as well as I could wish, but I thought with pains I could arrive at writing as well as my natural defects allowed. On taking thought it seemed to me that I must aim at lucidity, simplicity and euphony. I have put these three qualities in the order of the importance I assigned to them.

(1938)

8. Ford Madox FORD (*1873–1939*) æt. *64*

In the meantime poor Conrad, continuously groaning that the English language was no sort of a medium for a Polish gentleman and *prosateur*, pursued the desperate quest of just words that should make you see the ripples of wind running uphill on the golden russet of a wheatfield's whispering surface, in the sunlight, beneath a blue sky.[1] And Mr. James, too conscious of his ambassadorial position as between two great Republics of letters to say that the language of the country of his adoption was N.B.G.[2] for the *prosateur*-psychologist of a fictional vocation; and pursuing further and further his studies into the conversational methods of my Lady Maud Warrender[3] and her friends, who, since they included our sovereign lord Edward VII, might indeed be considered to speak, if I may use the phrase, the King's own English. . . . Mr. James got further and further from the limpid beauty and simplicity and force and gas and gaiters[4] of his original vernacular. Until,[5] unless you read him aloud, you could not make head or tail of his meanings, though, matchless Impressionist that he was, he succeeded in conveying to you the impression that some tremendous, tremulous, tenuous[6] game was, somewhere in the Index, being played. Crane went on—but for how short a time! —discharging his granitic phrases as if he had been a stick of dynamite in a quarry. And Hudson went on taking little words out of copybooks to substitute for other, more used words, and so achieving the supreme of beauty of English style. . . . As for me I went on working beside Conrad, trying, when his passionate and possessive material, mental and physical vicissitudes left me the leisure, to evolve for myself a vernacular of an extreme quietness that would suggest someone of some refinement talking in a low voice near the ear of someone else he

Ford Madox Ford, *Portraits from Life* (Boston, 1937), pp. 285–286.

liked a good deal. I don't really imagine that I really influenced Conrad at all. I suggested quite often colloquial synonyms for words of which he had only the literary versions—as you might say 'wire' or 'cable' for 'telegram.' . . . Only of course it was not usually as simple as that. And I corrected the syntax of his proofs and put in or took out commas. And—and, that is the only reason why I mention the collaboration at all—Messrs Garnett and Gosse and Galsworthy and Wells and Havelock Ellis, though the last rather unwittingly, all in varying degrees of loudness suggested that I was ruining Conrad's delicate Oriental style. I may have—but after a great deal of reflection I am pretty certain that I didn't.[7] Suggesting that a man write 'like me' instead of 'like I did' or 'different from' instead of 'different to' can't do him much harm. So that I don't believe I influenced him at all: he was too set on his own ways, on his gorgeous cadences and Elizabethan-Slav mental evolutions. No!

(*1937*)

9. Logan Pearsall SMITH (*1865–1946*) æt. *71*

The literary aspirants, of whom the world seems full to-day, are not lacking in advisers to guide their youthful pens and to warn them of the perils in their path. This path is, we are told, full of dreadful pitfalls into which the unwary may be too easily engulfed. Luckily two of our best-known contemporary critics, Mr. Middleton Murry[1] and Mr. Herbert Read,[2] have each written books on Style, and they, as well as several members of the flourishing school of Cambridge criticism,[3] have been at pains to place conspicuous danger-signals at the edge of these abysses.[4]

Their warnings are directed in particular against any attempts at what is called 'fine writing', any undue preoccupation with the technique of prose composition. Time spent in labouring to perfect one's style, or to make of it an instrument for the production of imaginative effects, is, Mr. Read tells us, just so much time wasted. Indeed, Mr. Middleton Murry says it is worse than this, for nothing could be more dangerous than the notion that the more poetic is prose, the finer it is: this is a heresy that cannot be too much deplored and combated. 'The terrible attraction of words', the impulse to use them for anything more than exact symbols of the things they stand for, is another danger; any sacrifice of sense to euphony being, these critics tell us, the beginning of decadence: 'it is a step on the downward path.' The histories and associations of words, are, Mr. Read says, entirely irrelevant to prose-style, their face-value in current usage being their only value. The young writer is also warned against rhythmical effects and the use of images, and is told that any conscious care for such devices, any playing, like Stevenson, of the sedulous ape to the masters of

Logan Pearsall Smith, "Fine Writing," *Society for Pure English Tracts* (Oxford, 1936), pp. 203–204.

this technique, must be carefully eschewed; though Mr. Read more generously admits that 'less talented writers like Stevenson and Gibbon' may indeed set themselves a standard in this fashion and feeble-mindedly ape it if they like.

Now all this preaching about dangers and decadence, and even 'downright wickedness', may seem to some of us uncalled for at the present time. There was supposed, indeed, about forty or fifty years ago, to exist somewhere a little cenacle of ill-conditioned young people, who were addicted to the fabrication of prose-patterns out of far-fetched and jewel-tinted words; and it was felt at the time, as I remember, that the police should be called upon to put a stop to their activities. I myself was not infrequently warned in my youth against the example of such polishers of fine phrases; but I do not recall any precise mention of the names of these miscreants, nor did I ever become aware of the least signs of their baleful influence upon contemporary letters. I used indeed to wonder sometimes whether—granted their existence—what might be wrong with them was not so much what they did, as the fact that they did it badly.

However that may be—and the whole affair still remains one of considerable obscurity—I cannot believe that this danger can be counted among the perils that are now threatening our civilization. Does any one seriously suppose that the youth of the present day are in the least tempted to retire to lonely garrets, to ascend stylite or stylistic columns,[5] in order to spend laborious years in meditating the thankless Muse of Prose? [6] Since, however, so large a part of criticism consists in repeating what has been said by former critics, may it not be that the battle-cries I have quoted are due to the fact that our modern critics are still engaged in a conflict with these defunct and, it may be, imaginary bogeys? And anyhow, suppose that there are still among us persons who feel an inclination to spend their lives in the study of perfection, do they deserve to be so severely warned and reprobated? Though they may be devoting themselves to an obscure and derided occupation, does not their enthusiasm, when compared with other forms of fascist and fanatical activities, seem almost innocuous after all? The fever of perfection is not catching; and if it be foolish for these astrophils to hitch their wagons (in Emerson's phrase) to this remotely glittering star, surely they cannot reasonably be supposed to inflict any serious damage on the solar system and the general scheme of things.

(1936)

10. Virginia WOOLF (*1882–1941*) æt. *50*

But if it were possible for Sterne to correct his manners, it was imposssible for him to correct his style.[1] That had become as much a part of himself as his large nose or his brilliant eyes.[2] With the first words [3]—They order, said I, this matter better in France—we are in the world of *Tristram Shandy*. It is a world in which anything may happen. We hardly know what jest, what jibe, what flash of poetry [4] is not going to glance suddenly through the gap which this astonishingly agile pen has cut in the thick-set hedge of English prose.[5] Is Sterne himself responsible? Does he know what he is going to say next for all his resolve to be on his best behaviour this time? [6] The jerky, disconnected sentences are as rapid and it would seem as little under control as the phrases that fall from the lips of a brilliant talker.[7] The very punctuation is that of speech, not writing, and brings the sound and associations of the speaking voice [8] in with it. The order of the ideas, their suddenness and irrelevancy, is more true to life [9] than to literature. There is a privacy in this intercourse which allows things to slip out unreproved that would have been in doubtful taste [10] had they been spoken in public. Under the influence of this extraordinary style the book becomes semi-transparent. The usual ceremonies and conventions which keep reader and writer at arm's length disappear. We are as close to life as we can be.[11]

That Sterne achieved this illusion [12] only by the use of extreme art and extraordinary pains is obvious without going to his manuscript to prove it. For though the writer is always haunted by the belief that somehow it must be possible to brush aside the ceremonies and conventions of writing and to speak to the reader as directly as by word of mouth, any one who has

Virginia Woolf, "The Sentimental Journey," *The Second Common Reader* (New York, 1932), pp. 81–82.

tried the experiment has either been struck dumb by the difficulty, or waylaid into disorder and diffusity unutterable.[13] Sterne somehow brought off the astonishing combination. No writing[14] seems to flow more exactly into the very folds and creases of the individual mind, to express its changing moods, to answer its lightest whim and impulse, and yet the result is perfectly precise and composed. The utmost fluidity exists with the utmost permanence. It is as if the tide raced over the beach hither and thither and left every ripple and eddy cut on the sand in marble.[15]

(1932)

11. D. H. LAWRENCE (*1885–1930*) æt. *43*

Literary criticism can be no more than a reasoned account [1] of the feeling produced upon the critic by the book he is criticizing. Criticism can never be a science: it is, in the first place, much too personal,[2] and in the second, it is concerned with values that science ignores.[3] The touchstone is emotion, not reason. We judge a work of art by its effect on our sincere and vital emotion, and nothing else.[4] All the critical twiddle-twaddle about style and form, all this pseudo-scientific classifying and analysing of books in an imitation-botanical fashion, is mere impertinence and mostly dull jargon.[5]

A critic must be able to *feel* the impact of a work of art in all its complexity and its force. To do so, he must be a man of force and complexity [6] himself, which few critics are. A man with a paltry, impudent nature will never write anything but paltry, impudent criticism.[7] And a man [8] who is *emotionally* educated is rare as a phœnix. The more scholastically educated a man is generally, the more he is an emotional boor.[9]

More than this, even an artistically and emotionally educated man must be a man of good faith. He must have the courage to admit what he feels, as well as the flexibility to *know* what he feels. So Sainte-Beuve [10] remains, to me, a great critic. And a man like Macaulay,[11] brilliant as he is, is unsatisfactory, because he is not honest. He is emotionally very alive, but he juggles his feelings. He prefers a fine effect to the sincere statement of the æsthetic and emotional reaction. He is quite intellectually capable of giving us a true account of what he feels. But not morally.[12] A critic must be emotionally alive in every fibre, intellectually capable and skilful in essential logic, and then morally very honest.

D. H. Lawrence, "John Galsworthy," *Selected Literary Criticism* (London, 1956), pp. 118–119.

Then it seems to me a good critic should give his reader a few standards to go by.[13] He can change the standards for every new critical attempt, so long as he keeps good faith. But it is just as well to say: This and this is the standard we judge by.

Sainte-Beuve, on the whole, set up the standard of the "good man". He sincerely believed that the great man was essentially[14] the good man in the widest range of human sympathy. This remained his universal standard. Pater's standard was the lonely philosopher of pure thought and pure æsthetic truth. Macaulay's standard was tainted by a political or democratic bias, he must be on the side of the weak. Gibbon tried a purely moral standard, individual morality.[15]

(1928)

12. T. S. ELIOT (*1888–1964*) æt. *31*

The death of Rostand[1] was the disappearance of the poet whom, more than any other in France, we treated as the exponent of "rhetoric," thinking of rhetoric as something recently out of fashion. And as we find ourselves looking back rather tenderly upon the author of *Cyrano* we wonder what this vice or quality is that is associated as plainly with Rostand's merits as with his defects. His rhetoric, at least, suited him at times so well, and so much better than it suited a much greater poet, Baudelaire, who is at times as rhetorical as Rostand. And we begin to suspect that the word is merely a vague term of abuse for any style that is bad, that is so evidently bad or second-rate that we do not recognize the necessity for greater precision in the phrases we apply to it.

Our own Elizabethan and Jacobean poetry—in so nice[2] a problem it is much safer to stick to one's own language—is repeatedly called "rhetorical." It had this and that notable quality, but, when we wish to admit that it had defects, it is rhetorical. It had serious defects, even gross faults, but we cannot be considered to have erased them from our language when we are so unclear in our perception of what they are. The fact is that both Elizabethan prose and Elizabethan poetry are written in a variety of styles[3] with a variety of vices. Is the style of Lyly,[4] is Euphuism, rhetorical? In contrast to the elder style of Ascham and Elyot[5] which it assaults, it is a clear, flowing, orderly and relatively pure style, with a systematic if monotonous formula of antitheses and similes.[6] Is the style of Nashe?[7] A tumid, flatulent, vigorous style very different from Lyly's. Or it is perhaps the strained and the mixed figures of speech in which Shakespeare indulged himself. Or it is perhaps the careful declamation of Jonson. The word simply cannot be used as

T. S. Eliot, "'Rhetoric' and Poetic Drama," *Selected Essays* (New York, 1932), pp. 25–27.

synonymous with bad writing. The meanings which it has been obliged to shoulder have been mostly opprobrious; but if a precise meaning can be found for it this meaning may occasionally represent a virtue. It is one of those words which it is the business of criticism to dissect and reassemble. Let us avoid the assumption that rhetoric is a vice of manner, and endeavour to find a rhetoric of substance also, which is right because it issues from what it has to express.

At the present time there is a manifest preference for the "conversational" in poetry—the style of "direct speech,"[8] opposed to the "oratorical" and the rhetorical; but if rhetoric is any convention of writing inappropriately applied, this conversational style can and does become a rhetoric—or what is supposed to be a conversational style, for it is often as remote from polite discourse as well could be. Much of the second and third rate in American *vers libre* is of this sort; and much of the second and third rate in English Wordsworthianism. There is in fact no conversational or other form which can be applied indiscriminately; if a writer wishes to give the effect of speech he must positively give the effect of himself talking in his own person or in one of his rôles; and if we are to express ourselves, our variety of thoughts and feelings, on a variety of subjects with inevitable rightness, we must adapt our manner to the moment with infinite variations. Examination of the development of Elizabethan drama shows this progress in adaptation, a development from monotony to variety, a progressive refinement in the perception of the variations of feeling, and a progressive elaboration of the means of expressing these variations. This drama is admitted to have grown away from the rhetorical expression, the bombast speeches, of Kyd and Marlowe to the subtle and dispersed utterance of Shakespeare and Webster. But this apparent abandonment or outgrowth of rhetoric is two things: it is partly an improvement in language and it is partly progressive variation in feeling. There is, of course, a long distance separating the furibund fluency of old Hieronimo and the broken words of Lear.

(*1919*)

13. George SAINTSBURY (*1845–1933*) æt. *71*

It is true that though the diffused admiration of him [1] has never wholly ceased, and has perhaps even (and so far fortunately) rather increased of late, thorough appreciation of his wisdom is not to be attained without a little difficulty. Boswell is no doubt a great stand-by, and his occasional summaries or collections of detached *Johnsoniana* are not merely valuable storehouses, but no mean works of art—the occasionally "green-goosish" [2] comments which the collector himself appends themselves contributing, though no doubt unconsciously, a positively artistic advantage of contrasted setting. But it is to be feared that the letters, which contain almost more [3] of this wisdom, are not uncommonly skipped; while even these letters require supplementing by the aid of his minor and miscellaneous works, which are very seldom read at all.

If this latter [4] is the case, it is no doubt very largely, if not mainly, due to the hasty acceptance of a far too common dictum, that Johnson, though a great conversationalist, was not really a great writer.[5] Perhaps also some defenders of his style have done him less service than they intended by over-exalting it for general use, and as a contribution to the main progress of English; while others of them have not fully appreciated the characteristics of the style itself. No doubt Macaulay's description [6] of it is one of the worst parts of his essay—so strangely compounded of good and bad. What he describes is not really Johnson's elaborate style at all; and the chief characteristic which (not indeed inventing it, but accepting it and "passing it on" with his own unique power of effective "vulgarisation") [7] he fixed upon—that of using Latinised diction [8]—is very far indeed from being the real *differentia*.[9] Johnson did, whether from the char-

George Saintsbury, *The Peace of the Augustans* (London, 1916), pp. 196–198.

acter of his favourite studies; from conscious or unconscious imitation of Browne; from a desire to lift English out of its drab vulgarity in the second quarter of the century; or from other reasons too many to mention—he did indulge[10] in such diction;[11] but it seems to have been at least as common in his praised conversation (though he sometimes "translated"[12] both ways there) as in his discredited writings; and it never was the staple or secret[13] of that writing at all. This staple or secret is to be found in the elaborate rhetorical *tesselation*[14] of his phrase—by which clauses and sentences were balanced against each other, and built up into larger sentences and paragraphs on a system of almost mathematical or military exactitude, file being drawn up against file, and squadron against squadron, while both the constituent clause-members and *their* constituents of substantive, adjective, and verb were balanced or "dressed"[15] against each other in pairs, triplets, even quaternions[16] of strictest equivalence and equilibrium in rhythm and thought.[17] This Palladian architecture of style is no doubt more imposing than delectable; and the artificial "art" of it sometimes invites Queen Gertrude's protest to Polonius,[18] except that "matter" is never deficient. But it is by no means omnipresent; and it may be doubted whether it[19] is ever very conspicuous in his really best passages.[20]

(1916)

14. Henry SWEET (*1845–1912*) æt. *54*

One result of language being partly rational, partly irrational, is that some of its phenomena can be brought under general rules, some cannot. Thus in English the fact that *tree* is made into *trees* when we speak of more than one tree is a general one; for we can add *s* in the same way and with the same change of meaning to nearly all other names of things. But the fact that *t*, *r*, *e*, *e* expresses the idea 'tree,' and not any other idea, is an isolated one; for, given these sounds, we cannot tell beforehand what the meaning will be, and given the idea 'tree,' we cannot tell beforehand what combination of sounds will express it.

This constitutes the whole distinction between grammar and dictionary. Grammar, like all other sciences, deals with what can be brought under general laws, and relegates all the other phenomena of language to that collection of isolated facts which we call the dictionary. It need hardly be said that there is no absolute line of demarcation between the two; thus the prepositions and many other particles belong both to the grammar and the dictionary. It also follows from our definition that what belongs only to the dictionary in one language may fall—partially, at least—under grammar in another, and *vice versa*. Thus in that remarkably symmetrical family of languages, the Semitic—of which classical Arabic is the best type—many of the details of the formation of roots and the structure of the primitive vocabulary are rightly included in the grammar. Again, such languages as German and Russian—though in many respects they fall short of the Semitic languages in word-forming power—still have great resources in the way of composition and derivation. In English, on the other hand—which, from the point of view of the vocabulary, must be regarded as a degenerate language—

Henry Sweet, *The Practical Study of Languages* (New York, 1899), pp. 74–76.

even such a simple matter as the formation of an adjective from a noun is often the business, not of the grammar, but of the dictionary, as in *sun, solar, man, human, virile.*

We see, then, that the existence of grammars and dictionaries is founded on the nature of language itself.

But many undeniable abuses in the use of these helps have led some reformers to a revolt not only against the use of grammars and dictionaries, but also against all system and method whatever in learning languages. This revolt against method has further led to an advocacy of the 'natural method' by which children learn their own language.

These enthusiasts forget that the process of learning one's native language is carried on under peculiarly favourable circumstances, which cannot be even approximately reproduced in the later study of foreign languages.

In learning our own language, we begin young, and we give our whole time to it. Our minds are perfect blanks, and we come to it with all our faculties fresh and unworn. The fact, too, that we generally learn new words and new ideas simultaneously, and that the word is often the key to the idea, gives a peculiar vividness and interest to the process of word-learning.

But the process has also its disadvantages. It is a very slow process; and the results are always imperfect. Indeed, so imperfect is this natural method, that even with the help of school-training and the incessant practice of everyday life, very few ever attain a really thorough mastery of their own language. When we say that any one is 'eloquent,' or that he 'has a good style,' or 'is a good speaker,' or 'can tell a story well,' we hardly mean more than that his command of his own language is rather less imperfect than that of his fellows. If languages were learnt perfectly by the children of each generation, then languages would not change: English children would still speak a language as old at least as 'Anglo-Saxon,' and there would be no such languages as French and Italian. The changes in languages are simply slight mistakes, which in the course of generations completely alter the character of the language.

The disadvantages we have to labour under when we learn a

foreign language are evident enough, and the later in life we begin, the more evident these disadvantages become. The power of imitation has greatly decreased, which is especially noticeable in the pronunciation. Not only has the power of imitation decreased, but also the desire to use it: the mind has lost its freshness and susceptibility to new impressions.

On the other hand, the mind is formed: it is capable of generalization and abstraction; it has an immensely wider and more accurate knowledge of the things and ideas represented by words and their combinations; it has greater powers of concentration and methodical perseverance. And these advantages more than compensate the disadvantages we have just mentioned.

Nevertheless, there is one disadvantage which turns the scale; that is, the fact that the student has already learnt another language—his own. Hence in learning the new language he has, as it were, to try to unlearn the other language, to struggle continually against the formidable difficulties caused by cross-associations. When he tries to pronounce a new sound, his tongue tends to slip back into the position for forming the nearest native sound. So also with word-order, grammatical construction generally, and the whole fabric of the language.

The fundamental objection, then, to the natural method is that it puts the adult into the position of an infant, which he is no longer capable of utilizing, and, at the same time, does not allow him to make use of his own special advantages. These advantages are, as we have seen, the power of analysis and generalization—in short, the power of using a grammar and dictionary.

(1899)

15. Oscar WILDE (*1854–1900*) æt. *37*

Life and Literature, life and the perfect expression of life. The principles of the former, as laid down by the Greeks, we may not realize in an age so marred by false ideals as our own. The principles of the latter,[1] as they laid them down, are, in many cases, so subtle that we can hardly understand them. Recognizing that the most perfect art is that which most fully mirrors man in all his infinite variety, they elaborated the criticism of language, considered in the light of the mere material of that art, to a point to which we, with our accentual system of reasonable or emotional emphasis, can barely if at all attain; studying, for instance, the metrical movements of a prose [2] as scientifically as a modern musician studies harmony and counterpoint, and, I need hardly say, with much keener æsthetic instinct. In this they were right, as they were right in all things. Since the introduction of printing,[3] and the fatal development of the habit of reading amongst the middle and lower classes of this country, there has been a tendency in literature to appeal more and more to the eye, and less and less to the ear which is really the sense which, from the standpoint of pure art, it should seek to please, and by whose canons of pleasure it should abide always. Even the work of Mr. Pater,[4] who is, on the whole, the most perfect master of English prose now creating amongst us, is often far more like a piece of mosaic than a passage in music, and seems, here and there, to lack the true rhythmical life of words and the fine freedom and richness of effect that such rhythmical life produces. We, in fact, have made writing a definite mode of composition,[5] and have treated it as a form of elaborate design. The Greeks, upon the other hand, regarded writing simply as a method of chronicling. Their test was al-

Oscar Wilde, "The Critic As Artist," *Intentions* (New York, 1905), pp. 112–114.

ways the spoken word in its musical and metrical relations. The voice was the medium, and the ear the critic. I have sometimes thought that the story of Homer's blindness might be really an artistic myth, created in critical days, and serving to remind us, not merely that the great poet is always a seer, seeing less with the eyes of the body than he does with the eyes of the soul, but that he is a true singer also, building his song out of music, repeating each line over and over again to himself till he has caught the secret of its melody, chaunting in darkness the words that are winged with light. Certainly, whether this be so or not, it was to his blindness, as an occasion if not as a cause, that England's great poet[6] owed much of the majestic movement and sonorous splendour of his later verse. When Milton could no longer write, he began to sing. Who would match the measures of *Comus* with the measures of *Samson Agonistes*, or of *Paradise Lost* or *Regained*? When Milton became blind he composed, as everyone should compose, with the voice purely, and so the pipe or reed of earlier days became that mighty many-stopped organ whose rich reverberant music has all the stateliness of Homeric verse, if it seeks not to have its swiftness, and is the one imperishable inheritance of English literature, sweeping through all the ages, because above them, and abiding with us ever, being immortal in its form. Yes: writing has done much harm to writers. We must return to the voice.[7] That must be our test, and perhaps then we shall be able to appreciate some of the subtleties of Greek art-criticism.

(1891)

16. Walter PATER (*1839–1894*) æt. *50*

There, we have the manner of Sir Thomas Browne, in exact expression of his mind! [1]—minute and curious in its thinking, but with an effect, on the sudden, of a real sublimity or depth. His style is certainly an unequal one. It has the monumental aim which charmed, and perhaps influenced, Johnson [2]—a dignity that can be attained only in such mental calm as follows long and learned pondering on the high subjects Browne loves to deal with. It has its garrulity, its various levels of painstaking, its mannerism, pleasant of its kind or tolerable, together with much, to us intolerable, but of which he was capable on a lazy summer afternoon down at Norwich. And all is so oddly mixed,[3] showing, in its entire ignorance of self, how much he, and the sort of literature he represents, really stood in need of *technique*, of a formed taste in literature, of a literary architecture.

And yet perhaps we could hardly wish the result different, in him, any more than in the books of Burton and Fuller, or some other similar writers of that age—mental abodes, we might liken, after their own manner, to the little old private houses of some historic town grouped about its grand public structures, which, when they have survived at all, posterity is loth to part with. For, in their absolute sincerity, not only do these authors clearly exhibit themselves ("the unique peculiarity of the writer's mind," being, as Johnson says of Browne, "faithfully reflected in the form and matter of his work") but, even more than mere professionally instructed writers, they belong to, and reflect, the age they lived in.[4] In essentials, of course, even Browne is by no means so unique among his contemporaries, and so singular, as he looks. And then, as the very condition of

Walter Pater, "Sir Thomas Browne," *Appreciations* (London, 1904), pp. 126–128.

their work, there is an entire absence of personal restraint in dealing with the public, whose humours they come at last in a great measure to reproduce. To speak more properly, they have no sense of a "public" to deal with, at all—only a full confidence in the "friendly reader," as they love to call him. Hence their amazing pleasantry, their indulgence in their own conceits; but hence also those unpremeditated wildflowers of speech we should never have the good luck to find in any more formal kind of literature.[5]

(1889)

17. John RUSKIN (*1819–1900*) æt. *66*

I have above said that had it not been for constant reading of the Bible, I might probably have taken Johnson for my model of English.[1] To a useful extent I have always done so; in these first essays, partly because I could not help it, partly of set, and well set, purpose.

On our foreign journeys, it being of course desirable to keep the luggage as light as possible, my father had judged that four little volumes of Johnson—the Idler and the Rambler [2]—did, under names wholly appropriate to the circumstances, contain more substantial literary nourishment than could be, from any other author, packed into so portable compass. And accordingly, in spare hours, and on wet days, the turns and returns [3] of reiterated Rambler and iterated Idler fastened themselves in my ears and mind; nor was it possible for me, till long afterwards, to quit myself of Johnsonian symmetry and balance in sentences intended, either with swordsman's or paviour's [4] blow, to cleave an enemy's crest, or drive down the oaken pile of a principle. I never for an instant compared Johnson to Scott, Pope, Byron, or any of the really great writers whom I loved. But I at once and for ever recognized in him a man entirely sincere, and infallibly wise in the view and estimate he gave of the common questions, business, and ways of the world. I valued his sentences not primarily because they were symmetrical, but because they were just, and clear; it is a method of judgment rarely used by the average public, who ask from an author always, in the first place, arguments in favour of their own opinions, in elegant terms; and are just as ready with their applause for a sentence of Macaulay's,[5] which may have no more sense in it than a blot pinched between doubled paper, as to reject one of Johnson's, telling against their own prejudice,—though its symmetry be as of thunder answering from two horizons.[6]

(*c. 1885*)

John Ruskin, *Praeterita* (London, 1949), pp. 210–211.

18. Matthew ARNOLD (*1822–1888*) æt. *58*

If we ask [1] ourselves wherein consists the immense superiority of Chaucer's poetry over the romance-poetry [2]—why it is that in passing from this to Chaucer we suddenly feel ourselves to be in another world,[3] we shall find that his superiority is both in the substance of his poetry and in the style [4] of his poetry.[5] His superiority in substance is given by [6] his large, free, simple, clear yet kindly [7] view of human life, [8]—so unlike the total want, in the romance-poets, of all intelligent command of it.[9] Chaucer has not their helplessness; he has gained the power to survey the world from a central, a truly human point of view.[10] We have only to call to mind the Prologue to *The Canterbury Tales*. The right comment upon it is Dryden's: 'It is sufficient to say, according to the proverb, that *here is God's plenty*.' And again: 'He is a perpetual fountain of good sense.' [11] It is by a large, free, sound [12] representation of things, that poetry, this high criticism of life, has truth of substance; [13] and Chaucer's poetry has truth of substance.

Of his style and manner,[14] if we think first of the romance-poetry and then of Chaucer's divine [15] liquidness of diction,[16] his divine fluidity of movement, it is difficult to speak temperately.[17] They are irresistible, and justify all the rapture [18] with which his successors speak of his 'gold dew-drops of speech.' [19] Johnson misses the point entirely when he finds fault with Dryden [20] for ascribing to Chaucer the first refinement of our numbers,[21] and says that Gower also can show smooth numbers and easy rhymes.[22] The refinement of our numbers means something far more than this. A nation may have versifiers with smooth numbers and easy rhymes, and yet may have no real poetry at all. Chaucer is the father [23] of our splendid English po-

Matthew Arnold, "The Study of Poetry," *Essays in Criticism* (London, 1905), pp. 27–29.

etry; he is our 'well of English undefiled,' [24] because by the lovely charm of his diction, the lovely charm [25] of his movement, he makes an epoch and founds a tradition.[26] In Spenser, Shakespeare, Milton, Keats, we can follow the tradition of the liquid diction, the fluid movement, of Chaucer; at one time it is his liquid diction of which in these poets we feel the virtue,[27] and at another time it is his fluid movement. And the virtue is irresistible.

(1880)

19. Anthony TROLLOPE (*1815–1882*) æt. *60*

The critics will again say that all this may be very well as to the rough work of the author's own brain, but will be very far from well in reference to the style in which that work is given to the public. After all, the vehicle which a writer uses for conveying his thoughts to the public should not be less important to him than the thoughts themselves. An author can hardly hope to be popular unless he can use popular language. That is quite true; but then comes the question of achieving a popular—in other words, I may say, a good and lucid style.[1] How may an author best acquire a mode of writing which shall be agreeable and easily intelligible to the reader? He must be correct, because without correctness he can be neither agreeable or intelligible. Readers will expect him to obey those rules which they, consciously or unconsciously, have been taught to regard as binding on language; and unless he does obey them, he will disgust. Without much labour, no writer will achieve such a style. He has very much to learn; and, when he has learned that much, he has to acquire the habit of using what he has learned with ease. But all this must be learned and acquired,—not while he is writing that which shall please, but long before. His language must come from him as music comes from the rapid touch of the great performer's fingers; as words come from the mouth of the indignant orator; as letters fly from the fingers of the trained compositor; as the syllables tinkled out by little bells form themselves to the ear of the telegraphist.[2] A man who thinks much of his words as he writes them will generally leave behind him work that smells of oil.[3] I speak here, of course, of prose; for in poetry we know what care is necessary, and we form our tastes accordingly.

Rapid writing no doubt will give rise to inaccuracy,—chiefly

Anthony Trollope, *An Autobiography* (London, 1950), pp. 176–178.

because the ear, quick and true as may generally be its operation, will occasionally break down under pressure, and, before a sentence be closed, will forget the nature of the composition with which it was commenced.[4] A singular nominative will be disgraced by a plural verb, because other pluralities have intervened and have tempted the ear into plural tendencies.[5] Tautologies [6] will occur, because the ear, in demanding fresh emphasis, has forgotten that the desired force has been already expressed. I need not multiply these causes of error, which must have been stumbling-blocks indeed when men wrote in the long sentences of Gibbon,[7] but which Macaulay, with his multiplicity of divisions,[8] has done so much to enable us to avoid. A rapid writer will hardly avoid these errors altogether. Speaking of myself, I am ready to declare that, with much training, I have been unable to avoid them. But the writer for the press is rarely called upon—a writer of books should never be called upon—to send his manuscript hot from his hand to the printer. It has been my practice to read everything four times at least—thrice in manuscript and once in print. Very much of my work I have read twice in print. In spite of this I know that inaccuracies have crept through,—not single spies, but in battalions. From this I gather that the supervision has been insufficient, not that the work itself has been done too fast. I am quite sure that those passages which have been written with the greatest stress of labour, and consequently with the greatest haste, have been the most effective and by no means the most inaccurate.

(c. 1865–76)

20. Charles MACKAY (*1814–1889*) æt. 55

It is one of the current assertions which, once started on high authority, are never again or very rarely questioned, that the writings of Chaucer are a "well of pure English undefiled." Chaucer's well, limpid and beautiful as it is, and undefiled as grammarians and critics may please to consider it, is not so much a fountain as a single stream. Chaucer, though so ancient in our eyes, was a neologist in his own day, and strove rather to increase the wealth of the written English, of which he was so great a master, by the introduction of words from the Norman-French, little understood by the bulk of the people, though familiar enough to the aristocracy, for whom he mainly wrote, than to fix in his pages for ever the strong simple words of his native Anglo-Saxon. The stream of English in his writings runs pure and cool; the stream of Norman-French runs pure and bright also; but the two currents that he introduced into his song never thoroughly intermingled in the language, and at least nine-tenths of the elegant Gallicisms which he employed found no favour with successive writers; and few of them have remained, except in the earlier poems of Milton. If we really wish to discover the true well of English undefiled, where the stream runs clear and unmixed, we must look to the author of *Piers Ploughman* rather than to Chaucer. We shall there find a large vocabulary of strong words, such as are plain to all men's comprehension at the present day, in the Bible as well as in the common speech of the peasantry; and, above all, in that ancient form of the English language which is known as the Scottish dialect.

Since the days of *Piers Ploughman*, a work invaluable to every English philologist, the spoken language of the peasantry has undergone but few changes as regards words, but very

Charles Mackay, "Lost Preterites," *Blackwood's*, CVI (1869), 258–260.

many changes as regards terminations and inflections. On the other hand, the language of literature and polite society has undergone changes so vast that uneducated people are scarcely able to understand the phraseology that occurs in the master-pieces of our great authors, or the Sunday sermons of their pastors, delivered, as the saying is, "above their heads," in words that are rarely or never employed in their everyday hearing. Among this class survive large numbers of verbs as well as of inflections that ought never to have been allowed to drop out of literature, and which it only needs the efforts of a few great writers and orators to restore to their original favour.

Among the losses which the English language has undergone are, first, the loss of the plurals in *n* and in *en,* and the substitution of the plural in *s;* secondly, the present participle in *and,* for which we have substituted the nasal and disagreeable *ing;* thirdly, the loss of the French negative *ne,* as in *nill,* for 'I will not;' *nould,* for 'I would not;' *n'am,* for 'I am not;' and of which the sole trace now remaining is 'willy-nilly;' and, fourthly, the substitution of the preterite in *d,* as in lov*ed* and admir*ed,* for the older and much stronger preterite formed by a change in the vowel sound of the infinitive and the present, as in run, ran; bite, bit; speak, spoke; take, took; and many others that still survive. And not only has the language lost the strong preterite in a great variety of instances where it would have been infinitely better to have retained it, but it has lost many hundred preterites altogether, as well as many whole verbs, which the illiterate sometimes use, but which literature for a hundred and fifty years has either ignored or despised. Of all the nouns that formerly formed their plural in *n,* as the German or Saxon nouns still for the most part do, very few survive —some in the Bible, some in poetical composition, some in the common conversation of the peasantry, and some, but very few, in polite literature. Among them may be mentioned 'oxen,' for oxes; 'kine,' for cows; 'shoon,' for shoes; 'hosen,' for stockings; 'een,' for eyes; 'housen,' for houses; and the words, as common to the vernacular as to literature, 'men,' 'women,' 'brethren,' and 'children.' In America, the word 'sistern,' as a companion to brethren, survives in the conventicle and the meeting-house. 'Lamben' and 'thumben,' for 'lambs' and 'thumbs,' were comparatively euphemistic words; but thumbs and lambs, and every noun which ends with a consonant in the singular, are syllables which set music, and sometimes pronunciation, at defiance. What renders the matter worse is, that the *s* in the French plural, from which this perversion of the English language was adopted, is not sounded, and that the plural is really marked by the change of the definite article, as *le champ, les champs.* Thus in borrowing an unpronounced consonant from the French, in order to pronounce it we have adulterated our language with a multitude of sibilations alien to its spirit and original structure. The substitution of *s* for *eth* as the terminal of the present person singular of every verb in the language is an aggravation of the evil. If this change had been repudiated by our forefathers, a grace much needed would have been retained in the language.

(1869)

21. Walter BAGEHOT (*1826–1877*) æt. *30*

A great deal of this vividness Macaulay of course owes to his style. Of its effectiveness there can be no doubt; its agreeableness no one who has just been reading it is likely to deny.[1] Yet it has a defect.[2] It is not, as Bishop Butler would have expressed it, such a style as "is suitable to such a being as man, in such a world as the present one." It is too omniscient. Everything is too plain. All is clear; nothing is doubtful.[3] Instead of probability being, as the great thinker expressed it, "the very guide of life," it has become a rare exception—an uncommon phenomenon.[4] You rarely come across anything which is not decided; and when you do come across it, you seem to wonder that the positiveness, which has accomplished so much, should have been unwilling to decide everything. This is hardly the style for history. The data of historical narratives, especially of modern histories, are a heap of confusion. No one can tell where they lie, or where they do not lie; what is in them, or what is not in them.[5] Literature is called the "fragment of fragments"; little has been written, and but little of that little has been preserved. So history is a vestige of vestiges; [6] few facts leave any trace of themselves, any witness of their occurrence; [7] of fewer still is that witness preserved; a slight track is all anything leaves, and the confusion of life, the tumult of change, sweeps even that away in a moment. It is not possible that these data can be very fertile in certainties. Few people would make anything of them: a memoir here, a MS. there—two letters in a magazine—an assertion by a person whose veracity is denied,—these are the sort of evidence out of which a flowing narrative is to be educed; and of course it ought not to be too flowing. "If you please, sir, tell me what you do *not* know," was the inquiry

"Thomas Babington Macaulay," *The Collected Works of Walter Bagehot* (Cambridge, Mass., 1965), I, 425–426.

of a humble pupil addressed to a great man of science. It would have been a relief to the readers of Macaulay if he had shown a little the outside of uncertainties, which there must be—the gradations of doubt, which there ought to be—the singular accumulation of difficulties, which must beset the extraction of a very easy narrative from very confused materials.[8]

This defect in style is, indeed, indicative of a defect in understanding. Macaulay's mind is eminently gifted, but there is a want of graduation in it. He has a fine eye for probabilities, a clear perception of evidence, a shrewd guess at missing links of fact; but each probability seems to him a certainty, each piece of evidence conclusive, each analogy exact. The heavy Scotch intellect is a little prone to this: one figures it as a heap of formulæ, and if fact *b* is reducible to formula B, that is all which it regards; the mathematical mill grinds with equal energy at flour perfect [9] and imperfect—at matter which is quite certain and at matter which is only a little probable. But the great cause of this error is, an abstinence from practical action. Life is a school of probability. In the writings of every man of patient practicality, in the midst of whatever other defects, you will find a careful appreciation of the degrees of likelihood; a steady balancing of them one against another; a disinclination to make things too clear, to overlook the debit side of the account in mere contemplation of the enormousness of the credit. The reason is obvious: action is a business of risk; the real question is the magnitude of that risk. Failure is ever impending; success is ever uncertain; there is always, in the very best of affairs, a slight probability of the former, a contingent possibility of the non-occurrence of the latter. For practical men, the problem ever is to test the amount of these inevitable probabilities; to make sure that no one increases too far; that by a well-varied choice the number of risks may in itself be a protection—be an insurance to you, as it were, against the capricious result of any one. A man like Macaulay, who stands aloof from life, is not so instructed; he sits secure: nothing happens in his study: he does not care to test probabilities; he loses the detective sensation.[10]

(1856)

22. Thomas Babington MACAULAY (*1800–1859*) æt. *31*

Johnson, as Mr. Burke [1] most justly observed,[2] appears far greater in Boswell's books [3] than in his own. His conversation appears to have been quite equal to his writings in matter, and far superior to them in manner.[4] When he talked, he clothed [5] his wit and his sense [6] in forcible [7] and natural expressions. As soon as he took his pen in his hand to write for the public, his style became systematically vicious.[8] All his books are written in a learned language—in a language which nobody hears from his mother or his nurse—in a language in which nobody ever quarrels, or drives bargains, or makes love—in a language in which nobody ever thinks.[9] It is clear,[10] that Johnson himself did not think in the dialect in which he wrote. The expressions which came first to his tongue [11] were simple, energetic, and picturesque.[12] When he wrote for publication,[13] he did his sentences out of English into Johnsonese.[14] His letters from the Hebrides [15] to Mrs. Thrale, are the original of that work of which the Journey to the Hebrides is the translation; and it is amusing to compare the two versions. "When we were taken up stairs," says he in one of his letters,[16] "a dirty fellow bounced out of the bed on which one of us was to lie." This incident is recorded in the Journey as follows: "Out of one of the beds on which we were to repose, started up, at our entrance, a man black as a Cyclops from the forge." Sometimes Johnson translated aloud. "The Rehearsal," he said, very unjustly, "has not wit enough to keep it sweet;" then, after a pause, "it has not vitality enough to preserve it from putrefaction." [17]

Mannerism [18] is pardonable, and is sometimes even agreeable, when the manner, though vicious, is natural. Few read-

Thomas Babington Macaulay, "Boswell's Life of Johnson," *Critical and Historical Essays* (London, 1856), I, 188–189.

ers,[19] for example, would be willing to part with the mannerism of Milton or of Burke. But a mannerism which does not sit easy on the mannerist, which has been adopted on principle, and which can be sustained only by constant effort, is always offensive.[20] And such [21] is the mannerism of Johnson.

The characteristic faults of his style are so familiar to all our readers, and have been so often burlesqued, that it is almost superfluous to point them out.[22] It is well known that he made less use than any other eminent writer of those strong plain words, Anglo-Saxon or Norman-French, of which the roots lie in the inmost depths of our language; and that he felt a vicious partiality for terms which, long after our own speech had been fixed, were borrowed from the Greek and Latin, and which, therefore, even when lawfully naturalized, must be considered as born aliens, not entitled to rank with the king's English.[23] His constant practice of padding out a sentence with useless epithets,[24] till it became as stiff as the bust of an exquisite; [25] his antithetical forms of expression, constantly employed even where there is no opposition in the ideas expressed; [26] his big words wasted on little things; his harsh inversions,[27] so widely different from those graceful and easy inversions which give variety, spirit, and sweetness to the expression of our great old writers—all these peculiarities [28] have been imitated by his admirers, and parodied by his assailants, till the public has become sick of the subject.

(1831)

23. Thomas CARLYLE (*1795–1881*) æt. *32*

To say how, with so peculiar a natural endowment, Richter should have shaped his mind by culture, is much harder than to say that he has shaped it wrong. Of affectation we will neither altogether clear him, nor very loudly pronounce him guilty. That his manner of writing is singular, nay in fact a wild complicated Arabesque, no one can deny.[1] But the true question is, How nearly does this manner of writing represent his real manner of thinking and existing? [2] With what degree of freedom does it allow this particular form of being to manifest itself; or what fetters and perversions does it lay on such manifestation? For the great law of culture is: Let each become all that he was created capable of being; expand, if possible, to his full growth; resisting all impediments, casting off all foreign, especially all noxious adhesions; and show himself at length in his own shape and stature, be these what they may. There is no uniform of excellence, either in physical or spiritual Nature: all *genuine* things are what they ought to be. The reindeer is good and beautiful, so likewise is the elephant. In Literature it is the same: 'every man,' says Lessing, 'has his own style, like his own nose.' True, there are noses of wonderful dimensions; but no nose can justly be amputated by the public,—not even the nose of Slawkenbergius [3] himself; so it *be* a real nose, and no wooden one put on for deception's sake and mere show!

To speak in grave language,[4] Lessing [5] means, and we agree with him, that the outward style is to be judged of by the inward qualities of the spirit which it is employed to body forth; that, without prejudice to critical propriety well understood, the former may vary into many shapes as the latter varies; that, in short, the grand point for a writer is not to be of this or that

Thomas Carlyle, "Jean Paul Richter," *Critical and Miscellaneous Essays* (London, 1887), I, 17–18.

external make and fashion, but, in every fashion,[6] to be genuine, vigorous, alive,—alive with his whole being, consciously, and for beneficial results.

Tried by this test,[7] we imagine Richter's wild manner will be found less imperfect than many a very tame one. To the man it may not be unsuitable. In that singular form there is a fire, a splendour, a benign energy, which persuades us into tolerance, nay into love, of much that might otherwise offend. Above all, this man, alloyed with imperfections as he may be, is consistent and coherent; he is at one with himself; he knows his aims, and pursues them in sincerity of heart, joyfully and with undivided will. A harmonious development of being, the first and last object of all true culture, has been obtained; if not completely, at least more completely than in one of a thousand ordinary men. Nor let us forget that, in such a nature, it was not of easy attainment; that where much was to be developed, some imperfection should be forgiven. It is true, the beaten paths of Literature lead the safeliest [8] to the goal; and the talent pleases us most, which submits to shine with new gracefulness through old forms. Nor is the noblest and most peculiar mind too noble or peculiar for working by prescribed laws: Sophocles, Shakspeare, Cervantes, and in Richter's own age, Goethe, how little did they innovate on the given forms of composition, how much in the spirit they breathed into them! All this is true; and Richter must lose of our esteem in proportion. Much, however, will remain; and why should we quarrel with the high, because it is not the highest? Richter's worst faults are nearly allied to his best merits; being chiefly exuberance of good, irregular squandering of wealth, a dazzling with excess of true light. These things may be pardoned the more readily, as they are little likely to be imitated.

(1827)

24. William HAZLITT (*1778–1830*) æt. *43*

It is not easy to write a familiar style. Many people mistake a familiar for a vulgar style, and suppose that to write without affectation is to write at random. On the contrary, there is nothing that requires more precision, and, if I may so say, purity of expression, than the style I am speaking of. It utterly rejects not only all unmeaning pomp, but all low, cant phrases, and loose, unconnected, *slipshod* allusions. It is not to take the first word that offers, but the best word in common use; it is not to throw words together in any combinations we please, but to follow and avail ourselves of the true idiom of the language. To write a genuine familiar or truly English style, is to write as any one would speak in common conversation, who had a thorough command and choice of words, or who could discourse with ease, force, and perspicuity, setting aside all pedantic and oratorical flourishes. Or to give another illustration, to write naturally is the same thing in regard to common conversation, as to read naturally is in regard to common speech. It does not follow that it is an easy thing to give the true accent and inflection to the words you utter, because you do not attempt to rise above the level of ordinary life and colloquial speaking. You do not assume indeed the solemnity of the pulpit, or the tone of stage-declamation: neither are you at liberty to gabble on at a venture, without emphasis or discretion, or to resort to vulgar dialect or clownish pronunciation. You must steer a middle course. You are tied down to a given and appropriate articulation, which is determined by the habitual associations between sense and sound, and which you can only hit by entering into the author's meaning, as you must find the proper words and style to express yourself by fixing your thoughts on the subject you have to write about. Any

"On Familiar Style," *The Collected Works of William Hazlitt* (London, 1903), VI, 242–245.

one may mouth out a passage with a theatrical cadence, or get upon stilts to tell his thoughts: but to write or speak with propriety and simplicity is a more difficult task. Thus it is easy to affect a pompous style, to use a word twice as big as the thing you want to express: it is not so easy to pitch upon the very word that exactly fits it. Out of eight or ten words equally common, equally intelligible, with nearly equal pretensions, it is a matter of some nicety and discrimination to pick out the very one, the preferableness of which is scarcely perceptible, but decisive. The reason why I object to Dr. Johnson's style [1] is, that there is no discrimination, no selection, no variety in it. He uses none but 'tall, opaque words,' taken from the 'first row of the rubric:'—words with the greatest number of syllables, or Latin phrases with merely English terminations. If a fine style depended on this sort of arbitrary pretension, it would be fair to judge of an author's elegance by the measurement of his words, and the substitution of foreign circumlocutions (with no precise associations) for the mother-tongue. How simple it is to be dignified without ease, to be pompous without meaning! Surely, it is but a mechanical rule for avoiding what is low to be always pedantic and affected. It is clear you cannot use a vulgar English word, if you never use a common English word at all. A fine tact is shewn in adhering to those which are perfectly common, and yet never falling into any expressions which are debased by disgusting circumstances, or which owe their signification and point to technical or professional allusions. A truly natural or familiar style can never be quaint or vulgar, for this reason, that it is of universal force and applicability, and that quaintness and vulgarity arise out of the immediate connection of certain words with coarse and disagreeable, or with confined ideas. The last form what we understand by *cant* or *slang* phrases.—To give an example of what is not very clear in the general statement. I should say that the phrase *To cut with a knife*, or *To cut a piece of wood*, is perfectly free from vulgarity, because it is perfectly common: but to *cut an acquaintance* is not quite unexceptionable, because it is not perfectly common or intelligible, and has hardly yet escaped out of the limits of slang phraseology. I should hardly therefore use the word in this sense without putting it in italics as a license of expression, to be received *cum grano salis*. All provincial or bye-phrases come under the same mark of reprobation—all such as the writer transfers to the page from his fire-side or a particular *coterie*, or that he invents for his own sole use and convenience. I conceive that words are like money, not the worse for being common, but that it is the stamp of custom alone that gives them circulation or value. I am fastidious in this respect, and would almost as soon coin the currency of the realm as counterfeit the King's English. I never invented or gave a new and unauthorised meaning to any word but one single one (the term *impersonal* applied to feelings) and that was in an abstruse metaphysical discussion to express a very difficult distinction. I have been (I know) loudly accused of revelling in vulgarisms and broken English. I cannot speak to that point: but so far I plead guilty to the determined use of acknowledged idioms and common elliptical expressions. I am not sure that the critics in question know the one from the other, that is, can distinguish any medium between formal pedantry and the most barbarous solecism. As an author, I endeavour to employ plain words and popular modes of construction, as were I a chapman and dealer, I should common weights and measures.

The proper force of words lies not in the words themselves, but in their application.[2] A word may be a fine-sounding word, of an unusual length, and very imposing from its learning and novelty, and yet in the connection in which it is introduced, may be quite pointless and irrelevant. It is not pomp or pretension, but the adaptation of the expression to the idea that clenches a writer's meaning:—as it is not the size or glossiness of the materials, but their being fitted each to its place, that gives strength to the arch; or as the pegs and nails are as necessary to the support of the building as the larger timbers, and more so than the mere shewy, unsubstantial ornaments. I hate any thing that occupies more space than it is worth. I hate to see a load of band-boxes go along the street, and I hate to see a parcel of big words without any thing in them. A person who does not deliberately dispose of all his thoughts alike in cumbrous draperies and flimsy disguises, may strike out twenty varieties of familiar everyday language, each coming somewhat nearer to the feeling he wants to convey, and at last not hit upon that particular and only one, which may be said to be identical with the exact impression in his mind. This would seem to shew that Mr. Cobbett is hardly right in saying that the first word that occurs is always the best. It may be a very good one; and yet a better may present itself on reflection or from time to time. It should be suggested naturally, however, and spontaneously, from a fresh and lively conception of the subejct. We seldom succeed by trying at improvement, or by merely substituting one word for another that we are not satisfied with, as we cannot recollect the name of a place or person by merely plaguing ourselves about it. We wander farther from the point by persisting in a wrong scent; but it starts up accidentally in the memory when we least expected it, by touching some link in the chain of previous association.

(1821)

25. Percy Bysshe SHELLEY (*1792–1822*)
æt. *29*

Language, colour, form, and religious and civil habits of action, are all the instruments and materials of poetry; they may be called poetry by that figure of speech [1] which considers the effect as a synonyme of the cause. But poetry in a more restricted sense expresses those arrangements of language, and especially metrical language, which are created by that imperial faculty,[2] whose throne is curtained within the invisible nature of man. And this springs from the nature itself of language, which is a more direct representation of the actions and passions of our internal being, and is susceptible of more various and delicate combinations, than colour, form, or motion, and is more plastic and obedient to the control of that faculty of which it is the creation. For language is arbitrarily produced by the imagination, and has relation to thoughts alone; but all other materials, instruments, and conditions of art, have relations among each other, which limit and interpose between conception and expression. The former [3] is as a mirror which reflects, the latter as a cloud which enfeebles, the light of which both are mediums of communication. Hence the fame of sculptors, painters, and musicians, although the intrinsic powers of the great masters of these arts may yield in no degree to that of those who have employed language as the hieroglyphic of their thoughts, has never equalled that of poets in the restricted sense of the term; as two performers of equal skill will produce unequal effects from a guitar and a harp.[4] The fame of legislators and founders of religions, so long as their institutions last, alone seems to exceed that of poets in the restricted sense; but it can scarcely be a question, whether, if we deduct the celebrity which

"A Defence of Poetry," *The Complete Works of Percy Bysshe Shelley,* ed. Roger Ingpen and Walter E. Peck (London, 1926–30), VII, 113–115.

their flattery of the gross opinions of the vulgar usually conciliates, together with that which belonged to them in their higher character of poets, any excess will remain.

We have thus circumscribed the meaning of the word Poetry within the limits of that art which is the most familiar and the most perfect expression of the faculty itself. It is necessary, however, to make the circle still narrower, and to determine the distinction between measured and unmeasured language; for the popular division into prose and verse is inadmissible in accurate philosophy.

Sounds as well as thoughts have relation both between each other and towards that which they represent, and a perception of the order of those relations has always been found connected with a perception of the order of those relations of thoughts. Hence the language of poets has ever affected a certain uniform and harmonious recurrence of sound, without which it were not poetry, and which is scarcely less indispensable to the communication of its action, than the words themselves, without reference to that peculiar order. Hence the vanity of translation; it were as wise to cast a violet into a crucible that you might discover the formal principle of its colour and odour, as seek to transfuse from one language into another the creations of a poet. The plant must spring again from its seed, or it will bear no flower—and this is the burthen of the curse of Babel.

An observation of the regular mode of the recurrence of this harmony in the language of poetical minds, together with its relation to music, produced metre, or a certain system of traditional forms of harmony of language. Yet it is by no means essential that a poet should accommodate his language to this traditional form, so that the harmony, which is its spirit, be observed. The practice is indeed convenient and popular, and to be preferred, especially in such composition as includes much form and action: but every great poet must inevitably innovate upon the example of his predecessors in the exact structure of his peculiar versification. The distinction between poets and prose writers is a vulgar error. The distinction between philosophers and poets has been anticipated. Plato was essentially a poet [5]—

the truth and splendour of his imagery, and the melody of his language, is the most intense that it is possible to conceive. He rejected the measure of the epic, dramatic, and lyrical forms, because he sought to kindle a harmony in thoughts divested of shape and action, and he forbore to invent any regular plan of rhythm which should include, under determinate forms, the varied pauses of his style. Cicero [6] sought to imitate the cadence of his periods, but with little success. Lord Bacon was a poet.[7] His language has a sweet and majestic rhythm, which satisfies the sense, no less than the almost superhuman wisdom of his philosophy satisfies the intellect; it is a strain which distends, and then bursts the circumference of the hearer's mind, and pours itself forth together with it into the universal element with which it has perpetual sympathy. All the authors of revolutions in opinion are not only necessarily poets as they are inventors, nor even as their words unveil the permanent analogy of things by images which participate in the life of truth; but as their periods are harmonious and rhythmical, and contain in themselves the elements of verse; being the echo of the eternal music. Nor are those supreme poets, who have employed traditional forms of rhythm on account of the form and action of their subjects, less capable of perceiving and teaching the truth of things, than those who have omitted that form. Shakspeare, Dante, and Milton (to confine ourselves to modern writers) are philosophers of the very loftiest power.[8]

A poem is the image of life expressed in its eternal truth. There is this difference between a story and a poem, that a story is a catalogue of detached facts, which have no other bond of connexion than time, place, circumstance, cause and effect; the other is the creation of actions according to the unchangeable forms of human nature, as existing in the mind of the creator, which is itself the image of all other minds. The one is partial, and applies only to a definite period of time, and a certain combination of events which can never again recur; the other is universal, and contains within itself the germ of a relation to whatever motives or actions have place in the possible varieties of human nature. Time, which destroys the beauty and the use of the story of particular facts, stript of the poetry which should invest them, augments that of Poetry, and for ever develops new and wonderful applications of the eternal truth which it contains. Hence epitomes have been called the moths of just history; they eat out the poetry of it! The story of particular facts is as a mirror which obscures and distorts that which should be beautiful: Poetry is a mirror which makes beautiful that which is distorted.

(1821)

26. Samuel Taylor COLERIDGE (*1772–1834*)

æt. *45*

If then I am compelled to doubt the theory, by which the choice of *characters* was to be directed, not only *a priori*, from grounds of reason, but both from the few instances in which the poet himself *need* be supposed to have been governed by it, and from the comparative inferiority of those instances; still more must I hesitate in my assent to the sentence which immediately follows the former citation; and which I can neither admit as particular fact, or as general rule. "The language too of these men is adopted (purified indeed from what appear to be its real defects, from all lasting and rational causes of dislike or disgust) because such men hourly communicate with the best objects from which the best part of language is originally derived; and because, from their rank in society and the sameness and narrow circle of their intercourse, being less under the action of social vanity, they convey their feelings and notions in simple and unelaborated expressions."[1] To this I reply[2]; that a rustic's language, purified from all provincialism and grossness, and so far reconstructed as to be made consistent with the rules of grammar (which are in essence no other than the laws of universal logic, applied to psychological materials) will not differ from the language of any other man of common-sense, however learned or refined he may be, except as far as the notions, which the rustic has to convey, are fewer and more indiscriminate. This will become still clearer, if we add the consideration (equally important though less obvious) that the rustic, from the more imperfect developement of his faculties, and from the lower state of their cultivation, aims almost solely to convey *insulated facts*, either those of his scanty experience or his traditional belief; while the educated man chiefly seeks to discover

Samuel Taylor Coleridge, *Biographia Literaria* (London, 1907), II, 38–43.

and express those *connections* of things, or those relative *bearings* of fact to fact, from which some more or less general law is deducible. For *facts* are valuable to a wise man, chiefly as they lead to the discovery of the indwelling *law*, which is the true *being* of things, the sole solution of their modes of existence, and in the knowledge of which consists our dignity and our power.

As little can I agree with the assertion, that from the objects with which the rustic hourly communicates the best part of language is formed. For first, if to communicate with an object implies such an acquaintance with it, as renders it capable of being discriminately reflected on; the distinct knowledge of an uneducated rustic would furnish a very scanty vocabulary. The few things, and modes of action, requisite for his bodily conveniences, would alone be individualized; while all the rest of nature would be expressed by a small number of confused general terms. Secondly, I deny that the words and combinations of words derived from the objects, with which the rustic is familiar, whether with distinct or confused knowledge, can be justly said to form the *best* part of language. It is more than probable, that many classes of the brute creation possess discriminating sounds, by which they can convey to each other notices of such objects as concern their food, shelter, or safety. Yet we hesitate to call the aggregate of such sounds a language, otherwise than metaphorically. The best part of human language, properly so called, is derived from reflection on the acts of the mind itself. It is formed by a voluntary appropriation of fixed symbols to internal acts, to processes and results of imagination, the greater part of which have no place in the consciousness of uneducated man; though in civilized society, by imitation and passive remembrance of what they hear from their religious instructors and other superiors, the most uneducated share in the harvest which they neither sowed or reaped. If the history of the phrases in hourly currency among our peasants were traced, a person not previously aware of the fact would be suprised at finding so large a number, which three or four centuries ago were the exclusive property of the universities and the schools; and, at the commencement of the Reformation, had been transferred from the school to the pulpit, and thus gradually passed into common life. The extreme difficulty, and often the impossibility, of finding words for the simplest moral and intellectual processes in the languages of uncivilized tribes has proved perhaps the weightiest obstacle to the progress of our most zealous and adroit missionaries. Yet these tribes are surrounded by the same nature as our peasants are; but in still more impressive forms; and they are, moreover, obliged to *particularize* many more of them. When, therefore, Mr. Wordsworth adds, "accordingly, such a language" (meaning, as before, the language of rustic life purified from provincialism) "arising out of repeated experience and regular feelings, is a more permanent, and a far more philosophical language, than that which is frequently substituted for it by poets, who think they are conferring honor upon themselves and their art in proportion as they indulge in arbitrary and capricious habits of expression:" it may be answered, that the language, which he has in view, can be attributed to rustics with no greater right, than the style of Hooker [3] or Bacon to Tom Brown or Sir Roger L'Estrange.[4] Doubtless, if what is peculiar to each were omitted in each, the result must needs be the same. Further, that the poet, who uses an illogical diction, or a style fitted to excite only the low and changeable pleasure of wonder by means of groundless novelty, substitutes a language of *folly* and *vanity*, not for that of the *rustic*, but for that of *good sense* and *natural feeling*.

Here let me be permitted to remind the reader, that the positions, which I controvert, are contained in the sentences—"*a selection of the* REAL *language of men;*"—"*the language of these men*" (i.e. men in low and rustic life) "*I propose to myself to imitate, and, as far as is possible, to adopt the very language of men.*" "*Between the language of prose and that of metrical composition, there neither is, nor can be any essential difference.*" It is against these exclusively that my opposition is directed.

I object, in the very first instance, to an equivocation in the use of the word "real." Every man's language varies, according to the extent of his knowledge, the activity of his faculties, and the depth or quickness of his feelings. Every man's language has, first, its *individualities;* secondly, the common properties of the *class* to which he belongs; and thirdly, words and phrases of *universal* use.[5] The language of Hooker, Bacon, Bishop Taylor, and Burke differs from the common language of the learned class only by the superior number and novelty of the thoughts and relations which they had to convey. The language of Algernon Sidney differs not at all from that, which every well-educated-gentleman would wish to write, and (with due allowances for the undeliberateness, and less connected train, of thinking natural and proper to conversation) such as he would wish to talk. Neither one nor the other differ half so much from the general language of cultivated society, as the language of Mr. Wordsworth's homeliest composition differs from that of a common peasant. For "real" therefore, we must substitute *ordinary,* or *lingua communis.* And this, we have proved, is no more to be found in the phraseology of low and rustic life than in that of any other class. Omit the peculiarities of each, and the result of course must be common to all. And assuredly the omissions and changes to be made in the language of rustics, before it could be transferred to any species of poem, except the drama or other professed imitation, are at least as numerous and weighty, as would be required in adapting to the same purpose the ordinary language of tradesmen and manufacturers. Not to mention, that the language so highly extolled by Mr. Wordsworth varies in every county, nay in every village, according to the accidental character of the clergyman, the existence or non-existence of schools; or even, perhaps, as the exciseman, publican, or barber, happen to be, or not to be, zealous politicians, and readers of the weekly newspaper *pro bono publico.* Anterior to cultivation, the lingua communis of every country, as Dante has well observed, exists every where in parts, and no where as a whole.

Neither is the case rendered at all more tenable by the addition of the words, *in a state of excitement.* For the nature of a man's words, where he is strongly affected by joy, grief, or anger, must necessarily depend on the number and quality of the general truths, conceptions and images, and of the words expressing them, with which his mind had been previously stored. For the property of passion is not to *create;* but to set in increased activity. At least, whatever new connections of thoughts or images, or (which is equally, if not more than equally, the appropriate effect of strong excitement) whatever generalizations of truth or experience, the heat of passion may produce; yet the terms of their conveyance must have pre-existed in his former conversations, and are only collected and crowded together by the unusual stimulation. It is indeed very possible to adopt in a poem the unmeaning repetitions,[6] habitual phrases, and other blank counters, which an unfurnished or confused understanding interposes at short intervals, in order to keep hold of his subject, which is still slipping from him, and to give him time for recollection; or in mere aid of vacancy, as in the scanty companies of a country stage the same player pops backwards and forwards, in order to prevent the appearance of empty spaces, in the procession of Macbeth, or Henry VIIIth. But what assistance to the poet, or ornament to the poem, these can supply, I am at a loss to conjecture. Nothing assuredly can differ either in origin or in mode more widely from the *apparent* tautologies of intense and turbulent feeling, in which the passion is greater and of longer endurance than to be exhausted or satisfied by a single representation of the image or incident exciting it. Such repetitions I admit to be a beauty of the highest kind; as illustrated by Mr. Wordsworth himself from the song of Deborah.[7] "*At her feet he bowed, he fell, he lay down; at her feet he bowed, he fell; where he bowed, there he fell down dead.*"

(1817)

27. Sidney SMITH (*1771–1845*) æt. *38*

Latin and Greek are, in the first place, useful, as they inure children to intellectual difficulties, and make the life of a young student what it ought to be, a life of considerable labour. We do not, of course, mean to confine this praise exclusively to the study of Latin and Greek; or to suppose that other difficulties might not be found which it would be useful to overcome: but though Latin and Greek have this merit in common with many arts and sciences, still they have it; and, if they do nothing else, they at least secure a solid and vigorous application at a period of life which materially influences all other periods.

To go through the grammar of one language thoroughly is of great use for the mastery of every other grammar; because there obtains, through all languages, a certain analogy to each other in their grammatical construction. Latin and Greek have now mixed themselves etymologically with all the languages of modern Europe—and with none more than our own; so that it is necessary to read these two tongues for other objects than themselves.

The two ancient languages are as mere inventions—as pieces of mechanism incomparably more beautiful than any of the modern languages of Europe: their mode of signifying time and case, by terminations, instead of auxiliary verbs and particles, would of itself stamp their superiority. Add to this, the copiousness of the Greek language, with the fancy, majesty, and harmony of its compounds; and there are quite sufficient reasons why the classics should be studied for the beauties of language. Compared to them, merely as vehicles of thought and passion, all modern languages are dull, ill-contrived, and barbarous.

That a great part of the Scriptures have come down to us in

Sidney Smith, "Classical Learning," *Essays, Social and Political* (London, 1882), pp. 59–61.

the Greek language, is of itself a reason, if all others were wanting, why education should be planned so as to produce a supply of Greek scholars.

The cultivation of style is very justly made a part of education. Everything which is written is meant either to please or to instruct. The second object it is difficult to effect, without attending to the first; and the cultivation of style is the acquisition of those rules and literary habits which sagacity anticipates, or experience shows to be the most effectual means of pleasing. Those works are the best which have longest stood the test of time, and pleased the greatest number of exercised minds. Whatever, therefore, our conjectures may be, we cannot be so sure that the best modern writers can afford us as good models as the ancients;—we cannot be certain that they will live through the revolutions of the world, and continue to please in every climate—under every species of government—through every stage of civilisation. The moderns have been well taught by their masters; but the time is hardly yet come when the necessity for such instruction no longer exists. We may still borrow descriptive power from Tacitus; dignified perspicuity from Livy; simplicity from Caesar; and from Homer some portion of that light and heat which, dispersed into ten thousand channels, has filled the world with bright images and illustrious thoughts. Let the cultivator of modern literature addict himself to the purest models of taste which France, Italy, and England could supply, he might still learn from Virgil to be majestic, and from Tibullus to be tender; he might not yet look upon the face of nature as Theocritus saw it; nor might he reach those springs of pathos with which Euripides softened the hearts of his audience. In short, it appears to us, that there are so many excellent reasons why a certain number of scholars should be kept up in this and in every civilised country, that we should consider every system of education from which classical education was excluded, as radically erroneous, and completely absurd.

That vast advantages, then, may be derived from classical learning there can be no doubt. The advantages which are derived from classical learning by the English manner of teaching involve another and a very different question; and we will venture to say, that there never was a more complete instance in any country of such extravagant and over-acted attachment to any branch of knowledge as that which obtains in this country with regard to classical knowledge. A young Englishman goes to school at six or seven years old; and he remains in a course of education till twenty-three or twenty-four years of age. In all that time, his sole and exclusive occupation is learning Latin and Greek: he has scarcely a notion that there is any other kind of excellence; and the great system of facts with which he is the most perfectly acquainted are the intrigues of the heathen Gods: with whom Pan slept?—with whom Jupiter?—whom Apollo ravished? These facts the English youth get by heart the moment they quit the nursery; and are most sedulously and industriously instructed in them till the best and most active part of life is passed away. Now, this long career of classical learning, we may, if we please, denominate a foundation; but it is a foundation so far above ground, that there is absolutely no room to put anything upon it. If you occupy a man with one thing till he is twenty-four years of age, you have exhausted all his leisure time: he is called into the world and compelled to act; or is surrounded with pleasures, and thinks and reads no more. If you have neglected to put other things in him, they will never get in afterwards;—if you have fed him only with words, he will remain a narrow and limited being to the end of his existence.

The bias given to men's minds is so strong that it is no uncommon thing to meet with Englishmen, whom, but for their grey hairs and wrinkles, we might easily mistake for schoolboys. Their talk is of Latin verses; and it is quite clear, if men's ages are to be dated from the state of their mental progress, that such men are eighteen years of age, and not a day older. Their minds have been so completely possessed by exaggerated notions of classical learning, that they have not been able, in the great school of the world, to form any other notion of real greatness. Attend, too, to the public feelings—look to all the terms of applause. A learned man!—a scholar!—a man of erudition! Upon whom are these epithets of approbation bestowed? Are they given to men acquainted with the science of government? thoroughly masters of the geographical and commercial relations of Europe? to men who know the properties of bodies, and their action upon each other? No: this is not learning; it is chemistry, or political economy—not learning. The distinguishing abstract term, the epithet of Scholar, is reserved for him who writes on the Æolic reduplication, and is familiar with Sylburgius, his method of arranging defectives in ω and μι. The picture which a young Englishman, addicted to the pursuit of knowledge, draws—his *beau idéal*, of human nature—his top and consummation of man's powers—is a knowledge of the Greek language. His object is not to reason, to imagine, or to invent; but to conjugate, decline, and derive. The situations of imaginary glory which he draws for himself, are the detection of an anapaest in the wrong place, or the restoration of a dative case which Cranzius had passed over, and the never-dying Ernesti failed to observe. If a young classic of this kind were to meet the greatest chemist or the greatest mechanician, or the most profound political economist of his time, in company with the greatest Greek scholar, would the slightest comparison between them ever come across his mind?—would he ever dream that such men as Adam Smith and Lavoisier were equal in dignity of understanding to, or of the same utility as Bentley and Heyne? We are inclined to think that the feeling excited would be a good deal like that which was expressed by Dr. George about the praises of the great King of Prussia, who entertained considerable doubts whether the King, with all his victories, knew how to conjugate a Greek verb in μι.

Another misfortune of classical learning, as taught in England, is, that scholars have come, in process of time, and from the effects of association, to love the instrument better than the end;—not the luxury which the difficulty incloses, but the difficulty;—not the filbert, but the shell;—not what may be read in Greek, but Greek itself. It is not so much the man who has mastered the wisdom of the ancients that is valued, as he who displays his knowledge of the vehicle in which that wisdom is conveyed. The glory is to show I am a scholar. The good sense and ingenuity I may gain by my acquaintance with ancient authors is matter of opinion; but if I bestow an immensity of pains upon a point of accent or quantity, this is something positive; I establish my pretensions to the name of Scholar, and gain the credit of learning, while I sacrifice all its utility.

(*1809*)

28. William WORDSWORTH (*1770–1850*)
æt. *30*

Having dwelt thus long on the subjects and aim of these Poems, I shall request the Reader's permission to apprize him of a few circumstances relating to their *style,* in order, among other reasons, that I may not be censured for not having performed what I never attempted. Except in a very few instances the Reader will find no personifications of abstract ideas [1] in these volumes, not that I mean to censure such personifications: they may be well fitted for certain sorts of composition, but in these Poems I propose to myself to imitate, and, as far as possible, to adopt the very language of men, and I do not find that such personifications make any regular or natural part of that language. I wish to keep my Reader in the company of flesh and blood, persuaded that by so doing I shall interest him. Not but that I believe that others who pursue a different track may interest him likewise: I do not interfere with their claim, I only wish to prefer a different claim of my own. There will also be found in these volumes little of what is usually called poetic diction; [2] I have taken as much pains to avoid it as others ordinarily take to produce it; this I have done for the reason already alleged, to bring my language near to the language of men, and further, because the pleasure which I have proposed to myself to impart is of a kind very different from that which is supposed by many persons to be the proper object of poetry. I do not know how without being culpably particular I can give my Reader a more exact notion of the style in which I wished these poems to be written than by informing him that I have at all times endeavoured to look steadily at my subject, consequently I hope it will be found that there is in these Poems little falsehood of description, and that my ideas are expressed in lan-

William Wordsworth, "Preface," *Lyrical Ballads,* ed. R. L. Brett and A. R. Jones (London, 1963), pp. 244–246.

guage fitted to their respective importance. Something I must have gained by this practice, as it is friendly to one property of all good poetry, namely good sense; [3] but it has necessarily cut me off from a large portion of phrases and figures of speech which from father to son have long been regarded as the common inheritance of Poets. I have also thought it expedient to restrict myself still further, having abstained from the use of many expressions, in themselves proper and beautiful, but which have been foolishly repeated by bad Poets till such feelings of disgust are connected with them as it is scarcely possible by any art of association to overpower.

If in a Poem there should be found a series of lines, or even a single line, in which the language, though naturally arranged and according to the strict laws of metre, does not differ from that of prose, there is a numerous class of critics who, when they stumble upon these prosaisms as they call them, imagine that they have made a notable discovery, and exult over the Poet as over a man ignorant of his own profession. Now these men would establish a canon of criticism which the Reader will conclude he must utterly reject if he wishes to be pleased with these volumes. And it would be a most easy task to prove to him that not only the language of a large portion of every good poem, even of the most elevated character, must necessarily, except with reference to the metre, in no respect differ from that of good prose, but likewise that some of the most interesting parts of the best poems will be found to be strictly the language of prose when prose is well written.[4] The truth of this assertion might be demonstrated by innumerable passages from almost all the poetical writings, even of Milton himself. I have not space for much quotation; but, to illustrate the subject in a general manner, I will here adduce a short composition of Gray,[5] who was at the head of those who by their reasonings have attempted to widen the space of separation betwixt Prose and Metrical composition, and was more than any other man curiously elaborate in the structure of his own poetic diction.

(*1800*)

29. Hester Lynch PIOZZI (*1741–1821*) æt. *53*

If then to the selection of words in conversation and elegant colloquial language a book may give assistance, the Author, with that deference she so justly owes a generous public, modestly [1] offers her's; persuaded that, while men teach to write with propriety, a woman may at worst be qualified—through long practice—to direct the choice of phrases in familiar talk. Nor has the *Ars recte loquendi*,[2] as Sanctius calls grammar, escaped her observation, though this may surely be setting talk somewhat too high; for grammar, that teaches us to analyse speech into her elements, and again synthetize her into that composite form we commonly find before us, might have pretensions to a higher title, terming itself *Ars recte scribendi* [3] rather—Province of men and scholars, some of whom have told me that Ammonius [4] has observed, I believe in *Com. de Prædic.* p. 28, that even a child knows how to put a sentence together, and say *Socrates walketh;* but how to resolve this sentence into noun and verb, these again into syllables, and syllables into letters or elements—here he is at a stand.[5] Of this, indeed, first of mundane sciences it befits me to be a learner, not a teacher, while one of the most desirable appellations in our unassuming tongue implies a pupil or student rather than a doctor or professor of philology; nor know I any term adequate to that of a good *scholar* in any modern language, whence one is often at a pause in explaining its meaning to foreigners.

Such excellence were in truth superfluous to a work like this, intended chiefly for a parlour window, and acknowledging itself unworthy of a place upon a library shelf. For Selden [6] says wisely, that to know which way the wind sits we throw up a straw, not a stone: my little book then—*levior cortice* [7]—may

Hester Lynch Piozzi, "Preface," *British Synonymy* (London, 1794), I, ii–iv.

on that principle suffice to direct travellers on their way, till a more complicated and valuable piece of workmanship be found to further their research.

(1794)

30. Samuel JOHNSON (*1709–1784*) æt. *72*

In his works, he has given very different specimens both of sentiment and expression.[1] His *Tale of a Tub*[2] has little resemblance[3] to his other pieces. It exhibits a vehemence and rapidity of mind, a copiousness of images, and vivacity of diction, such as he afterwards never possessed, or never exerted.[4] It is of a mode so distinct and peculiar, that it must be considered by itself; what is true of that, is not true of any thing else which he has written.

In his other works is found an equable tenour of easy language,[5] which rather trickles than flows. His delight was in simplicity.[6] That he has in his works no metaphor, as has been said, is not true; but his few metaphors seem to be received rather by necessity than choice.[7] He studied purity;[8] and though perhaps all his structures are not exact, yet it is not often that solecisms can be found; and whoever depends on his authority may generally conclude himself safe.[9] His sentences are never too much dilated or contracted; and it will not be easy to find any embarrassment in the complication of his clauses, any inconsequence in his connections, or abruptness in his transitions.[10]

His style was well suited to his thoughts,[11] which are never subtilised by nice disquisitions, decorated by sparkling conceits, elevated by ambitious sentences, or variegated by far-sought learning.[12] He pays no court to the passions;[13] he excites neither surprise nor admiration; he always understands himself, and his reader always understands him:[14] the peruser[15] of Swift wants[16] little previous knowledge; it will be sufficient

Samuel Johnson, "Swift," *The Lives of the Most Eminent English Poets* (London, 1781), III, 434–436.

that he is acquainted with common words and common things; [17] he is neither [18] required to mount elevations, nor to explore profundities; [19] his passage is always on a level, along solid ground,[20] without asperities, without obstruction.[21]

This easy and safe conveyance of meaning it was Swift's desire to attain,[22] and for having attained [23] he certainly deserves praise, though perhaps not the highest praise.[24] For purposes merely didactick,[25] when something is to be told that was not known before,[26] it is in the highest degree proper,[27] but against [28] that inattention by which known truths are suffered to lie neglected, it makes no provision; [29] it instructs, but does not persuade.[30]

(1781)

31. James Burnett, Lord MONBODDO (*1714–1799*) æt. *62*

By *style*,[1] I do not mean every combination of words expressing some sense; but I mean such a combination, as, in regard either of the words, or the composition of these words, or both, is some way different from ordinary discourse. It has a certain character by which we distinguish it, and denominate it the historical, the didactic, the poetic, the epistolary, and the like. Even dialogue writing, though it be in imitation of conversation, is nevertheless different from ordinary conversation upon the common affairs of life.

Style consists of two parts[2]; the choice of words, and the composition of those words. And, as the last of these two is of greatest variety, and distinguishes most the several kinds of style from one another, we commonly, in English, denominate the whole from that part, calling style, in general, by the name of *composition*.

Words taken singly are to be considered with respect either to their sound or their sense. As to the sound, they are varied in several different ways that have been observed by grammarians; but, with respect to the sense, or meaning, they are only either proper or tropical.[3]

As to the second part of style,[4] or composition, it is more various; but all its variety may be reduced under three heads. *First*, the sound of words in composition; *secondly*, the different ways in which the composition may be varied by grammatical construction; and, *lastly*, the several changes which are made in

[James Burnett, Lord Monboddo], *Of the Origin and Progress of Language* (London, 1786), III, 10–13.

the composition, by giving a different turn to the thought, and consequently to the expression. These last are called, by critics, *figures of the sense,* as the former are called *figures of construction.*

Of these materials all style is made; for it is of these materials, differently used, that the didactic and the historic style are composed; the rhetorical and the poetic, the sublime, the pathetic, the ethic, the familiar, the epistolary, the witty, the humorous, and whatever other difference of style can be imagined. All these may be called the *colours* of style [5]; and of these I propose to treat, after having explained the materials abovementioned, of which style is composed.

(*1773–1792*)

32. George CAMPBELL (*1719–1796*) æt. 57

No law of the English tongue relating to the disposition of words in a sentence, holds more generally than this, that the nominative has the first place, the verb the second, and the accusative, if it be an active verb that is employed, has the third; if it be a substantive verb, the participle, adjective, or predicate of whatever denomination it be, occupies the third place.[1] Yet this order, to the great advantage of the expression, is often inverted. Thus in the general uproar at Ephesus, on occasion of Paul's preaching among them against idolatry, we are informed, that the people exclaimed for some time without intermission, "Great is Diana of the Ephesians." Alter the arrangement,[2] restore the grammatic order, and say, "Diana of the Ephesians is great;" and you destroy at once the signature of impetuosity and ardour resulting, if you please to call it so, from the disarrangement of the words.

We are apt to consider the customary arrangement as the most consonant to nature,[3] in consequence of which notion we brand every departure from it as a transgression of the natural order. This way of thinking ariseth from some very specious causes, but is far from being just. "Custom," it hath been said, "becomes a second nature."[4] Nay, we often find it strong enough to suppress the first. Accordingly, what is in this respect accounted natural in one language, is unnatural in another.[5] In Latin, for example, the negative particle is commonly put before the verb, in English it is put after it; in French one negative is put before, and another after. If in any of these languages you follow the practice of any other, the order of the words will appear unnatural. We in Britain think it most suitable to nature to place the adjective before the substantive; the

George Campbell, *The Philosophy of Rhetoric* (London, 1776), II, 310–316.

French and most other Europeans think the contrary. We range the oblique cases [6] of the personal pronouns, as we do the nouns whose place they occupy, after the verb; they range them invariably before, notwithstanding [7] that when the regimen is a substantive,[8] they make it come after the verb, as we do. They and we have both the same reason, *custom*, which is different in different countries. But it may be said, that more than this can be urged in support of the ordinary arrangement of a simple sentence above explained. The nominative, to talk in the logicians' style, is the subject; the adjective, or participle, is the predicate; and the substantive verb, the copula. Now, is it not most natural,[9] that the subject be mentioned before the thing predicated of it? and what place so proper for the copula which unites them, as the middle? This is plausible, and, were the mind a pure intellect, without fancy, taste, or passion, perhaps it would be just. But as the case is different with human nature, I suspect there will be found to be little uniformity in this particular in different tongues, unless where, in respect either of matter or of form, they have been in a great measure derived from some common source. The Hebrew [10] is a very simple language, and hath not that variety either of moods or of conjunctions that is requisite for forming a complicated style. Here, therefore, if anywhere, one would expect to find an arrangement purely natural. Yet in this language, the most usual, and what would with them therefore be termed the grammatical disposition of the words, is not the disposition above mentioned. In the historic style, or when past events are related, they commonly place the verb first, then the nominative, afterwards the regimen, predicate, or attendant circumstances. The freedom which Greek and Latin allow on this article, renders it improper to denominate one order grammatical exclusively of others. I imagine, therefore, that perhaps the only principle in which on this subject we can safely rest, as being founded in nature, is, that whatever most strongly fixes the attention, or operates on the passion of the speaker, will first seek utterance by the lips. This is agreeable to a common proverb, which perhaps, to speak in Shakespeare's phrase, *is something musty*,[11] but significant enough, "Nearest the heart, nearest the mouth." [12] In these transpositions, therefore, I maintain, that the order will be found, on examination, to be more strictly natural, than when the more general practice in the tongue is followed.

1776)

33. Oliver GOLDSMITH (*1728–1774*) æt. *31*

From a desire in the critic, of grafting the spirit of ancient languages upon the English, have proceeded of late several disagreeable instances of pedantry.[1] Among the number I think we may reckon blank verse. Nothing but the greatest sublimity of subject can render such a measure pleasing; however, we now see it used upon the most trivial occasions. It has particularly found its way into our didactic poetry, and is likely to bring that species of composition into disrepute, for which the English are deservedly famous.[2]

Those who are acquainted with writing know that our language runs almost naturally into blank verse.[3] The writers of our novels, romances,[4] and all of this class who have no notion of style, naturally hobble into this unharmonious measure. If rhymes, therefore, be more difficult, for that very reason I would have our poets write in rhyme. Such a restriction upon the thought of a good poet often lifts and increases the vehemence of every sentiment; for fancy, like a fountain, plays highest by diminishing the aperture. But rhymes, it will be said, are a remnant of monkish stupidity,[5] an innovation upon the poetry of the ancients. They are but indifferently acquainted with antiquity who make the assertion. Rhymes are probably of older date than either the Greek or Latin dactyl and spondee. The Celtic, which is allowed to be the first language spoken in Europe, has ever preserved them, as we may find in the Edda of Iceland, and the Irish carols, still sung among the original inhabitants of that island.[6] Olaus Wormius gives us some of the Teutonic poetry in this way; and Pontoppidan, Bishop of Bergen, some of the Norwegian. In short, this jingle of sounds is almost natural to mankind, at least it is so to our language, if we may judge from many unsuccessful attempts to throw it off.

"The Present State of Polite Learning," *The Works of Oliver Goldsmith*, ed. P. Cunningham (New York, 1881), II, 61–62.

I should not have employed so much time in opposing this erroneous innovation, if it were not apt to introduce another in its train; I mean, a disgusting solemnity of manner into our poetry; and, as the prose writer has been ever found to follow the poet, it must consequently banish in both all that agreeable trifling which, if I may so express it, often deceives us into instruction.[7] The finest sentiment and the most weighty truth may put on a pleasant face; and it is even virtuous to jest when serious advice must be disgusting. But instead of this, the most trifling performance among us now assumes all the didactic stiffness of wisdom. The most diminutive son of fame or of famine has his *we* and his *us*,[8] his *firstlies* and his *secondlies*, as methodical as if bound in cowhide and closed with clasps of brass. Were these monthly reviews and magazines frothy, pert, or absurd, they might find some pardon; but to be dull and dronish is an encroachment on the prerogative of a folio. These things should be considered as pills to purge melancholy; they should be made up in our splenetic climate to be taken as physic, and not so as to be used when we take it.

(*1759*)

34. David HUME (*1711–1776*) æt. *31*

Fine writing, according to Mr. Addison, consists of sentiments, which are natural, without being obvious. There cannot be a juster, and more concise definition of fine writing.[1]

Sentiments, which are merely natural, affect not [2] the mind with any pleasure, and seem not worthy of our attention. The pleasantries of a waterman,[3] the observations of a peasant, the ribaldry of a porter or hackney coachman, all of these are natural, and disagreeable. What an insipid comedy should we make of the chit-chat of the tea-table,[4] copied faithfully and at full length? Nothing can please persons of taste, but nature drawn with all her graces and ornaments, *la belle nature;* or if we copy low life, the strokes must be strong and remarkable, and must convey a lively image to the mind. The absurd naivety of *Sancho Panza* is represented in such inimitable colours by Cervantes, that it entertains as much as the picture of the most magnanimous hero or softest lover.

The case is the same with orators, philosophers, critics, or any author who speaks in his own person, without introducing other speakers or actors. If his language be not elegant, his observations uncommon, his sense strong and masculine, he will in vain boast his nature and simplicity. He may be correct; but he never will be agreeable. It is the unhappiness of such authors, that they are never blamed or censured. The good fortune of a book, and that of a man, are not the same. The secret deceiving path of life, which Horace talks of, *fallentis semita vitæ,* may be the happiest lot of the one; but it is the greatest misfortune which the other can possibly fall into.

On the other hand, productions, which are merely surprising,

David Hume, "Of Simplicity and Refinement in Writing," *Essays, Moral, Political and Literary,* ed. T. H. Green and T. H. Grose (London, 1875), I, 240–241.

without being natural, can never give any lasting entertainment to the mind. To draw chimeras, is not, properly speaking, to copy or imitate. The justness of the representation is lost, and the mind is displeased to find a picture which bears no resemblance to any original. Nor are such excessive refinements more agreeable in the epistolary or philosophic style, than in the epic or tragic. Too much ornament is a fault in every kind of production. Uncommon expressions, strong flashes of wit, pointed similes, and epigrammatic turns, especially when they recur too frequently, are a disfigurement, rather than any embellishment of discourse. As the eye, in surveying a Gothic building,[5] is distracted by the multiplicity of ornaments, and loses the whole by its minute attention to the parts; so the mind, in perusing a work overstocked with wit, is fatigued and disgusted with the constant endeavour to shine and surprise. This is the case where a writer over-abounds in wit, even though that wit, in itself, should be just and agreeable. But it commonly happens to such writers, that they seek for their favourite ornaments, even where the subject does not afford them; and by that means have twenty insipid conceits for one thought which is really beautiful.

There is no object in critical learning more copious, than this of the just mixture of simplicity and refinement in writing; and therefore, not to wander in too large a field, I shall confine myself to a few general observations on that head.

(*1742*)

35. George BERKELEY (*1685–1753*) æt. *47*

Words are signs: They do or should stand for ideas; which so far as they suggest they are significant.[1] But words that suggest no ideas are insignificant. He who annexeth [2] a clear idea to every word he makes use of, speaks sense: But where such ideas are wanting, the speaker utters nonsense. In order, therefore, to know whether any man's speech be senseless and insignificant, we have nothing to do but lay aside the words and consider the ideas suggested by them. Men, not being able immediately to communicate their ideas one to another, are obliged to make use of sensible signs, or words; the use of which is to raise those ideas in the hearer, which are in the mind of the speaker: And if they fail of this end, they serve to no purpose. He, who really thinks hath a train of ideas succeeding each other and connected in his mind: And when he expresseth himself by discourse, each word suggests a distinct idea to the hearer or reader; who by that means hath the same train of ideas in his, which was in the mind of the speaker or writer. As far as this effect is produced, so far the discourse is intelligible, hath sense and meaning. Hence it follows, that whoever can be supposed to understand what he reads or hears, must have a train of ideas raised in his mind, correspondent to the train of words read or heard. These plain truths, to which men readily assent in theory, are but little attended to in practice, and therefore deserve to be enlarged on, and inculcated however obvious and undeniable. Mankind are generally averse from thinking, though apt enough to entertain discourse either in themselves or others: The effect whereof [3] is, that their minds are rather stored with names than ideas, the husk of science rather than the thing. And yet these words without meaning do often make distinctions of

"Alciphron, or The Minute Philosopher," *The Works of George Berkeley*, ed. Alexander Campbell Fraser (Oxford, 1901), II, 319–320.

parties, the subject matter of their disputes, and the object of their zeal. This is the most general cause of error, which doth not influence ordinary minds alone, but even those who pass for acute and learned philosophers are often employed about names instead of things or ideas, and are supposed to know when they only pronounce hard words, without a meaning.

(1732)

36. Jonathan SWIFT (*1667–1745*) æt. *53*

And[1] upon this Account it is, that among *hard Words*,[2] I number likewise those which are peculiar to Divinity as it is a Science; because I have observed several Clergymen, otherwise little fond of obscure terms, yet in their Sermons very liberal of those which they find in Ecclesiastical Writers, as if it were our Duty to understand them: Which I am sure it is not.[3] And I defy the greatest Divine, to produce any Law either of God or Man, which obliges me to comprehend the Meaning of *Omniscience, Omnipresence, Ubiquity, Attribute, Beatifick Vision*,[4] with a Thousand others so frequent in Pulpits; any more than that of *Excentrick, Idiosyncracy, Entity*, and the like.[5] I believe, I may venture to insist further, that many Terms used in Holy Writ, particularly by St. *Paul*, might with more Discretion be changed into plainer Speech, except when they are introduced as part of a Quotation.

I am the more earnest in this Matter, because it is a general Complaint, and the justest in the World.[6] For a Divine hath nothing to say to the wisest Congregation of any Parish in this Kingdom, which he may not express in a Manner to be understood by the meanest[7] among them. And this Assertion must be true, or else God requires from us more than we are able to perform. However, not to contend whether a Logician might possibly put a Case that would serve for an Exception; I will appeal to any Man of Letters, whether at least nineteen in twenty[8] of those perplexing Words might not be changed into easy ones, such as naturally first occur to ordinary Men, and probably did so at first to those very Gentlemen, who are so fond of the former.

We are often reproved by Divines from the Pulpits, on Ac-

Jonathan Swift, "A Letter to a Young Gentleman," *Irish Tracts 1720–1723 and Sermons* (Oxford, 1948), pp. 66–68.

count of our Ignorance in Things sacred; [9] and perhaps with Justice enough: [10] However, it is not very reasonable for them to expect, that *common Men* should understand Expressions, which are never made use of in *common Life*. No Gentleman thinks it safe or prudent to send a Servant with a Message, without repeating it more than once, and endeavouring to put it into Terms brought down to the Capacity of the Bearer: Yet after all this Care, it is frequent for Servants to mistake, and sometimes occasion Misunderstandings between Friends; although the common Domestics in some Gentlemen's Families,[11] may have more Opportunities of improving their Minds, than the ordinary Sort of Tradesmen.

It is usual for Clergymen who are taxed with this learned Defect, to quote Dr. *Tillotson*,[12] and other famous Divines in their Defence; without considering the Difference between elaborate Discourses upon important Occasions, delivered to Princes or Parliaments, written with a View of being made publick; and a plain Sermon intended for the Middle or lower Size of People. Neither do they seem to remember the many Alterations, Additions, and Expungings made by great Authors, in those Treatises which they prepare for the Publick. Besides, that excellent Prelate above-mentioned, was known to preach after a much more popular Manner in the City Congregations: And if in those Parts of his Works, he be any where [13] too obscure for the Understandings of many, who may be supposed to have been his Hearers; it ought to be numbered among his Omissions.

The Fear of being thought Pedants [14] hath been of pernicious Consequence to young Divines. This hath wholly taken many of them off from their severer Studies in the University; which they have exchanged for Plays, Poems, and Pamphlets, in order to qualify them for Tea-Tables and Coffee-Houses. This they usually call *Polite Conversation*,[15] *knowing the World*, and *reading Men instead of Books*. These Accomplishments, when applied in the Pulpit, appear by [16] a quaint, terse, florid Style,[17] rounded into Periods and Cadencies,[18] commonly without either Propriety or Meaning. I have listened with my utmost Attention for half an Hour to an Orator of this Species, without being able to understand, much less to carry away one single Sentence out of a whole Sermon. Others, to shew that their Studies have not been confined to Sciences, or ancient Authors, will talk in the Style of a gaming Ordinary,[19] and *White Friars;* [20] where I suppose the Hearers can be little edified by the Terms of *Palming, Shuffling, Biting, Bamboozling,*[21] and the like, if they have not been sometimes conversant among Pick-pockets and Sharpers. And truly, as they say, a Man is known by his Company; so it should seem, that a man's Company may be known by his Manner of expressing himself, either in publick Assemblies, or private Conversation.

It would be endless [22] to run over the several Defects of Style among us: I shall therefore say nothing [23] of the *mean* and the *paultry,* (which are usually attended by the *fustian,*) much less of the *slovenly* or *indecent.*[24] Two Things I will just warn you against: The first is, the Frequency of flat, unnecessary Epithets; [25] and the other is, the Folly of using old threadbare Phrases,[26] which will often make you go out of your Way to find and apply them; are nauseous to rational Hearers, and will seldom express your Meaning as well as your own natural Words.[27]

Although, as I have already observed, our *English* Tongue be too little cultivated in this Kingdom; [28] yet the Faults are nine in ten owing to Affectation,[29] and not to the want of Understanding. When a Man's Thoughts are clear, the properest Words will generally offer themselves first; and his own Judgment will direct him in what Order to place them, so as they may be best understood.[30] Where Men err against this Method, it is usually on Purpose, and to shew their Learning, their Oratory, their Politeness, or their Knowledge of the World. In short, that Simplicity, without which no human Performance can arrive to any great Perfection,[31] is no where more eminently useful than in this.

(1720)

37. Joseph ADDISON (*1672–1719*) æt. *39*

There is no kind of false Wit which has been so recommended by the Practice of all Ages, as that which consists in a Jingle of Words, and is comprehended under the general Name of *Punning*. It is indeed impossible to kill a Weed, which the Soil has a natural Disposition to produce. The Seeds of Punning are in the Minds of all Men, and tho'[1] they may be subdued by Reason, Reflection and good Sense,[2] they will be very apt to shoot up in the greatest Genius, that is not broken and cultivated by the Rules of Art. Imitation is natural to us, and when it does not raise the Mind to Poetry, Painting, Musick, or other more noble Arts, it often breaks out in Punns and Quibbles.

Aristotle, in the Eleventh Chapter of his Book of Rhetorick, describes two or three kinds of Punns, which he calls Paragrams, among the Beauties of good Writing, and produces Instances of them out of some of the greatest Authors in the *Greek* Tongue. *Cicero* has sprinkled several of his Works with Punns, and in his Book where he lays down the Rules of Oratory, quotes abundance of Sayings as Pieces of Wit, which also upon Examination prove arrant Punns. But the Age in which *the Punn* chiefly flourished, was the Reign of King *James* the First. That learned Monarch was himself a tolerable Punnster, and made very few Bishops or Privy-Counsellors that had not some time or other signalized themselves by a Clinch, or a *Conundrum*. It was therefore in this Age that the Punn appeared with Pomp and Dignity. It had before been admitted into merry Speeches and ludicrous Compositions, but was now delivered with great Gravity from the Pulpit, or pronounced in the most solemn manner at the Council-Table. The greatest Authors, in their most serious Works, made frequent use of Punns.

Joseph Addison, *The Spectator*, No. 61, *Works* (Birmingham, 1761), II, 491–492.

The Sermons of Bishop *Andrews*,[3] and the Tragedies of *Shakespear*, are full of them. The Sinner was punned into Repentance by the former, as in the Latter nothing is more usual than to see a Hero weeping and quibbling for a dozen Lines together.

I must add to these great Authorities, which seem to have given a kind of Sanction to this Piece of false Wit, that all the Writers of Rhetorick have treated of Punning with very great Respect, and divided the several kinds of it into hard Names,[4] that are reckoned among the Figures of Speech, and recommended as Ornaments in Discourse. I remember a Country School-master of my Acquaintance told me once, that he had been in Company with a Gentleman whom he looked upon to be the greatest *Paragrammatist* among the Moderns. Upon Enquiry, I found my learned Friend had dined that Day with Mr. *Swan*, the famous Punnster; and desiring him to give me some Account of Mr. *Swan's* Conversation, he told me that he generally talked in the *Paranomasia*, that he sometimes gave into the *Plocè*, but that in his humble Opinion he shined most in the *Antanaclasis*.

(*1711*)

38. Daniel DEFOE (*1661–1731*) æt. *37*

The Work of this Society shou'd be to encourage Polite Learning, to polish and refine the *English* Tongue, and advance the so much neglected Faculty of Correct Language, to establish Purity and Propriety of Stile, and to purge it from all the Irregular Additions that Ignorance and Affectation have introduc'd; and all those Innovations in Speech, if I may call them such, which some Dogmatic Writers have the Confidence to foster upon [1] their Native Language, as if their Authority were sufficient to make their own Fancy legitimate.

By such a Society I dare say the true Glory of our *English* Stile wou'd appear; and among all the Learned Part of the World, be esteem'd,[2] as it really is, the Noblest and most Comprehensive of all the Vulgar [3] Languages in the World.

Into this Society should be admitted none but Persons Eminent for Learning, and yet none, or but very few, whose Business or Trade was Learning: For I may be allow'd, I suppose, to say, We have seen many great Scholars, meer Learned Men, and Graduates in the last Degree of Study, whose *English* has been far from Polite, full of Stiffness and Affectation, hard Words,[4] and long unusual Coupling of *Syllables* and Sentences, which sound harsh and untuneable to the Ear, and shock the Reader both in Expression and Understanding.

In short, There should be room in this Society for neither *Clergyman*, *Physician*, or *Lawyer*. Not that I wou'd put an Affront upon the Learning of any of those Honourable Employments, much less upon their Persons: But if I do think that their several Professions do naturally and severally prescribe Habits of Speech to them peculiar to their Practice, and prejudicial to the Study I speak of, I believe I do them no wrong.

Daniel Defoe, *An Essay upon Projects* (London, 1697), pp. 233–235.

Nor do I deny but there may be, and now are among some of all those Professions, Men of Stile and Language, great Masters of *English*, whom few men will undertake to Correct; and where such do at any time appear, their extraordinary Merit shou'd find them a Place in this Society; but it shou'd be rare, and upon very extraordinary Occasions, that such be admitted.

(1698)

39. John LOCKE (*1632–1704*) æt. *58*

Besides words, which are names of ideas in the mind, there are a great many others that are made use of, to signify the connection that the mind gives to ideas, or propositions,[1] one with another. The mind, in communicating its thoughts to others, does not only need [2] signs of the ideas it has then before it, but others also, to shew [3] or intimate [4] some particular action of its own, at that time, relating to those ideas. This it does several ways; [5] as is,[6] and is not, are the general marks of the mind, affirming or denying. But besides affirmation or negation, without which there is in words [7] no truth or falshood, the mind does,[8] in declaring its sentiments to others, connect not only the parts of propositions, but whole sentences one to another, with their several relations and dependencies, to make a coherent discourse.

§ 2. THE WORDS, whereby it signifies what connection it gives to the several affirmations and negations,[9] that it unites in one continued reasoning, or narration,[10] are generally called particles; and it is in the right use of these, that more particularly consists the clearness and beauty of a good stile.[11] To think well, it is not enough that a man has ideas clear and distinct in his thoughts,[12] nor that he observes the agreement, or disagreement of some of them; but he must think in train,[13] and observe the dependence of his thoughts and reasonings one upon another. And to express well such methodical and rational thoughts, he must have words to shew what connection, restriction, distinction, opposition, emphasis, &c. he gives to each respective part of his discourse. To mistake in any of these, is to puzzle, instead of informing his hearer; and therefore it is [14] that those words, which are not truly by themselves the names

"Essay Concerning Human Understanding," *The Works of John Locke* (London, 1751), I, 218–219.

of any ideas, are of such constant and indispensible use in language, and do much contribute to men's well expressing themselves.[15]

§ 3. THIS part of grammar has been perhaps as much neglected, as some others over-diligently cultivated. It is easy for men to write, one after another,[16] of cases and genders, moods and tenses, gerunds and supines.[17] In these, and the like, there has been great diligence used; and particles themselves, in some languages, have been, with great shew of exactness, ranked[18] into their several orders. But, tho' prepositions and conjunctions, &c. are names well known in grammar, and the particles contained under them carefully ranked into their distinct subdivisions; yet, he who would shew the right use of particles, and what significancy[19] and force they have, must take a little more pains, enter into his own thoughts, and observe nicely[20] the several postures of his mind[21] in discoursing.

§ 4. NEITHER is it enough, for the explaining of these words, to render them, as is usual in dictionaries,[22] by words of another tongue, which come nearest to their signification: for what is meant by them, is commonly as hard to be understood in one, as another language. They are all marks of some action or intimation[23] of the mind; and therefore to understand them rightly, the several views, postures, stands, turns,[24] limitations and exceptions, and several other thoughts of the mind, for which we have either none, or very deficient names, are diligently to be studied. Of these there are a great variety, much exceeding the number of particles, that most languages have to express them by; and therefore it is not to be wondered, that most of these particles have divers, and sometimes almost opposite significations.[25] In the Hebrew tongue there is a particle consisting but of one single letter, of which there are reckoned up, as I remember, seventy, I am sure above fifty several significations.

§ 5. BUT is a particle, none more familiar in our language; and he that says it is a discretive conjunction, and that it answers sed in Latin, or mais in French, thinks he has sufficiently explained it. But it seems to me to intimate several relations, the mind gives to the several propositions, or parts of them, which it joins by this monosyllable.

FIRST, but [26] to say no more: here it intimates a stop of the mind in the course it was going, before it came to the end of it.

SECONDLY, I saw but [27] two plants: here it shews, that the mind limits the sense to what is expressed, with a negation of all other.

THIRDLY, you pray; but it is not that God would bring you to the true religion,

FOURTHLY, but [28] that he would confirm you in your own. The first of these Buts intimates a supposition in the mind of something otherwise than it should be; the latter shews, that the mind makes a direct opposition between that, and what goes before it.

FIFTHLY, all animals have sense; but [29] a dog is an animal: here it signifies little more, but that the latter proposition is joined to the former, as the minor of a syllogism.[30]

§ 6. To these, I doubt not, might be added a great many other significations of this particle, if it were my business to examine it in its full latitude, and consider it in all the places it is to be found, which if one should do, I doubt, whether, in all those manners it is made use of, it would deserve the title of discretive, which grammarians give to it. But I intend not here a full explication of this sort of signs. The instances I have given, in this one, may give occasion to reflect upon their use and force in language, and lead us into the contemplation of several actions of our minds in discoursing, which it has found a way to intimate to others, by these particles; some whereof constantly, and others in certain constructions, have the sense of a whole sentence [31] contained in them.

(1690)

40. John DRYDEN (*1631–1700*) æt. *49*

The Consideration of these difficulties, in a servile, literal Translation, not long since made two of our famous Wits,[1] Sir *John Denham*,[2] and Mr. *Cowley*[3] to contrive another way of turning Authours into our Tongue, call'd by the latter of them, Imitation. As they were Friends, I suppose they Communicated their thoughts on this Subject to each other, and therefore their reasons for it are little different: though the practice of one is much more moderate. I take Imitation of an Authour in their sense to be an Endeavour of a later Poet to write like one who has written before him on the same Subject: that is, not to Translate his words, or to be Confin'd to his Sense, but only to set him as a Patern, and to write, as he supposes, that Authour would have done, had he liv'd in our Age, and in our Country. Yet I dare not say that either of them have carried this libertine[4] way of rendring Authours (as Mr. *Cowley* calls it) so far as my Definition reaches. For in the *Pindarick Odes*, the Customs and Ceremonies of Ancient *Greece* are still preserv'd: but I know not what mischief may arise hereafter from the Example of such an Innovation, when writers of unequal parts to him,[5] shall imitate so bold an undertaking; to add and to diminish what we please, which is the way avow'd by him, ought only to be granted to Mr. *Cowley*, and that too only in his Translation of *Pindar*, because he alone was able to make him amends, by giving him better of his own, when ever he refus'd his Authours thoughts. *Pindar* is generally known to be a dark writer, to want Connexion, (I mean as to our understanding) to soar out of sight, and leave his Reader at a Gaze: So wild and ungovernable a Poet cannot be Translated litterally, his Genius is too strong to bear a Chain, and *Sampson* like he shakes it off: A

John Dryden, "Preface to the Translation of Ovid's Epistles," *The Poems of John Dryden* (Oxford, 1958), I, 184–185.

Genius [6] so Elevated and unconfin'd as Mr. *Cowley*'s, was but necessary to make *Pindar* speak *English*, and that was to be perform'd by no other way than Imitation. But if *Virgil* or *Ovid*, or any regular intelligible Authours be thus us'd 'tis no longer to be call'd their work, when neither the thoughts nor words are drawn from the Original: but instead of them there is something new produc'd, which is almost the creation of another hand. By this way 'tis true, somewhat that is Excellent may be invented perhaps more Excellent than the first design, though *Virgil* must be still excepted, when that perhaps takes place: Yet he who is inquisitive to know an Authours thoughts will be disapointed in his expectation. And 'tis not always that a man will be contented to have a Present made him, when he expects the payment of a Debt. To state it fairly, Imitation of an Authour is the most advantagious way for a Translator to shew himself, but the greatest wrong which can be done to the Memory and Reputation of the dead. Sir *John Denham* (who advis'd more Liberty than he took himself,) gives this Reason for his Innovation, in his admirable Preface before the Translation of the second *Æneid*: "Poetry is of so subtil a Spirit, that in pouring out of one Language into another, it will all Evaporate; and if a new Spirit be not added in the transfusion, there will remain nothing but a *Caput Mortuum*".[7] I confess this Argument holds good against a litteral Translation, but who defends it? Imitation and verbal Version [8] are in my Opinion the two Extreams, which ought to be avoided: and therefore when I have propos'd the mean betwixt them, it will be seen how far his Argument will reach.

No man is capable of Translating Poetry, who besides a Genius to that Art, is not a Master both of his Authours Language, and of his own: Nor must we understand the Language only of the Poet, but his particular turn of Thoughts, and of Expression, which are the Characters that distinguish,[9] and as it were individuate him from all other writers. When we are come thus far, 'tis time to look into our selves, to conform our Genius to his, to give his thought either the same turn if our tongue will bear it, or if not, to vary but the dress,[10] not to alter or destroy the substance. The like Care must be taken of the more outward Ornaments, the Words: when they appear (which is but seldom) litterally graceful, it were an injury to the Authour that they should be chang'd: But since every Language is so full of its own proprieties, that what is Beautiful in one, is often Barbarous, nay sometimes Nonsence in another, it would be unreasonable to limit a Translator to the narrow compass [11] of his Authours words: 'tis enough if he choose out some Expression which does not vitiate the Sense. I suppose he may stretch his Chain to such a Latitude, but by innovation of thoughts, methinks he breaks it. By this means the Spirit of an Authour may be transfus'd, and yet not lost: and thus 'tis plain that the reason alledg'd by Sir *John Denham*, has no farther force than to Expression: for thought, if it be Translated truly, cannot be lost in another Language, but the words that convey it to our apprehension (which are the Image and Ornament of that thought) may be so ill chosen as to make it appear in an unhandsome dress, and rob it of its native Lustre. There is therefore a Liberty to be allow'd for the Expression, neither is it necessary that Words and Lines should be confin'd to the measure of their Original. The sence of an Authour, generally speaking, is to be Sacred and inviolable. If the Fancy of *Ovid* be luxuriant, 'tis his Character to be so, and if I retrench it, he is no longer *Ovid*. It will be replyed that he receives advantage by this lopping of his superfluous branches, but I rejoyn that a Translator has no such Right: when a *Painter* Copies from the life, I suppose he has no priviledge to alter Features, and Lineaments, under pretence that his Picture will look better: perhaps the Face which he has drawn would be more Exact, if the Eyes, or Nose were alter'd, but 'tis his business to make it resemble the Original. In two Cases only there may a seeming difficulty arise, that is, if the thought be notoriously trivial or dishonest; But the same Answer will serve for both, that then they ought not to be Translated.

(*1680*)

41. Thomas SPRAT (*1635–1713*) æt. *32*

Thus they have directed, judg'd, conjectur'd upon, and improved *Experiments*. But lastly, in these and all other businesses that have come under their care, there is one thing more about which the *Society* has been most sollicitous, and that is the manner of their *Discourse*, which, unless they had been very watchful to keep in due temper, the whole spirit and vigour [1] of their *Design* had been soon eaten out by the luxury and redundance of *speech*. The ill effects of this superfluity of talking have already overwhelm'd most other *Arts* and *Professions*, insomuch that when I consider the means of *happy living* and the causes of their corruption, I can hardly forbear recanting what I said before, and concluding that *eloquence* ought to be banish'd out of all *civil Societies*, as a thing fatal to Peace and good Manners. To this opinion I should wholly incline, if I did not find that it is a Weapon which may be as easily procur'd by *bad* men as *good*, and that, if these should onely cast it away, and those retain it, the *naked Innocence* [2] of vertue would be upon all occasions expos'd to the *armed Malice* of the wicked. This is the chief reason that should now keep up the Ornaments of speaking [3] in any request,[4] since they are so much degenerated from their original usefulness. They were at first, no doubt, an admirable Instrument in the hands of *Wise Men*, when they were onely employ'd to describe *Goodness*, *Honesty*, *Obedience*, in larger, fairer and more moving Images; [5] to represent *Truth*, cloth'd with Bodies; and to bring *Knowledg* back again to our very senses, from whence it was at first deriv'd to our understandings. But now they are generally chang'd to worse uses: They make the *Fancy* disgust [6] the best things, if they come sound and unadorn'd; they are in open defiance against

Thomas Sprat, *The History of the Royal Society of London* (London, 1667), pp. 111–113.

Reason, professing not to hold much correspondence with that, but with its Slaves, *the Passions;*[7] they give the mind a motion too changeable and bewitching [8] to consist with *right practice*.[9] Who can behold without indignation how many mists and uncertainties these specious *Tropes* and *Figures* [10] have brought on our knowledg? How many rewards which are due to more profitable and difficult *Arts* have been still snatch'd away by the easie vanity [11] of *fine speaking?* For now I am warm'd with this just Anger, I cannot with-hold my self from betraying the shallowness of all these seeming Mysteries upon which *we Writers* and *Speakers* look so bigg. And, in few words, I dare say that, of all the Studies of men, nothing may be sooner obtain'd than this vicious abundance of *Phrase*,[12] this trick of *Metaphors*, this volubility of *Tongue*, which makes so great a noise in the World. But I spend words in vain, for the evil is now so inveterate that it is hard to know whom to *blame*, or where to begin to *reform*. We all value one another so much upon this beautiful deceipt,[13] and labour so long after it in the years of our education, that we cannot but ever after think kinder of it than it deserves. And indeed, in most other parts of Learning, I look on it to be a thing almost utterly desperate in its cure, and I think it may be plac'd amongst those *general mischiefs*, such as the *dissention* of Christian Princes, the *want of practice* in Religion, and the like, which have been so long spoken against that men are become insensible about them, every one shifting off the fault from himself to others, and so they are only made bare common places of complaint.[14] It will suffice my present purpose to point out what has been done by the *Royal Society* [15] towards the correcting of its excesses in *Natural Philosophy*,[16] to which it is, of all others, a most profest enemy.

They have therefore been most rigorous in putting in execution the only Remedy that can be found for this *extravagance*, and that has been a constant Resolution to reject all amplifications, digressions, and swellings of style; to return back to the primitive purity and shortness,[17] when men deliver'd so many *things* almost in an equal number of *words*.[18] They have exacted from all their members a close, naked, natural way of speaking, positive expressions, clear senses, a native easiness, bringing all things as near the Mathematical plainness[19] as they can, and preferring the language of Artizans,[20] Countrymen, and Merchants, before that of Wits or Scholars.

(1667)

42. Joseph GLANVILL (*1636–1680*) æt. *25*

Only to give an hint more of this verbal emptiness; a short view of a *definition* or two will be current evidence: which, though in *Greek* or *Latine* they amuse us, yet a *vernacular translation* unmasks them; and if we make them speak *English*, the cheat is transparent. Light is ἐνέργεια τοῦ διαφάνους saith that *Philosophy:* In *English*, the *Act of a perspicuous body*. Sure *Aristotle* here transgrest his *Topicks:* and if this definition be clearer, and more known then the thing defin'd; *midnight* may vye for conspicuity with *noon*. Is not *light* more known then this insignificant *Energie?* And what's a *diaphanous* body, but the *Lights medium*, the *Air?* So that *light* is the act of the *Air:* which *definition* spoils the *Riddle;* and makes it no wonder, a man should see by *night* as well as by *day*. Thus is *light* darkned by an *illustration;* and the *Sun* itself is wrap'd up in obscuring *clouds:* As if *light* were best seen by *darkness*, as *light inaccessible* is known by *Ignorance*. If *Lux* be *Umbra Dei;* this definition is *Umbra lucis*. The infant, that was last enlarged from its *maternal cels;* knows more what *light* is, then this *definition* teacheth. Again, that motion is ἐντελέχεια τῶν ὄντων ἐν δυνάμει, *&c.* is as insignificant as the former. By the most favourable interpretation of that unintelligible *Entelechy;* It is but an *act* of a being in *power*, as it is in *power:* The construing of which to any real meaning, is beyond the *criticisms* of a *Mother Tongue;* except it describes our modern Acts of Parliaments. Sure that definition is not very *conspicuous*, whose *Genus* pos'd the *Devil*. The *Philosopher*, that prov'd *motion* by walking, did in that action better *define* it: And that puzled *Candidate*, who being ask'd what a *circle* was, describ'd it by the *rotation* of his *hand;* gave an account more satisfying. In some things we must indeed give an allowance for words of Art: But

Joseph Glanvill, *The Vanity of Dogmatizing* (London, 1661), pp. 156–158.

in defining obvious appearances, we are to use what is most plain and easie; that the mind be not misled by *Amphibologies*, or ill conceived notions, into fallacious deductions. To give an account of all the insignificancies of this *Philosophy*, would be almost to transcribe it; a task that I should never engage in, though I ow'd no account for my idle hours. 'Twill need a pardon from the Ingenious for the minutes already spent, though in a *confutation*.

(*1661*)

43. Thomas HOBBES (*1588–1679*) æt. *63*

The generall use [1] of Speech, is to transferre our Mentall Discourse, into Verbal; or the Trayne of our Thoughts, into a Trayne of Words; and that for two commodities; [2] whereof [3] one is, the Registring of the Consequences of our Thoughts; which being apt to slip out of our memory, and put us to a new labour, may again be recalled, by such words as they were marked by. So that the first use of names, is to serve for *Markes*, or *Notes* of remembrance. Another is, when many use the same words, to signifie (by their connexion and order,) one to another, what they conceive, or think of each matter; and also what they desire, feare, or have any other passion [4] for. And for this use they are called *Signes*. Speciall uses of Speech are these; First, to Register, what by cogitation, wee find to be the cause of any thing, present or past; and what we find things present or past may produce, or effect: which in summe, is acquiring of Arts.[5] Secondly, to shew to others that knowledge which we have attained; which is, to Counsell, and Teach one another. Thirdly, to make known to others our wills, and purposes, that we may have the mutuall help of one another. Fourthly, to please and delight our selves, and others, by playing with our words, for pleasure or ornament,[6] innocently.

To these Uses, there are also foure correspondent Abuses. First, when men register their thoughts wrong, by the inconstancy of the signification of their words; by which they register for their conceptions, that which they never conceived; and so deceive themselves. Secondly, when they use words metaphorically; [7] that is, in other sense than that they are ordained for; and thereby deceive others. Thirdly, when by words they declare that to be their will, which is not. Fourthly, when they use them to grieve one another: for seeing nature hath armed living

Thomas Hobbes, *Leviathan* (Oxford, 1909), pp. 24–25.

creatures, some with teeth, some with horns, and some with hands, to grieve an enemy, it is but an abuse of Speech, to grieve him with the tongue, unlesse it be one whom wee are obliged to govern; and then it is not to grieve, but to correct and amend.

(1651)

44. John MILTON (*1608–1674*) æt. *33*

Lastly, I should not chuse this manner of writing,[1] wherin knowing my self inferior to my self, led by the genial power of nature to another task,[2] I have the use, as I may account it, but of my left hand. And though I shall be foolish in saying more to this purpose, yet since it will be such a folly as wisest men, going about to commit, have only confest and so committed, I may trust with more reason, because with more folly to have courteous pardon. For although a Poet soaring in the high region of his fancies with his garland and singing robes about him might without apology speak more of himself then I mean to do, yet for me sitting here below in the cool element of prose, a mortall thing among many readers of no Empyreall conceit,[3] to venture and divulge unusual things of my selfe, I shall petition to the gentler sort, it may not be envy [4] to me. I must say therefore that after I had from my first yeeres by the ceaselesse diligence and care of my father, whom God recompence, bin exercis'd to the tongues,[5] and some sciences, as my age would suffer,[6] by sundry masters and teachers both at home and at the schools, it was found that whether ought was impos'd me by them that had the overlooking, or betak'n to of mine own choise in English, or other tongue, prosing or versing, but chiefly this latter, the stile by certain vital signes it had, was likely to live.[7] But much latelier [8] in the privat Academies of *Italy*, whither I was favor'd to resort, perceiving that some trifles which I had in memory, compos'd at under twenty or thereabout (for the manner [9] is that every one must give some proof of his wit and reading there) met with acceptance above what was lookt for, and other things [10] which I had shifted [11] in scarsity [12] of books and conveniences to patch up amongst them, were receiv'd with

John Milton, *The Reason of Church-government Urg'd against Prelaty* (London, 1641), pp. 37–38.

written Encomiums, which the Italian is not forward to bestow on men of this side the *Alps*, I began thus farre to assent both to them and divers of my friends here at home, and not lesse to an inward prompting which now grew daily upon me, that by labour and intent study (which I take to be my portion in this life), joyn'd with the strong propensity of nature, I might perhaps leave something so written to aftertimes, as they should not willingly let it die. These thoughts at once possest me, and these other. That if *I* were certain to write as men buy Leases,[13] for three lives and downward, there ought no regard be sooner had, then to God's glory [14] by the honour and instruction of my country.[15] For which cause, and not only for that I knew it would be hard to arrive at the second rank among the Latines,[16] *I* apply'd my selfe to that resolution which *Ariosto* [17] follow'd against the perswasions of *Bembo*, to fix all the industry and art I could unite to the adorning of my native tongue: not to make verbal curiosities the end (that were a toylsom vanity), but to be an interpreter & relater of the best and sagest things among mine own Citizens throughout this Iland in the mother dialect: [18] That what the greatest and choycest wits of *Athens*, *Rome*, or modern *Italy*, and those Hebrews of old, did for their country, I in my proportion, with this over and above of being a Christian, might doe for mine; not caring to be once nam'd abroad,[19] though perhaps I could attaine to that, but content with these British Ilands as my world, whose fortune hath hitherto bin, that if the Athenians, as some say, made their small deeds great and renowned by their eloquent writers, *England* hath had her noble atchievments made small by the unskilfull handling of monks and mechanicks.[20]

(*1641*)

45. Sir William ALEXANDER (*1567–1640*)
æt. *67*

After a great Travel both of Body and of Mind, which (since not voluntary but imposed upon me) was the more painful, by retiring for a Time where I was born, of late, gladly embracing this rarely offered Opportunity to refresh my self, and being curious, as the most dainty Kind of Pleasure for such as are capable of their Delicacies, to recreate my self with the Muses, —I may justly say recreate, since they create new Spirits, which shaking off gross Affections, diving into the Depths, reaching the Heights, and contemplating both, are transported with these Things which are only worthy to Entertain so noble a Thing as the Mind of Man,—I began to renew my Acquaintance there, having of a long Time been a Stranger with them; so that at the first I could not begin to practise as one of their ordinary Train, but only to court with these whose Credit might procure my Access. I conversed with some of the Modern as well as with the Ancients, kindling my Fire at those Fires which do still burn out of the Ashes of ancient Authors, to whom I find them no Way inferior, though like affectioned Patriots, by writing in the vulgar Tongues, seeking to grace their own Country. I have pitied the Ignorance of some who might be admitted for Versifiers and Poets, that would extol as an excellent Piece of Poesy that which, wanting Life, had nothing but Language, masking Ignorance with *Greek* and *Latin*, whose Treasure long feeding upon, they had by Time digested, and converted to their own Use, though venting it but in Excrements.

Language is but the Apparel of Poesy, which may give Beauty, but not Strength: And when I censure any Poet, I first dissolve the general Contexture of his Work in several Pieces, to

Sir William Alexander, "Anacrisis," *Critical Essays of the Seventeenth Century*, ed. J. E. Spingarn (London, 1908), I, 181–183.

see what Sinews it hath, and to mark what will remain behind, when that external Gorgeousness, consisting in the Choice or Placing of Words, as if it would bribe the Ear to corrupt the Judgment, is first removed, or at least only marshalled in its own Degree. I value Language as a Conduit, the Variety thereof to several Shapes, and adorned Truth or witty Inventions that which it should deliver. I compare a Poem to a Garden, the disposing of the Parts of the one to the several Walks of the other: The Decorum kept in Descriptions, and representing of Persons, to the Proportions and Distances to be observed in such Things as are planted therein, and the Variety of Invention to the Diversity of Flowers thereof; whereof Three Sorts do chiefly please me: A grave Sentence, by which the Judgment may be bettered; a witty Conceit, which doth harmoniously delight the Spirits; and a generous Rapture expressing Magnanimity, whereby the Mind may be inflamed for great Things. All the rest, for the most Part, is but a naked Narration or gross Staff to uphold the general Frame, yet the more apt, if well contrived and eloquently delivered, to angle vulgar Readers, who perchance can scarce conceive the other.

I condemn their Opinions, who, as they would include all Perfection in one, do prefer someone with whom they sympathize, or whom they have most practised, to all others. There is none singular in all, and yet all are singular in some Things. There is none so excellent that is not excelled in some Pieces by some others, and every one hath his own particular Grace, none being positively but only comparatively to be praised, and that for Parts, not in the whole; Men's Works, like themselves, not being all of one Quality, nor ever alike.

(1634)

46. Ben JONSON (*1573–1637*) æt. *47*

Language most shewes a man: speake that I may see thee. It springs out of the most retired, and inmost parts of us, and is the Image of the Parent of it, the mind. No glasse renders a mans forme, or likenesse, so true as his speech. Nay, it is likened to a man; and as we consider feature, and composition in a man; so words in Language: in the greatnesse, aptnesse, sound, structure, and harmony of it. Some men are tall, and bigge, so some Language is high and great. Then the words are chosen, their sound ample, the composition full, the absolution plenteous, and powr'd out, all grave, sinnewye and strong. Some are little, and Dwarfes: so of speech it is humble, and low, the words poore and flat; the members and *Periods*, thinne and weake, without knitting, or number. The middle are of a just stature. There the Language is plaine, and pleasing: even without stopping, round without swelling; all well-torn'd, compos'd, elegant, and accurate. The vitious Language is vast, and gaping, swelling, and irregular; when it contends to be high, full of Rocke, Mountaine, and pointednesse: as it affects to be low, it is abject, and creeps, full of bogs, and holes. And according to their Subject, these stiles vary, and lose their names: For that which is high and lofty, declaring excellent matter, becomes vast and tumorous, speaking of petty and inferiour things: so that which was even, and apt in a meane and plaine subject, will appeare most poore and humble in a high Argument. Would you not laugh, to meet a great Counsellor of state in a flat cap, with his trunck hose, and a hobby-horse Cloake, his Gloves under his girdle, and yond Haberdasher in a velvet Gowne, furr'd with sables? There is a certaine latitude in these things, by which wee find the degrees. The next thing to the stature, is the figure and feature in Language: that is, whether it be round,

Timber, or Discoveries, Ben Jonson (Oxford, 1947), VIII, 625–627.

and streight, which consists of short and succinct *Periods*, numerous, and polish'd; or square and firme, which is to have equall and strong parts, every where answerable, and weighed. The third is the skinne, and coat, which rests in the well-joyning, cementing, and coagmentation of words; when as it is smooth, gentle, and sweet; like a Table, upon which you may runne your finger without rubs, and your nayle cannot find a joynt; not horrid, rough, wrinckled, gaping, or chapt. After these the flesh, blood, and bones come in question. Wee say it is a fleshy style, when there is much *Periphrasis*, and circuit of words; and when with more then enough, it growes fat and corpulent; *Arvina orationis*, full of suet and tallow. It hath blood, and juyce, when the words are proper and apt, their sound sweet, and the *Phrase* neat and pick'd. *Oratio uncta, &* *benè pasta*. But where there is Redundancy, both the blood and juyce are faulty, and vitious. *Redundat sanguine, quæ multò plus dicit, quàm necesse est.* Juyce in Language is somewhat lesse then blood; for if the words be but becomming, and signifying, and the sense gentle, there is Juyce: but where that wanteth, the Language is thinne, flagging, poore, starv'd, scarce covering the bone; and shewes like stones in a sack. Some men, to avoid Redundancy, runne into that; and while they strive to have no ill blood, or Juyce, they loose their good. There be some styles, againe, that have not lesse blood, but lesse flesh, and corpulence. These are bony, and sinnewy: *Ossa habent, et nervos.*

(*1620*)

47. The Translators of the King James Version of the Bible

An other thing we thinke good to admonish thee of (gentle Reader) that wee haue not tyed our selues to an vniformitie of phrasing, or to an identitie of words, as some peraduenture would wish that we had done, because they obserue, that some learned men some where, haue beene as exact as they could that way. Truly, that we might not varie from the sense of that which we had translated before, if the word signified the same thing in both places (for there bee some wordes that bee not of the same sense euery where) we were especially carefull, and made a conscience, according to our duetie. But, that we should expresse the same notion in the same particular word; as for example, if we translate the *Hebrew* or *Greeke* word once by *Purpose*, neuer to call it *Intent;* if one where *Iourneying*, neuer *Traueiling;* if one where *Thinke*, neuer *Suppose;* if one where *Paine*, neuer *Ache;* if one where *Ioy*, neuer *Gladnesse*, &c. Thus to minse the matter, wee thought to sauour more of curiositie then wisedome, and that rather it would breed scorne in the Atheist, then bring profite to the godly Reader. For is the kingdome of God become words or syllables? why should wee be in bondage to them if we may be free, vse one precisely when wee may vse another no lesse fit, as commodiously? A godly Father in the Primitiue time shewed himselfe greatly moued, that one of newfanglenes called κράββατον σκίμπους, though the difference be little or none; and another reporteth, that he was much abused for turning *Cucurbita* (to which reading the people had beene vsed) into *Hedera*. Now if this happen in better times, and vpon so small occasions, wee might iustly feare hard censure, if generally wee should make verball and vnnecessary chang-

Reasons inducing vs not to stand curiously vpon an identitie of phrasing.

"The Translators to the Reader," *The Authorised Version of the English Bible* (Cambridge, 1909), I, 28–29.

ings. We might also be charged (by scoffers) with some vnequall dealing towards a great number of good English wordes. For as it is written of a certaine great Philosopher, that he should say, that those logs were happie that were made images to be worshipped; for their fellowes, as good as they, lay for blockes behinde the fire: so if wee should say, as it were, vnto certaine words, Stand vp higher, haue a place in the Bible alwayes, and to others of like qualitie, Get ye hence, be banished for euer, wee might be taxed peraduenture with S. *Iames* his words, namely, *To be partiall in our selues and iudges of euill thoughts.* Adde hereunto, that nicenesse in wordes was alwayes counted the next step to trifling, and so was to bee curious about names too: also that we cannot follow a better patterne for elocution then God himselfe; therefore hee vsing diuers words, in his holy writ, and indifferently for one thing in nature: we, if wee will not be superstitious, may vse the same libertie in our English versions out of *Hebrew* & *Greeke,* for that copie or store that he hath giuen vs. Lastly, wee haue on the one side auoided the scrupulositie of the Puritanes, who leaue the olde Ecclesiasticall words, and betake them to other, as when they put *washing* for *Baptisme,* and *Congregation* in stead of *Church:* as also on the other side we haue shunned the obscuritie of the Papists, in their *Azimes, Tunike, Rational, Holocausts, Præpuce, Pasche,* and a number of such like, whereof their late Translation is full, and that of purpose to darken the sence, that since they must needs translate the Bible, yet by the language thereof, it may bee kept from being vnderstood. But we desire that the Scripture may speake like it selfe, as in the language of *Canaan,* that it may bee vnderstood euen of the very vulgar.

(1611)

48. Francis BACON (*1561–1626*) æt. *44*

There be therfore chiefely three vanities in Studies,[1] whereby learning hath been most traduced: For those things we do esteeme vaine which are either false or friuolous, those which either haue no truth or no vse; & those persons we esteem vain which are either credulous or curious; & curiositie is either in mater or words: so that in reason as wel as in experience there fal out to be these 3 distempers [2] (as I may tearm them) of learning: The first, fantastical learning; The second, contentious learning; & the last, delicate learning; vaine Imaginations, vaine Altercations, & vain affectations; & with the last I wil begin.[3] *Martin Luther,* conducted no doubt by an higher prouidence, but in discourse of reason, finding what a Prouince [4] he had vndertaken against the Bishop of *Rome* and the degenerate traditions of the Church, and finding his owne solitude being no waies ayded by the opinions of his owne time, was enforced to awake all Antiquitie, and to call former times to his succors to make a partie against the present time: so that the ancient Authors, both in Diuinitie and in Humanitie, which had long time slept in Libraries, began generally to be read and reuolued. This by consequence did draw on a necessitie of a more exquisite trauaile [5] in the languages originall wherin those Authors did write: For the better vnderstanding of those Authors, and the better aduantage of pressing and applying their words. And thereof grew againe a delight in their manner of Stile and Phrase,[6] and an admiration of that kinde of writing; [7] which was much furthered & precipitated by the enmity & opposition that the propounders of those primitiue but seeming new opinions had against the Schoole-men,[8] who were generally of the contrarie part, and whose Writings were altogether in a

The Two Books of Sir Francis Bacon Of the Proficience and Advancement of Learning, Divine and Humane (London, 1629), pp. 34–37.

differing Stile and fourme,[9] taking libertie to coyne and frame new tearms of Art[10] to expresse their own sence, and to auoide circuite of speech without regard to the purenesse, pleasantnesse, and (as I may call it) lawfulnesse[11] of the Phrase or word: And againe, because the great labour that then was with the people (of whome the Pharisees were wont to say, *Execrabilis ista turba quæ non nouit legem*),[12] for the winning and perswading of them there grewe of necessitie in cheefe price and request eloquence and varietie of discourse, as the fittest and forciblest accesse into the capacitie of the vulgar sort; so that these foure causes concurring, the admiration of ancient Authors, the hate of the Schoole-men, the exact studie of Languages, and the efficacie of Preaching did bring in an affectionate studie of eloquence and copie of speech, which then began to flourish. This grew speedily to an excesse; for men began to hunt more after wordes than matter,[13] and more after the choisenesse of the Phrase, and the round and cleane composition of the sentence, and the sweet falling of the clauses, and the varying and illustration of their workes with tropes and figures, then after the weight of matter, worth of subiect, soundnesse of argument, life of inuention, or depth of iudgement. Then grew the flowing and watrie vaine of *Osorius,* the Portugall Bishop, to be in price;[14] then did *Sturmius*[15] spend such infinite and curious paines vpon *Cicero* the Orator and *Hermogenes* the Rhetorician, besides his owne Bookes of Periods and imitation and the like; Then did *Car* of *Cambridge,*[16] and *Ascham,* with their Lectures and Writings, almost deifie *Cicero*[17] and *Demosthenes,* and allure all young men that were studious vnto that delicate and pollished kinde of learning. Then did *Erasmus*[18] take occasion to make the scoffing Eccho, *Decem annos consumpsi in legendo Cicerone,*[19] and the Eccho answered in Greeke, *One* (*Asine*).[20] Then grew the learning of the Schoolemen to be vtterly despised as barbarous. In summe, the whole inclination and bent of those times was rather towards copie than weight.

Here, therefore, is the first distemper of learning, when men studie words and not matter; whereof though I haue represented an example of late times, yet it hath beene and will be, *Secundum maius & minus,*[21] in all time. And how is it possible but this should haue an operation to discredite learning, euen with vulgar capacities, when they see learned mens workes like the first Letter[22] of a Patent or limmed Booke, which, though it hath large flourishes, yet it is but a Letter. It seemes to me that *Pigmalions* frenzie[23] is a good embleme or portraiture of this vanitie; for wordes are but the Images of matter, and except they haue life of reason and inuention, to fall in loue with them is all one as to fall in loue with a Picture.

(*1605*)

49. George PUTTENHAM (*1530–1590*)
æt. *59*

And because our chiefe purpose herein is for the learning of Ladies and young Gentlewomen, or idle Courtiers, desirous to become skilful in their owne mother tongue, and for their priuate recreation to make now & then ditties of pleasure, thinking for our parte none other science so fit for them & the place as that which teacheth *beau* semblant, the chiefe profession aswell of Courting as of poesie, since to such manner of mindes nothing is more combersome then tedious doctrines and schollarly methodes of discipline, we haue in our owne conceit deuised a new and strange modell of this arte, fitter to please the Court then the schoole, and yet not vnnecessarie for all such as be willing themselues to become good makers in the vulgar, or to be able to iudge of other mens makings: wherefore, intending to follow the course which we haue begun, thus we say: that though the language of our Poet or maker be pure & clenly, & being not disgraced by such vicious parts as haue bene before remembred in the Chapter of language, be sufficiently pleasing and commendable for the ordinarie vse of speech; yet is not the same so well appointed for all purposes of the excellent Poet, as when it is gallantly arrayed in all his colours which figure can set vpon it, therefore we are now further to determine of figures and figuratiue speeches. Figuratiue speech is a noueltie of language euidently (and yet not absurdly) estranged from the ordinarie habite and manner of our dayly talke and writing and figure it selfe is a certaine liuely or good grace set vpon wordes, speaches and sentences to some purpose and not in vaine, giuing them ornament or efficacie by many maner of alterations in shape, in sounde, and also in sence, sometime by way of sur-

George Puttenham, *The Arte of English Poesie*, ed. Gladys Doidge Willcock and Alice Walker (Cambridge, 1936), pp. 158–161.

plusage, sometime by defect, sometime by disorder, or mutation, & also by putting into our speaches more pithe and substance, subtilitie, quicknesse, efficacie or moderation, in this or that sort tuning and tempring them, by amplification, abridgement, opening, closing, enforcing, meekening or otherwise disposing them to the best purpose: whereupon the learned clerks who haue written methodically of this Arte in the two master languages, Greeke and Latine, haue sorted all their figures into three rankes, and the first they bestowed vpon the Poet onely: the second vpon the Poet and Oratour indifferently: the third vpon the Oratour alone. And that first sort of figures doth serue th'eare onely and may be therefore called *Auricular* your second serues the conceit onely and not th'eare, and may be called *sensable,* not sensible nor yet sententious: your third sort serues as well th'eare as the conceit, and may be called *sententious figures,* because not only they properly apperteine to full sentences, for bewtifying them with a currant & pleasant numerositie, but also giuing them efficacie, and enlarging the whole matter besides with copious amplifications. I doubt not but some busie carpers will scorne at my new deuised termes: *auricular* and *sensable,* saying that I might with better warrant haue vsed in their steads these words, *orthographicall* or *syntacticall,* which the learned Grammarians left ready made to our hands, and do importe as much as th'other that I haue brought, which thing peraduenture I deny not in part, and neuerthelesse for some causes thought them not so necessarie but with these maner of men I do willingly beare, in respect of their laudable endeuour to allow antiquitie and flie innouation: with like beneuolence I trust they will beare with me writing in the vulgar speach and seeking by my nouelties to satisfie not the schoole but the Court: whereas they know very well all old things soone waxe stale & lothsome, and the new deuises are euer dainty and delicate, the vulgar instruction requiring also vulgar and communicable termes, not clerkly or vncouthe, as are all these of the Greeke and Latine languages primitiuely receiued, vnlesse they be qualified or by much vse and custome allowed and our eares made acquainted with them. Thus then I say that *auricular* figures be those which worke alteration in th'eare by sound, accent, time, and slipper volubilitie in vtterance, such as for that respect was called by the auncients numerositie of speach. And not onely the whole body of a tale in poeme or historie may be made in such sort pleasant and agreable to the eare, but also euery clause by it selfe, and euery single word carried in a clause, may haue their pleasant sweetenesse apart. And so long as this qualitie extendeth but to the outward tuning of the speach reaching no higher then th'eare and forcing the mynde little or nothing, it is that vertue which the Greeks call *Enargia* and is the office of the *auricular* figures to performe. Therefore as the members of language at large are whole sentences, and sentences are compact of clauses, and clauses of words, and euery word of letters and sillables, so is the alteration (be it but of a sillable or letter) much materiall to the sound and sweetenesse of vtterance. Wherefore beginning first at the smallest alterations which rest in letters and sillables, the first sort of our figures *auricular* we do appoint to single words as they lye in language; the second to clauses of speach; the third to perfit sentences and to the whole masse or body of the tale be it poeme or historie written or reported.

(1589)

50. "E.K." (author unknown)

And firste of the wordes to speake, I graunt they be something hard, and of most men vnused, yet both English, and also vsed of most excellent Authors and most famous Poetes. In whom, whenas this our Poet hath bene much traueiled and throughly redd, how could it be (as that worthy Oratour sayde) but that walking in the sonne, although for other cause he walked, yet needes he mought be sunburnt; and, hauing the sound of those auncient Poetes still ringing in his eares, he mought needes, in singing, hit out some of theyr tunes. But whether he vseth them by such casualtye and custome, or of set purpose and choyse, as thinking them fittest for such rusticall rudenesse of shepheards, eyther for that theyr rough sounde would make his rymes more ragged and rustical, or els because such olde and obsolete wordes are most vsed of country folke, sure I think, and think I think not amisse, that they bring great grace, and, as one would say, auctoritie to the verse. For albe, amongst many other faultes, it specially be obiected of Valla against Liuie, and of other against Saluste, that with ouer much studie they affect antiquitie, as coueting thereby credence and honor of elder yeeres, yet I am of opinion, and eke the best learned are of the lyke, that those auncient solemne wordes are a great ornament, both in the one and in the other; the one labouring to set forth in hys worke an eternall image of antiquitie, and the other carefully discoursing matters of grauitie and importaunce. For, if my memory faile not, Tullie, in that booke wherein he endeuoureth to set forth the paterne of a perfect Oratour, sayth that ofttimes an auncient worde maketh the style seeme graue, and as it were reuerend, no otherwise then we honour and

"E.K." (author unknown), "Epistle Dedicatory" to *The Shepheards Calendar* (1579), in Edmund Spenser, *The Works: The Minor Poems*, ed. Charles Grosvenor Osgood and Henry Gibbons Lotspeich (Baltimore, 1943), I, 7–9.

reuerence gray heares, for a certein religious regard which we haue of old age. Yet nether euery where must old words be stuffed in, nor the common Dialecte and maner of speaking so corrupted therby, that, as in old buildings, it seme disorderly and ruinous. But all as in most exquisite pictures they vse to blaze and portraict not onely the daintie lineaments of beautye, but also rounde about it to shadow the rude thickets and craggy clifts, that, by the basenesse of such parts, more excellency may accrew to the principall; for oftimes we fynde ourselues, I knowe not how, singularly delighted with the shewe of such naturall rudenesse, and take great pleasure in that disorderly order. Euen so doe those rough and harsh termes enlumine, and make more clearly to appeare, the brightnesse of braue and glorious words. So oftentimes a dischorde in Musick maketh a comely concordaunce: so great delight tooke the worthy Poete Alceus to behold a blemish in the ioynt of a wel shaped body. But if any will rashly blame such his purpose in choyse of old and vnwonted words, him may I more iustly blame and condemne, or of witlesse headinesse in iudging or of heedelesse hardinesse in condemning; for, not marking the compasse of hys bent, he wil iudge of the length of his cast: for in my opinion it is one special prayse of many whych are dew to this Poete, that he hath laboured to restore, as to theyr rightfull heritage, such good and naturall English words as haue ben long time out of vse and almost cleane disherited. Which is the onely cause that our Mother tonge, which truely of it self is both ful enough for prose and stately enough for verse, hath long time ben counted most bare and barrein of both. Which default when as some endeuoured to salue and recure, they patched up the holes with peces and rags of other languages, borrowing here of the French, there of the Italian, every where of the Latine; not weighing how il those tongues accorde with themselues, but much worse with ours: So now they haue made our English tongue a gallimaufray or hodgepodge of al other speches. Other some, not so wel sene in the English tonge as perhaps in other languages, if they happen to here an olde word, albeit very naturall and significant, crye out streightway that we speak no

English, but gibbrish, or rather such as in old time Euanders mother spake: whose first shame is, that they are not ashamed, in their own mother tonge, straungers to be counted and alienes. The second shame, no lesse then the first, that what so they vnderstand not they streight way deeme to be sencelesse and not at al to be vnderstode. Much like to the Mole in Æsopes fable, that, being blynd her selfe, would in no wise be perswaded that any beast could see. The last, more shameful then both, that of their owne country and natural speach, which together with their Nources milk they sucked, they haue so base regard and bastard iudgement, that they will not onely themselues not labor to garnish and beautifie it, but also repine that of other it shold be embellished. Like to the dogge in the maunger, that him selfe can eate no hay, and yet barketh at the hungry bullock that so faine would feede: whose currish kind, though it cannot be kept from barking, yet I conne them thanke that they refrain from byting.

(1579)

51. Roger ASCHAM (*1515–1568*) æt. *c.* 50

Imitation is a facultie to expresse liuelie and perfitelie that example: which ye go about to folow. And of it selfe, it is large and wide: for all the workes of nature, in a maner be examples for arte to folow.

But to our purpose, all languages, both learned and mother tonges,[1] be gotten, and gotten onelie by *Imitation*. For as ye vse to heare, so ye learne to speake: if ye heare no other, ye speake not your selfe: and whom ye onelie heare, of them ye onelie learne.[2]

And therefore, if ye would speake as the best and wisest do, ye must be conuersant where the best and wisest are: but if yow be borne or brought vp in a rude contrie, ye shall not chose but speake rudelie: the rudest man of all knoweth this to be trewe.

Yet neuerthelesse, the rudenes of common and mother tonges is no bar for wise speaking.[3] For in the rudest contrie, and most barbarous mother language, many be found can speake verie wiselie: but in the Greeke and Latin tong, the two onelie learned tonges, which be kept, not in common taulke, but in priuate bookes, we finde alwayes, wisdome and eloquence, good matter and good vtterance, neuer or seldom asonder.[4] For all soch Authors, as be fullest of good matter and right iudgement in doctrine, be likewise alwayes, most proper in wordes,[5] most apte in sentence, most plaine and pure in vttering the same.

And contrariwise, in those two tonges, all writers, either in Religion, or any sect of Philosophie, who so euer be founde fonde [6] in iudgement of matter, be commonlie found as rude in vttering their mynde. For Stoickes, Anabaptistes, and Friers with Epicures, Libertines and Monkes,[7] being most like in learning and life, are no fonder and pernicious in their opinions, than they be rude and barbarous in their writinges. They be not

Roger Ascham, *The Scholemaster* (London, 1570), 45 verso–47 recto.

wise,[8] therefore that say, what care I for a mans wordes and vtterance, if his matter and reasons be good. Soch men, say so, not so moch of ignorance, as eyther of some singular pride in themselues, or some speciall malice or other, or for some priuate and perciall matter, either in Religion or other kinde of learning. For good and choice meates, be no more requisite for helthie bodies than proper and apte wordes be for good matters, and also plaine and sensible vtterance for the best and depest reasons: in which two pointes standeth perfite eloquence, one of the fairest and rarest giftes that God doth geue to man.

Ye know not, what hurt ye do to learning, that care not for wordes, but for matter, and so make a deuorse betwixt the tong and the hart. For marke all aiges: looke vpon the whole course of both the Greeke and Latin tonge, and ye shall surelie finde, that, whan apte and good wordes began to be neglected,[9] and properties of those two tonges to be confounded, than also began, ill deedes to spring: strange maners to oppresse good orders, newe and fond opinions to striue with olde and trewe doctrine, first in Philosophie: and after in Religion: right iudgement of all thinges to be peruerted, and so vertue with learning is contemned,[10] and studie left of: of ill thoughtes cummeth peruerse iudgement: of ill deedes springeth lewde taulke. Which fower misorders, as they mar mans life, so destroy they good learning withall.

But behold the goodnesse of Gods prouidence for learning: all olde authors and sectes of Philosophy, which were fondest in opinion, and rudest in vtterance, as Stoickes and Epicures, first contemned of wise men, and after forgotten of all men, be so consumed by tymes, as they be now, not onelie out of vse, but also out of memorie of man: which thing, I surelie thinke, will shortlie chance, to the whole doctrine and all the bookes of phantasticall Anabaptistes and Friers, and of the beastlie Libertines and Monkes.

Againe behold on the other side, how Gods wisdome hath wrought, that of *Academici* and *Peripatetici*,[11] those that were wisest in iudgement of matters, and purest in vttering their myndes, the first and chiefest, that wrote most and best, in either tong, as *Plato* and *Aristotle* in Greeke, *Tullie* in Latin, be so either wholie or sufficiently left vnto vs, as I neuer knew yet scholer, that gaue himselfe to like, and loue, and folowe chieflie those three Authors but he proued, both learned, wise, and also an honest man,[12] if he ioyned with all the trewe doctrine of Gods holie Bible, without the which, the other three be but fine edge tooles in a fole or mad mans hand.

(*1570*)

52. Thomas WILSON (*1525–1581*) æt. *28*

Among al other lessons, this should first be learned, that we never affect any strange ynkehorne termes, but so speake as is commonly received: neither sekyng to be over fine, nor yet livyng over carelesse, usyng our speache as most men do, and ordryng our wittes, as the fewest have doen. Some seke so farre for outlandishe Englishe, that thei forget altogether their mothers language. And I dare swere this, if some of their mothers were alive, thei were not able to tell, what thei say, and yet these fine Englishe clerkes, wil saie thei speake in their mother tongue, if a man should charge them for counterfeityng the kynges English. Some farre iorneid ientlemen at their returne home, like as thei love to go in forrein apparell, so thei wil pouder their talke with oversea language. He that commeth lately out of France, wil talke Frenche English, and never blushe at the matter. Another choppes in with Angleso Italiano: the lawyer wil store his stomack with the pratyng of Pedlers. The Auditour in makyng his accompt and rekenyng, commeth in with sise sould, and cater denere, for vi. s iiii. d. The fine Courtier will talke nothyng but Chaucer. The misticall wise menne, and Poeticall Clerkes, will speake nothyng but quaint proverbes, and blynd allegories, delityng muche in their awne darkenesse, especially, when none can tell what thei dooe saie. The unlearned or foolishe phantasticall, that smelles but of learnyng (suche felowes as have seen learned men in their daies) will so latine their tongues, that the simple cannot but wonder at their talke, and thynke surely thei speake by some Revelacion. I knowe them that thynke Rhetorique, to stande holy upon darke woordes, and he that can catche an ynke horne terme by the taile, hym thei compte to bee a fine Englishe man, and a good Rhetorician. And the rather to set out this folie, I

Thomas Wilson, *The Arte of Rhetorique* ([London], 1553), Fo. 86, ii–87, i.

will adde here suche a letter, as Willyam Sommer himself, could not make a better for that purpose. Some will thinke and swere it to, that there was never any suche thyng written, well I wil not force any man to beleve it, but I will saie thus muche, and abide by it to, the like have been made heretofore, and praised above the Moone.

(1553)

53. Richard SHERRY (*fl. 1550*)

I doubt not but that the title of this treatise all straunge unto our Englyshe eares, wil cause some men at the fyrst syghte to marvayle what the matter of it should meane: yea, peradventure if they be rashe of iudgement to cal it some newe fangle, and so casting it hastily from them, wil not once vouch safe to reade it: and if they do, yet perceivynge nothing to be therin that pleaseth their phansy, wyl count it but a tryfle, and a tale of Robynhoode. But of thys sorte as I doubte not to fynde manye, so perhaps there wyll be other, whiche moved with the noveltye thereof, wyll thynke it worthye to be looked upon, and se what is contained therin. These words, *Scheme* and *Trope*, are not used in our Englishe tongue, neither bene they Englyshe words. No more be manye whiche nowe in oure tyme be made by continual use, very familier to most men, and come so often in speakyng, that aswel is knowen amongest us the meanyng of them, as if they had bene of oure owne native broode. Who hath not in hys mouthe nowe thys worde Paraphrasis, homelies, usurped, abolyshed, wyth manye other lyke. And what marvail is it if these words have not bene used here tofore, seynge there was no such thynge in oure Englishe tongue where unto they shuld be applyed. Good cause have we therefore to gyve thankes unto certayne godlye and well learned men, whych by their greate studye enrychynge our tongue both wyth matter and wordes, have endevoured to make it so copyous and plentyfull that therein it maye compare wyth anye other whiche so ever is the best. It is not unknowen that oure language for the barbarousnes and lacke of eloquence hathe bene complayned of, and yet not trewely, for anye defaut in the toungue it selfe, but rather for slackenes of our countrimen, whiche have alwayes set

Richard Sherry, *A Treatise of Schemes and Tropes* [London, 1550], Aiv–Aiiiv.

lyght by searchyng out the elegance and proper speaches that be ful many in it: as plainly doth appere not only by the most excellent monumentes of our auncient forewriters, Gower, Chawcer and Lydgate, but also by the famous workes of many other later: inespeciall of that ryght worshipful knyght syr Thomas Eliot, which first in hys dictionarye as it were generallye searchinge oute the copye of oure language in all kynde of wordes and phrases, after that setting abrode goodlye monumentes of hys wytte, lernynge and industrye, aswell in historycall knowledge, as of eyther the Philosophies, hathe herebi declared the plentyfulnes of our mother toungue, love toward hys country, hys tyme not spent in vanitye and tryfles.

(*1550*)

54. William LILY (*1468–1522*)

To exhorte everye man to the learnynge of Grammar, that intendeth to attayne to the understandyng of the tongues (wherein is contayned a great treasurye of wysedome and knowledge), it shoulde seeme muche vayne and lyttle needefull: for so muche as it is knowen, that nothinge can surelye be ended, whose beginning is eyther feeble or faultye: and no buyldynge bee perfect, when as the foundacion and grounde worke is readye to fall, and unable to upholde the burthen of the frame. Wherefore it were better for the thynge itselfe, and more profitable to the learner, to understand how he may best come to that which he ought moste necessaryly to have, and to learne the gaynest ways of obtaynynge that whiche muste be hys beste and certaynest guyde, bothe of reading and speakinge, then to fall in doubte of the goodnesse and necessity thereof. Whiche I doubte whether hee shall more lament that he lacketh, or esteeme that he hath it: and whether he shal oftenner stumble in tryfles and be deceyved in lyght matters when he hathe it not, or iudge truelye and faythfully of dyvers wayghtye thynges when he hathe it. The which hathe seemed to manye verye harde to compasse aforetyme, bycause that they, who professed this arte of teachinge Grammar, did teache divers Grammers and not one: and yf by chaunce they taught one Grammar, yet they did it diversly, and so could not do it all beste, for so muche as there is but one bestenes, not only in every thing, but also in the manner of every thing.

As for the diversitye of Grammars, it is wel and profitably taken away by the Kinges Maiesties wisdome, who foreseing the inconvenience, and favourablye providinge the remedy, caused one kinde of Grammar by sundry learned men to be diligently

William Lily, *A Shorte Introduction of Grammar* ([London], 1567), Sig. aii.

drawen, and so to be set out, onely every where to be taught for the use of learners, and for the hurte in chaunging of Schoolemaisters.

(*1567*)

55. Thomas ELYOT (*1490–1546*) æt. *41*

Nowe let us retourne to the order of learning, apt for a gentleman. Wherin I am of Quintilians opinion, that I wold haue him lerne greke and latine authors, both at one time, or els to begin with greke, forasmuche as that is hardest to come by: by reason of the diuersitie of tungues, whyche be fiue in numbre,[1] and all muste bee knowen, or els uneth [2] anye poete can be well understande. And if a chyld doe begyn therin at seuen yeres of age, he maye continuallye learne greke authors thre yeres, and in the meane tyme use the Latin tungue as a familiar language: whyche in a noble mans son maye well come to passe, hauynge none other persons to serue hym or kepe him company, but suche as can speake latin elegantly. And what doubt is there: but so maye he as sone speke good Latin, as he may do pure french, whiche now is brought into as many rules and figures,[3] and as longe a grammer, as is latin or greke. I wyll not contende, who amonge them that doe write grammers of greke (whyche nowe allmoste bee innumerable) is the best: but that I refer to the discretion of a wyse maister. Alwaye I wolde aduise hym, not to deteine the chyld to longe in that tedious labors, eyther in the greeke or latin grammer. For a gentill wit is therwith soone fatigate.[4]

Grammer, beyng but an introduction to the understandyng of autours, if it be made to long or exquisite [5] to the lerner, it in a maner mortifieth his courage: And by that tyme he cometh to the moste swete and pleasant redyng of olde auctours, the sparkes of feruent desyre of learnyng, is extinct, with the burdeyne of grammer, like as a litle fire is sone quenched with a great heape of smal stickes: so that it can neuer come to the principal logges, wher it shulde long burne in a great pleasant fire.

(*1531*)

Thomas Elyot, *The Boke, Named the Gouvernour* (London, 1557), Fo. 25 recto-verso.

56. Leonard COX (*fl. 1572*)

Whosomeuer desyreth to be a good oratour or to dyspute and *com*mune of any maner thynge [1] / hym behoueth [2] to haue foure thynges. The fyrste is called Inuencyon, for he muste fyrste of al imagyne or inuent in his mynde what he shall saye. The .ii. is named iudgement / for he muste haue wyt to discerne and iudge whether tho thinges that he hathe founde in his mynde be conuenient to the purpose or nat / for often tymes yf a man lake thys propriete he may aswell tell that that is agaynste hym / as with hym / as experience doth dayly shew. The .iii. is dysposycyon wherby he maye knowe howe to ordre and set euery thynge in his due place. Leste thoughe his inuencyon and iudgement be neuer so goode he maye happen to be counted as the co*m*mune prouerbe sayeth To put the carte afore the horse.[3] The .iiii. & is such thynges laste as he hathe Inuentid and by iudgement knowen apte to his purpose when they ar set in theyr ordre so to speke them that it maye be pleasant and delectable to the audience. So that it maye be sayde of hym that historyes make mencion that an olde woman sayd ons by demosthenes and syns hathe bene a co*m*mune prouerbe amo*n*ge the grekes ουτοσ εστι whiche is asmoch to saye as (This is he). And this laste propriete is callyd amonge lernyd men eloquence.[4] Of these .iiii. the most difficile [5] or harde is to inuente what thou muste saye, wherfore of this parte the Rhetoryciens whiche be maysters of this arte haue written very moche and diligently.

Inuencyon is co*m*prehended in certayn placys [6] / as the Rhetoriciens call the*m* / out of who*m* he that knoweth the facultye may fetche easyly suche thynges as be mete for the mater that he shal speke of / which mater the Oratour calleth the theme and in oure vulgayre tonge it is callyd improprely the

Leonard Cox, *The Arte or Crafte of Rhethoryke*, ed. Frederic Ives Carpenter (Chicago, 1899), pp. 43–44.

antytheme. The theme proposed we muste after the rules of Rhetoryke go to oure placys that shal anone shew vnto vs what shalbe to oure purpose.

(1524)

57. William CAXTON (*1422–1491*) æt. *68*

And whan I had aduysed me in this sayd boke. I delybered and concluded to translate it in to englysshe And forthwyth toke a penne & ynke and wrote a leef or tweyne / whyche I ouersawe agayn to correcte it / And wha*n* I sawe the fayr & straunge termes therin / I doubted that it sholde not please some gentylmen whiche late blamed me sayeng y^{t} [1] in my translacyons I had ouer curyous termes whiche coude not be vnderstande of comyn peple / and desired me to vse olde and homely termes in my translacyons. and || fayn wolde I satysfye euery man / and so to doo toke an olde boke and redde therin / and certaynly the englysshe was so rude and brood [2] that I coude not wele vnderstande it. And also my lorde abbot of westmynster ded do shewe [3] to me late certayn euydences wryton in olde englysshe for to reduce it in to our englysshe now vsid / And certaynly it was wreton in suche wyse that it was more lyke to dutche than englysshe I coude not reduce ne brynge it to be vnderstonden [4] / And certaynly our langage now vsed varyeth ferre from that. whiche was vsed and spoken whan I was borne / For we englysshe men / ben borne vnder the domynacyon of the mone. whiche is neuer stedfaste / but euer wauerynge / wexynge one season / and waneth & dyscreaseth another season / And that comyn englysshe that is spoken in one shyre varyeth from a nother. In so moche that in my dayes happened that certayn marchau*n*tes were in a shipp*e* in tamyse [5] for to haue sayled ouer the see into zelande [6] / and for lacke of wynde thei taryed atte forlond.[7] and wente to lande for to refreshe them And one of theym named sheffelde a mercer cam in to an hows and axed for mete.[8] and specyally he axyd after eggys [9] And the good wyf answerde. that she coude speke no frenshe. And the marchau*n*t

"Prologue" to *Eneydos, The Prologues and Epilogues of William Caxton*, ed. W.J.B. Crotch (London, 1928), pp. 107–109.

was angry. for he also coude speke no frenshe. but wold haue hadde egges / and she vnderstode hym not / And thenne at laste a nother sayd that he wolde haue eyren / then the good wyf sayd that she vnderstod hym wel / Loo what sholde a man in thyse dayes now wryte. egges or eyren / certaynly it is harde to playse euery man / by cause of dyuersite & chau*n*ge of langage. For in these dayes euery man that is in ony reputacyon in his cou*n*tre. wyll vtter his co*m*mynycacyon and maters in suche maners & termes / that fewe men shall vnderstonde theym / And som ho||nest and grete clerkes [10] haue ben wyth me and desired me to wryte the moste curyous termes that I coude fynde / And thus bytwene playn rude / & curyous I stande abasshed. but in my Iudgemente / the comyn termes that be dayli vsed ben lyghter to be vnderstonde than the olde and au*n*cyent englysshe / And for as moche as this present booke is not for a rude vplondyssh [11] man to laboure therin / ne rede it / but onely for a clerke & a noble gentylman that feleth and vnderstondeth in faytes [12] of armes in loue & in noble chyualrye / Therfor in a meane bytwene bothe I haue reduced & translated this sayd booke in to our englysshe not ouer rude ne curyous but in suche termes as shall be vnderstanden by goddys grace accordynge to my copye. And yf ony man wyll enter mete [13] in redyng of hit and fyndeth suche termes that he can not vnderstande late hym goo rede and lerne vyrgyll / or the pystles of ouyde [14] / and there he shall see and vnderstonde lyghtly all / Yf he haue a good redar & enformer [15] / For this booke is not for e[u]ery rude [and] vnconnynge [16] man to see / but to clerkys and very gentylmen that vnderstande gentylnes and scyence. . . .[17]

(*1490*)

58. Samuel BUTLER (*1835–1902*) æt. *62*

In this day's silly *Sunday Times* (p. 2) there is an article on Mrs. Browning's letters which begins with some remarks about style. 'It is recorded,' says the writer, 'of Plato, that in a rough draft of one of his Dialogues, found after his death, the first paragraph was written in seventy different forms. Wordsworth spared no pains to sharpen and polish to the utmost the gifts with which nature had endowed him; and Cardinal Newman, one of the greatest masters of English style, has related in an amusing essay the pains he took to acquire his style.'

I never knew a writer yet who took the smallest pains with his style and was at the same time readable. Plato's having had seventy shies at one sentence is quite enough to explain to me why I hate him. A man may, and ought to take a great deal of pains to write clearly, tersely and euphemistically: he will write many a sentence three or four times over—to do much more than this is worse than not re-writing at all: he will be at great pains to see that he does not repeat himself, to arrange his matter in the way that shall best enable the reader to master it, to cut out superfluous words and, even more, to eschew irrelevant matter: but in each case he will be thinking not of his own style but of his reader's convenience.

Men like Newman and R. L. Stevenson seem to have taken pains to acquire what they called a style as a preliminary measure—as something that they had to form before their writings could be of any value. I should like to put it on record that I never took the smallest pains with my style, have never thought about it, do not know nor want to know whether it is a style at all or whether it is not, as I believe and hope, just common, simple, straightforwardness. I cannot conceive how any

Samuel Butler's Notebooks (London, 1951), pp. 290–291.

man can take thought for his style without loss to himself and his readers.

I have, however, taken all the pains that I had patience to endure in the improvement of my handwriting (which, by the way, has a constant tendency to resume feral characteristics) and also with my MS. generally to keep it clean and legible. Alfred and I are having a great tidying just now, in the course of which the MS. of *Erewhon* turned up, and I was struck with the great difference between it and the MS. of *The Authoress of the Odyssey*. I have also taken much pains, with what success I know not, to correct impatience, irritability and other like faults in my own character—and this not because I care two straws about my own character, but because I find the correction of such faults as I have been able to correct makes life easier and saves me from getting into scrapes, and attaches nice people to me more readily. But I suppose this really is attending to style after all.[1]

(1897)

59. Walter RALEIGH (*1861–1922*) æt. *36*

Let the truth be said outright: there are no synonyms, and the same statement can never be repeated in a changed form of words. Where the ignorance of one writer has introduced an unnecessary word into the language, to fill a place already occupied, the quicker apprehension of others will fasten upon it, drag it apart from its fellows, and find new work for it to do. Where a dull eye sees nothing but sameness, the trained faculty of observation will discern a hundred differences worthy of scrupulous expression. The old foresters had different names for a buck during each successive year of its life, distinguishing the fawn from the pricket, the pricket from the sore, and so forth, as its age increased. Thus it is also in that illimitable but not trackless forest of moral distinctions, language halts far behind the truth of things, and only a drowsy perception can fail to devise a use for some new implement of description. Every strange word that makes its way into a language spins for itself a web of usage and circumstance, relating itself from whatsoever centre to fresh points in the circumference. No two words ever coincide throughout their whole extent. If sometimes good writers are found adding epithet to epithet for the same quality, and name to name for the same thing, it is because they despair of capturing their meaning at a venture, and so practise to get near it by a maze of approximations. Or, it may be, the generous breadth of their purpose scorns the minuter differences of related terms, and includes all of one affinity, fearing only lest they be found too few and too weak to cover the ground effectively. Of this sort are the so-called synonyms of the Prayer-Book, wherein we "acknowledge and confess" the sins we are forbidden to "dissemble or cloke"; and the beadroll of the lawyer, who huddles together "give, devise, and bequeath," lest

Walter Raleigh, *Style* (London, 1897), pp. 46–50.

the cunning of litigants should evade any single verb. The works of the poets yield still better instances. When Milton praises the *Virtuous Young Lady* of his sonnet in that the spleen of her detractors moves her only to "pity and ruth," it is not for the idle filling of the line that he joins the second of these nouns to the first. Rather he is careful to enlarge and intensify his meaning by drawing on the stores of two nations, the one civilised, the other barbarous; and ruth is a quality as much more instinctive and elemental than pity as pitilessness is keener, harder, and more deliberate than the inborn savagery of ruthlessness.

It is not chiefly, however, for the purposes of this accumulated and varied emphasis that the need of synonyms is felt. There is no more curious problem in the philosophy of style than that afforded by the stubborn reluctance of writers, the good as well as the bad, to repeat a word or phrase. When the thing is, they may be willing to abide by the old rule and say the word, but when the thing repeats itself they will seldom allow the word to follow suit. A kind of interdict, not removed until the memory of the first occurrence has faded, lies on a once used word. The causes of this anxiety for a varied expression are manifold. Where there is merely a column to fill, poverty of thought drives the hackney author into an illicit fulness, until the trick of verbiage passes from his practice into his creed, and makes him the dupe of his own puppets. A commonplace book, a dictionary of synonyms, and another of phrase and fable equip him for his task; if he be called upon to marshal his ideas on the question whether oysters breed typhoid, he will acquit himself voluminously, with only one allusion (it is a point of pride) to the oyster by name. He will compare the succulent bivalve to Pandora's box, and lament that it should harbour one of the direst of ills that flesh is heir to. He will find a paradox and an epigram in the notion that the darling of Apicius should suffer neglect under the frowns of Æsculapius. Question, hypothesis, lamentation, and platitude dance their allotted round and fill the ordained space, while Ignorance masquerades in the garb of criticism, and Folly proffers her ancient epilogue of chastened hope. When all is said, nothing is said; and Montaigne's *Que sçais-je*, besides being briefer and wittier, was infinitely more informing.[1]

(*1897*)

60. Frederic HARRISON (*1831–1923*) æt. *63*

He was essentially the consummate literary artist who transmutes mountains of exact research into a complex mass, glowing with life in all its parts, and glorious to contemplate as a whole. This is a literary, rather than a philosophical, feat; and as such it must be judged. Its art is akin to that of the epic poet who works out a grand plot in symmetrical order, with episodes, incidents, digressions, but on a consistent scheme, with beauty in each part and memorable form in each line. Now, it is beyond dispute that Gibbon's subject and scheme far transcend in breadth and importance to humanity those of any other historian, even those of Herodotus and Livy, Henri Martin, Grote or Milman, if we put aside such manuals as those of Heeren, Becker, Ranke, and Freeman. This is also beyond doubt, that no historian of ancient or modern times has ever shown the creative and formative imagination triumphing over such transcendent difficulties and working on so grand a scale. Carlyle's *French Revolution* is perhaps a typical example of this power to infuse exact record with poetic vitality, but Carlyle's masterpiece gives us the story of five, or at most of twenty years, and of one country, or, rather, of one city. Gibbon's epic history is the story of mankind over the planet during thirteen centuries. And Gibbon's story is even more accurate, more brilliant, more organic, more truly a work of art than is Carlyle's.

And what vigour, what wit, what a clarion ring in every sentence from the first line of the first volume to the closing phrase of the last! How it holds the attention, how it leaves its imprint on the memory, how it conjures up scenes to the eye. It is like watching some interminable procession, as of a Roman triumph —some Cæsar returning from his Eastern victories, with war-

Frederic Harrison, "The Centenary of Gibbon," *Memories and Thoughts* (London, 1894), pp. 85–87.

riors of all races, costumes, and colours, and the trophies of barbaric peoples, and the roar of many tribes, strange beasts, the pomp of war, and the spoils of cities. We need not insist that it is a perfect style, or a style without grave limitations or defects. It has not the lucid simplicity of Voltaire and of Hume, nor the grace of Addison, nor the pathos of Burke. It is too elaborate, too stiff with jewelry, and too uniform in texture. And perhaps these defects have induced the most versatile of living critics to put on record his memorable saying that he did not care for Gibbon except for his *Memoirs*. This is as if one said that he did not care for Shakespeare except for the *Sonnets*.

A famous authority on the beautiful was disappointed with the Atlantic; but we must not take these purists too literally. The Atlantic becomes rather grandiose, and at last somewhat monotonous; and so, Gibbon's interminable antithesis and unbending majesty do pall upon the constant reader, if he takes in too much at a sitting. But how splendid is the vigour, the point, the precision of the language; and, with all its faults, how well fitted to rehearse these "strange stories of the deaths of kings," how akin to the theme and to the glowing scheme of the painter's colouring! It is impossible to hurry through your Gibbon; you cannot skip; you cannot take in a description at a glance; you cannot leave out the adjectives, or jump the second half of a clause. You may take up your *Decline and Fall*, of which you can repeat pages by heart; you may have read it fifteen times, but the sixteenth reading will give you a phrase of which you had not previously caught the full sense, or throw light on something which has long been a puzzle. And how fixed in the memory are the quips and innuendos, the epigrams and the epithets, with which the page coruscates like a piece of jewelry. It may not be a pure style, it is certainly not a model style, but it is one that gives a gorgeous colour to a supremely organic composition.[1]

(*1894*)

61. George Bernard SHAW (*1856–1950*)
æt. *47*

However, I am digressing, as a man with a grievance always does. And after all, the main thing in determining the artistic quality of a book is not the opinions it propagates, but the fact that the writer has opinions. The old lady from Colchester was right to sun her simple soul in the energetic radiance of Bradlaugh's genuine beliefs and disbeliefs rather than in the chill of such mere painting of light and heat as elocution and convention can achieve. My contempt for belles lettres, and for amateurs who become the heroes of the fanciers of literary virtuosity, is not founded on any illusion of mind as to the permanence of those forms of thought (call them opinions) by which I strive to communicate my bent to my fellows. To younger men they are already outmoded; for though they have no more lost their logic than an eighteenth century pastel has lost its drawing or its color, yet, like the pastel, they grow indefinably shabby, and will grow shabbier until they cease to count at all, when my books will either perish, or, if the world is still poor enough to want them, will have to stand, with Bunyan's, by quite amorphous qualities of temper and energy. With this conviction I cannot be a bellettrist. No doubt I must recognize, as even the Ancient Mariner did, that I must tell my story entertainingly if I am to hold the wedding guest spellbound in spite of the siren sounds of the loud bassoon. But "for art's sake" alone I would not face the toil of writing a single sentence. I know that there are men who, having nothing to say and nothing to write, are nevertheless so in love with oratory and with literature that they keep desperately repeating as much as they can understand of what others have said or written aforetime. I know that the leisurely tricks which their want of conviction leaves them free

George Bernard Shaw, "Epistle Dedicatory," *Man and Superman* (New York, 1904), pp. xxxiv–xxxvi.

to play with the diluted and misapprehended message supply them with a pleasant parlor game which they call style. I can pity their dotage and even sympathize with their fancy. But a true original style is never achieved for its own sake: a man may pay from a shilling to a guinea, according to his means, to see, hear, or read another man's act of genius; but he will not pay with his whole life and soul to become a mere virtuoso in literature, exhibiting an accomplishment which will not even make money for him, like fiddle playing. Effectiveness of assertion is the Alpha and Omega of style. He who has nothing to assert has no style and can have none: he who has something to assert will go as far in power of style as its momentousness and his conviction will carry him. Disprove his assertion after it is made, yet its style remains. Darwin has no more destroyed the style of Job nor of Handel than Martin Luther destroyed the style of Giotto. All the assertions get disproved sooner or later; and so we find the world full of a magnificent débris of artistic fossils, with the matter-of-fact credibility gone clean out of them, but the form still splendid. And that is why the old masters play the deuce with our mere susceptibles. Your Royal Academician thinks he can get the style of Giotto without Giotto's beliefs, and correct his perspective into the bargain. Your man of letters thinks he can get Bunyan's or Shakespear's style without Bunyan's conviction or Shakespear's apprehension, especially if he takes care not to split his infinitives. And so with your Doctors of Music, who, with their collections of discords duly prepared and resolved or retarded or anticipated in the manner of the great composers, think they can learn the art of Palestrina from Cherubini's treatise. All this academic art is far worse than the trade in sham antique furniture; for the man who sells me an oaken chest which he swears was made in the XIII century, though as a matter of fact he made it himself only yesterday, at least does not pretend that there are any modern ideas in it, whereas your academic copier of fossils offers them to you as the latest outpouring of the human spirit, and, worst of all, kidnaps young people as pupils and persuades them that his limitations are rules, his observances dexterities, his timidities good taste, and his emptinesses purities. And when he declares that art should not be didactic, all the people who have nothing to teach and all the people who dont want to learn agree with him emphatically.[1]

(1903)

62. Henry BRADLEY (*1845–1923*) æt. *59*

It is a truth often overlooked, but not unimportant, that every addition to the resources of a language must in the first instance have been due to an act (though not necessarily a voluntary or conscious act) of some one person. A complete history of the Making of English would therefore include the names of the Makers, and would tell us what particular circumstances suggested the introduction of each new word or grammatical form, and of each new sense or construction of a word.

Of course no such complete history could possibly be written. We shall never know anything about the myriads of obscure persons who have contributed to the development of the English tongue. And even if it were possible to discover the author of every new feature that has been introduced into the language since the earliest times, and the exact conditions under which it arose, the information would in all probability only very rarely have even the slightest interest or value.

But there are some Makers of English of whose personality we do know something: namely, the authors of literary works that are still in existence. The investigation of the extent of their influence on the language has a double interest. It not only gratifies our natural curiosity about the origin of the mechanism of English speech, but it also contributes in some small degree to our knowledge of the mental character of the writers, and thus enables us to attain a more complete understanding of their works.

Now there are two ways in which an author may contribute to the enrichment of the language in which he writes. He may do so *directly* by the introduction of new words or new applications of words, or *indirectly* by the effect of his popularity in giving to existing forms of expression a wider currency and a new

Henry Bradley, *The Making of English* (London, 1904), pp. 215–219.

value. If a popular writer happens to employ some comparatively rare word in a striking connexion, it will very likely come into the common vocabulary of the multitude and then undergo a development in sense which would have been impossible if the word had continued to be confined to purely literary use. Moreover, when a passage of a poet or prose-writer becomes widely familiar as a quotation, the words of which it consists are apt to be used by later generations with a recollection of their particular context, and so to become either specialized or enriched in meaning.

In this chapter we shall give some samples of what certain literary Makers of English have done for the language. It is comparatively seldom that a word can be proved to have been used for the first time by a particular author; but it can often be shown that a writer has brought a word into general use, or that a current sense of a word is derived from a literary allusion. Of course it is not always the greatest writers whose works are in this indirect way most powerful in their effect on the language; literary excellence counts for less in this matter than popularity, and the ability to write passages that lend themselves to quotation.

It is important to point out that a great part of the work done by individual writers in the improvement of the language is of too subtle a nature to admit of being analysed or accurately estimated. A literary language has to meet requirements which do not arise in ordinary speech. The structure of sentences which suffices for the needs of oral intercourse is inadequate for written composition, where the thought to be expressed is continuous and complex, and where the aids to intelligibility furnished by intonation and gesture are wanting. As the art of literary composition advances, and the tasks to which it addresses itself become more ambitious, there is a constantly increasing need of devices for exhibiting more clearly the connexion of thought. The particles used for linking one sentence to another become more precise in their force, and new turns of expression, new syntactical constructions, alien to the language of conversation, are continually being introduced. Now every one of these improvements in a language is an invention of some one person; but it is obviously impossible, in most cases, to trace them to their authors. And hence it follows that, although we may be able to say what new words or meanings, or what phraseological combinations, are due to the influence of a particular writer, the effect of his works on the language may be far more important than it can be proved to be.[1]

(1904)

63. Isaac D'ISRAELI (*1766–1848*) æt. *30*

The History of English Style since it's first elegance may, perhaps, be traced in the following concise manner.

When the national literature has attained to a certain point, there arises a simple elegance of Style, which in it's progress displays richer ornaments, and often becomes refined to a vicious excess. It may be traced through four schools.

The first writers who attempt elegance, and polish the asperities of a language, excel in a natural sweetness and amiable simplicity. But the Style is not yet castigated, for it still retains many colloquial terms and many negligent expressions, which either were not such in their day, or their ear, not being yet accustomed to a continued elegance, received no pain from familiar and unstudied expressions. In time these defects become sensible; yet as these writers are placed among the first classics of their nation, they are regarded with veneration, and often pointed out as the model for young writers. Among such authors we may place Tillotson, Swift, and Addison.

The second school introduces a more diffuse and verbose manner; these writers solicit the ear by a numerous prose, and expand their ideas on a glittering surface. As elegance can only be obtained by diffusion, it's concomitant is feebleness, and an elegant writer enervates his sentiments. Beauty is inconsistent with Force. Elevated emotions these writers rarely awaken, but a graceful manner in composition is their peculiar charm. Genius may be supposed at this period, to be somewhat impaired by the excursions of their predecessors, and they attempt to supply by the charms of amenity, and a copious diffusion of beautiful expression, the demand for novelty, as well as that taste for elegance of diction which the public now possess. Among these

Isaac D'Israeli, "Of Style," *Miscellanies* (London, 1796), pp. 37–41.

pleasing writers may be ranked Sir William Temple, though prior to Addison, Usher, Melmoth, &c.

Satiated with the nerveless beauty and the protracted period, a third school appears, the votaries of artificial embellishment and elaborated diction. At once, magisterially pompous, and familiarly pointed; concise and swelling; sparkling and solid; massy and light. Sometimes they condense ideas, by throwing into one vast thought, several intermediate ones; sometimes their rotundity of period is so arranged that the mind, with the ear, seems to rise on a regular ascent. The glare of art betrays itself; while sometimes the thoughts are more subtile than substantial, more airy than penetrating; the expressions new, and the ideas old. This school abounds with mannerists; such are Johnson, Hawkesworth, Robertson, and Gibbon.

When this taste for ornamented prose prevails, a fourth school arises, composed of inferior writers. As it is less difficult to collect words, than to create ideas, this race becomes versed in all the mysteries of diction; trivial thoughts are ridiculously invested by magnificent expressions, and they consider that blending the most glaring colours, without harmony or design, is an evidence of higher art. They colour like the distracted painter in Bedlam, who delighted in landscapes of golden earths, and vermilion skies. They tell us that their colours are vivid, and we reply that their figures are chimeras. These fantastic novelties flourish in the warmth of a fashionable circle, but once placed in the open air, they are killed by the popular gale. Writers of this class are not to be mentioned, as they are all dead authors who are yet living.

We may here observe that every period of literature has it's peculiar Style, derived from some author of reputation; and the history of a language as an object of taste, might be traced through a collection of ample quotations, from the most celebrated authors of each period. We should as rarely find an original Style, as an original Genius; and we should be enabled to perceive the almost insensible variations which at length produce an original Style.[1]

(1796)

64. William GODWIN (*1756–1836*) æt. *41*

No literary enquiry can be more interesting to an inhabitant of Great-Britain, than that respecting the history of the English language, and particularly that branch of its history, which may enable us to decide, at what time it has been written and spoken in the greatest purity and perfection.

The stream of opinion seems to be unfavourable to the age in which we live. The judgment of Swift and the most eminent writers in the first part of the present century, seems to have been, that the period of queen Elizabeth was the golden age of the English language. Ask the scholars and men of taste of the present day; they will perhaps for the most part give their suffrage to the reign of queen Anne.

Men of taste of the present day think they see, as Swift believed he saw before them, the influx of a corrupt and barbarous style. The mode of writing which is now practised, we are told, is dazzling and gaudy, not of intrinsic value. Our language is infected with a motley train of foreign phraseology. We adopt expressions with eagerness, which, at the same time that they are opposed to all just analogy, are in their own nature bad and contemptible. We hunt after unreal beauties. The dignified simplicity, which characterised the language of our forefathers, is no more.

It may be allowable to suspect the justice of this invective, when it is recollected, how universally the prejudice has spread, in favour of former times and distant ages. This prejudice has however suffered grievous defalcations. It is pretty generally acknowledged, that science and the improvement of the human mind, are in a progessive state. It has come to be vehemently suspected, that the political maxims and the moral conduct of our ancestors, were not altogether so perfect as they have been

William Godwin, *The Enquirer*, No. XII (London, 1797), pp. 368–374.

represented. May it not then happen, that the opinion in favour of their language may prove equally hasty and unfounded?

It is the purpose of this Essay to show, that the English language was never in so high a state of purity and perfection, as in the present reign of king George the third.

This can only be satisfactorily done by adducing a series of instances.

We will confine ourselves to prose examples. The licence of poetry, and the fetters of versification, have equally in all ages seduced the poets, in some degree to deviate from the received language of the age in which they wrote.

Before we enter upon our examples, let us endeavour to fix an idea of the laws of just composition or style.

And here I would lay it down as a maxim, that the beauty of style consists in this, to be free from unnecessary parts and excrescencies, and to communicate our ideas with the smallest degree of prolixity and circuitousness. Style should be the transparent envelop of our thoughts; and, like a covering of glass, is defective, if, by any knots and ruggedness of surface, it introduce an irregularity and obliquity into the appearances of an object, not proper to the object itself. The forming of an excellent composition, may be compared to the office of a statuary according to the fanciful idea of one of the ancients, who affirmed, that the statue was all along in the block of marble, and the artist did nothing more than remove those parts which intercepted our view of it. If he left any portion of the marble which ought to have been cut away, the statue was in some degree disfigured.

In the mean while this maxim is not to be so construed as to recommend or vindicate the cutting away any words or expressions that are necessary to render the grammatical construction of a sentence complete. As little does it apply to those metaphors and ornaments of composition, which shall be found to increase the clearness or force with which an author's ideas are communicated to his readers. It applies only to those superfluities which, like dead flesh upon the limb of a human body, would call upon the skilful surgeon for the exercise of the knife or the caustic.

The writers of the sixteenth and seventeenth centuries had for the most part a custom, of entering upon their subject with an enumeration of the branches into which, as they supposed, it most naturally divided itself, or rather into which the genus of which it was a branch divided itself; and then dwelling, with tedious accuracy and minuteness, upon those parts which in no sort belonged to their purpose, but which they thought must be described, because they were connected with it. This is an insupportable fault. It is formal, phlegmatic and repulsive. It detains us painfully in discussing all those things which we had no desire to know, and then dismisses us with a tired attention to consider what was material to the purpose. A skilful writer proceeds directly to his object. He shakes off with vigorous exertion every thing that would impede him, every thing that is, in the strict sense of the words, foreign and digressive.

The bad taste which displays itself in the phrases of the old writers, is of a similar nature to the bad taste which displays itself in the plan of their compositions. It is an ill mode of composition, where we find an author expressing his thought in ten words, when it might have been expressed with equal discrimination and grammatical propriety in five. The five additional words are so much dead and worthless matter mixed up with the true and genuine substance. They cloud the understanding, and are an inconceivable bar against passion and sympathy. Nothing will upon examination appear more certain, than that the forcible expression of passion demands closeness and compression. This is so true, that it will be found impossible to convey a great and electrical burst of the soul, in phrases, in which polysyllabic words, words, as Horace calls them, of a foot and a half long, are freely employed. It is not only necessary in this respect for the poet and the orator, where they would give their strongest shocks, to divest themselves of unnecessary words, but even of unnecessary syllables.

Another fault, which is perhaps more or less imputable to every English writer before the present age, is, that they were prone to tell their story or unfold their argument in a relaxed and disjointed style, more resembling the illiterate effusions of the nurse or the rustic, than those of a man of delicate perceptions and classical cultivation, who watched with nice attention the choice of his words and the arrangement of his phrases. The English language has lately assumed a loftier port. We may now often meet with it, though simple and elegant, yet with its nerves well strung, and its step at once skilful and firm. It is not unfrequent in examining an accidental pamphlet, or a news-paper correspondence, to find the language characterised by that clearness, propriety and compression, which command our thoughts, and seize upon a portion of our esteem.[1]

(*1797*)

65. Alexander Fraser Tytler, Lord WOODHOUSELEE (*1747–1813*) æt. *50*

From the consideration of those general rules of translation which in the foregoing essay I have endeavoured to illustrate, it will appear no unnatural conclusion to assert, that he only is perfectly accomplished for the duty of a translator who possesses a genius akin to that of the original author. I do not mean to carry this proposition so far as to affirm, that in order to give a perfect translation of the works of Cicero, a man must actually be as great an orator, or inherit the same extent of philosophical genius; but he must have a mind capable of discerning the full merits of his original, of attending with an acute perception to the whole of his reasoning, and of entering with warmth and energy of feeling into all the beauties of his composition. Thus we shall observe invariably, that the best translators have been those writers who have composed original works of the same species with those which they have translated. The mutilated version which yet remains to us of the Timæus of Plato translated by Cicero, is a masterly composition, which, in the opinion of the best judges, rivals the merit of the original. A similar commendation cannot be bestowed on those fragments of the Phænomena of Aratus translated into verse by the same author; for Cicero's poetical talents were not remarkable: but who can entertain a doubt, that had time spared to us his versions of the orations of Demosthenes and Æschines, we should have found them possessed of the most transcendent merit?

We have observed, in the preceding part of this essay, that poetical translation is less subjected to restraint than prose translation, and allows more of the freedom of original composition.

[Alexander Fraser Tytler, Lord Woodhouselee], *Essay on the Principles of Translation*, 2nd ed. (London, 1797), pp. 361–365.

It will hence follow, that to exercise this freedom with propriety, a translator must have the talent of original composition in poetry; and therefore, that in this species of translation, the possession of a genius akin to that of his author, is more essentially necessary than in any other. We know the remark of Denham, that the subtle spirit of poesy evaporates entirely in the transfusion from one language into another, and that unless a new, or an original spirit, is infused by the translator himself, there will remain nothing but a *caput mortuum*. The best translators of poetry, therefore, have been those who have approved their talents in original poetical composition. Dryden, Pope, Addison, Rowe, Tickell, Pitt, Warton, Mason, and Murphy, rank equally high in the list of original poets, as in that of the translators of poetry.[1]

(*1797*)

66. John Horne TOOKE (*1736–1812*) æt. *62*

We had formerly but two. But so great is the convenience and importance of this useful *abbreviation;* that our authors have borrowed from other languages and incorporated with our own, *four* other participles of equal value. We are obliged to our old translators for these new participles. I wish they had understood what they were doing at the time: and had been taught by their wants, the nature of the advantages which the learned languages had over ours. They would then perhaps have adopted the *contrivance* itself into our own language: instead of contenting themselves with taking individually the terms which they found they could not translate. But they proceeded in the same manner with these new participles, as with the new adjectives I before mentioned to you: they did not *abbreviate* their own language in imitation of the others; but took from other languages their *abbreviations* ready made. And thus again the foreigner, after having learned all our English verbs, must again have recourse to other languages in order to understand the meaning of many of our participles.

I cannot however much blame my countrymen for the method they pursued: because the very nations who enjoyed these advantages over us, were not themselves aware of the nature of what they possessed: at least so it appears by all the accounts which they have left us of the nature of speech; and by their distribution and definitions of the parts of which it is composed: and their posterity (the modern Greeks and the Italians) have been punished for the ignorance or carelessness of their ancestors, by the loss of great part of these advantages: which I suppose they would not have lost, had they known what they were.

John Horne Tooke, *Epea Pteroenta, or The Diversions of Purley* (Philadelphia, 1807), pp. 415–418.

As for the term PARTICIPLE, I should very willingly get rid of it: for it never was the proper denomination of this sort of word. And this improper title, I believe, led the way to its faulty definition: and both together have caused the obstinate and still unsettled disputes concerning it; and have prevented the improvement of language, in this particular, generally through the world.

The elder Stoics called this word. . . . "*modum verbi casualem.*" And, in my opinion, they called it well: except only that, instead of *casualem,* they should have said *adjectivum:* for the circumstance of its having *cases* was only a consequence of its *adjection.* But this small error of theirs cannot be wondered at in them, who, judging from their own transposed language, had no notion of a *noun,* much less of an *adjective* of any kind, without *cases.*

I desire therefore, instead of PARTICIPLE, to be permitted to call this word generally a *verb adjective.* And I call it by this new name; because I think it will make more easily intelligible what I conceive to be its office and nature.

This kind of word, of which we now speak, is a very useful *abbreviation:* for we have the same occasion to *adjective* the VERB as we have to *adjective* the NOUN. And, by means of a distinguishing termination, not only the simple *verb* itself, but every *mood,* and every *tense* of the verb, may be made *adjective,* and well as the *noun.* And accordingly some languages have *adjectived* more, and some languages have *adjectived* fewer of these *moods* and *tenses.*

And here I must observe that the *moods* and *tenses* themselves are merely *abbreviations*: I mean that they are nothing more than the circumstances of *manner* and *time,* added to the *verb* in some languages by distinguishing terminations.

When it is considered that our language has made but small progress, compared either with the Greek or with the Latin (or some other languages) even in this *modal* and *temporal* abbreviation; (for we are forced to perform the greatest part of it by what are called *auxiliaries,* i.e. separate words signifying the added circumstances;) when this is considered; it will not be wondered at, that the English, of itself, could not proceed to the next *abbreviating* step, viz. of *adjectiving* those first *abbreviations* of *mood* and *tense*, which our language had not: and that it has therefore been obliged to borrow many of the advantages of this kind which it now enjoys, either *mediately* or immediately from those two first-mentioned languages. And when it is considered, that the nature of these advantages was never well understood, or at least not delivered down to us, even by those who enjoyed them; it will rather be matter of wonder that we have adopted into our language so many, than that we have not taken all.[1]

(1798)

67. Nathan DRAKE (*1766–1836*) æt. *39*

The style of SWIFT, though it claim appropriate praise, has been extravagantly, and therefore injudiciously, applauded. Lowth has declared him the *most correct* of our prose writers; and Blair says that "he knew, almost, beyond any man, the purity, the extent, the *precision* of the English language; and therefore, to such as wish to attain a pure and correct style, he is one of the most useful models." Of this latter encomium, part is true and part unfounded. No man has equalled Swift in the knowledge of the force and purity of English words, or in fecundity of idiomatic expression; but in collocation and grammatical accuracy, it were absurd, in the present day, to consider him as a model. Of his wit, humour, and intellectual powers, I entertain the highest opinion; and I deem his works a rich *copia verborum,* which displays, in an unprecedented degree, the independent wealth of his native tongue; but, in the arrangement of these words into sentences he is not only inattentive to harmony and grace, but he is for the most part singularly negligent and harsh. It is true, the plainness of his style frequently sets off to advantage the keenness of his wit; but except where the vulgarity of the character may require it, it will not be contended, I imagine, that careless construction can assist his views; and yet, notwithstanding the great authorities abovementioned, I have little hesitation in asserting, that, in point of grammatical precision, he is inferior to several of his contemporaries. Mr. Sheridan, though an ardent admirer of the Doctor, and a repeater of the common idea with regard to his correctness, has in his preface and notes to the edition of 1784, with great propriety, pointed out many of his grammatical errors, solecisms, and inaccuracies; a service which might be con-

Nathan Drake, *Essays, Biographical, Critical and Historical* (London, 1805), III, 80–82.

siderably extended, and which, were prejudice set aside, would militate strongly against the popular opinion.

Great *verbal* purity and copiousness, a most extensive knowledge of idiom, and diction plain, forcible, and clear, form the *merits* of the Dean's style; a slovenly arrangement of sentences, an almost total want of modulation or smoothness, and frequent laxity in grammatical construction, are its *defects*.[1]

(*1805*)

68. William WOTTON (*1666–1727*) æt. *28*

Grammar is one of the Sciences which Sir *William Temple* says that *no Man ever disputed with the Ancients.*

As this Assertion is expressed, it is a little ambiguous: It may be understood of the Skill of the Moderns in the Grammatical Analogy of *Latin* and *Greek* or of their Skill in the *Grammar* of their Mother-Tongues. Besides, *Grammar* may either be considered *Mechanically*, or *Philosophically*. Those consider it *Mechanically* who only examine the Idiotisms and Proprieties of every particular Language, and lay down Rules to teach them to others. Those consider it as *Philosophers* who run over the several Steps by which every Language has altered its *Idiom;* who enquire into the several Perfections and Imperfections of those Tongues with which they are acquainted, and (if they are living Languages) propose Methods how to remedy them, or at least remove those Obscurities which are thereby occasioned in such Discourses where Truth is only regarded, and not Eloquence.

Now, this *Mechanical Grammar* of *Greek* and *Latin* has been very carefully studied by Modern Criticks. *Sanctius*, *Scioppius*, and *Gerhard Vossius*, besides a great Number of others, who have occasionally shown their Skill in their Illustrations of Ancient Authors, have given evident Proofs how well they understood the *Latin* Tongue: So have *Caninius*, *Clenard*, and abundance more, in *Greek:* Wherein they have gone upon sure Grounds, since, besides a great Number of Books in both Languages upon other Subjects, abundance of Grammatical Treatises, such as *Scholia upon difficult Authors*, *Glossaries*, *Onomasticons*, *Etymologicons*, *Rudiments of Grammar*, *&c.*, have been preserved, and published by skilful Men (most of them at

William Wotton, *Reflections upon Ancient and Modern Learning* (London, 1694), pp. 55–59.

least) with great Care and Accuracy. So that there is Reason to believe that some Modern Criticks may have understood the Grammatical Construction of *Latin* as well as *Varro*, or *Cæsar* and of *Greek* as well as *Aristarchus*, or *Herodian*. But this cannot be pretended to be a new Invention; for the *Grammar* of dead Languages can be only learned by Books: And since their Analogy can neither be increased nor diminished, it must be left as we find it.

So that when Sir *William Temple* says, *That no Man ever disputed Grammar with the Ancients;* if he means that we cannot make a new Grammar of a dead Language, whose Analogy has been determined almost Two Thousand Years, it is what can admit of no Dispute. But if he means, that Modern Languages have not been Grammatically examined; at least, not with that Care that some Ancient Tongues have been; that is a Proposition which may, perhaps, be very justly questioned. For, in the first place, it ought to be considered, that every Tongue has its own peculiar Form, as well as its proper Words; not communicable to, nor to be regulated by the Analogy of another Language: Wherefore he is the best Grammarian, who is the perfectest Master of the Analogy of the Language which he is about; and gives the truest Rules, by which another Man may learn it. Next, To apply this to our own Tongue, it may be certainly affirmed that the *Grammar* of *English* is so far our own, that Skill in the Learned Languages is not necessary to comprehend it. *Ben. Johnson* was the first Man, that I know of, that did any Thing considerable in it; but *Lilly's Grammar* was his Pattern: and for want of Reflecting upon the Grounds of a Language which he understood as well as any Man of his Age, he drew it by Violence to a dead Language that was of a quite different Make; and so left his Work imperfect. After him, came Dr. *Wallis;* who examined the *English* Tongue like a Grammarian and a Philosopher at once, and showed great Skill in that Business: And of his *English Grammar* one may venture to say, That it may be set against any Thing that is extant of the Ancients, of that kind: For, as Sir *William Temple* says upon another Occasion, there is *a Strain of Philosophy, and curious*

Thought, in his previous *Essay of the Formation of the Sounds of Letters;* and of Subtilty in the *Grammar*, in the reducing of our Language under Genuine Rules of Art, that one would not expect in a Book of that kind.[1]

(*1694*)

69. John HUGHES (*1677–1720*) æt. *21*

Elegance of *Thought* is what we commonly call *Wit*, which adds to Propriety, Beauty, and pleases our Fancy, while Propriety entertains our Judgment. This depends so much on Genius, that 'tis impossible to teach it by Rules. To the Elegance of Words, or Style, belong all the Figures of *Rhetorick*, and to use these to Advantage requires a Judgment well form'd by Observation. In this therefore, as in learning the Graces upon an Instrument of Musick, good Examples are the best Instruction. Thus a Man may write *Metaphors*, *Tropes*, *Hyperboles*, and all the other Figures, without the Trouble of studying a System of *Rhetorick;* and I believe better too, for to attend to a great many Rules whilst you are writing, is the way to make your Style stiff and constrain'd, whereas Elegance consists very much in a genteel Ease and Freedom of Expression; it is like a coy Mistress, of so nice a Humour, that to court her too much, is the surest way to lose her; and as Success in Love is owing to good Fortune, and the natural Happiness of pleasing, rather than to Fidelity and Attendance, so the Art of chusing, out of several Expressions equally proper, that which is the most graceful, is best call'd a *Curiosa Felicitas*, which two Words seem to comprehend all that can be said upon this Head.

The last Qualification I mention'd is *Cadence*, in Poetry call'd *the Numbers*. It consists in a Disposing of the Words in such Order, and with such Variation of Periods, as may strike the Ear with a sort of musical Delight, which is a considerable Part of Eloquence. This is chiefly that which makes a Style smooth, and not merely the avoiding of harsh Words. The best way to attain it, is to prepare yourself, before you begin to write,

John Hughes, "Of Style," *Poems on Several Occasions* (London, 1735), I, 251–254.

by reading in some harmonious Style, that so you may get your Ear well in Tune.

Besides all these Qualifications, there is something in Language, which, to borrow a Word from Singing, may be call'd *a Manner*. This, like the Air of Faces, is a Mark of Distinction, by which every one has somewhat peculiar to it self from all others. For, besides the manifest Difference between Beauty and Deformity, there is a wonderful Variety even among good Faces, for which reason the Painters have learn'd, from many scatter'd Beauties, to collect one perfect Idea, which is hard to be found in any Individual.

To apply this; Sir *William Temple,* Sir *Roger L'Estrange,* and Dr. *Sprat* (to mention no more) are each of them allow'd Masters in the Tongue, and yet every one has a different Manner, as may be seen by a short Character of each.

The Style of Sir *William Temple* is very harmonious and sweet, full of Spirit, and *Raciness of Wit,* to use a Word of his own. His Similies are particularly fine, his Allusions graceful, his Words significant, and the whole has a kind of Charm, which amuses the Reader with serious Pleasure, puts him in a good Humour while he is reading, and leaves him thoughtful when he breaks off.

L'Estrange's Talent is Humour, in which his Vein flows very freely; agreeably to this he is a perfect Master of all the Idioms and Proverbial Expressions which are peculiar to our Tongue; these he often applies happily enough, tho' sometimes not without Affectation; yet, generally speaking, his Style is pleasant, smooth, and natural; and that Gaiety and seeming Negligence, which is peculiar to him, entertains you with a similar sort of Delight, like that of witty and facetious Company. There is the same Difference in the Styles of these two, as in those of *Cicero* and *Terence* in the *Latin;* in the first you find more of the *Orator,* and in the latter more of the *Englishman.*

The elegant Dr. *Sprat* is, in my Judgment, one of the most genteel and exact Writers we have. His Style is grave and manly, infinitely preferable to Sir *Roger*'s, and having all that is beautiful in Sir *William Temple,* only (if 'tis possible) with more Correctness and Decency. There appears in him all the Sweetness and Fluency, handsom Turns and apt Expressions, that can be desir'd. He has united the most charming Elegance to the strictest Propriety, and is witty without the least Shadow of Affectation. The soft Cadence of his Periods, methinks, resembles the Current of a pleasant Stream; It makes but little Noise, yet affects you with a calm Delight, which, if it were heard louder, wou'd be lost.

There are several other Writers, which may be read with great Profit; and above all, the Incomparable *Tillotson*, who always writes the best Sense, and in the best Manner. That which particularly recommends him is an Easiness and beautiful Simplicity in all his Expressions, which every one that reads him is apt to think may be imitated without much Difficulty, and yet nothing perhaps is so hard in the Experiment.[1]

(1698)

70. Richard BENTLEY (*1662–1742*) æt. *37*

But since tyrants will not be confined by laws; let us suppose, if you will, that our Phalaris might make use of the Attic, for no reason at all, but his own arbitrary humour and pleasure: yet we have still another indictment against the credit of the epistles. For even the Attic of the true Phalaris's age is not there represented; but a more recent idiom and style, that by the whole thread and colour of it betrays itself to be many centuries younger than he. Every living language, like the perspiring bodies of living creatures, is in perpetual motion and alteration; some words go off, and become obsolete; others are taken in, and by degrees grow into common use; or the same word is inverted to a new sense and notion, which in tract of time makes as observable a change in the air and features of a language, as age makes in the lines and mien of a face. All are sensible of this in their own native tongues, where continual use makes every man a critic. For what Englishman does not think himself able, from the very turn and fashion of the style, to distinguish a fresh English composition from another a hundred years old? now there are as real and sensible differences in the several ages of Greek, were there as many that could discern them. But very few are so versed and practised in that language, as ever to arrive at that subtilty of taste. And yet as few will be content to relish or dislike a thing, not by their own sense, but by another man's palate. So that should I affirm, that I know the novity of these epistles from the whole body and form of the work; none, perhaps, would be convinced by it, but those that without my indication could discover it by themselves. I shall let that alone then, and point only at a few particular marks and moles in the letters, which every one that pleases may know them by. In the

Richard Bentley, *A Dissertation upon the Epistles of Phalaris* (London, 1699), pp. 310–311.

very first epistle; ὧν ἐμοὶ προτρέπεις, which you accuse me of, is an innovation in language; for which the ancients used προφέρεις. In the cxlii. among other presents to a bride, he sends θυγατέρας τέτταρας ὁμήλικας; which would antiently have signified daughters: but he here means it of virgins or maidens; as "fille" and "figlia" signify in French and Italian: which is a most manifest token of a later Greek. Even Tzetzes, when he tells the story out of this epistle, interprets it maids, θεραπαίνας. In the seventy-seventh, πολλοὶ παίδων ὄντες ἐραταί, many that are fond of their children; for that is his sense of the words; which of old, would have been taken for a flagitious love of boys; as if he had said, πολλοὶ ὄντες παίδερασαί. They that will make the search, may find more of this sort; but I suppose these are sufficient to unmask the recent sophist under the person of the old tyrant.[1]

(1699)

John DENNIS (*1657–1734*) æt. *44*

But, Secondly, At the same Time, that the *French* has been growing almost an universal Language, the *English* has been so far from diffusing itself in so vast a manner, that I know by Experience, that a Man may travel o'er most of these Western Parts of *Europe*, without meeting with Three Foreigners, who have any tolerable Knowledge of it. And yet the *English* is more strong, more full, more sounding, more significant, and more harmonious than the *French*. I know very well, that a great many will be unwilling to allow the last; but I appeal to your Lordship, if this is not a convincing Proof of it, that we have Blank Verse which is not inharmonious, and the *French* pretend to no Poetical Numbers, without the Assistance of Rhime.

But it may perhaps be alledg'd, that the Reason why the *French* has got the Advantage of our Language, is partly from their Situation on the Continent, partly from the Intrigues and Affairs which they have with their Neighbours, and partly, because their Language has more Affinity with one of the Learned Languages. But to this I answer, That the *Germans* are as advantageously seated as the *French*, for diffusing their Language; and the *Spanish* Tongue is rather nearer related to the *Latin* than is the *French;* and all the World knows, that towards the Beginning of the last Century, the House of *Austria*, was full as busie with their Neighbours, as the House of *Bourbon* is now; and yet then neither the *German* nor the *Spanish* Tongue made any considerable Progress. I will not deny, but that the Situation and Affairs of the *French*, may have been of Advantage to them in the diffusing their Language; but 'tis certainly, the Learning of any Nation that is most instrumental in

The Advancement and Reformation of Modern Poetry, *The Critical Works of John Dennis*, ed. Edward Niles Hooker (Baltimore, 1939), I, 204–205.

it. I make no doubt, but that in Learning, which is useful and necessary, and barely solid, without Ornament, we far surpass the *French*. Our practical Physicians have more Reputation than theirs, even in *France* itself; and our practical Divines, have acquir'd more Fame, throughout the Northern Countries of *Europe*, than either the Natives of those Places, or any of the Modern *French* Divines, whether they are Reform'd or Papistical. And this last, is therefore the more considerable, because they writ in our Mother Tongue, whereas the Physicians have employ'd a learned Language. But I am very much inclin'd to believe, that 'tis the Polite Learning of any Nation, that contributes most to the extending its Language, and Poetry is the Branch of Polite Learning, which is the most efficacious in it. In order to the proving this, I desire your Lordship's Leave, to examine who they are, who are most instrumental, in making a Language pass the Bounds which confine the Original Speakers of it. And they seem to me to be the Gentlemen of Neighbouring Nations, who have Time and Opportunity to visit Foreign Countries, and are capacitated by their Fortunes and their Educations, to cultivate Languages, which they were not born to speak. For, besides that these are the Persons who are the most capacitated to learn them, they have, by the Variety and Multiplicity of their Conversation, most Opportunities to spread them. Now the Motives that for the most Part incite Gentlemen to Study, are Two, Pleasure and Vanity. But Pleasure and Vanity, will find their Account abundantly more in Polite Learning, than in Literature which is barely Solid. For, Polite Learning is more easy, and has more of Imagination in it, and instructs them much better how to varnish their Defects, and render them agreeable to one another. 'Tis chiefly then, the Polite Learning of any Nation, that ingages the Gentlemen of foreign Countries to apply themselves to study the Language of that Nation. But even of Polite Learning, Poetry appears to be the most agreeable, and most attractive Branch, because it is the most moving. And we find by Experience, that in the Learning of those Languages which have been most generally known, Poetry has made a very considerable Figure. Gentlemen then, in all likelihood, will apply themselves most eagerly to the Study of that Language, whose Poetry is very agreeable to them. But that Poetry must be most agreeable to the Generality of Gentlemen, which is most moving, and most instructive. For, tho' Gentlemen study to please themselves, yet if they are Men of Sense, they will not be for empty Pleasure, but will endeavour to be instructed and delighted together. Besides, when Gentlemen begin to study the Poetry of any Language, the first thing they understand is the reasonable Part of it. For the Fineness of the Imaginative Part, which depends in great measure upon Force of Words, and upon the Beauty of Expression, must lie conceal'd from them in a good Degree, till they are perfect in the Language. Thus the Poetry of that Language, which is most reasonable and most instructive, must, in all likelihood, have most Attraction for the Gentlemen of neighboring Nations; and we have shewn above, that that is the most reasonable, and most instructive Poetry, which is the most Regular.[1]

(1701)

72. Isaac WATTS (*1674–1748*) æt. *42*

In the *Poems of heroic measure*, I have attempted, in rhyme, the same variety of cadence, comma and period, which blank verse glories in as its peculiar elegance and ornament. It degrades the excellency of the best versification, when the lines run on by couplets, twenty together, just in the same pace, and with the same pauses. It spoils the noblest pleasure of the sound: The reader is tired with the tedious uniformity, or charmed to sleep with the unmanly softness of the numbers, and the perpetual chime of even cadences.

In the *Essays without rhyme*, I have not set up Milton for a perfect pattern; though he shall be forever honoured as our deliverer from the bondage. His works contain admirable and unequalled instances of bright and beautiful diction, as well as majesty and sereneness of thought. There are several episodes in his longer works, that stand in supreme dignity without a rival; yet all that vast reverence with which I read his *Paradise Lost*, cannot persuade me to be charmed with every page of it. The length of his periods, and sometimes of his parenthesis, runs me out of breath: Some of his numbers seem too harsh and uneasy. I could never believe that roughness and obscurity added anything to the true grandeur of a poem: Nor will I ever affect archaisms, exoticisms and a quaint uncouthness of speech, in order to become perfectly *Miltonian*. 'Tis my opinion, that blank verse may be written, with all due elevation of thought, in a modern stile, without borrowing anything from Chaucer's Tales, or running back so far as the days of Colin *the shepherd*, and the reign of the *Fairy Queen*. The oddness of an antique sound gives but a false pleasure to the ear, and abuses the true relish, even when it works delight.[1]

(*1706*)

Isaac Watts, "Preface," *Horae Lyricae* (London, 1736), pp. xxi–xxii.

73. Tom WOLFE (*b. 1931*) æt. *34*

But! That is the beauty of the man! On the *outside* he is quiet and homey, easy-going. Underneath, however—William Shawn is not nodding for a moment. Like the time the people in the Checking Department started having these weekly *skits,* sort of spoofing some of the old hands—does one really wish to know about how long that kind of thing lasted? That is a . . . *rhetorical question.* Shawn is not nodding. William Shawn has not lapsed for a moment from the labor to which he dedicated himself 13 years ago upon the death of *The New Yorker's* founder, Harold Ross:

To preserve *The New Yorker* just as Ross left it; exactly in . . . perpetuity.

Yes! And to do so, William Shawn has done nothing half-way. He has devised an editing system that is in some ways more completely *group journalism,* or *org-edit,* as it is called at *Novy Mir,* than anything *Time* magazine ever even contemplated.

To start with, one can believe, most assuredly, that no little . . . comedians in the Checking Department are going to schmarf around in there doing skits about the old hands—the men who worked under Ross, many of them. Those men play an important part in Shawn's system. The *physical* part of the preservation—such as preserving The Thurber Room (see *New York,* April 11)—that was easy. Shawn's hardest task was to preserve the literary style of Ross' *New Yorker.* The thing to do, of course, was to adopt, as models, the styles of the men on the magazine who had been working under Ross—the so-called Tiny Giants, viz., E. B. White, Joseph Mitchell, Wolcott Gibbs, James Thurber, A. J. Liebling, people of that sort.

Tom Wolfe, "The New Yorker II: Lost in the Whichy Thicket," *New York, Herald Tribune,* April 18, 1965, pp. 16–18.

Well, Shawn's first step was brilliantly simple. In effect, he has established lifetime tenure—purity!—for nearly everybody who served under Ross. Seniority! Columnists and so forth at *The New Yorker* have lifetime seniority, and if any ambitious kids there *aspire*, they wait it out, earn their first pair of hard finished worsteds by working and waiting for them; one understands? This has led to a certain amount of awkwardness. *The New Yorker's* movie, theater and art sections have come to have an eccentric *irrelevance* about them. They have a kind of knit-sweater, stoke-the-coal-grate charm, but . . . somehow they are full of Magooisms. Such as, "It was evidently intended to be a very funny account of a lower-middle-class London family jam-packed with lovable eccentrics, but when, after 30 minutes, I found that nothing funny had happened and that my accustomed high spirits were being reduced to audible low moans, I got up and made my way out of the theater, which, as far as laughter was concerned, had been, and I suspect remained, as silent as a tomb." Evidently intended; audible low moans; as silent as a tomb: huckleberry preserves! mom's jowls are on the doilie!

The "Letter From London" and "Letter From Paris" features, written by two more seniors, have the same trouble. They started off in the 1930s, when not too many Americans were traveling to London or Paris, the idea being to introduce readers to what was current in the way of Culture and *modes* in Europe. Today all sorts of people fly to London and Paris all the time, and these "Letters" from abroad have taken on the tone of random sights seen from the window of a second-best hotel.

Shawn, of course, is well aware of all this. It is just that he has a more . . . specific mission. Museum curator! He apparently wanted a permanent mold for *The New Yorker's* essays, profiles and so forth, and he did it with unerring taste. Lillian Ross! The last really impressive thing *The New Yorker* published under Harold Ross was Lillian Ross' profile of Ernest Hemingway, published in 1950. Lillian Ross was no kin to Harold Ross, by the way. This piece of hers was terrific, and the technique influenced a lot of the best journalists in the country.

She gave up the usual historical format of the profile entirely, and instead, wrote a running account of a couple of days she spent following Hemingway around New York. She put in all his little asides, everything, a lot of terrific dialogue. This story gave a wonderful picture of this big egomaniac garruling around town and batting everybody over the head with his ego as if it were a pig bladder. The piece impressed Ross, and that gave Lillian Ross the right cachet around *The New Yorker*, right off. A small, quiet, inconspicuous, sympathetic girl from Syracuse, whose father had run a filling station and kept a lot of animals, she had a great deal of womanly concern for underdogs. Also, her prose style had a nice flat-out quality about it, none of those confounded curlicues of the man at the other extreme, Liebling. Liebling verged on Ross' Anglo-Saxon sin of "excess," straining at the brain, as they say. Anyway, Lillian Ross' style became the model for *The New Yorker* essay.

That was all right, but most of the boys never really *caught on*. All they picked up were some of her throw-away mannerisms. She piles up details and dialogue, dialogue mainly, but piles it all up very carefully, building up toward a single point; such as, Ernest Hemingway is a Big Boy and a fatuous ass. All that the vergers who have followed her seem to think is that somehow if you get in enough details, enough random fact—somehow this *trenchant portrait* is going to rise up off the pages. They miss her strong points, namely, her ear for dialogue and her point of view, and just run certain *sport* devices of hers into the ground. The fact-gorged sentence is one of them. Lillian Ross wrote another essay, that also had a lot of impact, about the making of a moving picture, *The Red Badge of Courage*, and the opening sentence of that story was the ruination of at least 50 "letters" and "profiles" by *The New Yorker* foot soldiers who followed in her path. That sentence read:

> "The making of the Metro-Goldwyn-Mayer movie 'The Red Badge of Courage,' based on the Stephen Crane novel about the Civil War, was preceded by routine disclosures about its production plans from the columnist Louella Parsons ('John Huston is writing a screen treatment of Stephen Crane's classic, "The Red Badge of Courage,"

as a possibility for an M-G-M picture'), from the columnist Hedda Hopper ('Metro has an option on "The Red Badge of Courage" and John Huston's working up a budget for it. But there's no green light yet'), and from *Variety* ('Pre-production work on "Red Badge of Courage" commenced at Metro with thesp-tests for top roles in drama'), and it was preceded, in the spring of 1950, by a routine visit by John Huston, who is both a screen writer and a director, to New York, the headquarters of Loew's, Inc., the company that produces and distributes M-G-M pictures."

Miss Ross was just funning around with that one, but *The New Yorker*'s line troops started writing *whole stories* that way. Unbelievable! All those clauses, appositions, amplifications, qualifications, asides, God knows what else, hanging inside the poor old skeleton of one sentence like some kind of Spanish moss. They are still doing it. One of the latest is an essay in the March 13 issue. It began with what has become *The New Yorker* formula lead:

"One afternoon just after the spring semester began at the University of California, I passed on my way to the Berkeley campus to make a tour of the card tables that had been set up that day by student political organizations on the Bancroft strip—a wide brick sidewalk, outside the main entrance to the campus, that had been the original battlefield of a free-speech controversy that embroiled and threatened the university for the entire fall semester."

That is just the warmup, though. It proceeds to a *New Yorker* style specialty known as the "whichy thicket":

"But, unlike COFO workers, *who* still can't be sure that their civil-rights campaign has made any significant change in Mississippi, F.S.M. workers need only walk a block or two to witness unrestricted campus political activity of the kind that was the goal of their movement, and, to anyone *who* has spent some time listening to their reminiscences, the F.S.M. headquarters, *which* is a relatively recent acquisition, seems to be a make-work echo of the days *when* the F.S.M. had a series of command posts, with names like Strike Central and Press Central—a system of walkie-talkies for communication among its scouts on the campus—and an emergency telephone number, called Nexus, to be used *when* the regular number was busy."

Wh-wh-wh-wh-wh-whoooaaaaaaagh!—piles of whichy whuh words—*which, when, where, who, whether, whuggheeee,* the living whichy thickets. All that was from a story called "Letter From Berkeley" by Calvin Trillin, but it is not a rare case or even Trillin's fault. Trillin can write very clearly, very directly, left to his own devices. But nobody is left to his own devices at *The New Yorker* today.

(1965)

74. Alfred KAZIN (*b. 1915*) æt. *45*

There is still something glorious and incomparably free about that early period—above all, about the years before the First World War, when modernism had not yet lost its connection with revolutionary thinking in all social and ethical fields, had not yet taken on the desperation of the late 1920s, was a long way from the safe investment in established taste that it has become today.

Yet by now the record of Gertrude Stein's influence on so many famous writers is not only familiar but mysterious. Consider how much she is supposed to have done for others, and how little she ultimately achieved for herself! I would suggest that one reason for her influence is the fact that these writers were usually men, and that despite her spectacular outward lack of female charm, it was as a woman with a deep rudimentary common sense that she influenced so many male writers. Whatever the sterilities and the self-infatuations in her work, she was a woman of extraordinary insight. She understood men who were writers, she understood fellow minds. Her influence was enormous because writers could pick up extraordinary suggestions from her thinking. She studied the world, from her mind as its center, with an intensity that literally made her a stream of consciousness, and writers could find particles of thought anywhere in this stream. Because of her quickness and her social sense, she was able to size up people quickly, and many of her verbal judgments on people—carefully repeated in her more popular books—are unforgettable. She said of a well-known novelist who has been "promising" all his life—"He has a certain syrup, but does not pour."

But if Gertrude Stein herself has become finally unreadable,

Alfred Kazin, "The Mystery of Gertrude Stein," *Contemporaries* (Boston, 1962), pp. 102–104.

it is because she did not think in terms of books at all but in orphic sayings, sentences, rhythmic paragraphs that brought home the sound of herself thinking to herself. She was fascinated by ideas, the outlines of things, the possibilities inherent in all subjects, the hidden voice of the individual beneath his social personality. Unlike so many writers today, who see their opportunity only in the generally accepted, she was utterly fearless and tried everything; there was nothing she ever found in her own mind that seemed alien to literature. If courage were the same as creativity, Gertrude Stein would have been Homer. But creativity is a matter of achieving whole works, not of ideas for books or brilliant passages in books. Gertrude Stein could make a Hemingway or Anderson or Fitzgerald—at times even a Picasso—glow with ideas. But when she sat down to write, she let the stream of all her thoughts flow as if a book were only a receptacle of her mind. One came to suspect that her wisdom was more in the realm of theory than of actuality.

Gertrude Stein's genius for suggestion actually stays more with poets than it does with novelists. Poetry, by its very character, deals with a world of essences that can be intimated but not always communicated, and the critical writing of poets is always essentially philosophical. It is noteworthy that Mr. Brinnin, a poet himself, thinks that the only luster today in literature comes from poets, and that in writing about Gertrude Stein's work he communicates more enthusiasm for her intentions—which are pure literary ideas—than for her books, which are usually dead novels. Gertrude Stein may have tried to inject into the novel as a form some of the power that poetry always exerts on the unconscious. So did Joyce and Proust. But both these writers were able to carry through epic works. Even *Finnegans Wake,* though often termed a failure except as "poetry," exists as a shape, is connected from the first word to the last, in the way that Gertrude Stein's works never were.

(1960)

75. Dwight MACDONALD (*b. 1906*) æt. 52

This fascination with the law is perhaps a clue to Cozzens'[1] defects as a novelist. It explains the peculiar aridity of his prose, its needless qualifications, its clumsiness, its defensive qualifications (a lawyer qualifies negatively—so he can't be caught out later; but a novelist qualifies positively—to make his meaning not safer but clearer). And his sensibility is lawyer-like in its lack of both form and feeling, its peculiar combination of a brutal domineering pragmatism ("Just stick to the facts, please!") with abstract fancywork, a kind of Victorian jigsaw decoration that hides more than it reveals. I, too, think the law is interesting, but as an intellectual discipline, like mathematics or crossword puzzles. I feel Cozzens uses it as a defense against emotion ("sentimentality"). Confusing it with philosophy, he makes it bear too heavy a load, so that reality is distorted and even the law's own qualities are destroyed, its logic and precision blurred, its technical elegance coarsened. There's too much emotion in his law and too much law in his emotion.

The three earlier Cozzens novels I've read, *The Last Adam*, *The Just and the Unjust*, and *Guard of Honor*, were written in a straightforward if commonplace style.[2] But here Cozzens has tried to write Literature, to develop a complicated individual style, to convey deeper meanings than he has up to now attempted. Slimly endowed as either thinker or stylist, he has succeeded only in fuzzing it up, inverting the syntax, dragging in Latin-root polysyllables. Stylistically, *By Love Possessed* is a neo-Victorian cakewalk. A cakewalk by a singularly awkward contestant.[3] Confusing laboriousness with profundity, the reviewers have for the most part not detected the imposture.

Dwight MacDonald, "By Cozzens Possessed," *Against the American Grain* (New York, 1965), pp. 199–201.

There is some evidence, if one reads closely and also between the lines, that some of the reviewers had their doubts. But they adopted various strategies for muffling them. Messrs. Gill, Fischer, and Balliett,[4] while applauding the style in general, refrained from quoting anything. The last-named, after praising the "compact, baked, fastidious sentences," went into a long, worried paragraph which implied the opposite. "The unbending intricacies of thought . . . seem to send his sentences into impossible log-jams," he wrote, which is like saying of a girl, "She doesn't seem pretty." Jessamyn West warned, "You may come away with a certain feeling of tiredness," and left it at that. Malcolm Cowley managed to imply the book is a masterpiece without actually saying so—the publishers couldn't extract a single quote. With that cooniness[5] he used to deploy in the 'thirties when he was confronted with an important work that was on the right (that is, the "left") side but was pretty terrible, Cowley, here also confronted with a conflict between his taste and his sense of the *Zeitgeist*,[6] managed to praise with faint damns.[7] One magisterial sentence, in particular, may be recommended to all ambitious young book reviewers: "His style used to be as clear as a mountain brook; now it has become a little weed-grown and murky, like the brook when it wanders through a meadow." A meadowy brook is pretty *too*—it shows the mature Cozzens now feels, in Cowley's words, that "life is more complicated than he once believed."

A favorite reviewer's gambit was that Cozzens' prose may be involved but so is James's. "One drawback is the style," *Time* admitted, "which is frosted with parenthetical clauses, hump-backed syntax, Jamesian involutions, Faulknerian meanderings." I am myself no foe of the parenthesis, nor do I mind a little syntactical humping at times, but I feel this comparison is absurd. James's involutions are (a) necessary to precisely discriminate his meaning; (b) solid parts of the architecture of the sentence; and (c) controlled by a fine ear for euphony. Faulkner does meander, but there is emotional force, descriptive richness behind his wanderings. They both use words that are not only in the dictionary[8] but also in the living language, and use them in conversational rhythms. Their style is complex because they are saying something complicated, not, as with Cozzens, because they cannot make words do what they want them to do.

(1958)

76. *The New Yorker (1925–date)* æt. *43*

Notes and Comment

As rhetoric has become an increasingly dispensable member of the liberal arts, people have abandoned the idea, held so firmly by the ancient Greeks and Romans, that eloquence is indispensable to politics. Perhaps President Kennedy's achievements in both spheres will revive a taste for good oratory—a taste that has been alternately frustrated by inarticulateness and dulled by bombast. There have been a few notable orators in our day—most recently, Adlai Stevenson—but they have been the exceptions, and it has taken Mr. Kennedy's success as a politician to suggest that the power to "enchant souls through words" (Socrates) may soon be at a premium once more. Whatever the impact of the Inaugural Address on contemporary New Frontiersmen, we find it hard to believe that an Athenian or Roman citizen could have listened to it unmoved, or that Cicero, however jealous of his own reputation, would have found reason to object to it.

We are all familiar by now with the generally high praise the President received for his first speech, but before the responsibility for a final judgment is yielded to Time it would be a shame not to seek the opinion of a couple of true professionals. Both Aristotle and Cicero, the one a theorist and the other a theorizing orator, believed that rhetoric could be an art to the extent that the orator was, first, a logician and, second, a psychologist with an appreciation and understanding of words. Cicero felt, further, that the ideal orator was the thoroughly educated man. (He would be pleased by Mr. Kennedy's background, with its strong emphasis on affairs of state: the philosopher-orator-statesman.) Of the three types of oratory defined by the ancients—political, forensic, and display (in which

"The Talk of the Town," *The New Yorker,* Feb. 4, 1961, pp. 23–24.

audience participation was limited to a judgment of style)—the political was esteemed most highly, because it dealt with the loftiest of issues; namely, the fate of peoples, rather than of individuals. ("Now the trumpet summons us again . . . against the common enemies of man. . . .") The ideal speech was thought to be one in which three kinds of persuasion were used by the speaker: logical, to present the facts of the case and construct an argument based on them; emotional, to reach the audience psychologically; and "ethical," to appeal to the audience by establishing one's own integrity and sincerity. The Inaugural Address, being a variation on the single theme of man's rights and obligations, is not primarily logical, although it contains no illogic; it is an appeal to men's souls rather than to their minds. During the Presidential campaign, Mr. Kennedy tested and patented an exercise in American psychology that proved to be all the emotional appeal he required for the inaugural speech: "And so, my fellow-Americans, ask not what your country can do for you, ask what you can do for your country." His ethical persuasion, or indication of his personal probity, consisted of an extension of that appeal ". . . ask of us here the same high standards of strength and sacrifice which we ask of you."

Aristotle recognized only one (good) style, while Cicero thought that there were three styles—the plain, the middle, and the grand. To Aristotle, who considered it sufficient for a style to be clear and appropriate, avoiding undue elevation (whence bombast) and excessive lowliness, it would have seemed that Mr. Kennedy had achieved the Golden Mean. The formality of the Inaugural Address ("To that world assembly of sovereign states, the United Nations . . .") is appropriate to the subject; the language ("In your hands, my fellow-citizens, more than mine, will rest the final success or failure of our course") is clear and direct. Cicero's ideal orator was able to speak in all three styles, in accordance with the demands of his subject, and in that respect Mr. Kennedy filled the role by speaking plainly on the practical ("All this will not be finished in the first one hundred days"), by speaking formally but directly on the purpose of national defense ("For only when our arms are sufficient beyond doubt can we be certain beyond doubt that they will never be employed"), and by speaking grandly on the potential accomplishments of the movement toward the New Frontier ("The energy, the faith, the devotion which we bring to this endeavor will light our country and all who serve it—and the glow from that fire can truly light the world").

The address, however, is largely in the grand style, which is characterized by Cicero as the ultimate source of emotional persuasion, through figures of speech [1] and a certain degree of dignified periodic rhythm, not iambic ("The world is very different now. For man holds in his mortal hands the power to abolish all forms of human poverty, and all forms of human life"). The oration is so rich in figures of speech—the many metaphors include a torch, a beachhead, jungles, a trumpet, a tiger—that we can imagine students of the future studying it for examples of antithesis ("If a free society cannot help the many who are poor, it cannot save the few who are rich"), personification (". . . the hand of mankind's final war"), and anaphora ("Not as a call to bear arms, though arms we need; not as a call to battle, though embattled we are . . ."). "Battle" and "embattled"—an excellent example of paronomasia.

And so we leave the speech to the students of rhetoric, having invoked for Mr. Kennedy the blessings of Aristotle and Cicero, and for ourself [2] the hope that he has reestablished the tradition of political eloquence.

(Feb. 4, 1961)

77. Herbert Marshall McLUHAN (*b. 1911*)
æt. *49*

Medieval universities were oral in their procedures; they were little hampered by rigidities of administrative apparatus; and they were not grounded by the need for large libraries. Today young lawyers in setting up offices are advised to keep books out of sight: "*You* are the law, the source of all knowledge of the law, so far as your clients are concerned." This was the natural attitude of student to teacher when books were few. It's becoming the attitude again when books are so numerous they are difficult to use or consult.

At Oxford under the Tudors, Mallet tells us, "The old lawless democratic spirit yielded unwillingly to discipline. The Renaissance set up new ideas of learning." The macadamized regularity of administrative procedures, which banished oral variety in prose by 1700, had begun to regulate school and college life much earlier. In place of the lively disputation came the lecture—the single lecturer reading written notes to silent listeners who spent their remaining time in silent reading.

Print enabled one man to speak to many, whereas the readers of any one manuscript were few. Similarly print enabled one reader to read many authors in a few years with the resulting awareness that we now label "historical." One reader speeding through whole eras of the past could return with the illusion of having grasped the unified character of peoples or periods. The manuscript reader went too slowly, traveled too little to develop much time sense. Whatever of the past was discussed was felt as present, just as today the simultaneity and inclusive-

Herbert Marshall McLuhan, "The Effect of the Printed Book on Language in the 16th Century," *Explorations in Communication,* ed. H. M. McLuhan and E. S. Carpenter (Boston, 1960), pp. 128–129.

ness of our historical knowledge makes it all felt as being now. We have arrived once more at the oral via what appear as non-auditory means.

In 16th century dictionaries a word was cited in a series of usable phrases with authors indicated. No attempt was made to isolate meaning in a definition. Before print the very concept of word definition was meaningless, since no single author was read by many people at one period of time. Moreover, it would have been impossible for many people to have consulted any one lexicon. Medievalists say that even nowadays a medieval dictionary would be impossible, since individual writers assumed they were free to define and develop any given term as their thought proceeded.

Print meant the possibility of uniform texts, grammars, and lexicons visually present to as many as asked for them. The classroom, as we know it, was entirely the by-product of print.

It was almost a century after print from movable type began before printers thought to use pagination for readers. Before then pagination was for bookbinders only. With print, the book ceased to be something to be memorized and became a work of reference.

Individual writers throughout the 16th century varied tone sentence by sentence, even phrase by phrase, with all the oral freedom and flexibility of pre-print days. Not until the later 17th century did it become apparent that print called for a stylistic revolution.[1] The speeding eye of the new reader favored not shifting tones but steadily maintained tone, page by page, throughout the volume. It was a change of scenery comparable to that of the motorist who shifts from a road sprinkled with Burma Shave yelps and siren gestures from Miss Rheingold to a throughway or turnpike. By the 18th century the reader could depend on a writer controlling the purr of his sentences and giving him a swift, smooth ride. Prose became urbane, macadamized. The plunging, rearing horses of 16th century journalese were more like a rodeo.[2]

Ingenioso in *The Returne from Parnassus* says, "Ile have my pen run like a spigot and my invention answer it quicke as a drawer," while Nashe gallops breathless and inconsequential in a style calling for the utmost agility of mind and attention:

> Verie devout Asses they were, for all they were so dunstically set forth, and such as thought they knew as much of God's minde as richer men: why inspiration was their ordinarie familiar, and buzd in their eares like a Bee in a boxe everie hower what newes from heaven, hell and the land of whipperginnie, displease them who durst, he should have his mittimus to damnation *ex tempore*, they would vaunt there was not a pease difference betwixt them and the Apostles, they were as poor as they, of as base trades as they, and no more inspired than they, and with God there is no respect of persons, onely herein may seem some little diversitie to lurk, that *Peter* wore a sword, and they count it flat hel fire for anie man to weare a dagger: nay, so grounded and gravlled were they in this opinion, that now when they should come to Battell, theres never a one of them would bring a blade (no, not an onion blade) about hym to dye for it.

A popular writer like Shakespeare was free of humanist obsessions about imitation of the ancients. He could exploit the old popular idiom and the huge new tapestry of polyglot effects that poured from the press. Many of his typical effects resulted from pouring the visual masques and pageants of the court and high-life through the new medium of spoken or orated poetry. The learned of the 16th century were obsessed by the need not only to imitate classical poets, but also to adapt this verse to song. Verse had no status at all as recited. It had to be sung. Owing to print, spoken verse became popular on the stage. Song is speech slowed down and adapted to a single tone or pitch. Print made possible the rapid reading of verse. In speeding up song, print fostered oratorically delivered poetry.

While the learned devised laborious reconstructions of Greek theatre in the form of grand opera, Shakespeare played with the new fabric and colors of the vernacular as enriched by a flood of translation from Latin, Spanish, French, Italian. When Donne and the Metaphysicals took over this new spoken verse for lyric poetry, they took over its heavy visual emphasis. So conscious were they of this visual stress, they reverted to the pictorial lore of the primitive *Biblia Pauprum.*

Between the 13th and 16th centuries word order substituted for word inflection as a principle of grammatical syntax. The same tendency occurred with word formation. After printing both tendencies accelerated greatly, and there was a shift from audible to visual means of syntax.

(*1960*)

78. E. B. WHITE (*b. 1899*) æt. *60*

If the student doubts that style is something of a mystery,[1] let him try rewriting a familiar sentence and see what happens. Any much-quoted sentence will do. Suppose we take "These are the times that try men's souls." Here we have eight short, easy words, forming a simple declarative sentence.[2] The sentence contains no flashy [3] ingredient, such as "Damn the torpedoes!" and the words, as you see, are ordinary.[4] Yet in that arrangement they have shown great durability; the sentence is well along in its second century. Now compose a few variations: [5]

> Times like these try men's souls.
> How trying it is to live in these times!
> These are trying times for men's souls.
> Soulwise, these are trying times.

It seems unlikely that Thomas Paine [6] could have made his sentiment stick [7] if he had couched [8] it in any of these forms. But why not? No fault of grammar can be detected in them, and in every case the meaning is clear. Each version is correct, and each, for some reason that we can't readily put our finger on,[9] is marked for oblivion.[10] We could, of course, talk about "rhythm" and "cadence," [11] but the talk would be vague and unconvincing. We could declare "soulwise" to be a silly word, inappropriate to the occasion; but even that won't do—it does not answer the main question.[12] Are we even sure "soulwise" is silly? If "otherwise" is a serviceable word, what's the matter with "soulwise?" [13]

(*1959*)

William Strunk, Jr. and E. B. White, "An Approach to Style," *The Elements of Style* (New York, 1959), pp. 53–54.

79. Jack KEROUAC (*b. 1922*) æt. *36*

TIMING.[1] Nothing is muddy that *runs in time* and to laws of *time*—Shakespearian stress of dramatic need to speak now in own unalterable way or forever hold tongue—*no revisions* (except obvious rational mistakes, such as names or *calculated* insertions in act of not writing but *inserting*).

CENTER OF INTEREST. Begin not from preconceived idea of what to say about image but from jewel center [2] of interest in subject of image at *moment* of writing, and write outwards swimming in sea of language to peripheral release and exhaustion—Do not afterthink [3] except for poetic or P.S. reasons.[4] Never afterthink to "improve" or defray [5] impressions, as, the best writing is always the most painful personal wrung-out tossed from cradle warm protective mind—tap from yourself the song of yourself *blow!* [6]—*now!*—*your* way is your only way—"good"—or "bad" [7]—always honest, ("ludicrous"), spontaneous, "confessional" interesting, because not "crafted." Craft *is* craft.

STRUCTURE OF WORK. Modern bizarre structures (science fiction, etc.) arise from language being dead, "different" themes give illusion of "new" life. Follow roughly outlines in outfanning [8] movement over subject, as river rock, so mindflow over jewel-center need (run your mind over it, *once*) arriving at pivot, where what was dim formed "beginning" becomes sharp-necessitating "ending" and language shortens in race to wire of time-race of work, following laws of Deep Form, to conclusion, last words, last trickle—Night is The End.

MENTAL STATE. If possible write "without consciousness" in semi-trance (as Yeats' later "trance writing") allowing subconscious to admit in own uninhibited interesting necessary and so

Jack Kerouac, "Essentials of Spontaneous Prose," *Evergreen Review*, II, No. 5 (Summer 1958), 72–73.

"modern" language what conscious art would censor, and write excitedly, swiftly, with writing-or-typing-cramps, in accordance (as from center to periphery) with laws of orgasm, Reich's "beclouding of consciousness." *Come* from within, out—to relaxed and said.

SET-UP. The object is set before the mind, either in reality, as in sketching (before a landscape or teacup or old face) or is set in the memory wherein it becomes the sketching from memory of a definite image-object.

PROCEDURE. Time being of the essence in the purity of speech, sketching language is undisturbed flow from the mind of personal secret idea-words, *blowing* (as per jazz musician) on subject of image.

METHOD. No periods separating sentence-structures already arbitrarily riddled by false colons [9] and timid usually needless commas—but the vigorous space dash separating rhetorical breathing (as jazz musician drawing breath between outblown phrases)—"measured pauses which are the essentials of our speech"—"divisions of the *sounds* we hear"—"time and how to note it down." (William Carlos Williams)

SCOPING. Not "selectivity" of expression but following free deviation (association) of mind into limitless blow-on-subject seas of thought, swimming in sea of English with no discipline other than rhythms of rhetorical exhalation and expostulated statement, like a fist coming down on a table with each complete utterance, bang! (the space dash)—Blow as deep as you want—write as deeply, fish [10] as far down as you want, satisfy yourself first, then reader cannot fail to receive telepathic shock and meaning-excitement by same laws operating in his own human mind.

LAG IN PROCEDURE. No pause to think of proper word but the infantile pileup of scatalogical buildup words till satisfaction is gained, which will turn out to be a great appending rhythm to a thought and be in accordance with Great Law of timing.

(*1958*)

80. Mary McCARTHY (*b. 1912*) æt. *42*

The notion that life is senseless, a tale told by an idiot—the under-theme of twentieth-century literature—is affirmed again by Faulkner in *The Sound and the Fury*. Yet here, as in *Ulysses*, characters appear from the mists of their own reveries and sensations: the idiot Benjy, Jason, Dilsey, the Negro cook. And a plot, even, is indicated for the reader to piece together from clues dropped here and there: the story of Caddy and the castration of Benjy and Quentin's suicide. The materialization of plot and character prove that there *is* being, after all, beyond the arbitrary flux of existence. Following Joyce and Faulkner, the imitation-from-within became almost standard practice for writers who were impatient with the fragmented impressionist novel and who had assimilated nonetheless some of its techniques. To use the technique of impressionism to create something quite different—a character study—seems the manifest intention of Joyce Cary in *The Horse's Mouth*, where the author, as it were, impersonates the eye of Gulley Jimson, an old reprobate painter down on his luck; the dancing, broken surface is only a means, like the muttering of an inner dialogue, to show the man in action, incessantly painting in his mind's eye as he boozily peregrinates the docks and streets. Something very similar is John Updike's *The Poorhouse Farm*, which is seen through the resentful hyperopic eye of an old man sitting on the porch of a county poorhouse. The sign of this kind of writing, the mark of its affiliation with the pure impressionist or stream-of-consciousness novel, is that when you start the book you do not know where you are. It takes you quite a few pages to get your bearings, just as if you were bumping along inside a sack in some fairy story; then you awake to the fact that the

Mary McCarthy, "Characters in Fiction," *On the Contrary* (New York, 1954), pp. 280–283.

consciousness you have been thrust into is named Benjy and is feebleminded or is a criminal old painter with a passion for William Blake's poetry or a charity patient whose eyesight, owing to the failing muscles of old age, bends and distorts everything in the immediate foreground and can only focus clearly on what is far off. Once you know where you are, you can relax and study your surroundings, though you must watch out for sudden, disorienting jolts and jerks—an indication that the character is in movement, colliding or interacting with objective reality.

The reader, here, as in *Ulysses,* is restricted to a narrow field of vision or to several narrow fields in succession. Now something comparable happens in recent books that, on the surface, seem to owe very little to the stream-of-consciousness tradition and to take no interest in the mechanics of perception or the field of vision as such. I mean such books as *Augie March, Henderson the Rain King, The Catcher in the Rye, Lolita,* and two of my own novels, *The Groves of Academe* and *A Charmed Life.* These books are impersonations, ventriloquial acts; the author, like some prankster on the telephone, is speaking in an assumed voice—high or deep, hollow or falsetto, but in any case not his own. He is imitating the voice of Augie or of Holden Caulfield and the book is written in Augie's or Holden's "style." The style is the man (or the boy), and the author, pretending to be Augie or Holden or Humbert Humbert, remains "in character" throughout the book, unless he shifts to another style, that is, to another character. These books, in short, are dramatic monologues or series of dramatic monologues. The reader, tuned in, is left in no doubt as to where he is physically, and yet in many of these books he finds himself puzzled by the very vocal consciousness he has entered: is it good or bad, impartial or biased? Can it be trusted as Huck Finn or Marcel or David Copperfield could be trusted? He senses the author, cramped inside the character like a contortionist in a box, and suspects (often rightly) some trick. In short, it is not all straight shooting, as it was with the old novelists.

This is not a defect, yet it points to the defects of the method, which can be summed up as a lack of straightforwardness.

There is something burglarious about these silent entries into a private and alien consciousness. Or so I feel when I do it myself. It is exhilarating but not altogether honest to make believe I am a devious red-haired man professor with bad breath and bits of toilet paper on his face, to talk under my breath his sibilant, vindictive thought-language and draw his pale lips tightly across my teeth. "So *this* is how the world looks to a man like that!" I can say to myself, awestruck, and so, I expect, John Updike, twenty-five years old, must have felt when he discovered what it felt like to be an old pauper with loosened eye-muscles sitting on a poorhouse porch. But I cannot know, really, what it feels like to be a vindictive man professor, any more than a young man can know what it is to be an old man or Faulkner can know what it is to be a feeble-minded adult who has had his balls cut off. All fictions, of course, are impersonations, but it seems to me somehow less dubious to impersonate the outside of a person, say Mrs. Micawber with her mysterious "I will never leave Mr. Micawber," than to claim to know what it feels like to *be* Mrs. Micawber. These impersonations, moreover, are laborious; to come at a character circuitously, by a tour de force, means spending great and sometimes disproportionate pains on the method of entry. I read somewhere that Salinger spent ten years writing *The Catcher in the Rye;* that was eight years too long. Granted, the book is a feat, but it compels admiration more as a feat than as a novel, like the performance of a one-armed violinist or any other curiosity. This could not be said of *Huckleberry Finn;* Mark Twain's imitation of Huck's language is never, so to speak, the drawing card. In the cases of Salinger, Updike, myself, one wonders whether the care expended on the mechanics of the imitation, on getting the right detail, vocabulary, and so on, does not constitute a kind of advertisement for the author, eliciting such responses as "Think of the work that went into it!" or "Imagine a twenty-five-year-old being able to take off an old man like that!" One is reminded of certain young actors whose trademark is doing character parts, or, vice versa, of certain old actresses whose draw can be summed up in the sentence "You would never guess she was sixty."

(*1954*)

81. William FAULKNER (*1897–1962*) æt. *56*

This time he was already sitting on the bench, laughing. He told me what it was at once: a dream:[1] he had dreamed the night before that he was walking for miles along country roads, leading a horse which he was trying to swap for a night's sleep —not for a simple bed for the night, but for the sleep itself; and with me to listen now, went on from there, elaborating it, building it into a work of art with the same tedious (it had the appearance of fumbling but actually it wasn't: it was seeking, hunting) almost excruciating patience and humility with which he did all his writing, me listening and believing no word of it: that is, that it had been any dream dreamed in sleep.[2] Because I knew better.[3] I knew that he had invented it, made it;[4] he had made most of it or at least some of it while I was there watching and listening to him. He didn't know why he had been compelled, or anyway needed, to claim it had been a dream, why there had to be that connection with dream and sleep, but I did. It was because he had written his whole biography into an anecdote or perhaps a parable: the horse (it had been a racehorse at first, but now it was a working horse, plow carriage and saddle, sound and strong and valuable, but without recorded pedigree) representing the vast rich strong docile sweep of the Mississippi Valley, his own America, which he in his bright blue racetrack shirt and vermilion-mottled Bohemian Windsor tie, was offering with humor and patience and humility, but mostly with patience and humility,[5] to swap for his own dream of purity and integrity and hard and unremitting work and accomplishment,[6] of which *Winesburg, Ohio* and *The Triumph of the Egg*[7] had been symptoms and symbols.

He would never have said this, put it into words, himself. He

William Faulkner, "A Note on Sherwood Anderson," *Essays, Speeches and Public Letters* (New York, 1965), pp. 3–6.

may never have been able to see it even, and he certainly would have denied it, probably pretty violently, if I had tried to point it out to him. But this would not have been for the reason that it might not have been true, nor for the reason that, true or not, he would not have believed it. In fact, it would have made little difference whether it was true or not or whether he believed it or not. He would have repudiated it for the reason which was the great tragedy of his character. He expected people to make fun of, ridicule him. He expected people nowhere near his equal in stature or accomplishment or wit or anything else, to be capable of making him appear ridiculous.

That was why he worked so laboriously and tediously and indefatigably at everything he wrote. It was as if he said to himself: 'This anyway will, shall, must be invulnerable.' It was as though he wrote not even out of the consuming unsleeping appeaseless thirst for glory for which any normal artist would destroy his aged mother, but for what to him was more important and urgent: not even for mere truth, but for purity, the exactitude of purity. His was not the power and rush of Melville, who was his grandfather, nor the lusty humor for living of Twain, who was his father; he had nothing of the heavy-handed disregard for nuances of his older brother, Dreiser.[8] His was that fumbling for exactitude, the exact word and phrase within the limited scope of a vocabulary controlled and even repressed by what was in him almost a fetish of simplicity, to milk them both dry, to seek always to penetrate to thought's uttermost end. He worked so hard at this that it finally became just style:[9] an end instead of a means: so that he presently came to believe that, provided he kept the style pure and intact and unchanged and inviolate, what the style contained would have to be first rate: it couldn't help but be first rate, and therefore himself too.

At this time in his life, he had to believe this. His mother had been a bound girl,[10] his father a day laborer; this background had taught him that the amount of security and material success which he had attained was, must be, the answer and end of life. Yet he gave this up, repudiated and discarded it at a later age, when older in years than most men and women who make that decision, to dedicate himself to art, writing. Yet, when he made the decision, he found himself to be only a one- or two-book man. He had to believe that, if only he kept that style pure, then what the style contained would be pure too, the best. That was why he had to defend the style. That was the reason for his hurt and anger at Hemingway about Hemingway's *The Torrents of Spring*,[11] and at me in a lesser degree since my fault was not full book-length but instead was merely a privately-printed and -subscribed volume which few people outside our small New Orleans group would ever see or hear about, because of the book of Spratling's caricatures which we titled *Sherwood Anderson & Other Famous Creoles* and to which I wrote an introduction in Anderson's primer-like style.[12] Neither of us—Hemingway or I—could have touched, ridiculed, his work itself. But we had made his style look ridiculous; and by that time, after *Dark Laughter*, when he had reached the point where he should have stopped writing, he had to defend that style at all costs because he too must have known by then in his heart that there was nothing else left.

(*1953*)

82. Lionel TRILLING (*b. 1905*) æt. *43*

As for the style of the book, it is not less than definitive in American literature. The prose of *Huckleberry Finn* established for written prose the virtues of American colloquial speech. This has nothing to do with pronunciation or grammar. It has something to do with ease and freedom in the use of language. Most of all it has to do with the structure of the sentence, which is simple, direct, and fluent, maintaining the rhythm of the word-groups of speech and the intonations of the speaking voice.

In the matter of language, American literature had a special problem. The young nation was inclined to think that the mark of the truly literary product was a grandiosity and elegance not to be found in the common speech. It therefore encouraged a greater breach between its vernacular and its literary language than, say, English literature of the same period ever allowed. This accounts for the hollow ring one now and then hears even in the work of our best writers in the first half of the last century. English writers of equal stature would never have made the lapses into rhetorical excess that are common in Cooper and Poe and that are to be found even in Melville and Hawthorne.

Yet at the same time that the language of ambitious literature was high and thus always in danger of falseness, the American reader was keenly interested in the actualities of daily speech. No literature, indeed, was ever so taken up with matters of speech as ours was. "Dialect," which attracted even our serious writers, was the accepted common ground of our popular humorous writing. Nothing in social life seemed so remarkable as the different forms which speech could take—the brogue of the immigrant Irish or the mispronunciation of the German, the

Lionel Trilling, "Huckleberry Finn," *The Liberal Imagination* (New York, 1950), pp. 115–117.

"affectation" of the English, the reputed precision of the Bostonian, the legendary twang of the Yankee farmer, and the drawl of the Pike County man. Mark Twain, of course, was in the tradition of humor that exploited this interest, and no one could play with it nearly so well. Although today the carefully spelled-out dialects of nineteenth-century American humor are likely to seem dull enough, the subtle variations of speech in *Huckleberry Finn,* of which Mark Twain was justly proud, are still part of the liveliness and flavor of the book.

Out of his knowledge of the actual speech of America Mark Twain forged a classic prose. The adjective may seem a strange one, yet it is apt. Forget the misspellings and the faults of grammar, and the prose will be seen to move with the greatest simplicity, directness, lucidity, and grace. These qualities are by no means accidental. Mark Twain, who read widely, was passionately interested in the problems of style; the mark of the strictest literary sensibility is everywhere to be found in the prose of *Huckleberry Finn.*

It is this prose that Ernest Hemingway had chiefly in mind when he said that "all modern American literature comes from one book by Mark Twain called *Huckleberry Finn.*" Hemingway's own prose stems from it directly and consciously; so does the prose of the two modern writers who most influenced Hemingway's early style, Gertrude Stein and Sherwood Anderson (although neither of them could maintain the robust purity of their model); so, too, does the best of William Faulkner's prose, which, like Mark Twain's own, reinforces the colloquial tradition with the literary tradition. Indeed, it may be said that almost every contemporary American writer who deals conscientiously with the problems and possibility of prose must feel, directly or indirectly, the influence of Mark Twain. He is the master of the style that escapes the fixity of the printed page, that sounds in our ears with the immediacy of the heard voice, the very voice of unpretentious truth.

(1948)

83. Henry MILLER (*b. 1891*) æt. *50*

I haven't the slightest idea what my future books will be like, even the one immediately to follow. My charts and plans are the slenderest sort of guides: I scrap them at will, I invent, distort, deform, lie, inflate, exaggerate, confound and confuse as the mood seizes me.[1] I obey only my own instincts and intuitions. I know nothing in advance. Often I put down things which I do not understand myself, secure in the knowledge that later they will become clear and meaningful to me. I have faith in the man who is writing, who is myself, the writer. I do not believe in words, no matter if strung together by the most skillful man: I believe in language, which is something beyond words, something which words give only an inadequate illusion of. Words do not exist separately, except in the minds of scholars, etymologists, philologists, etc. Words divorced from language are dead things, and yield no secrets. A man is revealed in his style, the language which he has created for himself. To the man who is pure at heart I believe that everything is as clear as a bell,[2] even the most esoteric scripts. For such a man there is always mystery, but the mystery is not mysterious, it is logical, natural, ordained, and implicitly accepted. Understanding is not a piercing of the mystery, but an acceptance of it, a living blissfully with it,[3] in it, through and by it. I would like my words to flow along in the same way that the world flows along, a serpentine movement through incalculable dimensions,[4] axes, latitudes, climates, conditions. I accept a priori my inability to realize such an ideal. It does not bother me in the least. In the ultimate sense, the world itself is pregnant with failure, is the perfect manifestation of imperfection, of the consciousness of failure. In the realization of this, failure is itself eliminated. Like the

Henry Miller, "Reflections on Writing," *The Wisdom of the Heart* (Norfolk, Conn., 1941), pp. 22–28.

primal spirit of the universe, like the unshakable Absolute, the One, the All, the creator, i.e., the artist, expresses himself by and through imperfection. It is the stuff of life, the very sign of livingness. One gets nearer to the heart of truth, which I suppose is the ultimate aim of the writer, in the measure that he ceases to struggle, in the measure that he abandons the will. The great writer is the very symbol of life, of the non-perfect. He moves effortlessly, giving the illusion of perfection, from some unknown center [5] which is certainly not the brain center but which is definitely a center, a center connected with the rhythm of the whole universe and consequently as sound, solid, unshakable, as durable, defiant, anarchic, purposeless, as the universe itself. Art teaches nothing, except the significance of life. The great work must inevitably be obscure, except to the very few, to those who like the author himself are initiated into the mysteries. Communication then is secondary: it is perpetuation which is important. For this only one good reader is necessary.

If I am a revolutionary, as has been said, it is unconsciously. I am not in revolt against the world order. "I revolutionize," as Blaise Cendrars said of himself. There is a difference. I can as well live on the minus side of the fence as on the plus side. Actually I believe myself to be just above these two signs, providing a ratio between them which expresses itself plastically, non-ethically, in writing. I believe that one has to pass beyond the sphere and influence of art. Art is only a means to life, to the life more abundant. It is not in itself the life more abundant. It merely points the way, something which is overlooked not only by the public, but very often by the artist himself. In becoming an end it defeats itself. Most artists are defeating life by their very attempt to grapple with it. They have split the egg in two. All art, I firmly believe, will one day disappear. But the artist will remain, and life itself will become not "an art," but *art,* i.e., will definitely and for all time usurp the field. In any true sense we are certainly not yet alive. We are no longer animals, but we are certainly not yet *men.* Since the dawn of art every great artist has been dinning that into us, but few are they who have understood it. Once art is really accepted it will cease to be. It is only a substitute, a symbol-language, for something which can be seized directly. But for that to become possible man must become thoroughly religious, not a believer, but a prime mover, a god in fact and deed. He will become that inevitably. And of all the detours along this path art is the most glorious, the most fecund, the most instructive. The artist who becomes thoroughly aware consequently ceases to be one. And the trend is towards awareness, towards that blinding consciousness in which no present form of life can possibly flourish, not even art.

To some this will sound like mystification, but it is an honest statement of my present convictions. It should be borne in mind, of course, that there is an inevitable discrepancy between the truth of the matter and what one thinks, even about himself: but it should also be borne in mind that there exists an equal discrepancy between the judgment of another and this same truth. Between subjective and objective there is no vital difference. Everything is illusive [6] and more or less transparent. All phenomena, including man and his thoughts about himself, are nothing more than a movable, changeable alphabet. There are no solid facts to get hold of. Thus, in writing, even if my distortions and deformations be deliberate, they are not necessarily less near to the truth of things. One can be absolutely truthful and sincere even though admittedly the most outrageous liar. Fiction and invention are of the very fabric of life. The truth is no way disturbed by the violent perturbations of the spirit.

Thus, whatever effects I may obtain by technical device are never the mere results of technique, but the very accurate registering by my seismographic needle of the tumultuous, manifold, mysterious and incomprehensible experiences which I have lived through and which, in the process of writing, are lived through again, differently, perhaps even more tumultuously, more mysteriously, more incomprehensibly. The so-called core of solid fact, which forms the point of departure as well as repair, is deeply embedded in me: I could not possibly lose it, alter it, disguise it, try as I may. And yet it *is* altered, just as the face of the world is altered, with each moment that we breathe. To record it then, one must give a double illusion—one of arrestation and one of flow. It is this dual trick, so to speak, which gives the illusion of falsity: it is this lie, this fleeting, metamorphic [7] mask, which is of the very essence of art. One anchors oneself in the flow: one adopts the lying mask in order to reveal the truth.

I have often thought that I should like one day to write a book explaining how I wrote certain passages in my books, or perhaps just one passage. I believe I could write a good-sized book on just one small paragraph selected at random from my work. A book about its inception, its genesis, its metamorphosis, its accouchement,[8] of the time which elapsed between the birth of the idea and its recording, the time it took to write it, the thoughts I had between times while writing it, the day of the week, the state of my health, the condition of my nerves, the interruptions that occurred, those of my own volition and those which were forced upon me, the multifarious varieties of expression which occurred to me in the process of writing, the alterations, the point where I left off and in returning, completely altered the original trend, or the point where I skillfully left off, like a surgeon making the best of a bad job, intending to return and resume some time later, but never doing so, or else returning and continuing the trend unconsciously some few books later when the memory of it had completely vanished.[9] Or I might take one passage against another, passages which the cold eye of the critic [10] seizes on as examples of this or that, and utterly confound them, the analytical-minded critics, by demonstrating how a seemingly effortless piece of writing was achieved under great duress whereas another difficult, labyrinthian passage was written like a breeze, like a geyser erupting. Or I could show how a passage originally shaped itself when in bed, how it became transformed upon arising, and again transformed at the moment of sitting down to record it. Or I could produce [11] my scratch pad to show how the most remote, the most artificial stimulus produced a warm, life-like human flower. I could produce certain words discovered by hazard while riffling the pages of a book, show how they set me off—but who on earth could ever guess how, in what manner, they were to set me off? All that the critics write about a work of art, even at the best, even when most sound, convincing, plausible, even when done with love, which is seldom, is as nothing compared to the actual mechanics, the real genetics of a work of art. I remember my work, not word for word, to be sure, but in some more accurate, trustworthy way; my whole work has come to resemble a terrain of which I have made a thorough, geodetic survey, not from a desk, with pen and ruler, but by touch, by getting down on all fours, on my stomach, and crawling over the ground inch by inch, and this over an endless period of time in all conditions of weather. In short, I am as close to the work now as when I was in the act of executing it—closer perhaps. The conclusion of a book was never anything more than a shift of bodily position. It might have ended in a thousand different ways. No single part of it is finished off: I could resume the narrative at any point, carry on, lay canals, tunnels, bridges, houses, factories, stud it with other inhabitants, other fauna and flora, all equally true to fact. I have no beginning and no ending, actually. Just as life begins at any moment, through an act of realization, so the work. But each beginning, whether of book, page, paragraph, sentence or phrase, marks a vital connection, and it is in the vitality, the durability, the timelessness and changelessness of the thoughts and events that I plunge anew each time. Every line and word is vitally connected with my life, my life only, be it in the form of deed, event, fact, thought, emotion, desire, evasion, frustration, dream, revery, vagary, even the unfinished nothings which float listlessly in the brain like the snapped filaments of a spider's web.[12] There is nothing really vague or tenuous—even the nothingnesses are sharp, tough, definite, durable. Like the spider I return again and again to the task, conscious that the web I am spinning is made of my own substance, that it will never fail me, never run dry.

(1941)

84. Henry L. MENCKEN (*1880–1956*)
æt. *56*

Of the intrinsic differences that separate American from English the chief have their roots in the obvious disparity between the environment and traditions of the American people since the Seventeenth Century and those of the English. The latter have lived under a relatively stable social order, and it has impressed upon their souls their characteristic respect for what is customary and of good report. Until the World War brought chaos to most of their institutions, their whole lives were regulated, perhaps more than those of any other people save the Spaniards, by regard for precedent. The Americans, though partly of the same blood, have felt no such restraint, and acquired no such habit of conformity. On the contrary, they have plunged to the other extreme, for the conditions of life in their country have put a high value upon the precisely opposite qualities of curiosity and daring, and so they have acquired that character of restlessness, that impatience of forms, that disdain of the dead hand, which now broadly marks them. From the first, says a literary historian, they have been "less phlegmatic, less conservative than the English. There were climatic influences, it may be; there was surely a spirit of intensity everywhere that made for short effort." [1] Thus, in the arts, and thus in business, in politics, in daily intercourse, in habits of mind and speech. The American is not, of course, lacking in a capacity for discipline; he has it highly developed; he submits to leadership readily, and even to tyranny. But, by a curious twist, it is not the leadership that is old and decorous that commonly fetches him, but the leadership that is new and extravagant. He will resist dictation out of the past, but he will follow a new messiah with

Henry L. Mencken, *The American Language*, 4th ed. (New York, 1936), pp. 91–93.

almost Russian willingness, and into the wildest vagaries of economics, religion, morals and speech. A new fallacy in politics spreads faster in the United States than anywhere else on earth, and so does a new fashion in hats, or a new revelation of God, or a new means of killing time, or a new shibboleth, or metaphor, or piece of slang. Thus the American, on his linguistic side, likes to make his language as he goes along, and not all the hard work of the schoolmarm can hold the business back. A novelty loses nothing by the fact that it is a novelty; it rather gains something, and particularly if it meets the national fancy for the terse, the vivid, and, above all, the bold and imaginative. The characteristic American habit of reducing complex concepts to the starkest abbreviations was already noticeable in colonial times, and such highly typical Americanisms as *O.K.*, *N.G.*, and *P.D.Q.*, have been traced back to the early days of the Republic. Nor are the influences that shaped these tendencies invisible today, for institution-making is yet going on, and so is language-making. In so modest an operation as that which has evolved *bunco* from *buncombe* and *bunk* from *bunco* there is evidence of a phenomenon which the philologian recognizes as belonging to the most lusty stages of speech.

But of more importance than the sheer inventions, if only because much more numerous, are the extensions of the vocabulary, both absolutely and in ready workableness, by the devices of rhetoric. The American, from the beginning, has been the most ardent of recorded rhetoricians. His politics bristles with pungent epithets; his whole history has been bedizened with tall talk; his fundamental institutions rest far more upon brilliant phrases than upon logical ideas. And in small things as in large he exercises continually an incomparable capacity for projecting hidden and often fantastic relationships into arresting parts of speech. Such a term as *rubberneck* is almost a complete treatise on American psychology; it reveals the national habit of mind more clearly than any labored inquiry could ever reveal it. It has in it precisely the boldness and contempt for ordered forms that are so characteristically American, and it has too the grotesque humor of the country, and the delight in devastating opprobriums, and the acute feeling for the succinct and savory. The same qualities are in *rough-house, water-wagon, has-been, lame-duck, speed-cop* and a thousand other such racy substantives, and in all the great stock of native verbs and adjectives. There is, indeed, but a shadowy boundary in these new coinages between the various parts of speech. *Corral,* borrowed from the Spanish, immediately becomes a verb and the father of an adjective. *Bust,* carved out of *burst,* erects itself into a noun. *Bum,* coming by way of an earlier *bummer* from the German, becomes noun, adjective, verb and adverb. Verbs are fashioned out of substantives by the simple process of prefixing the preposition: *to engineer, to stump, to hog, to style, to author.* Others grow out of an intermediate adjective, as *to boom.* Others are made by torturing nouns with harsh affixes, as *to burglarize* and *to itemize,* or by groping for the root, as *to resurrect* and *to jell.* Yet others are changed from intransitive to transitive; a sleeping-car *sleeps* thirty passengers. So with the adjectives. They are made of substantives unchanged: *codfish, jitney.* Or by bold combinations: *down-and-out, up-state, flat-footed.* Or by shading down suffixes to a barbaric simplicity: *scary, classy, tasty.* Or by working over adverbs until they tremble on the brink between adverb and adjective: *right, sure* and *near* are examples.

(*1936*)

85. Thomas WOLFE (*1900–1938*) æt. *36*

Cutting had always been the most difficult and distasteful part of writing to me; my tendency had always been to write rather than to cut. Moreover, whatever critical faculty I may have had concerning my own work had been seriously impaired, for the time being at least, by the frenzied labor of the past four years. When a man's work has poured from him for almost five years like burning lava from a volcano; when all of it, however superfluous, has been given fire and passion by the white heat of his own creative energy, it is very difficult suddenly to become coldly surgical, ruthlessly detached.

To give a few concrete illustrations of the difficulties that now confronted us: The opening section of the book describes the journey of a train across the State of Virginia at night. Its function in the book is simply to introduce some of the chief characters, to indicate a central situation, to give something of the background from which the book proceeds, and perhaps through the movement of the train across the stillness of the earth to establish a certain beat, evoke a certain emotion which is inherent to the nature of the book. Such a section, therefore, undoubtedly serves an important function, but in proportion to the whole purport of the book, its function is a secondary one and must be related to the whole book in a proportionate way.

Now in the original version, the manuscript which described the journey of the train across Virginia at night was considerably longer than the average novel. What was needed was just an introductory chapter or two, and what I had written was over 100,000 words in length, and this same difficulty, this lack of proportion, was also evident in other parts of the manuscript.

What I had written about the great train was really good. But what I had to face, the very bitter lesson that every one

Thomas Wolfe, *The Story of a Novel* (New York, 1936), pp. 78–85.

who wants to write has got to learn, was that a thing may in itself be the finest piece of writing one has ever done, and yet have absolutely no place in the manuscript one hopes to publish. This is a hard thing, but it must be faced, and so we faced it.

My spirit quivered at the bloody execution.[1] My soul recoiled before the carnage of so many lovely things cut out upon which my heart was set. But it had to be done, and we did it.

The first chapter [2] in the original manuscript, a chapter which the editor, himself, admitted was as good a single piece of writing as I had ever done, was relentlessly kicked out, and the reason it was kicked out was that it was really not a true beginning for the book but merely something which led up to the true beginning; therefore it had to go. And so it went all up and down the line. Chapters 50,000 words long were reduced to ten or fifteen thousand words, and having faced this inevitable necessity, I finally acquired a kind of ruthlessness of my own, and once or twice, myself, did more cutting than my editor was willing to allow.

Another fault that has always troubled me in writing is that I have often attempted to reproduce in its entirety the full flood and fabric [3] of a scene in life itself. Thus, in another section of the book, four people were represented as talking to each other for four hours without a break or intermission. All were good talkers; often all talked, or tried to talk, at the same time. The talk was wonderful and living talk [4] because I knew the life and character and the vocabulary of all these people from its living source, and I had forgotten nothing. Yet all the time, all that was actually happening in this scene was that a young woman had got out of her husband's motor car and gone into her mother's house and kept calling to the impatient man outside every time he honked his horn, "All right. All right. I'll be with you in five minutes." These five minutes really lengthened into four hours, while the unfortunate man outside honked upon his horn, and while the two women and two young men of the same family inside carried on a torrential discourse [5] and discussed exhaustively the lives and histories of almost everyone in town, their memories of the past, adventures of the present, and speculations of the future. I put it all down in the original manuscript just as I had seen and known and lived it a thousand times, and even if I do say so myself, the nature of the talk, the living vitality and character of the language, the utter naturalness, the flood-tide river of it all was wonderful, but I had made four people talk 80,000 words—200 printed pages of close type in a minor scene of an enormous book, and of course, good as it was, it was all wrong and had to go.

Such, then, were some of our major difficulties with the manuscript we had in hand, and although since its publication there have been many declarations to the effect that the book would have benefited by a much more radical cutting, the cutting we did do was much more drastic than I had dreamed was possible.

Meanwhile I was proceeding at full speed with the work of completing my design, finishing the unfinished parts and filling in the transition links which were essential.

This in itself was an enormous job and kept me writing all day long as hard as I could go for a full year. Here again the nature of my chief fault was manifest. I wrote too much again. I not only wrote what was essential, but time and time again my enthusiasm for a good scene, one of those enchanting vistas which can open up so magically to a man in the full flow of his creation, would overpower me, and I would write thousands of words upon a scene which contributed nothing of vital importance to a book whose greatest need already was ruthless condensation.

During the course of this year, I must have written well over a half million words [6] of additional manuscript, of which, of course, only a small part was finally used.

The nature of my method, the desire fully to explore my material, had led me into another error. The whole effect of those five years of incessant writing had been to make me feel not only that everything had to be used, but that everything had to be told, that nothing could be implied. Therefore, at the end, there were at least a dozen additional chapters which I felt had to be completed to give the book its final value. A thousand times I debated this question desperately with my editor. I told him that these chapters had to go in simply because I felt the book would not be complete without them, and with every argument he had, he tried to show me that I was wrong. I see now that on the whole he was right about it, but at the time I was so inextricably involved in my work, that I did not have the detachment necessary for a true appraisal.

(1936)

86. Gertrude STEIN (*1874–1946*) æt. *61*

It is true that generations are not of necessity existing that is to say if the actual movement within a thing is alive enough. A motor goes inside of an automobile and the car goes. In short this generation has conceived an intensity of movement so great that it has not to be seen against something else to be known, and therefore, this generation does not connect itself with anything,[1] that is what makes this generation what it is and that is why it is American, and this is very important in connection with portraits of anything. I say portraits and not description and I will gradually explain why. Then also there is the important question of repetition and is there any such thing. Is there repetition or is there insistence.[2] I am inclined to believe there is no such thing as repetition. And really how can there be. This is a thing about which I want you to think before I go on telling about portraits of anything. Think about all the detective stories everybody reads. The kind of crime is the same, and the idea of the story is very often the same, take for example a man like Wallace, he always has the same theme, take a man like Fletcher he always has the same theme, take any American ones, they too always have the scene, the same scene, the kind of invention that is necessary to make a general scheme is very limited in everybody's experience, every time one of the hundreds of times a newspaper man makes fun of my writing and of my repetition he always has the same theme, always having the same theme, that is, if you like, repetition, that is if you like the repeating that is the same thing, but once started expressing this thing, expressing any thing there can be no repetition because the essence of that expression is insistence, and if you insist you must each time use emphasis and if you use emphasis it is not possible while anybody is alive that they should use exactly the

Gertrude Stein, *Lectures in America* (Boston, 1957), pp. 166–169.

same emphasis.[3] And so let us think seriously of the difference between repetition and insistence.

Anybody can be interested in a story of a crime because no matter how often the witnesses tell the same story the insistence is different. That is what makes life that the insistence is different, no matter how often you tell the same story if there is anything alive in the telling the emphasis is different. It has to be, anybody can know that.

It is very like a frog hopping he cannot ever hop exactly the same distance or the same way of hopping at every hop. A bird's singing is perhaps the nearest thing to repetition but if you listen they too vary their insistence. That is the human expression saying the same thing and in insisting and we all insist varying the emphasising.

I remember very well first beginning to be conscious of this thing. I became conscious of these things, I suppose anybody does when they first really know that the stars are worlds and that everything is moving, that is the first conscious feeling of necessary repetition, and it comes to one and it is very disconcerting. Then the second thing is when you first realize the history of various civilizations, that have been on this earth,[4] that too makes one realize repetition and at the same time the difference of insistence. Each civilization insisted in its own way before it went away. I remember the first time I really realized this in this way was from reading a book we had at home of the excavations of Nineveh, but these emotions although they tell one so much and one really never forgets them, after all are not in one's daily living, they are like the books of Jules Verne terribly real terribly near but still not here. When I first really realized the inevitable repetition in human expression that was not repetition but insistence when I first began to be really conscious of it was when at about seventeen years of age, I left the more or less internal and solitary and concentrated life I led in California and came to Baltimore and lived with a lot of my relations and principally with a whole group of very lively little aunts who had to know anything.

If they had to know anything and anybody does they naturally had to say and hear it often, anybody does, and as there were ten and eleven of them they did have to say and hear said whatever was said and any one not hearing what it was they said had to come in to hear what had been said. That inevitably made everything said often. I began then to consciously listen to what anybody was saying and what they did say while they were saying what they were saying. This was not yet the beginning of writing but it was the beginning of knowing what there was that made there be no repetition. No matter how often what happened had happened any time any one told anything there was no repetition. This is what William James calls the Will to Live. If not nobody would live.

And so I began to find out then by listening the difference between repetition and insisting and it is a very important thing to know. You listen as you know.

(1935)

87. Ezra POUND (*b. 1885*) æt. *49*

Literature does not exist in a vacuum. Writers as such have a definite social function exactly proportioned to their ability AS WRITERS. This is their main use. All other uses are relative, and temporary, and can be estimated only in relation to the views of a particular estimator.[1]

Partisans of particular ideas may value writers who agree with them more than writers who do not, they may, and often do, value bad writers of their own party or religion more than good writers of another party or church.

But there is one basis susceptible of estimation and independent of all questions of viewpoint.[2]

Good writers are those who keep the language efficient. That is to say, keep it accurate, keep it clear. It doesn't matter whether the good writer wants to be useful, or whether the bad writer wants to do harm.

Language is the main means of human communication. If an animal's nervous system does not transmit sensations and stimuli, the animal atrophies.

If a nation's literature declines, the nation atrophies and decays.[3]

Your legislator can't legislate for the public good, your commander can't command, your populace [4] (if you be a democratic country) can't instruct its 'representatives',[5] save by language.

The fogged language of swindling classes [6] serves only a temporary purpose.

A limited amount of communication *in re* special subjects, passes via mathematical formulae, via the plastic arts, via diagrams, via purely musical forms, but no one proposes substituting these for the common speech, nor does anyone suggest that it would be either possible or advisable.

Ezra Pound, *ABC of Reading* (Norfolk, Conn., [1934]), pp. 32–35.

UBICUNQUE LINGUA ROMANA, IBI ROMA[7]

GREECE and Rome civilized BY LANGUAGE. Your language is in the care of your writers.

['Insults o'er dull and speechless tribes'][8]

but this language is not merely for records of great things done. Horace and Shakespeare[9] can proclaim its monumental and mnemonic[10] value, but that doesn't exhaust the matter.

Rome rose with the idiom of Caesar, Ovid, and Tacitus, she declined in a welter of rhetoric, the diplomat's 'language to conceal thought',[11] and so forth.[12]

The man of understanding can no more sit quiet and resigned while his country lets its literature decay, and lets good writing meet with contempt, than a good doctor could sit quiet and contented while some ignorant child was infecting itself with tuberculosis under the impression that it was merely eating jam tarts.

It is very difficult to make people understand the *impersonal* indignation that a decay of writing can cause men who understand what it implies, and the end whereto it leads. It is almost impossible to express any degree of such indignation without being called 'embittered',[13] or something of that sort.

Nevertheless the 'statesman cannot govern, the scientist cannot participate his discoveries, men cannot agree on wise action without language',[14] and all their deeds and conditions are affected by the defects or virtues of idiom.

A people that grows accustomed to sloppy writing is a people in process of losing grip on its empire and on itself. And this looseness and blowsiness is not anything as simple and scandalous as abrupt and disordered syntax.[15]

It concerns the relation of expression to meaning. Abrupt and disordered syntax can be at times very honest, and an elaborately constructed sentence can be at times merely an elaborate camouflage.

The sum of human wisdom is not contained in any one language, and no single language is CAPABLE of expressing all forms and degrees of human comprehension.

This is a very unpalatable and bitter doctrine. But I cannot omit it.

People occasionally develop almost a fanaticism in combating the ideas 'fixed' in a single language. These are generally speaking 'the prejudices of the nation' (any nation).

Different climates and different bloods have different needs, different spontaneities, different reluctances, different ratios between different groups of impulse and unwillingness, different constructions of throat,[16] and all these leave trace in the language, and leave it more ready and more unready for certain communications and registrations.

(1934)

88. Ernest HEMINGWAY (*1898–1961*)

æt. *34*

What about the Old Lady? [1] She's gone. We threw her out of the book, finally. A little late you say. Yes, perhaps a little late. What about the horses? They are what people always like to talk about in regard to the bullfight. Has there been enough about the horses? Plenty about the horses, you say. They like it all but the poor horses. Should we try to raise the general tone? What about higher things?

Mr. Aldous Huxley writing in an essay entitled "Foreheads Villainous Low" [2] commences: "In [naming a book by this writer] Mr. H. ventures, once, to name an Old Master. There is a phrase, quite admirably expressive [here Mr. Huxley inserts a compliment], a single phrase, no more, about 'the bitter nail-holes' of Mantegna's [3] Christs; then quickly, quickly, appalled by his own temerity, the author passes on (as Mrs. Gaskell [4] might hastily have passed on, if she had somehow been betrayed into mentioning a water-closet), passes on, shamefacedly, to speak once more of Lower Things.

"There was a time, not so long ago, when the stupid and uneducated aspired to be thought intelligent and cultured. The current of aspiration has changed its direction. It is not at all uncommon now to find intelligent and cultured people doing their best to feign stupidity and to conceal the fact that they have received an education"—and more; more in Mr. Huxley's best educated vein which is a highly educated vein indeed.

What about that, you say? Mr. Huxley scores there, all right, all right. What have you to say to that? Let me answer truly.[5] On reading that [6] in Mr. Huxley's book I obtained a copy of the volume he refers to and looked through it and could not

Ernest Hemingway, *Death in the Afternoon* (New York, 1932), pp. 190–192.

find the quotation he mentions. It may be there, but I did not have the patience nor the interest to find it, since the book was finished and nothing to be done.[7] It sounds very much like the sort of thing one tries to remove in going over the manuscript. I believe it is more than a question of the simulation or avoidance of the appearance of culture.[8] When writing a novel a writer should create living people; people not characters. A *character* is a caricature. If a writer can make people live there may be no great characters in his book, but it is possible that his book will remain as a whole; as an entity; as a novel. If the people the writer is making [9] talk of old masters; of music; of modern painting; of letters; or of science then they should talk of those subjects in the novel. If they do not talk of those subjects and the writer makes them talk of them he is a faker, and if he talks [10] about them himself to show how much he knows then he is showing off. No matter how good a phrase or a simile [11] he may have if he puts it in where it is not absolutely necessary and irreplaceable [12] he is spoiling his work for egotism. Prose is architecture, not interior decoration, and the Baroque [13] is over. For a writer to put his own intellectual musings, which he might sell for a low price as essays, into the mouths of artificially constructed characters which are more remunerative when issued as people in a novel is good economics, perhaps, but does not make literature. People in a novel, not skillfully constructed *characters*, must be projected from the writer's assimilated experience, from his knowledge, from his head, from his heart and from all there is of him. If he ever has luck as well as seriousness and gets them out entire they will have more than one dimension and they will last a long time. A good writer should know as near everything as possible. Naturally he will not. A great enough writer seems to be born with knowledge. But he really is not; he has only been born with the ability to learn in a quicker ratio to the passage of time than other men and without conscious application, and with an intelligence to accept or reject what is already presented as knowledge. There are some things which cannot be learned quickly and time, which is all we have, must be paid heavily for their acquiring.[14]

They are the very simplest things and because it takes a man's life to know them the little new that each man gets from life is very costly and the only heritage he has to leave. Every novel which is truly written [15] contributes to the total of knowledge which is there at the disposal of the next writer who comes, but the next writer must pay, always, a certain nominal percentage in experience to be able to understand and assimilate what is available as his birthright and what he must, in turn, take his departure from. If a writer of prose knows enough about what he is writing about he may omit things that he knows and the reader, if the writer is writing truly enough, will have a feeling of those things as strongly as though the writer had stated them. The dignity of movement of an ice-berg is due to only one-eighth of it being above water. A writer who omits things because he does not know them only makes hollow places in his writing. A writer who appreciates the seriousness of writing so little that he is anxious to make people see he is formally educated, cultured or well-bred is merely a popinjay. And this too remember; [16] a serious writer is not to be confounded with a solemn writer. A serious writer may be a hawk or a buzzard or even a popinjay,[17] but a solemn writer is always a bloody owl.[18]

(1932)

89. Sherwood ANDERSON (*1876–1941*)
æt. *43*

In my own boyhood in an Ohio town I went about delivering newspapers at kitchen doors, and there were certain houses to which I went—old brick houses with immense old-fashioned kitchens—in which I loved to linger. On Saturday mornings I sometimes managed to collect a fragrant cooky at such a place but there was something else that held me. Something got into my mind connected with the great light kitchens and the women working in them that came sharply back when, last year, I went to visit an American woman, Miss Gertrude Stein, in her own large room in the house at 27 rue de Fleurus in Paris. In the great kitchen of my fanciful world in which, ever since that morning, I have seen Miss Stein standing there is a most sweet and gracious aroma.[1] Along the walls are many shining pots and pans, and there are innumerable jars of fruits, jellies and preserves. Something is going on in the great room, for Miss Stein is a worker in words [2] with the same loving touch in her strong fingers that was characteristic of the women of the kitchens of the brick houses in the town of my boyhood. She is an American woman of the old sort, one who cares for the hand-made goodies and who scorns the factory-made foods, and in her own great kitchen she is making something with her materials, something sweet to the tongue and fragrant to the nostrils.

That her materials are the words of our English speech and that we do not, most of us, know or care too much what she is up to does not greatly matter to me. The impression I wish now to give you of her is of one very intent and earnest in a matter most of us have forgotten.[3] She is laying word against word, relating sound to sound, feeling for the taste, the smell, the

Sherwood Anderson, "Four American Impressions," *Sherwood Anderson's Notebook* (New York, 1926), pp. 48–51.

rhythm of the individual word.[4] She is attempting to do something for the writers of our English speech that may be better understood after a time, and she is not in a hurry.

And I have always [5] that picture of the woman in the great kitchen of words, standing there by a table, clean, strong, with red cheeks and sturdy legs, always quietly and smilingly at work. If her smile has in it something of a mystery, to the male at least, of the Mona Lisa, I remember that the women in the kitchens on the wintry mornings wore often that same smile.

She is making new, strange and to my ears sweet combinations of words. As an American writer I admire her because she, in her person, represents something sweet and healthy [6] in our American life, and because I have a kind of undying faith that what she is up to in her word kitchen in Paris is of more importance to writers of English than the work of many of our more easily understood and more widely accepted word artists.

When it comes to our Mr. Ring Lardner, here is something else again. Here is another word fellow, one who cares about the words of our American speech and who is perhaps doing more than any other American to give new force to the words of our everyday life.

There is something I think I understand about Mr. Ring Lardner. The truth is that I believe there is something the matter [7] with him and I have a fancy I know what it is. He is afraid of the highbrows. They scare him to death. I wonder why. For it is true that there is often, in a paragraph of his, more understanding of life, more human sympathy, more salty wisdom than in hundreds of pages of, say Mr. Sinclair Lewis's dreary prose—and I am sure Mr. Lewis would not hesitate to outface any highbrow in his lair.

I said that I thought I knew what was the matter with Mr. Ring Lardner. He comes from out in my country, from just such another town as the one in which I spent my own boyhood, and I remember certain shy lads of my own town who always made it a point to consort mostly with the town toughs—and for a reason. There was in them something extremely sensitive that did not want to be hurt. Even to mention the fact that there was in such a one a real love of life, a quick sharp stinging hunger for beauty would have sent a blush of shame to his cheeks. He was intent upon covering up, concealing from everyone, at any cost, the shy hungry child he was carrying about within himself.

And I always see [8] our Mr. Ring Lardner as such a fellow. He is covering up, sticking to the gang, keeping out of sight. And that is all right too, if in secret and in his suburban home he is really using his talent for sympathetic understanding of life, if in secret he is being another Mark Twain and working in secret on his own *Huckleberry Finn.* Mark Twain wrote and was proclaimed for writing his *Innocents Abroad, Following the Equator, Roughing It,* etc., etc., and was during his lifetime most widely recognized for such secondary work. And Mark Twain was just such another shy lad, bluffed by the highbrows —and even the glorious Mark had no more sensitive understanding of the fellow in the street, in the hooch joint, the ballpark and the city suburb than our Mr. Ring Lardner.

(*1919*)

90. Henry JAMES (*1843–1916*) æt. *62*

Of the degree [1] in which a society is civilized the vocal form, the vocal tone, the personal, social accent and sound of its intercourse, have always been held to give a direct reflection. That sound, that vocal form, the touchstone of manners, is the note, the representative note—representative of its having (in our poor, imperfect human degree) achieved civilization.[2] Judged in this light, it must frankly be said, our civilization remains strikingly *un*achieved: the last of American idiosyncrasies, the last by which we can be conceived as "represented" in the international concert of culture, would be the pretension to a tone-standard, to our wooing comparison with that of other nations. The French, the Germans, the Italians, the English perhaps in particular, and many other people, Occidental and Oriental, I surmise, not excluding the Turks and the Chinese, have for the symbol of education, of civility, a tone-standard; we alone flourish in undisturbed and—as in the sense of so many other of our connections—in something like sublime unconsciousness of any such possibility.

It is impossible, in very fact,[3] to have a tone-standard without the definite preliminary of a *care* for tone, and against a care for tone, it would very much appear, the elements of life in this country, as at present conditioned, violently and increasingly militate. At one or two reasons [4] for this strange but consummate conspiracy I shall in a moment ask you to glance with me, but in the meanwhile I should go any length in agreeing with you about any such perversity, on the part of parents and guardians, pastors and masters, as their expecting the generations, whether of young women or young men, to arrive at a position of such comparative superiority alone—unsupported and unguided. There is no warrant for the placing on these inevit-

Henry James, *The Question of Our Speech* (Boston, 1905), pp. 11–20.

ably rather light heads and hearts, on any company of you, assaulted, in our vast vague order, by many pressing wonderments, the *whole* of the burden of a care for tone. A care for tone is part of a care for many other things besides; for the fact, for the value, of good breeding, above all, as to which tone unites with various other personal, social signs to bear testimony. The idea of good breeding—without which intercourse fails to flower into fineness, without which human relations bear but crude and tasteless fruit—is one of the most precious conquests of civilization, the very core of our social heritage; but in the transmission of which it becomes us much more to be active and interested than merely passive and irresponsible participants. It is an idea, the idea of good breeding (in other words, simply the idea of *secure* good manners), for which, always, in every generation, there is yet more, and yet more, to be done; and no danger would be more lamentable than that of the real extinction, in our hands, of so sacred a flame. Flames, however, even the most sacred, do not go on burning of themselves; they require to be kept up; handed on the torch [5] needs to be from one group of patient and competent watchers to another. The possibility, the preferability, of people's speaking as people speak when their speech has had for them a signal importance, is a matter to be kept sharply present; from that comes support, comes example, comes authority—from that comes the inspiration of those comparative beginners of life, the hurrying children of time, who are but too exposed to be worked upon, by a hundred circumstances, in a different and inferior sense. You don't speak soundly and agreeably, you don't speak neatly and consistently, unless you *know* how you speak, how you may, how you should, how you shall speak, unless you have discriminated, unless you have noticed differences and suffered from violations and vulgarities; and you have not this positive consciousness, you are incapable of any reaction of taste or sensibility worth mentioning, unless a great deal of thought of the matter has been taken *for* you.[6]

Taking thought, in this connection, is what I mean by obtaining a tone-standard—a clear criterion of the best usage and example: which is but to recognize, once for all, that avoiding vulgarity, arriving at lucidity, pleasantness, charm, and contributing by the mode and the degree of utterance a colloquial, a genial value even to an inevitably limited quantity of intention, of thought, is an art to be acquired and cultivated, just as much as any of the other, subtler, arts of life. There are plenty of influences round about us that make for an imperfect disengagement of the human side of vocal sound, that make for the confused, the ugly, the flat, the thin, the mean, the helpless, that reduce articulation to an easy and ignoble minimum, and so keep it as little distinct as possible from the grunting, the squealing, the barking or the roaring of animals. I do not mean to say that civility of utterance may not become an all but unconscious beautiful habit—I mean to say, thank goodness, that this is exactly what it *may* become. But so to succeed it must be a collective and associated habit; for the greater the number of persons speaking well, in given conditions, the more that number will tend to increase, and the smaller the number the more that number will tend to shrink and lose itself in the desert of the common. Contact and communication, a beneficent contagion, bring about the happy state—the state of sensibility to tone, the state of recognizing, and responding to, certain vocal sounds *as* tone, and recognizing and reacting from certain others as negations of tone: negations the more offensive in proportion as they have most enjoyed impunity. You will have, indeed, in any at all aspiring cultivation of tone, a vast mass of assured impunity, of immunity on the wrong side of the line, to reckon with. There are in every quarter, in our social order, impunities of aggression and corruption in plenty; but there are none, I think, showing so unperturbed a face—wearing, I should slangily [7] say, if slang were permitted me here, so impudent a "mug"—as the forces assembled to make you believe that no form of speech is provably better than another, and that just this matter of "care" is an affront to the majesty of sovereign ignorance. Oh, I don't mean to say that you will find in the least a clear field and nothing but favor! The difficulty of your case is exactly the ground of my venturing thus to appeal to you. That there is difficulty, that there is a great blatant, blowing dragon to slay, can only constitute, as it appears to me, a call of honor for generous young minds, something of a trumpet-sound for tempers of high courage.

And now, of course, there are questions you may ask me: as to what I more intimately mean by speaking "well," by speaking "ill;" as to what I more definitely mean by "tone" and by the "negation" of tone; [8] as to where you are to recognize the presence of the exemplary rightness I have referred you to—as to where you are to see any standard raised to the breeze; and above all, as to my reasons for referring with such emphasis to the character of the enemy you are to overcome. I am able, I think, to satisfy you all the way; but even in so doing I shall still feel our question to be interesting, as a whole, out of proportion to any fractions of an hour we may now clutch at; feel that if I could only treat it with a freer hand and more margin I might really create in you a zeal to follow it up. I mean, then, by speaking well, in the first place, speaking under the influence of *observation*—your own. I mean speaking with consideration for the forms and shades of our language, a consideration so inbred that it has become instinctive and well-nigh unconscious and automatic, as all the habitual, all the inveterate amenities of life become. By the forms and shades of our language I mean the innumerable differentiated, discriminated units of sound and sense that lend themselves to audible production, to enunciation, to intonation: those innumerable units that have, each, an identity, a quality, an outline, a shape, a clearness, a fineness, a sweetness, a richness, that have, in a word, a value, which it is open to us, as lovers of our admirable English tradition, or as cynical traitors to it, to preserve or to destroy.

(*1905*)

91. Mark TWAIN [pseudonym of Samuel L. Clemens] (*1835–1910*) æt. *59*

No, the remark about the swiftness of their flight was not necessary; neither was the one which said that the Indian found an opportunity; neither was the one which said he *struck* the fawn; neither was the one which explained that it was a "straggling" fawn; neither was the one which said the striking was done with an arrow; neither was the one which said the Indian bore the "fragments"; nor the remark that they were preferable fragments; nor the remark that they were *more* preferable fragments; nor the explanation that they were fragments of the "victim"; nor the overparticular explanation that specifies the Indian's "shoulders" as the part of him that supported the fragments; nor the statement that the Indian bore the fragments patiently.[1] None of those details has any value. We don't care what the Indian struck the fawn with; we don't care whether it was a straggling fawn or an unstraggling one; we don't care which fragments the Indian saved; we don't care why he saved the "more" preferable ones when the merely preferable ones would have amounted to just the same thing and couldn't have been told from the more preferable ones by anybody, dead or alive; we don't care whether the Indian carried them on his shoulders or in his handkerchief; and finally, we don't care whether he carried them patiently or struck for higher pay and shorter hours. We are indifferent to that Indian and all his affairs.[2]

There was only one fact[3] in that long sentence that was worth stating, and it could have been squeezed into these few words—and with advantage to the narrative, too: "During the flight one of the Indians had killed a fawn and he brought it into camp."

Mark Twain, "Cooper's Prose Style," *Letters from the Earth* (New York, 1962), pp. 139–141.

You will notice [4] that "During the flight one of the Indians had killed a fawn and he brought it into camp," is more straightforward and business-like, and less mincing and smirky, than it is to say, "Notwithstanding the swiftness of their flight, one of the Indians had found an opportunity to strike a straggling fawn with an arrow, and had borne the more preferable fragments of the victim, patiently on his shoulders, to the stopping-place." You will notice that the form "During the flight one of the Indians had killed a fawn and he brought it into camp" holds up its chin and moves to the front with the steady stride of a grenadier, whereas the form "Notwithstanding the swiftness of their flight, one of the Indians had found an opportunity to strike a straggling fawn with an arrow, and had borne the more preferable fragments of the victim, patiently on his shoulders, to the stopping-place" simpers along with an airy, complacent, monkey-with-a-parasol gait which is not suited to the transportation of raw meat.

I beg to remind you that an author's way of setting forth a matter is called his Style, and that an author's style is a main part of his equipment for business. The style of some authors has variety in it, but Cooper's style is remarkable for the absence of this feature. Cooper's style is always grand and stately and noble. Style may be likened to an army, the author to its general, the book to the campaign. Some authors proportion an attacking force to the strength or weakness, the importance or unimportance, of the object to be attacked; but Cooper doesn't. It doesn't make any difference to Cooper whether the object of attack is a hundred thousand men or a cow; he hurls his entire force against it. He comes thundering down with all his battalions at his back, cavalry in the van, artillery on the flanks, infantry massed in the middle, forty bands braying, a thousand banners streaming in the wind; and whether the object be an army or a cow you will see him come marching sublimely in, at the end of the engagement, bearing the more preferable fragments of the victim patiently on his shoulders, to the stopping-place.[5] Cooper's style is grand, awful, beautiful; but it is sacred to Cooper, it is his very own, and no student of the Veterinary College of Arizona[6] will be allowed to filch it from him.

In one of his chapters Cooper throws an ungentle slur at one Gamut because he is not exact enough in his choice of words. But Cooper has that failing himself, as remarked in our first lecture.[7] If the Indian had "struck" the fawn with a brick, or with a club, or with his fist, no one could find fault with the word used. And one cannot find much fault when he strikes it with an arrow; still it sounds affected, and it might have been a little better to lean to simplicity and say he shot it with an arrow.

"Fragments" is well enough, perhaps, when one is speaking of the parts of a dismembered deer, yet it hasn't just exactly the right sound—and sound is something; in fact sound is a good deal. It makes the difference between good music and poor music, and it can sometimes make the difference between good literature and indifferent literature. "Fragments" sounds all right when we are talking about the wreckage of a breakable thing that has been smashed; it also sounds all right when applied to cat's meat; but when we use it to describe large hunks and chunks like the fore- and hindquarters of a fawn, it grates upon the fastidious ear.

"Without any aid from the science of cookery, he was immediately employed, in common with his fellows, in gorging himself with this digestible sustenance."

This was a mere statistic; just a mere cold, colorless statistic; yet you see Cooper has made a chromo out of it. To use another figure, he has clothed a humble statistic in flowing, voluminous and costly raiment, whereas both good taste and economy suggest that he ought to have saved these splendors for a king, and dressed the humble statistic in a simple breech-clout.[8] Cooper spent twenty-four words here on a thing not really worth more than eight. We will reduce the statistic to its proper proportions and state it in this way:

"He and the others ate the meat raw."

"Digestible sustenance" is a handsome phrase, but it was out of place there, because we do not know these Indians or care for them; and so it cannot interest us to know whether the meat was going to agree with them or not. Details which do not assist a story are better left out.

"Magua alone sat apart, without participating in the revolting meal" is a statement which we understand, but that is our merit, not Cooper's. Cooper is not clear. He does not say who it is that is revolted by the meal. It is really Cooper himself, but there is nothing in the statement to indicate that it isn't Magua. Magua is an Indian and likes raw meat.

The word "alone" could have been left out and space saved. It has no value where it is.

(c. 1894)

92. Walt WHITMAN (*1819–1892*) æt. *69*

View'd freely, the English language is the accretion and growth of every dialect, race, and range of time, and is both the free and compacted composition of all. From this point of view, it stands for Language in the largest sense, and is really the greatest of studies. It involves so much; is indeed a sort of universal absorber, combiner, and conqueror. The scope of its etymologies is the scope not only of man and civilization, but the history of Nature in all departments, and of the organic Universe, brought up to date; for all are comprehended in words, and their backgrounds. This is when words become vitaliz'd, and stand for things, as they unerringly and soon come to do, in the mind that enters on their study with fitting spirit, grasp, and appreciation.

Slang, profoundly consider'd, is the lawless germinal element, below all words and sentences, and behind all poetry, and proves a certain perennial rankness and protestantism in speech. As the United States[1] inherit by far their most precious possession—the language they talk and write—from the Old World, under and out of its feudal institutes, I will allow myself to borrow a simile even of those forms farthest removed from American Democracy. Considering Language then as some mighty potentate, into the majestic audience-hall of the monarch ever enters a personage like one of Shakspere's clowns, and takes position there, and plays a part even in the stateliest ceremonies. Such is Slang, or indirection, an attempt of common humanity to escape from bald literalism, and express itself illimitably, which in highest walks produces poets and poems, and doubtless in pre-historic times gave the start to, and perfected, the whole immense tangle of the old mythologies. For,

Walt Whitman, "Slang in America," *November Boughs*, in *Complete Prose Works* (Boston, 1891), pp. 406–407.

curious as it may appear, it is strictly the same impulse-source, the same thing. Slang, too, is the wholesome fermentation or eructation [2] of those processes eternally active in language, by which froth and specks are thrown up, mostly to pass away; though occasionally to settle and permanently crystallize.

To make it plainer, it is certain that many of the oldest and solidest words we use, were originally generated from the daring and license of slang. In the processes of word-formation, myriads die, but here and there the attempt attracts superior meanings, becomes valuable and indispensable, and lives forever. Thus the term *right* [3] means literally only straight. *Wrong* primarily meant twisted, distorted. *Integrity* meant oneness. *Spirit* meant breath, or flame. A *supercilious* person was one who rais'd his eyebrows. To *insult* was to leap against. If you *influenc'd* a man, you but flow'd into him. The Hebrew word which is translated *prophesy* meant to bubble up and pour forth as a fountain. The enthusiast bubbles up with the Spirit of God within him, and it pours forth from him like a fountain. The word prophecy is misunderstood. Many suppose that it is limited to mere prediction; that is but the lesser portion of prophecy. The greater work is to reveal God. Every true religious enthusiast is a prophet.

Language, be it remember'd, is not an abstract construction of the learn'd, or of dictionary-makers, but is something arising out of the work, needs, ties, joys, affections, tastes of long generations of humanity, and has its bases broad and low, close to the ground. Its final decisions are made by the masses, people nearest the concrete, having most to do with actual land and sea. It impermeates all, the Past as well as the Present, and is the grandest triumph of the human intellect.

(1888)

93. James Russell LOWELL (*1819–1891*)
æt. *46*

I have just been renewing my recollection of Mr. Thoreau's writings, and have read through his six volumes in the order of their production. I shall try to give an adequate report of their impression upon me both as critic and as mere reader. He seems to me to have been a man with so high a conceit of himself that he accepted without questioning, and insisted on our accepting, his defects and weaknesses of character as virtues and powers peculiar to himself. Was he indolent,[1] he finds none of the activities which attract or employ the rest of mankind worthy of him. Was he wanting in the qualities that make success, it is success that is contemptible, and not himself that lacks persistency and purpose. Was he poor, money was an unmixed evil. Did his life seem a selfish one, he condemns doing good as one of the weakest of superstitions. To be of use was with him the most killing bait of the wily tempter Uselessness. He had no faculty of generalization from outside of himself, or at least no experience which would supply the material of such, and he makes his own whim the law, his own range the horizon of the universe. He condemns a world, the hollowness of whose satisfactions he had never had the means of testing, and we recognize Apemantus [2] behind the mask of Timon. He had little active imagination; of the receptive he had much. His appreciation is of the highest quality; his critical power, from want of continuity of mind, very limited and inadequate. He somewhere cites a simile from Ossian,[3] as an example of the superiority of the old poetry to the new, though, even were the historic evidence less convincing, the sentimental melancholy of those poems should be conclusive of their modernness. He had none of the artistic mastery

James Russell Lowell, "Thoreau," *Literary Essays*, I (Boston, 1899), 368–375.

which controls a great work to the serene balance of completeness, but exquisite mechanical skill in the shaping of sentences [4] and paragraphs, or (more rarely) short bits of verse for the expression of a detached thought, sentiment, or image. His works give one the feeling of a sky full of stars,—something impressive and exhilarating certainly, something high overhead and freckled thickly with spots of isolated brightness; but whether these have any mutual relation with each other, or have any concern with our mundane matters, is for the most part matter of conjecture,—astrology as yet, and not astronomy.

It is curious, considering what Thoreau afterwards became, that he was not by nature an observer.[5] He only saw the things he looked for, and was less poet than naturalist. Till he built his Walden shanty, he did not know that the hickory grew in Concord. Till he went to Maine, he had never seen phosphorescent wood, a phenomenon early familiar to most country boys. At forty he speaks of the seeding of the pine as a new discovery, though one should have thought that its gold-dust of blowing pollen might have earlier drawn his eye. Neither his attention nor his genius was of the spontaneous kind. He discovered nothing. He thought everything a discovery of his own, from moonlight to the planting of acorns and nuts by squirrels. This is a defect in his character, but one of his chief charms as a writer. Everything grows fresh under his hand. He delved in his mind and nature; he planted them with all manner of native and foreign seeds, and reaped assiduously. He was not merely solitary, he would be isolated, and succeeded at last in almost persuading himself that he was autochthonous.[6] He valued everything in proportion as he fancied it to be exclusively his own. He complains in "Walden" that there is no one in Concord with whom he could talk of Oriental literature, though the man was living within two miles of his hut who had introduced him to it. This intellectual selfishness becomes sometimes almost painful in reading him. He lacked that generosity of "communication" which Johnson admired in Burke. De Quincey tells us that Wordsworth was impatient when any one else spoke of mountains, as if he had a peculiar property in them. And we can readily understand why it should be so: no one is satisfied with another's appreciation of his mistress. But Thoreau seems to have prized a lofty way of thinking (often we should be inclined to call it a remote one) not so much because it was good in itself as because he wished few to share it with him. It seems now and then as if he did not seek to lure others up "above our lower region of turmoil," but to leave his own name cut on the mountain peak as the first climber. This itch of originality infects his thought and style. To be misty is not to be mystic. He turns commonplaces end for end, and fancies it makes something new of them. As we walk down Park Street, our eye is caught by Dr. Winship's dumb-bells, one of which bears an inscription testifying that it is the heaviest ever put up at arm's length by any athlete; and in reading Mr. Thoreau's books we cannot help feeling as if he sometimes invited our attention to a particular sophism or paradox as the biggest yet maintained by any single writer. He seeks, at all risks, for perversity of thought, and revives the age of *concetti* [7] while he fancies himself going back to a pre-classical nature. "A day," he says, "passed in the society of those Greek sages, such as described in the Banquet of Xenophon, would not be comparable with the dry wit of decayed cranberry-vines and the fresh Attic salt of the moss-beds." It is not so much the True that he loves as the Out-of-the-Way. As the Brazen Age [8] shows itself in other men by exaggeration of phrase, so in him by extravagance of statement. He wishes always to trump your suit and to *ruff* [9] when you least expect it. Do you love Nature because she is beautiful? He will find a better argument in her ugliness. Are you tired of the artificial man? He instantly dresses you up an ideal in a Penobscot Indian, and attributes to this creature of his otherwise-mindedness as peculiarities things that are common to all woodsmen, white or red, and this simply because he has not studied the pale-faced variety.

This notion of an absolute originality, as if one could have a patent-right in it, is an absurdity. A man cannot escape in thought, any more than he can in language, from the past and the present. As no one ever invents a word, and yet language somehow grows by general contribution and necessity, so it is with thought. Mr. Thoreau seems to me to insist in public on going back to flint and steel, when there is a match-box in his pocket which he knows very well how to use at a pinch. Originality consists in power of digesting and assimilating thought, so that they become part of our life and substance. Montaigne, for example, is one of the most original of authors, though he helped himself to ideas in every direction. But they turn to blood and coloring in his style, and give a freshness of complexion that is forever charming. In Thoreau much seems yet to be foreign and unassimilated, showing itself in symptoms of indigestion. A preacher-up of Nature, we now and then detect under the surly and stoic garb something of the sophist and the sentimentalizer. I am far from implying that this was conscious on his part. But it is much easier for a man to impose on himself when he measures only with himself. A greater familiarity with ordinary men would have done Thoreau good, by showing him how many fine qualities are common to the race. The radical vice of his theory of life was that he confounded physical with spiritual remoteness from men. A man is far enough withdrawn from his fellows if he keep himself clear of their weaknesses. He is not so truly withdrawn as exiled, if he refuse to share in their strength. "Solitude," says Cowley,[10] "can be well fitted and set right but upon a very few persons. They must have enough knowledge of the world to see the vanity of it, and enough virtue to despise all vanity." It is a morbid self-consciousness that pronounces the world of men empty and worthless before trying it, the instinctive evasion of one who is sensible of some innate weakness, and retorts the accusation of it before any has made it but himself. To a healthy mind, the world is a constant challenge of opportunity. Mr. Thoreau had not a healthy mind, or he would not have been so fond of prescribing. His whole life was a search for the doctor. The old mystics had a wiser sense of what the world was worth. They ordained a severe apprenticeship to law, and even ceremonial, in order to the gaining of freedom and mastery over these. Seven years of service [11] for Rachel were to be rewarded at last with

Leah. Seven other years of faithfulness with her were to win them at last the true bride of their souls. Active Life was with them the only path to the Contemplative.

Thoreau had no humor, and this implies that he was a sorry logician.[12] Himself an artist in rhetoric, he confounds thought with style when he undertakes to speak of the latter. He was forever talking of getting away from the world, but he must be always near enough to it, nay, to the Concord corner of it, to feel the impression he makes there. He verifies the shrewd remark of Sainte-Beuve,[13] "On touche encore à son temps et très-fort, même quand on le repousse." This egotism of his is a Stylites pillar[14] after all, a seclusion which keeps him in the public eye. The dignity of man is an excellent thing, but therefore to hold one's self too sacred and precious is the reverse of excellent. There is something delightfully absurd in six volumes addressed to a world of such "vulgar fellows" as Thoreau affirmed his fellowmen to be. I once had a glimpse of a genuine solitary who spent his winters one hundred and fifty miles beyond all human communication, and there dwelt with his rifle as his only confidant. Compared with this, the shanty on Walden Pond has something the air, it must be confessed, of the Hermitage of La Chevrette.[15] I do not believe that the way to a true cosmopolitanism carries one into the woods or the society of musquashes.[16] Perhaps the narrowest provincialism is that of Self; that of Kleinwinkel is nothing to it. The natural man, like the singing birds, comes out of the forest as inevitably as the natural bear and the wildcat stick there. To seek to be natural implies a consciousness that forbids all naturalness forever. It is as easy—and no easier—to be natural in a *salon*[17] as in a swamp, if one do not aim at it, for what we call unnaturalness always has its spring in a man's thinking too much about himself. "It is impossible," said Turgot,[18] "for a vulgar man to be simple."

(*1865*)

94. Edgar Allan POE (*1809–1849*) æt. *40*

Boccalini,[1] in his "Advertisements from Parnassus," tells us that Zoilus[2] once presented Apollo with a very caustic review of a very admirable poem. The god asked to be shown the beauties of the work; but the critic replied that he troubled himself only about the errors. Hereupon Apollo gave him a sack of unwinnowed wheat—bidding him pick out all the chaff for his pains.

Now this fable does very well as a hit at the critics; but I am by no means sure that the Deity was in the right. The fact is, that the limits of the strict critical duty are grossly misapprehended. We may go so far as to say that, while the critic is *permitted* to play, at times, the part of the mere commentator—while he is *allowed*, by way of merely *interesting* his readers, to put in the fairest light the merits of his author—his *legitimate* task is still, in pointing out and analyzing defects and showing how the work might have been improved, to aid the general cause of Letters, without undue heed of the individual literary men. Beauty to be brief, should be considered in the light of an axiom, which, to become at once evident, needs only to be distinctly *put*. It is *not* Beauty, if it require to be demonstrated as such:—and thus to point out too particularly the merits of a work, is to admit that they are *not* merits altogether.

When I say that both Mr. Jones and Mr. Whipple[3] are, in some degree, imitators of Macaulay, I have no design that my words should be understood as disparagement. The style and general conduct of Macaulay's critical papers could scarcely be improved. To call his manner "conventional," is to do it gross injustice. The manner of Carlyle *is* conventional—with himself. The style of Emerson is conventional—with himself *and* Carlyle-

Edgar Allan Poe, "About Critics and Criticism," *Graham's Magazine*, in *Complete Works* (New York, 1902), VI, 194–196.

lyle. The style of Miss Fuller [4] is conventional—with herself and *Emerson* and Carlyle:—that is to say, it is a triple-distilled conventionality:—and by the word "conventionality," as here used, I mean very nearly what, as regards personal conduct, we style "affectation"—that is, an assumption of airs or *tricks* which have no basis in reason or common sense. The quips, quirks, and curt oracularities [5] of the Emersons, Alcotts and Fullers, are simply Lyly's Euphuisms [6] revived. Very different, indeed, are the *peculiarities* of Macaulay.[7] He has his mannerisms; but we see that, by dint of them, he is enabled to accomplish the extremes of unquestionable excellences—the extreme of clearness, of vigor (dependent upon clearness) of grace, and very especially of thoroughness. For his short sentences, for his antitheses, for his modulations, for his climaxes—for every thing that he does—a very slight analysis suffices to show a distinct reason. His manner, thus, is simply the perfection of that justifiable rhetoric which has its basis in common sense; and to say that such rhetoric is never called in to the aid of *genius*, is simply to disparage genius, and by no means to discredit the rhetoric. It is nonsense to assert that the highest genius would not be benefited by attention to its modes of manifestation—by availing itself of that Natural Art which it too frequently despises. Is it not evident that the more intrinsically valuable the rough diamond, the more gain accrues to it from polish?

Now, since it would be nearly impossible to vary the rhetoric of Macaulay, in any material degree, without deterioration in the *essential* particulars of clearness, vigor, etc., those who write *after* Macaulay have to choose between the two horns of a dilemma:—they must be weak and original, or imitative and strong:—and since imitation in a case of this kind, is merely adherence to *Truth* and *Reason* as pointed out by one who feels their value, the author who should forego the advantages of the "imitation" for the mere sake of being erroneously original, "*n'est pas si sage qu'il croit.*" [8]

The true course to be pursued by our critics—justly sensible of Macaulay's excellences—is *not*, however, to be content with tamely following in his footsteps—but to outstrip him in his own path—a path not so much his as Nature's. We must not fall into the error of fancying that he is *perfect* merely because he excels (in point of style) all his British cotemporaries.[9]

(1850)

95. Henry David THOREAU (*1817–1862*)
æt. *32*

A perfectly healthy sentence,[1] it is true, is extremely rare. For the most part we miss the hue and fragrance of the thought; as if we could be satisfied with the dews of the morning or evening without their colors, or the heavens without their azure. The most attractive sentences are, perhaps, not the wisest, but the surest and roundest. They are spoken firmly and conclusively, as if the speaker had a right to know what he says, and if not wise, they have at least been well learned. Sir Walter Raleigh [2] might well be studied, if only for the excellence of his style, for he is remarkable in the midst of so many masters. There is a natural emphasis in his style, like a man's tread, and a breathing space between the sentences, which the best of modern writing does not furnish. His chapters are like English parks, or say rather like a Western forest, where the larger growth keeps down the underwood, and one may ride on horseback through the openings. All the distinguished writers of that period possess a greater vigor and naturalness than the more modern, —for it is allowed to slander our own time,—and when we read a quotation from one of them in the midst of a modern author, we seem to have come suddenly upon a greener ground, a greater depth and strength of soil. It is as if a green bough were laid across the page, and we are refreshed as by the sight of fresh grass in midwinter or early spring. You have constantly the warrant of life and experience in what you read. The little that is said is eked out by implication of the much that was done. The sentences are verdurous and blooming as evergreen and flowers, because they are rooted in fact and experience, but our false and florid sentences have only the tints of flowers without

A Week on the Concord and Merrimack Rivers, The Writings of Henry David Thoreau (Boston, 1906), I, 106–110.

their sap or roots.[3] All men are really most attracted by the beauty of plain speech,[4] and they even write in a florid style in imitation of this. They prefer to be misunderstood rather than to come short of its exuberance. Hussein Effendi praised the epistolary style of Ibrahim Pasha [5] to the French traveler Botta, because of "the difficulty of understanding it; there was," he said, "but one person at Jidda who was capable of understanding and explaining the Pasha's correspondence." A man's whole life is taxed for the least thing well done. It is its net result.[6] Every sentence is the result of a long probation. Where shall we look for standard English but to the words of a standard man? The word which is best said came nearest to not being spoken at all, for it is cousin to a deed which the speaker could have better done. Nay, almost it must have taken the place of a deed by some urgent necessity, even by some misfortune, so that the truest writer will be some captive knight, after all. And perhaps the fates had such a design, when, having stored Raleigh so richly with the substance of life and experience, they made him a fast prisoner, and compelled him to make his words his deeds, and transfer to his expression the emphasis and sincerity of his action.

Men have a respect for scholarship and learning greatly out of proportion to the use they commonly serve. We are amused to read how Ben Jonson engaged that the dull masks [7] with which the royal family and nobility were to be entertained should be "grounded upon antiquity and solid learning." Can there be any greater reproach than an idle learning? Learn to split wood, at least. The necessity of labor and conversation with many men and things to the scholar is rarely well remembered; steady labor with the hands, which engrosses the attention also, is unquestionably the best method of removing palaver [8] and sentimentality out of one's style, both of speaking and writing. If he has worked hard from morning till night, though he may have grieved that he could not be watching the train of his thoughts during that time, yet the few hasty lines which at evening record his day's experience will be more musical and true [9] than his freest but idle fancy could have furnished. Surely the writer is to address a world of laborers, and such therefore must be his own discipline. He will not idly dance at his work who has wood to cut and cord before nightfall in the short days of winter; but every stroke will be husbanded, and ring soberly through the wood; and so will the strokes of that scholar's pen, which at evening record the story of the day, ring soberly, yet cheerily, on the ear of the reader, long after the echoes of his axe have died away. The scholar may be sure that he writes the tougher truth for the calluses on his palms. They give firmness to the sentence. Indeed, the mind never makes a great and successful effort, without a corresponding energy of the body.[10] We are often struck by the force and precision of style to which hard-working men,[11] unpracticed in writing, easily attain when required to make the effort. As if plainness and vigor and sincerity, the ornaments of style, were better learned on the farm and in the workshop than in the schools. The sentences written by such rude hands are nervous and tough, like hardened thongs, the sinews of the deer, or the roots of the pine. As for the graces of expression, a great thought is never found in a mean dress; but though it proceed from the lips of the Wolofs,[12] the nine Muses and the three Graces will have conspired to clothe it in fit phrase. Its education has always been liberal, and its implied wit can endow a college. The world, which the Greeks called Beauty, has been made such by being gradually divested of every ornament which was not fitted to endure. The Sibyl,[13] "speaking with inspired mouth, smileless, inornate, and unperfumed, pierces through centuries by the power of the god." The scholar might frequently emulate the propriety and emphasis of the farmer's call to his team, and confess that if that were written it would surpass his labored sentences. Whose are the truly *labored* sentences? [14] From the weak and flimsy periods of the politician and literary man, we are glad to turn even to the description of work, the simple record of the month's labor in the farmer's almanac, to restore our tone and spirits. A sentence should read as if its author, had he held a plow instead of a pen, could have drawn a furrow deep and straight to the end. The scholar requires hard and serious labor to give an impetus to his thought. He will learn to grasp the pen firmly so, and wield it gracefully and effectively, as an axe or a sword. When we consider the weak and nerveless periods of some literary men, who perchance in feet and inches come up to the standard of their race, and are not deficient in girth also, we are amazed at the immense sacrifice of thews and sinews. What! these proportions, these bones,—and this their work! Hands which could have felled an ox have hewed this fragile matter which would not have tasked a lady's fingers! Can this be a stalwart man's work, who has a marrow in his back and a tendon Achilles in his heel? They who set up the blocks of Stonehenge [15] did somewhat, if they only laid out their strength for once, and stretched themselves.

(1849)

96. Ralph Waldo EMERSON (*1803–1882*)
æt. *33*

Because of this radical [1] correspondence between visible things and human thoughts, savages,[2] who have only what is necessary, converse in figures. As we go back in history, language becomes more picturesque, until its infancy,[3] when it is all poetry; or all spiritual facts are represented by natural symbols. The same symbols [4] are found to make the original elements of all languages. It has moreover been observed, that the idioms of all languages [5] approach each other in passages of the greatest eloquence and power. And as this is the first language, so is it the last. This immediate dependence of language upon nature, this conversion of an outward phenomenon into a type of somewhat in human life, never loses its power to affect us. It is this which gives that piquancy to the conversation of a strong-natured farmer or back-woodsman,[6] which all men relish.

A man's power to connect his thought with its proper symbol, and so to utter it, depends on the simplicity of his character, that is, upon his love of truth and his desire to communicate it without loss. The corruption of man is followed by the corruption of language.[7] When simplicity of character and the sovereignty of ideas is broken up by the prevalence of secondary desires, the desire of riches, of pleasure, of power, and of praise,—and duplicity and falsehood take place of simplicity and truth, the power over nature as an interpreter of the will is in a degree lost; new imagery ceases to be created, and old words are perverted to stand for things which are not; a paper currency is employed, when there is no bullion in the vaults. In due time the fraud is manifest, and words lose all power to stimulate the understanding or the affections. Hundreds of writers may be

Ralph Waldo Emerson, *Nature, Addresses and Lectures, Works* (Cambridge, Mass., 1883), I, 34–36.

found in every long-civilized nation who for a short time believe and make others believe that they see and utter truths, who do not of themselves clothe one thought in its natural garment, but who feed unconsciously on the language created by the primary writers of the country, those, namely, who hold primarily on nature.

But wise men pierce this rotten diction and fasten words again to visible things; [8] so that picturesque language [9] is at once a commanding certificate that he who employs it is a man in alliance with truth and God. The moment our discourse rises above the ground line of familiar facts and is inflamed with passion or exalted by thought, it clothes itself in images. A man conversing in earnest, if he watch his intellectual processes, will find that a material image [10] more or less luminous arises in his mind, contemporaneous with every thought, which furnishes the vestment of the thought.[11] Hence, good writing and brilliant discourse are perpetual allegories. This imagery is spontaneous. It is the blending of experience with the present action of the mind. It is proper creation. It is the working of the Original Cause through the instruments he has already made.

(1836)

97. James Fenimore COOPER (*1789–1851*)
æt. *39*

If the people of this country were like the people of any other country on earth, we should be speaking at this moment a great variety of nearly unintelligible patois; but, in point of fact, the people of the United States, with the exception of a few of German and French descent, speak, as a body, an incomparably better English than the people of the mother country. There is not, probably, a man (of English descent) born in this country, who would not be perfectly intelligible to all whom he should meet in the streets of London, though a vast number of those he met in the streets of London would be nearly unintelligible to him. In fine, we speak our language, as a nation, better than any other people speak their language. When one reflects on the immense surface of country that we occupy, the general accuracy, in pronunciation and in the use of words, is quite astonishing. This resemblance in speech can only be ascribed to the great diffusion of intelligence, and to the inexhaustible activity of the population, which, in a manner, destroys space.

It is another peculiarity of our institutions, that the language of the country, instead of becoming more divided into provincial dialects, is becoming, not only more assimilated to itself as a whole, but more assimilated to a standard which sound general principles, and the best authorities among our old writers, would justify. The distinctions in speech between New England and New York, or Pennsylvania, or any other state, were far greater twenty years ago than they are now. Emigration alone would produce a large portion of this change; but emigration would often introduce provincialisms without correcting them, did it not also, by bringing acute men together, sharpen wits,

James Fenimore Cooper, *Notions of the Americans* (London, 1828), II, 164–167.

provoke comparisons, challenge investigations, and, finally, fix a standard.

It has been a matter of hot dispute, for the last twenty years, in which of our large towns the best English is spoken. The result of this discussion has been to convince most people who know any thing of the matter, that a perfectly pure English is spoken no where, and to establish the superiority, on one point, in favour of Boston, on another in favour of New York, and so on to the end of the chapter. The effect of all this controversy is, to make men think seriously on the subject, and thinking seriously is the first step in amendment. We do amend, and each year introduces a better and purer English into our country. We are obliged, as you may suppose, to have recourse to some standard to settle these contentions. What shall this standard be? It is not society, for that itself is divided on the disputed points; it cannot be the church, for there is none that will be acknowledged by all parties; it cannot be the stage, for that is composed of foreigners, and possesses little influence on morals, politics, or any thing else; nor the universities, for they are provincial, and parties to the dispute; nor congress, for that does not represent the fashion and education of the nation; nor the court, for there is none but the president, and he is often a hot partizan; nor the fashions of speech in England, for we often find as much fault with them as we do with our own. Thus, you see, we are reduced to the necessity of consulting reason, and authority, and analogy, and all the known laws of language, in order to arrive at our object. This we are daily doing, and I think the consequence will be, that, in another generation or two, far more *reasonable* English will be used in this country than exists here now. How far this melioration or purification of our language will affect the mother country, is another question.

(1828)

98. Noah WEBSTER (*1758–1843*) æt. *31*

It must be confessed that languages are changing, from age to age, in proportion to improvements in science. Words, as Horace observes, are like leaves of trees; the old ones are dropping off and new ones growing. These changes are the necessary consequence of changes in customs, the introduction of new arts, and new ideas in the sciences. Still the body of a language and its general rules remain for ages the same, and the new words usually conform to these rules; otherwise they stand as exceptions, which are not to overthrow the principle of analogy [1] already established.

But when a language has arrived at a certain stage of improvement, it must be stationary or become retrograde; for improvements in science either cease, or become slow and too inconsiderable to affect materially the tone of a language. This stage of improvement is the period when a nation abounds with writers of the first class, both for abilities and taste. This period in England commenced with the age of Queen Elizabeth and ended with the reign of George II.[2] It would have been fortunate for the language, had the stile of writing and the pronunciation of words been fixed, as they stood in the reign of Queen Ann and her successor.[3] Few improvements have been made since that time; but innumerable corruptions in pronunciation have been introduced by Garrick,[4] and in stile, by Johnson, Gibbon and their imitators.

The great Sidney [5] wrote in a pure stile; [6] yet the best models [7] of purity and elegance, are the works of Sir William Temple, Dr. Middleton, Lord Bolingbroke, Mr. Addison and

Noah Webster, *Dissertations on the English Language* (Boston, 1789), pp. 29–36.

Dean Swift. But a little inferior to these, are the writings of Mr. Pope,[8] Sir Richard Steele,[9] Dr. Arbuthnot,[10] with some of their cotemporaries. Sir William Blackstone [11] has given the law stile all the elegance and precision of which it is capable. Dr. Price and Dr. Priestley [12] write with purity, and Sir William Jones [13] seems to have copied the ease, simplicity and elegance of Middleton and Addison.

But how few of the modern writers have pursued the same manner of writing? Johnson's stile [14] is a mixture of Latin and English; an intolerable composition of Latinity, affected smoothness, scholastic accuracy and roundness of periods. The benefits derived from his morality and his erudition, will hardly counterbalance the mischief done by his manner of writing. The names of a Robertson, a Hume, a Home and a Blair,[15] almost silence criticism; but I must repeat what a very learned Scotch gentleman once acknowledged to me, "that the Scotch writers are not models of the pure English stile." Their stile is generally stiff, sometimes very awkward, and not always correct. Robertson labors his stile and sometimes introduces a word merely for the sake of rounding a period. Hume has borrowed French idioms without number; in other respects he has given an excellent model of historical stile. Lord Kaims' manner is stiff; and Dr. Blair, whose stile is less exceptionable in these particulars, has however introduced, into his writings, several foreign idioms and ungrammatical phrases. The Scotch writers now stand almost the first for erudition; but perhaps no man can write a foreign language [16] with genuin purity.

Gibbon's harmony of prose [17] is calculated to delight our ears; but it is difficult to comprehend his meaning and the chain of his ideas, as fast as we naturally read; and almost impossible to recollect them, at any subsequent period. Perspicuity, the first requisite in stile, is sometimes sacrificed to melody; the mind of a reader is constantly dazzled by a glare of ornament, or charmed from the subject by the music of the language. As he is one of the *first*, it is hoped he may be the *last*, to attempt the gratification of our *ears*, at the expense of our *understanding*.

Such however is the taste of the age; simplicity of stile is neglected for ornament, and sense is sacrificed to sound.

Altho stile, or the choice of words and manner of arranging them, may be necessarily liable to change, yet it does not follow that pronunciation and orthography [18] cannot be rendered in a great measure permanent. An orthography, in which there would be a perfect correspondence between the spelling and pronunciation, would go very far towards effecting this desireable object. The Greek language suffered little or no change in these particulars, for about a thousand years; and the Roman was in a great degree fixed for several centuries.

Rapid changes of language proceed from violent causes; but these causes cannot be supposed to exist in North America. It is contrary to all rational calculation, that the United States will ever be conquered by any one nation, speaking a different language from that of the country. Removed from the danger of corruption by conquest, our language can change only with the slow operation of the causes beforementioned and the progress of arts and sciences, unless the folly of imitating our parent country should continue to govern us, and lead us into endless innovation.[19] This folly however will lose its influence gradually, as our particular habits of respect for that country shall wear away, and our *amor patriæ* acquire strength and inspire us with a suitable respect for our own national character.

We have therefore the fairest opportunity of establishing a national language, and of giving it uniformity and perspicuity, in North America, that ever presented itself to mankind. Now is the time to begin the plan. The minds of the Americans are roused by the events of a revolution; the necessity of organizing the political body and of forming constitutions of government that shall secure freedom and property, has called all the faculties of the mind into exertion: and the danger of losing the benefits of independence, has disposed every man to embrace any scheme that shall tend, in its future operation, to reconcile the people of America to each other, and weaken the prejudices which oppose a cordial union.

(*1789*)

99. Benjamin FRANKLIN (*1706–1790*)
æt. *65*

There was another Bookish Lad in the Town, John Collins by Name, with whom I was intimately acquainted. We sometimes disputed, and very fond we were of Argument, and very desirous of confuting [1] one another. Which disputacious Turn, by the way, is apt to become a very bad Habit, making People often extreamly disagreeable in Company, by the Contradiction that is necessary to bring it into Practice, and thence, besides souring and spoiling the Conversation, is productive of Disgusts [2] and perhaps Enmities where you may have occasion for Friendship.[3] I had caught it by reading my Father's Books of Dispute about Religion. Persons of good Sense, I have since observ'd, seldom fall into it, except Lawyers, University Men, and Men of all Sorts that have been bred at Edinborough. A Question was once some how or other started between Collins and me, of the Propriety of educating the Female Sex in Learning, and their Abilities for Study. He was of Opinion that it was improper; and that they were naturally unequal to it. I took the contrary Side, perhaps a little for Dispute sake. He was naturally more eloquent, had a ready Plenty of Words, and sometimes as I thought bore me down more by his Fluency than by the Strength of his Reasons. As we parted without settling the Point, and were not to see one another again for some time, I sat down to put my Arguments in Writing, which I copied fair and sent to him. He answer'd and I reply'd. Three or four Letters of a Side had pass'd, when my Father happen'd to find my Papers, and read them. Without entring into the Discussion, he took occasion to talk to me about the Manner of my Writing, observ'd that tho' I had the Advantage of my Antagonist in correct Spelling and pointing [4] (which I ow'd to the Printing House) I fell far short in elegance of Expression, in Method

The Autobiography of Benjamin Franklin (New Haven, 1964), pp. 60–62.

and in Perspicuity, of which he convinc'd me by several Instances. I saw the Justice of his Remarks, and thence grew more attentive to the *Manner* in Writing, and determin'd to endeavour at Improvement.

About this time I met with an odd Volume of the Spectator. It was the third. I had never before seen any of them. I bought it, read it over and over, and was much delighted with it. I thought the Writing excellent, and wish'd if possible to imitate it. With that View, I took some of the Papers, and making short Hints [5] of the Sentiment [6] in each Sentence, laid them by a few Days, and then without looking at the Book, try'd to compleat the Papers again, by expressing each hinted Sentiment at length and as fully as it had been express'd before, in any suitable Words, that should come to hand.

Then I compar'd my Spectator with the Original, discover'd some of my Faults and corrected them. But I found I wanted a Stock of Words or a Readiness in recollecting and using them, which I thought I should have acquir'd before that time, if I had gone on making Verses, since the continual Occasion for Words of the same Import but of different Length, to suit the Measure, or of different Sound for the Rhyme, would have laid me under a constant Necessity of Searching for Variety, and also have tended to fix that Variety in my Mind, and make me Master of it. Therefore I took some of the Tales and turn'd them into Verse: And after a time, when I had pretty well forgotten the Prose, turn'd them back again. I also sometimes jumbled my Collections of Hints into Confusion, and after some Weeks, endeavour'd to reduce them into the best Order, before I began to form the full Sentences, and compleat the Paper. This was to teach me Method in the Arrangement of Thoughts. By comparing my work afterwards with the original, I discover'd many faults and amended them; but I sometimes had the Pleasure of Fancying that in certain Particulars of small Import, I had been lucky enough to improve the Method or the Language and this encourag'd me to think I might possibly in time come to be a tolerable English Writer, of which I was extreamly ambitious.[7]

(*c. 1771*)

100. Cotton MATHER (*1663–1728*) æt. *63*

There has been a deal of a do about a STYLE; So much, that I must offer you my Sentiments upon it. There is a *Way of Writing*, wherein the Author endeavours, that the Reader may have *something to the Purpose* in every Paragraph. There is not only a *Vigour* sensible in every *Sentence*, but the Paragraph is embellished with *Profitable References*, even to something beyond what is *directly spoken*. Formal and Painful *Quotations* are not studied; [1] yet all that could be learnt from them is insinuated. The Writer pretends not unto *Reading*, yet he could not have writ as he does if he had not *Read* very much in his Time; and his Composures [2] are not only a *Cloth of Gold*, but also stuck with as many *Jewels*, as the Gown of a Russian Embassador. This *Way of Writing* has been decried by many, and is at this Day more than ever so, for the same Reason, that in the old Story, the *Grapes* [3] were decried, *That they were not Ripe*. A Lazy, Ignorant, Conceited Sett of Authors, would perswade the whole Tribe, to lay aside that *Way of Writing*, for the same Reason that one would have perswaded his Brethren to part with the Encumbrance of their *Bushy Tails*.[4] But however *Fashion* and *Humour* may prevail, they must not think that the Club at their *Coffee-House* is, *All the World;* but there will always be those, who will in this Case be governed by *Indisputable Reason;* And who will think that the real Excellency of a Book will never ly in *saying of little;* That the less one has for his Money in a Book, 'tis really the more Valuable for it; and that the less one is instructed in a Book, and the more of Superfluous *Margin*, and Superficial *Harangue*, and the less of *Substantial Matter* one has in it, the more tis to be accounted of.[5] And if a more Massy [6] *Way of Writing* be never so much disgusted [7] at This Day, a *Better Gust* [8] will come on, as will some

Cotton Mather, *Manuductio ad Ministerium* (Boston, 1726), pp. 40–47.

other Thing, *quæ jam Cecidere.*[9] In the mean time, Nothing appears to me more Impertinent and Ridiculous than the *Modern Way,* [I cannot say, *Rule;* For they have *None!*] of *Criticising.* The Blades that set up for *Criticks,* I know not who constituted or commission'd 'em!—they appear to me, for the most part as *Contemptible,* as they are a *Supercilious* Generation. For indeed no Two of them have the same *Style;* and they are as intollerably Cross-grain'd and severe in their Censures upon one another, as they are upon the rest of Mankind. But while each of them, conceitedly enough, sets up for the *Standard of Perfection,* we are entirely at a Loss which *Fire* to follow. Nor can you easily find any one thing wherein they agree for their *Style,* except perhaps a perpetual Care to give us Jejune[10] and Empty Pages, without such *Touches of Erudition* (to speak in the *Style* of an Ingenious Traveller) as may make the Discourses less *Tedious,* and more *Enriching,* to the Mind of him that peruses them. There is much Talk of a *Florid Style,* obtaining among the Pens, that are most in Vogue; but how often would it puzzle one, even with the best Glasses to find the *Flowres!*[11] And if they were to be Chastized for it, it would be with much what as much of Justice,[12] as *Jerom*[13] was, for being a *Ciceronian.* After all, Every Man will have his own *Style,*[14] which will distinguish him as much as his *Gate:*[15] And if you can attain to that which I have newly described, but always writing so as to give an *Easy Conveyance* unto your *Idea's,* I would not have you by any *Scourging* be driven out of your *Gate,* but if you must confess a *Fault* in it, make a Confession like that of the Lad, unto his Father while he was beating him for his *Versifying.*

However, since every Man will have his own Style, I would pray, that we may learn to treat one another with mutual *Civilities,* and *Condescensions,*[16] and handsomely *indulge* one another in this, as *Gentlemen* do in other Matters.

I wonder what ails People, that they can't let *Cicero* write in the *Style* of *Cicero,* and *Seneca* write in the (much other!) *Style* of *Seneca;*[17] and own that *Both* may please in their *several Ways.*—But I will freely tell you; what has made me consider the *Humourists* that set up for *Criticks upon Style,* as the most *Unregardable Set of Mortals* in the World, is This! Far more Illustrious *Criticks* than any of those to whom I am now bidding Defiance, and no less Men than your *Erasmus's,* and your *Grotius's,*[18] have taxed[19] the *Greek Style* of the *New Testament,* with I know not what *Solœcisms* and *Barbarisms;*[20] And how many *learned Folks* have Obsequiously run away with the Notion! Whereas 'tis an Ignorant and an Insolent *Whimsey;* which they have been guilty of. It may be (and particularly by an Ingenious *Blackwal,*[21] it has been) Demonstrated, That the Gentlemen are mistaken in every one of their pretended Instances; All the Unquestionable *Classicks,* may be brought in, to convince them of their Mistakes. Those Glorious Oracles are as *pure Greek* as ever was written in the World; and so Correct, so Noble, to Sublime is their *Style,* that never any thing under the Cope of Heaven, but the *Old Testament,* has equall'd it.

(*1726*)

ANNOTATIONS

Note

[For the purpose of cross reference, the names of the 100 stylists are printed in small capitals followed by their selection number when they first appear in an annotation.

Rhetorical terms are printed in bold face type on first appearance in a note. Other reference to these terms may be found in the index.]

GRAVES (No. 1, p. 27)

Robert Graves was elected Professor of Poetry at Oxford in 1960 over the objections of some who desired a more academic critic, rather than a poet of Mr. Graves's earthy stamp, for this prestigious but largely honorary post whose occupant is required only to give three lectures a year. The selection is from the first lecture, entitled "The Dedicated Poet," which cites John Skelton as a praiseworthy example. In the second lecture, Virgil is unsympathetically described as "The Anti-Poet," the Apollonian devotee of reason, contrasted with the poet of passion guided by the Muse, such as Skelton (and Graves). A dedicated poet, says Graves in the paragraph preceding the selection, is a man "who needs food, drink, lodging, and even domestic happiness—none of which are bestowed on him without payment. But though he may make concessions to authority by wearing academic robes, or Court dress, or even a cassock, he must never smother poetic principle. . . ."

It seems evident that Graves is using Skelton to represent himself and that the lecture contains both self-justification and defense against his critics and detractors. Possibly this accounts for the thickness of allusion in the selection and for its occasional obscurity. An incidental question of some interest: If Graves identifies himself with Skelton, whom is Virgil intended to depict?

1. *society.* The three items separated by commas after *vacuum* constitute a series. In English prose, a series is any sequence of grammatically equivalent items, e.g., the nouns in line 21: "court, university, public house, or gipsy camp." Ideally, the items in a series fulfill two conditions: they are identical in form; the last item is preceded by a conjunction, which serves as a terminal marker. When both these conditions are strictly fulfilled, the series conveys its meaning most clearly but with the minimum of expressive effect. Expressiveness is the result of making the reader attentive; he is least attentive when what he reads fulfills his formal expectations. Thus, rhetorical expressiveness depends to a great extent on departure from neutral or conventional forms of expression. At the same time, such departure may result in obscurity and confuse the reader, whose heightened attentiveness is thus put to no constructive use.

In the series under consideration, the three elements ("discarding all tradition, all knowledge, rejecting society") must be construed as an expansion of the first clause, "Dedicated poets cannot exist in a vacuum." The series, however, violates both of the conditions mentioned above: the three elements are not grammatically equivalent; there is no terminal marker. The three elements of the series may be set out as follows:

discarding all tradition	(participle with noun as object)
all knowledge	(second noun object of participle)
rejecting society	(participle with noun as object).

The constructions are not grammatically identical and are only equivalent if the series is interpreted as consisting of two participle phrases, the first with two objects.

Series which violate the normal conditions become ambiguous, usually because of the grammatical convention that two constructions in sequence, unless they are part of a series, are considered in apposition. That is, the second is taken to be an explanation of the first. In the present case, this would create this kind of arrangement:

1. *discarding all knowledge*	(first element)
2. *all tradition*	(in apposition with *all knowledge*)
3. *rejecting society*	(in apposition with 1 and 2).

The absence of the terminal marker does not preclude the possibility of a series, for one of the two traditional departures from convention in the construction of series is the omission of the terminal conjunction. This rhetorical figure is called **asyndeton** and contrasts with **polysyndeton,** in which all adjacent items are linked by a connective. The consequence of both *asyndetic* and *polysyndetic* construction is to interfere with the reader's ability to know when the series will end. In *asyndetic* series, it is difficult to be sure that a series is actually involved, rather than a set of appositives.

Because of these considerations, the reader of this sentence cannot be sure whether Graves intended him to interpret the second half as meaning

1. that is, discarding (or rejecting) tradition, knowledge and society, *or*
2. that is, they cannot discard all traditional knowledge without discarding society.

Does Graves gain or lose by this ambiguity?

2. *Psalter.* How many books does Graves name in this series?
3. *Clare.* Does the mention of the obscure John Clare really help to clarify the allusion to Shakespeare?
4. *grammatic.* Note the unusual form of this adjective.
5. *woman.* Try to describe the structure of this series, noting especially the verb parallelism and the dependence on certain elements of the sequence.
6. *Welshman's hose.* Earlier, Graves defines "to use Welshman's hose" as "to

take liberties with solemn texts—a Welshman's hose is one that will fit any leg." As above, there is an ambiguous construction after the colon. Are the two items in apposition or in asyndetic series? In either case, they are intended to define *humour*. Do they?

7. *refined.* Note the structural ambiguity of the second *refined.*

8. *improve it.* What does this sentence mean? Try rewriting it more simply, possibly as more than one sentence.

9. *gipsy camp.* This series of four items, which fulfills the two necessary conditions for series, exemplifies an additional aspect of series, which may be called semantic, or notional. The first two items (*court, university*) are drawn from respectable society. The third item (*public house;* Amer. *bar* or *saloon*) and the fourth (*gipsy camp*) are hardly in the same class. This descent into the lower strata is unexpected and is similar in effect to the formal manipulations of the series discussed above: to increase the reader's attentiveness by frustrating his expectations. The effect is often humorous. Note, by the way, that Graves did not select this option in the definition of the dedicated poet quoted above: "by wearing academic robes, or Court dress, or even a cassock."

10. *Naaman.* In the story of the powers of Elisha, the Syrian general Naaman was cured of his leprosy by the prophet and converted to the worship of the god of Israel. In making this declaration, Naaman added: "In this thing the Lord pardon thy servant, that when my master goeth into the house of Rimmon to worship there, and he leaneth on my hand, and I bow myself in the house of Rimmon: when I bow down myself in the house of Rimmon, the Lord pardon they servant in this thing" (II Kings 5:18). The allegory likens Skelton to Naaman and something unspecified (God, the Church, the Establishment) to Rimmon. The allusion, once the reader has the necessary information, is clear enough. But the form of the sentence seems to make Skelton bow in the house of Rimmon rather than in its equivalent, whatever it may be. The grammatical construction of the sentence would be thus:

Subject **Verb**

1. Skelton, like Naaman, bowed in the House of Rimmon,

Absolute phrase

his fingers humorously crossed.

If Naaman, not Skelton, is in the house of the Assyrian thunder god, the sentence must be construed another way:

Subject **Participle phrase** (modifying *Naaman*)

2. Skelton, like Naaman, bowed in the House of Rimmon,

Direct object **Verb**

his fingers humorously crossed.

The second version, with its unusual inverted word order, seems less likely than the first, but is made a possibility by the allusion.

11. *humorously.* This is the third reference to "humour." Are all three instances consistent, deliberate?

12. *piously.* This adverb obviously corresponds to *humorously* in the previous sentence. Are both to be taken literally?

13. *beatnik.* Is this word made more effective by the use of *so-called* in front of it? How does the word fit the diction of the rest of the selection?

Is it possible to develop any conclusions about Graves as a prose writer on the basis of observations made on this selection? Does the possible oral delivery of this lecture have any influence on its form?

It is fundamental to an effective analysis of style that a propositional reduction of the selection analyzed take place first. The following is a suggested version:

Propositional Reduction

¶ 1. Poets must live in society.
2. Poets should be as well educated as the self-educated Shakespeare.
3. Shakespeare and John Clare are special cases of poets with limited education.
4. Poets should study the great English writers, learn grammar, travel widely, be familiar with many kinds of people, and have both suffered from and enjoyed love relationships.
5. A poet's greatest ability is his awareness of the identity of opposites.
6. After long effort by the poet, a poem can become so completely balanced in its meaning that the addition of a negative may make no difference.

¶ 7. Good manners require that visitors (including especially poets) obey the customs of the society they are in.
8. Skelton obeyed the laws of his society.
9. I recommend that poets behave like polite guests and disapprove of bohemians who take pride in being impolite.

Logical Diagram

	A	B	C	D
¶ 1.	( )			
2.	(+)			
3.			(×)	

4.		(=)		
5.	(+)			
6.		(=)		
¶ 7.	( )			
8.			(×)	
9.				(:)

RUSSELL (No. 2, p. 29)

1. *I cannot pretend to know.* This announcement of ignorance by a man like Bertrand Russell implies no shame, regret or modesty but is rather a criticism of the thing he does not know. Anything Russell does not know is hardly worth the effort to find out, one may infer. Compare the similar introductory sentence by MAUGHAM (No. 7).
2. *smallest number of words.* Again, compare Maugham.
3. *Logan Pearsall Smith.* For his views and writing, see No. 9.
4. *Walter Pater.* Like Smith, an admirer and practitioner of an ornate manner of writing (see No. 16).
5. *Having.* This dangling participle may be an example of Russell's proclaimed carelessness of form.
6. *different from that of our time.* Another formulation might be that imitation is bad because even if we could manage to duplicate another's style, we would find it suited to express his ideas and not ours.

ORWELL (No. 3, p. 33)

This famous essay originally appeared in *Horizon* (April 1946), which was edited by Cyril CONNOLLY (see No. 6), and has been very often reprinted since, especially in collections used by students of composition. Like RUSSELL and MAUGHAM (and unlike Connolly and L. P. SMITH), Orwell favors the plain style and much of the essay is devoted to recommending ways to make writing *clearer,* which Orwell thinks is synonymous with *simpler.* The selection provided is followed by a list of six rules which may be summarized as follows: avoid figurative language often seen in print; prefer short to long words; cut out words when possible; prefer the active voice; prefer everyday

English to foreign or scientific jargon; avoid barbarism, even at the risk of breaking these rules (39 words for Orwell's 84).

Like most good writers, Orwell does not trouble to follow his own rules. Even the statement of the rules violates his rules, especially the third one. This is not because Orwell does not know what good writing is. He knows—in that he can practice it. But he does not know what he is doing when he writes and therefore he cannot tell anyone else. His recommendations are directed entirely at one type of writing: diplomatic or bureaucratic prose, one purpose of which is to conceal (facts, intentions, events) or to present things in a favorable light. The points Orwell discusses hardly touch even that kind of writing effectively. Jargon, long words, passives—these are hardly of great enough importance in describing a style to justify Orwell's interest or to account for his success.

The basis for the success of this essay is the general recognition among the reading public that there is a great deal of bad writing and that it would be desirable to find a simple recipe for curing it. Orwell's six rules or E. B. WHITE's twenty-one (see No. 78) seem to promise this panacea and they find a ready audience, particularly because the cure is presented so persuasively. The same rules would be unacceptable from a hack writer.

1. *protesting against.* Why does Orwell make this admission rather than correct the faults?
2. *jeers of a few journalists.* Is it possible that expressions like those cited could be "killed" by the disapproval of "a few" people of whatever sort? What does *killed* mean in this context?
3. *flyblown metaphors.* By this expression, we must suppose that Orwell means clichés or stereotyped phrases, but he does not really specify where he would draw the line. For example, he speaks (sent. 1, para. 2) of *decadence* as *curable,* surely a figurative usage and mixed at that (since decadence is not a disease). In the next sentence, he speaks of *tinkering* with words, which is literally impossible, since words are not such objects as a tinker works with. In the sentence previous to this, *examples* are *killed* by *jeers,* undoubtedly a very unorthodox arrangement. What Orwell is doing here is what everyone who uses the language inescapably does—he forgets about its very large figurative component. The very use of *flyblown* in "flyblown metaphor" is figurative and hackneyed, which does not prevent us from understanding.
4. *grammar and syntax.* It is difficult to interpret Orwell's meaning here. How can one make one's meaning clear without grammar or syntax, which Orwell says are of no importance? Compare Lionel TRILLING's statement (No. 82, sent. 3), claiming that some feature of Mark TWAIN's style has nothing to do with grammar. It may be an ambiguity in the word *grammar* that makes

literary men so unwilling to accept its importance; or it may be (more likely is) simply ignorance about the formal structure of the language they are writing in. While literary men are always interesting when they write about language, they are seldom on firm ground there.

5. *exact words that seem to fit it.* Orwell's psycholinguistic hypothesis is based on a clear-cut distinction between concrete objects and abstract entities. Can such a distinction be justified? Even if it could, is there any evidence at all that the writing process is preceded by such a sequence as Orwell describes? According to his account, we think in pictures (or we should) and then we find the proper words to describe the pictures, the result being good vivid writing. When we do not see pictures, as when we write about abstract things, existing language networks provide ready-made phrases and the outcome is unsatisfactory, in that the intended meaning may be distorted. Even if it were true that we could think graphically, would not that process be limited to certain kinds of mental activity (description, narration), leaving the most difficult (exposition, argumentation) unattended? It is unlikely, however, that the process Orwell describes actually takes place. Probably writing would be impossible if the visual implications of every phrase and word had to be explored first. In its most common forms, language is properly used as a system of signs without extensive symbolic meaning, quasi-algebraically, so to speak. To use it, we merely need to know reference (meaning) and syntax (grammatical rules), without troubling ourselves about etymology, connotation, imagery, and other literary and linguistic features. To use it well, as a poet or careful essayist might, we must take account of the possible advantages of manipulated implications and the danger of conveying unwanted meanings. (See next note.)

6. *vagueness generally.* This last sentence of the selection offers an illustration of the contention in the previous note, that most writing is algebraic. Parenthetically, it also shows that Orwell does not follow his own injunction. The first phrase ("this last effort of the mind") might have been avoided by a more careful writer because it vaguely echoes MILTON'S line in *Lycidas,* "that last infirmity of noble mind." Moreover, *cuts* and *stale* are metaphors from the kitchen whereas *mixed* and *images* are literal abstractions. *Prefabricated* is effective, suggesting shoddy and uniform construction, even when it is allied to the colorless *phrases.* Of course, it merely duplicates the information in the previous segment, making it a "needless repetition." Both *humbug* and *vagueness* (and perforce *generally*) are examples of abstraction and vagueness themselves. Having committed himself to an impossible ideal, on the basis of an untenable hypothesis, Orwell is unable to avoid the very faults he proscribes.

BOWRA (No. 4, p. 37)

Perhaps the best quality of the two paragraphs in this selection is their organization. Nowadays, paragraph structure is largely imaginary, mainly taught as a discipline for freshmen in college. Even good writers paragraph by intuition rather than by principle and in some writings paragraphs are deliberately kept down to a sentence or two. But it was not always so. Of course, if we go back far enough in the history of English we shall find no paragraphing at all (see CAXTON, No. 57, or PUTTENHAM, No. 49). Even MILTON (No. 44) paragraphed in a way that can be called chaotic. But by the time of LOCKE (No. 39) or ADDISON (No. 37), the principles of paragraphing were established, and the form of the paragraph was maintained in the same way for over two centuries.

The main purpose of this standard in paragraphing was to provide the reader with guidance to the steps of the writer's thought. To that end, each step was embodied in a separate paragraph and summarized in a (topic) sentence usually placed near the beginning. Each paragraph then proceeded to explain, illustrate, or otherwise develop the idea in the topic sentence. A transition often consisting of a connective word or phrase bridged the space between paragraphs. Sometimes, summary sentences were added to follow or to conclude a sequence of paragraphs. The whole structure conveyed the sense that the writer controlled both the material and the response of the reader. (See ARNOLD, No. 18, for another good example.)

In this selection, the first sentence announces the subject of the two paragraphs taken together. The second sentence is the topic sentence of the first paragraph: "the poet who writes for readers. . . ." The rest of the paragraph develops the topic by restatement, illustration, and contrast of Virgil with Homer. The paragraph closes with a repetition of the theme: "his aim was to compose a poem which could be read with . . . care. . . ."

The second paragraph opens with a transitional sentence. The point—that Virgil is modern compared with Homer—is stressed by the inserted *in fact*. The second sentence contains the topic, the contrast between reader and listener. The development is antithetic: oral, written, Homer, Virgil. The substance of the two paragraphs is reviewed in the last sentence, which is characterized by a set of oppositions illustrating the two kinds of epic. The effect is successful, though of course it is not due solely to organization.

CONNOLLY (No. 6, p. 41)

Cyril Connolly founded the journal *Horizon* in 1939 and edited it until 1950, when it closed. Among its well known contributors were Mary MC CARTHY and George ORWELL. The book from which this selection was taken is dedicated to Logan Pearsall SMITH and is concerned with declaring the virtues of what Connolly calls the "Mandarin style":

> The Mandarin style at its best yields the richest and most complex expression of the English language. It is the diction of Donne, Browne, Addison, Johnson, Gibbon, de Quincey, Landor, Carlyle, and Ruskin as opposed to that of Bunyan, Dryden, Locke, Defoe, Cowper, Cobbett, Hazlitt, Southey, and Newman. It is characterized by long sentences with many dependent clauses, by the use of the subjunctive and conditional, by exclamations and interjections, quotations, allusions, metaphors, long images, Latin terminology, subtlety and conceits. Its cardinal assumption is that neither the writer nor the reader is in a hurry, that both are in possession of a classical education and a private income. It is Ciceronian English. (pp. 29–30, Penguin ed.)

The last great writers in this style, writes Connolly (in 1938), were Walter PATER and Henry JAMES, but they became victims of their habituation to it, "grew prisoners of their style, committed to a tyranny of euphonious nothings" (p. 30). They were, moreover, overtaken by a change in reading habits influenced by journalism. Modern writing became journalistic, colloquial, plain, as in BUTLER, SHAW, Wells, Bennett, MAUGHAM. Subsequently, a new Mandarin generation arose (Joyce, Strachey, Huxley, Virginia WOOLF), to be replaced by a new vernacular group (Isherwood, HEMINGWAY, Orwell), whose tenure is now insecure. In predicting the demise of the current style, Connolly proposes that the writer anxious to see his work survive for half a generation must write "against the current, in a prose that makes demands both on the resources of our language and the intelligence of the reader" (p. 92). Such a writer would avoid some of the Mandarins' failings (indolence, egotism, exhibitionism) but borrow from them artistic conscience, dislike of the stereotype, pleasure in the creative use of the long and complicated sentence. Their rivals will similarly provide him with things to use and things to avoid. That is the content of the selection. In the three decades since the book was published such Mandarin writers as E. B. WHITE, the two Thomas WOLFES,

Mary MC CARTHY and William FAULKNER have reached the highest levels of appreciation. Perhaps the oscillation between Mandarin and Puritan that Connolly describes is an actual fact of literary experience.

Connolly mentions in the Introduction to the revised edition (London, 1949), "On every page I have retouched the writing itself. . . ." The notes which follow represent the changes made in the revision.

1. *pruning:* "constant pruning"
2. *the imagination reverts to the wilderness:* "the imagination like a tea-rose reverts to the wilderness."
3. *must eventually come:* "must eventually sidle."
4. *controversies:* "such controversies"
5. *there is action:* "there continue action"
6. *necessary as it was:* "necessary though it were"
7. *victorious though it seems:* "victorious as it may appear"
8. *this is not inevitable:* "this is not inevitably so"
9. *Now the moment has come:* "now has come the moment"
10. *It is not a question of taking sides about one way of writing or another:* "It is no more a question of taking sides about one way or another of writing"
11. *it is important to know at any given moment:* "at any given moment it is important to know"
12. *Experiment and adventure is indicated:* "Experiment and adventure are indicated"
13. *let us try and break:* "let us try then to break"

MAUGHAM (No. 7, p. 43)

In this book of reminiscences, Maugham explains how he taught himself to write English. Though of British parents, Maugham spent the first ten years of his life as a native speaker of French. To improve his style, he tried to imitate the archaic and unusual vocabulary of PATER and WILDE and of Jeremy Taylor.

1. *Taylor.* "I studied Jeremy Taylor's *Holy Dying.* In order to assimilate his style I copied down passages and then tried to write them down from memory."
2. *The Tale of a Tub.* Properly known as *A Tale of a Tub,* this work con-

sists of a satiric history of the Christian Church in the form of an allegory about three brothers (Peter, Martin and Jack), interspersed with digressions on various subjects. Outwardly, it has seemed to many critics unlike SWIFT'S other prose. Samuel JOHNSON, one of the earliest critics of Swift's work, expresses quite a different opinion from Maugham. (See No. 30, para. 1.) Most readers agree that the prose of *A Tale of a Tub* appears to be quite different from all of Swift's other prose, at least on the levels of diction, imagery, and sentence length. Maugham's description is so general that it could fit any writer of whom one approved. To enable the reader to compare that description with the original, here follows the first paragraph of "A Digression Concerning Criticks":

> Tho' I have been hitherto as cautious as I could, upon all Occasions, most nicely to follow the Rules and Methods of Writing, laid down by the Example of our illustrious moderns; yet has the unhappy shortness of my Memory led me into an Error, from which I must immediately extricate my self, before I can decently pursue my Principal Subject. I confess with Shame, it was an unpardonable Omission to proceed so far as I have already done, before I had performed the due Discourses, Expostulatory, Supplicatory, or Deprecatory with my good Lords the Criticks. Towards some Atonement for this grievous Neglect, I do here make humbly bold to present them with a short Account of themselves and their Art, by looking into the Original and Pedigree of the Word, as it is generally understood among us, and very briefly considering the antient and present State thereof.

3. *place.* An allusion to Swift's dictum: "Proper words in proper places is the true definition of a style."

4. *impeccable prose.* Note Maugham's system of sentence construction. There are not many sentences in this selection as long as the first one. Most are shorter and a number are very short. In this first paragraph, there are four of seven words or less:

1. The prose of Swift enchanted me.
2. I chose *The Tale of a Tub.*
3. But the style is admirable.
4. It is an impeccable prose.

Number 1 is the second sentence in the paragraph, number 4 the last. The distribution of sentence lengths suggests an attempt to achieve a rhythm by the variation in numbers of words per sentence. Sentence length and complexity are common means of achieving variety and rhythm—of creating patterns—in prose.

A related phenomenon is the connection of sentences to each other. In expository and especially in argumentative writing, the relationship of sentences to each other is important and must be indicated unambiguously to the reader. Although all sentences begin with a capital letter and end with a period or other full stop, they are not all of equal importance in a discourse, nor do they fulfill identical purposes. Some sentences state important points, others merely restate, illustrate, or exemplify and might be easily omitted if space were in short supply. Connectives serve to make clear the nature of each sentence.

In the use of connectives, there have long been two tendencies, one of which is called the Plain Style; its opposite has no standard name, though Cyril CONNOLLY (No. 6, notes) has called it the *Mandarin* style. The Plain Style may be recognized by its shorter sentences, less complicated syntax, commoner vocabulary, greater use of idiom, and low use of connectives. In a sense, the Plain Style is a way of distrusting the artifice of language. In ancient rhetoric, the two tendencies were called the Attic and Asiatic styles. In the Renaissance, they appeared as the Ciceronian and Senecan movements. Whatever their names, the alternation between these tendencies seems inevitable as long as expression remains less than ideally effective.

In the first paragraph, Maugham reveals his affinity with the Plain Style by his steady avoidance of initial connectives. Of its eighteen sentences, only two begin with a connective (*but, as*); nine begin with pronouns, four with expletives (*there, it*), two with *the.* This procedure has two kinds of consequences: monotony of sentence structure and ambiguity of logical sequence. The avoidance of connectives is associated with the minimal use of the resources of syntax. The result is the repetition of a limited set of sentence patterns. Also, as might be expected, if the relationship between successive sentences is not specified, it will be obscure. Consider the first three sentences of paragraph 3, of which the first begins with *the,* and the next two with *I.* Without connective guidance, it is not possible to determine whether Maugham intended to say:

1. I now began to write better, but I still did not write well, too stiffly and self-consciously.
2. I now began to write better. In the past, I did not write well: too stiffly and self-consciously.

In expository writing, this kind of ambiguity is no advantage. The Plain writer is deliberately sacrificing variety and at times clarity in the interests of appearing simple. But it should be carefully noted that the Plain Style is not simple in the sense of artless. It substitutes one set of artful mannerisms for another. It is not really simple nor is it "natural." "Natural" writing is a contradiction in terms. All writing is artificial. But the Plain writer gives the impression of restraint, of telling less than he could, whereas the other writer wants to tell everything about everything. He is intent on one hundred percent Expression. Perhaps he should be called the Expressive writer.

5. *country*. How effective is Maugham's analogy? If Swift's prose is the canal, what are the poplars, the country? How well in mind does Maugham have Swift's works? Did he have *A Tale of a Tub* open in front of him as he wrote? How can you tell?

6. *You go on. . . .* Why does Maugham slip into the second person here? Can you think of other writers who do this? Here is one example: "All that the vergers who have followed her seem to think is that somehow if you get in enough details, enough random fact—somehow this *trenchant portrait* is going to rise up off the pages." (WOLFE, No. 73, p. 231.)

7. *affectation*. Try to define *lucidity, terseness, naturalness,* and *lack of affectation* without using any of the following terms or their derivatives: "clear, simple, plain, natural."

8. *Addison*. Look up the passages of SWIFT, ADDISON and DRYDEN (Nos. 36, 7, 40) and see whether you can apply Maugham's descriptive phrases to these writers. "Perfection," "easy elegance," "springtime gaiety," "conversational ease," "blithe spontaneousness": Are these qualities in the writing or in the reader?

9. *in England*. Do you feel any awkwardness about the placing of this modifier here? Where else could it be placed? If it were moved toward the end of the clause, what would happen to the antithesis between *before* and *since?*

10. *French*. Maugham, whose English was influenced by French, praises Dryden's French-influenced English. (See GRAVES on Skelton.)

11. *England*. Dryden, whose English is influenced by French, is more like England than Swift, whose English is likened to a French canal. What is the point of this paradox? Why is it not more stressed?

12. *evident*. Does *see* in this sentence mean *realize* or *arrange?* Does *evident* mean *visible* or *already present?* How do you account for the lack of clarity in the beginning of this paragraph?

13. *facts*. Here is the credo of the Plain writer, including the desire for verbal self-restraint, here shown in the pointless desire to avoid adjectives.

14. *naturally*. In this context, this seems to mean "written with the appearance of lack of art," an appearance which would be supported by grammatical errors. In the sense that they contribute to an evaluation of the author as a Plain Stylist, grammatical errors are a rhetorical device.

15. *embellishments*. In the first part of this paragraph, Maugham describes the practice of the Expressive writer. Does he describe it as if he regretted that he could not emulate it? What is another way of saying "farfetched tropes"?

In the last part of the paragraph, Maugham explains once more the ideals of the Plain Stylist. The terms "lucidity, simplicity, and euphony" can be interpreted as meaning the following:

1. The writing must be easily understood. (lucidity)
2. The writing should be simple. (simplicity)
3. The writing should sound good. (euphony)

What does number two accomplish, that is not already done by number one? Note that this is the only series in this selection. This fact suggests a certain attitude toward seriation by the all-out Plain Stylist.

Propositional Reduction (first paragraph)

¶ 1. I studied the writers of the early 18th century.
2. I especially liked the prose of Swift.
3. I studied Swift as I had Taylor.
4. I selected Swift's *A Tale of a Tub.*
5. In old age Swift said about *A Tale of a Tub:* "What genius I had then!"
6. Some of Swift's other works are better than *A Tale of a Tub.*
7. The allegory and irony of *A Tale of a Tub* are boring.
8. The style of *A Tale of a Tub* is excellent.
9. There is no better English than that of *A Tale of a Tub.*
10. *A Tale of a Tub* contains no unusual imagery.
11. The prose of *A Tale of a Tub* is "civilized."
12. The vocabulary of *A Tale of a Tub* is commonplace.
13. In *A Tale of a Tub* Swift used words properly.
14. The excellence of the sentences in *A Tale of a Tub* is due to Swift's taste.
15. I copied passages from *A Tale of a Tub* and tried to write them out from memory.
16. I tried to change the words or the word order.
17. I found that Swift's words and word order were the best.
18. Swift's prose is faultless.

Logical Diagram

	A	B	C	D
¶ 1.	( )			
2.			(×)	

3.		(=)		
4.			(×)	
5.	(+)			
6.	(–)			
7.		(=)		
8.	(–)			
9.	(!)			
10.			(×)	
11.	(+)			
12.		(=)		
13.		(+)		
14.	(+)			
15.	(+)			
16.	(+)			
17.	(–)			
18.				(:)

FORD (No. 8, p. 47)

In his essay on the centenary of George SAINTSBURY, Edmund Wilson says: "The only other writer I know who has created a style similar to Saintsbury's is the late Ford Madox Ford. Both these men are worth attention as writers because they found out how to manage a fine and flexible English prose on the rhythms of informal speech rather than on those of literary convention." Whether the description is apt or not, it calls attention to the quality that united these two men, the quality of eccentricity. The modern version of Ford is Tom WOLFE (No. 73). Note the frequent ellipsis points and the final "No!"

1. *blue sky.* A parody of the sort of writing Conrad apparently wished to do.
2. *N. B. G.* The British vulgarism "no bloody good."
3. *Lady Maud* [Ethel M.] *Warrender* (1870–1945) may have been a mistress of King Edward VII. She is the author of *My First Sixty Years* (London, 1933).
4. *gas and gaiters.* Eric Partridge's *Dictionary of Slang and Unconventional*

English defines this expression as "nonsense; mere verbiage, redundancy; exaggerated rubbish."

5. *Until.* Though this is punctuated as a sentence, it is merely a dependent clause.

6. *tremendous, tremulous, tenuous.* Alliterative jocularity.

7. *pretty certain that I didn't.* Vernacular features like these are also characteristic of the "casual style" of the *New Yorker.*

SMITH (No. 9, p. 49)

Logan Pearsall Smith by any account must be considered an eccentric. He is one of a small band of our writers (like Henry JAMES, T. S. ELIOT), who have chosen to live in England and to become Englishmen. Born in New Jersey, of an old family of Philadelphia Quakers, Smith studied at Haverford and Harvard, then at Balliol College, Oxford, where he received the B.A. and M.A. He became a naturalized Englishman in 1913. Matthew ARNOLD and Whistler were among his friends. The president of Bryn Mawr was a cousin of his. Bernard Berenson and Bertrand RUSSELL married his sisters. He himself never married but became a founding member of the Society for Pure English (among whose tracts the present selection was printed) and the author of a number of books, on Milton, Shakespeare, the English language, and various literary topics. He loved poetic prose and excelled in the writing of the short pieces he published in several volumes titled *Trivia, More Trivia, Afterthoughts,* and *Last Words.* The following are some typical examples:

HUMILIATION

'My own view is,' I began, but no one listened. At the next pause, 'I always say,' I remarked, but again the loud talk went on. Someone told a story. When the laughter had ended, 'I often think—'; but looking around the table I could catch no friendly, no attentive eye. It was humiliating, but more humiliating the thought that Sophocles and Goethe would have always commanded attention, while the lack of it would not have troubled Spinoza, nor Abraham Lincoln.

REASSURANCE

I look at my overcoat and my hat hanging in the hall with reassurance; for although I go out of doors with one individuality today, when yesterday I had quite another, yet my clothes keep my various selves buttoned up together, and enable all these otherwise irreconcilable aggregates of psychological phenomena to pass themselves off as one person.

ACTION

I am no mere thinker, no mere creature of dreams and imagination. I pay bills, post letters; I buy new bootlaces and put them in my boots. And when I set out to get my hair cut, it is with the iron face of those men of empire and unconquerable will, those Caesars and Napoleons, whose footsteps shake the earth.

ROUTINE

I live by the clock; all my activities, my exits and entrances, my times for smoking cigarettes and reading murder-stories, are synchronized and set in harmony with the earth's motion and the sun's. Much more than happiness I love my habits, the timely routine and oscillation of the hours which carry me on through months and seasons. Thus my life spins silent on its axle; but at the least dislocation or jar—if the Post is late, or the Morning Paper doesn't turn up—I am giddy, I am undone; the ground rocks beneath my feet.

PHRASES

Is there, after all, any solace like the solace and consolation of Language? When I am disconcerted by the unpleasing aspects of existence, when to me, as to Hamlet, this earth seems a sterile promontory, it is not in Metaphysics nor in Religion that I seek for reassurance, but in fine phrases. The thought of gazing on life's Evening Star makes of ugly old age a pleasing prospect; if I call Death mighty and unpersuaded, it has no terrors for me; I am perfectly content to be cut down as a flower, to flee as a shadow, to be swallowed like a snowflake on the sea. These similes soothe and effectually console me. I am sad only at the thought that Words must perish like all things mortal; that the most perfect Metaphors must be forgotten when the human race is dust.

'But the iniquity of Oblivion blindly scattereth her poppy.' [Sir Thomas Browne: *Urne Buriall*]

From these and from the substance and style of the selection, it should be clear that Smith is what CONNOLLY (No. 6) calls a "Mandarin."

1. *Middleton Murry.* Author of *The Problem of Style* (1922).

2. *Herbert Read.* Author of *English Prose Style* (1928).

3. *Cambridge Criticism.* F. L. Lucas and F. W. Bateson, among others.

4. *abysses.* Together with *path, pitfalls, engulfed, danger-signals* and *edge,* this word completes the extended metaphor in this paragraph wherein a young

writer is identified with someone engaged in travelling. Though this is a rather common image, Smith's carefulness as a writer is evident in his ability to keep the metaphor consistent while he extends it. In this respect, Smith is using the language symbolically rather than algebraically. If he had not been so careful, he might have abandoned the image along the way and have written "This path is full of dreadful dangers into which the unwary may be too easily seduced," or "pitfalls into which the unwary may be too easily lured." (Compare ORWELL, No. 3.)
5. *stylite or stylistic columns.* A deliberate pun on the curious origin of the wrong spelling of the word *style* (properly *stile* from Latin *stilus*) by assimilation with the word for column (*style* from Greek *stulos*). A stylite was an ascetic who lived on the top of a column.
6. *Muse of Prose.* An allusion to the lines from Milton's *Lycidas:* "Alas! what boots it with uncessant care/To tend the homely, slighted, shepherd's trade,/And strictly meditate the thankless Muse?"

As a preliminary to advocating his views about ornamental writing, Smith attacks two critics he has isolated as detractors of Fine Writing and supporters of the Plain Style. The method of his argument consists of misrepresenting his opponents by attributing to them beliefs they do not hold or by making their opinions seem absurdly extreme and finally by deriding the ridiculous consequences of these views.

He begins ironically, by pretending to an alarm he does not feel about the dangers to which young writers are exposed and to a relief which is equally insincere that Herbert Read and Middleton Murry are available to protect these apprentices. **Irony** is a figure in the old rhetoric as well as a common precedure in the discourse of all times. In the technical sense, it is a group term covering a multitude of departures from literal statement, such as understatement and overstatement, sarcasm and irony proper, in which the speaker but not the hearer is aware of the two opposed meanings of the utterance. In common parlance, especially since Milton's time, irony has been an attitude of aloof criticism (as in Voltaire and SWIFT) rather than a specific device of rhetoric.

The irony of the first paragraph is a hint to the reader that Read and Murry are being criticized and that further comment about their opinions will be essentially unfavorable, whatever it may seem to be on the surface. Smith then turns to the substance of Read's and Murry's warnings to new writers with a show of objectivity, such as seeming to quote their words, providing definitions. . . . But the quotations are merely phrases taken out of context and the definitions are tendentious. Their position is that excessive attention to technique at the expense of meaning is dangerous to good writing. He redefines this so as to make it seem as if they were unalterably opposed to careful attention to style, such as imaginative effects, euphony, rhythm, imagery, diction, the search for perfection itself. Plainly, this was not what they meant, but he has skilfully represented them to hold these views and he has no trouble defeating them. He does this both by showing that they are against writing itself and at the same time that they have exaggerated the dangers (e.g., the last sentence with its reference to the solar system).

The ironic effect and the argumentative reductions are both achieved in part by careful choice of word, by the use of what have been called "loaded words." Such words tend to stimulate readers or hearers into automatic reactions which further the wanted effect by closing the mind to doubt. Propaganda, advertising, political speaking are much given to loaded diction. Words like *progress, communism, nation, on sale* trigger automatic reactions. The words *heresy, decadence, preaching, miscreants,* and phrases like *threatening our civilization, lonely garrets, serious damage on the solar system,* are intended to exploit the reader's unconscious responses and to subvert any tendency on his part to be judicious or fair to the objects of Smith's disapproval.

WOOLF (No. 10, p. 53)

Virginia Woolf's style has been compared to Laurence Sterne's. William York Tindall, for instance, believes that Sterne's rebellion against the rationalism of his time "provided her with a model of free association, [and] subjective vagary . . ." (*Forces in Modern British Literature* [New York, 1947], p. 304). Her admiration for Sterne's style is evident in this selection, which was originally an introduction to the "World's Classics" edition of *A Sentimental Journey*. In the preceding paragraph, which begins the essay, she suggests that Sterne's outlook had undergone a change since writing the wayward and bawdy *Tristram Shandy*. His passion for a lady who sailed for India caused him to approach his new work in a spirit of deepened sensibility.

1. *were possible . . . was impossible.* The rules for the "subjunctive" in English are quite complicated and like many writers Virginia Woolf failed to master them. The *were* in the *if*-clause is only used with conditions that have not happened or cannot happen, which is plainly not applicable here since he did "correct his manners." The sentence should read: "But if it was possible. . . ."

2. *brilliant eyes.* Virginia Woolf had a long (if not a large) nose and large, liquid, brown eyes. Some kind of self-identification with Sterne seems certain here.

3. *first words.* The matter between dashes is the first sentence of Sterne's *Sentimental Journey* (1758).

4. *flash of poetry.* There seems to be an unconscious reference here, both in the meaning of this sentence and in the words *jibe* and *flash,* to Hamlet's meditation on Yorick: "Where be your gibes now? your gambols? your songs? your flashes of merriment . . ." (*Hamlet,* V, i, 208–10). Sterne, of course, had adopted the disguise of "Mr. Yorick," first in the publication of his Sermons and later on the title page of *A Sentimental Journey.*

5. *hedge of English prose.* The imagery of this sentence (jokes and poetical flashes jumping through the gap cut in a hedge by a pen) is of some interest, partly because it is so outlandishly mixed. The personification of a writer as a pen is hardly a problem—it is merely an algebraic image (see ORWELL, No. 3, notes 5 and 6). The gap, however, is troublesome, for it depends on the concrete existence of the hedge. If we cannot see English prose as a hedge (surrounding a building? a barrier to keep out strangers?), we cannot interpret the gap. Since we do not have the hedge in view until we are past the gap, the immediacy of the whole image is compromised. Its weakness is known to the writer or she would not have troubled to identify the hedge as English prose. We are distracted by the characterization of the hedge as "thick-set." The expression is mysterious but it has a charm which sustains the whole image. More literally, if we were not puzzled by the meaning of "thick-set," we would easily detect how mixed and unsatisfactory the image is.

6. *behaviour this time?* Why is Virginia Woolf's doubt about the consciousness of Sterne's art put in the form of a question?—two questions (for the second merely restates the first).

7. *brilliant talker.* Another occurrence of the claim that a style one approves of is based on speech, perhaps here with more justice than usual. The reader should satisfy himself that Virginia Woolf's description of Sterne's style ("jerky, disconnected sentences . . .") is accurate. Incidentally, an artistic reproduction of speech would probably have avoided the disturbing assonance in "order this *matter better.*" (See SAINTSBURY, No. 13, notes, conclusion.)

8. *speaking voice.* As Virginia Woolf suggests, Sterne's punctuation seems oral rather than formal, both in the very frequent use of the dash and in the unorthodox placement of the comma at points where a speaker is generally supposed to pause. Linguists have observed, however, that pauses in speech generally occur within constructions rather than between: to simulate oral delivery the first dash in the following illustrative paragraph should come before rather than after *mystery.*

> There were two other circumstances which entangled this mystery—the one was, he told every woman what he had to say in her ear, and in a way which had much more the air of a secret than a petition—the other was, it was always successful—he never stopp'd a woman, but she pull'd out her purse, and immediately gave him something. (*A Sentimental Journey,* ed. G. Stout [Berkeley, 1967], p. 240.)

9. *true to life.* As can be seen in the second paragraph, this naive formulation is merely a red herring that the writer brings in to throw us off the scent. It is worth noting that the three sentences following the two questions are vaguely parallel. Each supplies one ingredient of Sterne's style (jerky sentences, speech punctuation, incoherence of ideas) and each is more or less in declarative order with the verb *to be* following the subject. This parallelism helps to organize the paragraph and to give it a jerkiness not unlike what has been asserted of Sterne.

10. *doubtful taste.* Sterne's lewdness has been censured by many critics. Only a devoted Sternian, like Virginia Woolf, would go out of his way to defend him.

11. *close to life.* By saying that the book becomes "semi-transparent," that the reader is not kept "at arm's length" and that we are "close to life," Virginia Woolf seems to be saying only that the language is idiomatic and that she finds it effective.

12. *Sterne achieved this illusion.* Having brought the reader to the point where he is almost ready to believe that Sterne was unconscious of any art and that his writing was merely life represented accurately, our author lets us have the truth very suddenly. To bring it to us more quickly, she inverts the sentence, putting the important information ("Sterne achieved this illusion . . .") in a noun clause serving as subject when the normal order might have been, "it is obvious that Sterne. . . ."

13. *diffusity unutterable.* "Unspeakable vagueness." The odd terminal (post-nominal) placement of the adjective which governs both *disorder* and *diffusity* gives an elaborateness to the sentence which perhaps is intended to counterpoise the pedestrian "brush aside," "word of mouth," "struck dumb." Moreover it prepares a suitable contrast for the short sentence that follows and makes it (with its slangy "brought off") stand out effectively.

14. *No writing.* A typical hyperbole of the critic of style, meaning more exactly "no writing that I have read and that I can think of at the moment."

15. *cut on the sand in marble.* The shortage of information in the last three sentences is concealed or offset by a great display of imagery: "folds and creases of the mind," "fluidity . . . permanence," "tide . . . beach . . . ripple and eddy cut on the sand in marble." Despite the folds and creases, which recall the physical brain, the words are all drawn from the same area of experience, the

sea, an interest that Virginia Woolf shared with Sterne. Note the words *flow, fluidity, tide, beach, ripple, eddy, sand.* Compare Sterne's fondness for "ebbs and flows." (*A Sentimental Journey,* ed. Stout, p. 70 n. 6.)

LAWRENCE (No. 11, p. 55)

D. H. Lawrence is best known as the novelist of the instincts, though he also wrote travel books, poems, and critical prose. His criticism is unorthodox but interesting. Lawrence is aware that criticism is primarily reasoning, but he is on principle opposed to reason and committed to the instinct. Thus he rejects the method by which criticism proceeds but has nothing to replace it with except emotionality, which does not lead to criticism but to appreciation or rapture. Fortunately, however, Lawrence adopts in practice what he rejects in principle.

1. *reasoned account.* Despite his violent rejection of reason, Lawrence allows himself this emergency exit. It sounds as if he were saying that criticism is feeling and not reason. Actually, he is saying that criticism is the critic's analysis ("reasoned account") of his feelings. This is scarcely revolutionary.
2. *too personal.* This must mean subjective: without reference to external standards.
3. *science ignores.* This can mean values that science has (a) no knowledge of, or (b) no interest in. In either case, it seems to be saying much the same as the item "in the first place." Lawrence does not scruple to use a facsimile of logical argument in showing the superiority of emotion to reason.
4. *sincere and vital emotion.* Lawrence intends to distinguish the emotion he means from other kinds, but his description does not succeed. It seems to say merely that the emotion he speaks of is genuine and not spurious.
5. *critical twiddle-twaddle.* To Lawrence, the appearance of analytic procedure, such as the study of form and style calls forth from its responsible practitioners, was objectionable and elicited this derogatory noun. Several other words in this sentence represent mere name-calling: *pseudo-scientific, imitation-botanical, impertinence, jargon.* The attitude reflected by this procedure is hardly a reasonable one, as might be expected. The excess is also revealed more subtly, by the considerable number of words indicating extremes or absolutes. The first paragraph includes the following: *no more, never, much too, nothing else, all* (twice). How do the other paragraphs compare?

6. *force and complexity.* In the previous sentence, the work of art was possessed of complexity and force. In the present one, the critic needs force and complexity. Why the rearrangement? Compare with the repetition of the qualities of the inferior critic. (See next note.)
7. *paltry, impudent criticism.* Compare the opinions of SHAW (No. 62) on the relation between style and force of personality. Incidentally, what is the relation between the qualities of the good critic (complexity and force) and the repetition of the two adjectives characterizing the poor critic?
8. *And a man.* There is a string of subjects of the form "a man." Is there any significance to this? Is it art or accident?
9. *emotional boor.* Lawrence wants to get this proportion off his chest despite its lack of logic in the context.
10. *Sainte-Beuve.* The best-known French critic of the nineteenth century, inventor of an undogmatic criticism which presented the reader with vast amounts of information without insisting that he draw any particular conclusion. Proust disliked him intensely and mentions him many times in his novels.
11. *Macaulay.* Another blow at Macaulay, who seems to have been a favorite target. See, also, BAGEHOT (No. 21), SAINTSBURY (No. 13), and the notes under MACAULAY (No. 22). Part of his attractiveness as a target was his tremendous reputation as a writer and his still great readability. POE's praise of him (No. 94) reflects grudging admiration. Lawrence attacks his honesty and sincerity, a reproach which many others levelled at him, but he credits him with emotional life. Lytton Strachey, who deplored Macaulay's rhetorical quality, disagreed with Lawrence on the question of emotion: "one cannot resist the conclusion that the absence from his make-up of intense physical emotion brought a barrenness upon his style." (*Portraits in Miniature* [New York, 1931], p. 174.)
12. *But not morally.* A fragmentary sentence, perhaps designed to display Lawrence's contempt for standards of literary form.
13. *a few standards.* The notion of standards contradicts the previously-stated principle of criticism by feeling. The standards he cites, of course, do not offer very secure guidance.
14. *sincerely . . . essentially.* The effect of these two adverbial modifiers is to undermine the sentence in which they occur. In the previous sentence, the parenthetical "on the whole" gives the same effect. It sounds as if Lawrence is not very sure about what Sainte-Beuve thought.
15. *individual morality.* The lame ending of this paragraph is partly due to the structure and punctuation of the last sentence, and partly to the monotonous repetition of subject constructions: *Sainte-Beuve, He, This, Pater's standard, Macaulay's standard, Gibbon.* The repetition subserves no rhetorical

purpose—it seems merely artless. An inspection of the sentences in the rest of the selection will show that Lawrence seldom opened a sentence with anything but a subject, unless it was with a coordinating conjunction. Compare this practice with that of another novelist, Virginia WOOLF (No. 10) or Somerset MAUGHAM (No. 7).

ELIOT (No. 12, p. 57)

1. *Rostand.* Edmond Rostand (1868–1918), French playwright, wrote *Cyrano de Bergerac.*
2. *nice.* An archaic word meaning "delicate."
3. *variety of styles.* Eliot here questions, with justice, the notion of the period style.
4. *Lyly.* The following is the first paragraph of John Lyly's *Euphues:* The *Anatomy of Wit* (1578):

> There dwelt in Athens a young gentleman of great patrimony and of so comely a personage that it was doubted whether he were more bound to Nature for the lineaments of his person or to Fortune for the increase of his possessions. But Nature, impatient of comparisons, and as it were disdaining a companion or copartner in her working, added to this comeliness of his body such a sharp capacity of mind that not only she proved Fortune counterfeit but was half of that opinion that she herself was only current. This young gallant, of more wit than wrath, and yet of more wrath than wisdom, seeing himself inferior to none in pleasant conceits thought himself superior to all in honest conditions, insomuch that he deemed himself so apt to all things that he gave himself almost to nothing but practising of those things commonly which are incident to these sharp wits—fine phrases, smooth quipping, merry taunting, using jesting without mean, and abusing mirth without measure. As therefore the sweetest rose has his prickle, the finest velvet his brack, the fairest flour his bran, so the sharpest wit hath his wanton will and the holiest his wicked way. And true it is that some men write, and most men believe, that in all perfect shapes a blemish bringeth rather a liking every way to the eyes than a loathing any way to the mind. Venus had her mole in her cheek which made her more amiable; Helen her scar on her chin which Paris called *cos amoris,* the whetstone of love; Aristippus his wart, Lycurgus his wen. So likewise in the disposition of the mind, either virtue is overshadowed with some vice or vice overcast with some virtue: Alexander valiant in war, yet

> given to wine; Tully eloquent in his glozes, yet vainglorious; Solomon wise, yet too too wanton; David holy, but yet an homicide; none more witty than Euphues, yet at the first none more wicked.

5. *Ascham and Elyot.* See numbers 51 and 55.

6. *antithesis and similes.* Euphuism was a highly developed type of Ciceronianism, characterized mainly by three kinds of devices: **isocolon,** successive structural elements (phrases, clauses) equal in length (of words or syllables); **parison,** successive elements identical in syntactic structure; **paromoion,** similarity of sound (syllables of parts of words) in corresponding items in successive structural elements. Lyly's particular version was also notable for **antithesis** and **similes** drawn from history or science. All these devices are exemplified in the paragraph quoted above.

7. *Nashe.* Thomas Nashe (1567–1601) was a master at invective and disputation. He writes in what is believed to be the colloquial Elizabethan style. The following is from *Strange News* (1592), part of a controversy with Gabriel Harvey (the friend of Edmund Spenser), whose **inkhorn terms** Nashe attacks vigorously:

> Thou art mine enemy, Gabriel, and that which is more, a contemptible underfoot enemy or else I would teach thy old Truantship the true use of words, as also how more inclinable verse is than prose to dance after the horrisonant pipe of inveterate antiquity. It is no matter, since thou hast brought godly instruction out of love with thee; use thy own destruction, reign sole emperor of Inkhornism! I wish unto thee all superabundant increase of the singular gifts of absurdity and vainglory; from this time forth for ever, ever, ever, evermore mayest thou be canonized as the nonpareil of impious epistlers, the short shredder-out of sandy sentences without lime, as Quintilian termed Seneca all lime and no sand, all matter and no circumstance; the factor for the fairies and night-urchins in supplanting and setting aside the true children of the English, and suborning inkhorn changelings in their stead; the gallimauferyer of all styles in one standish, as imitating everyone and having no separate form of writing of thy own; and, to conclude, the only feather-driver of phrases and putter-of-a-good-word-to-it-when-thou-hast-once-got-it that is betwixt this and the Alps. So be it, world without end. Chroniclers, hear my prayers; good Master Stowe, be not unmindful of him. (See also MC LUHAN, No. 77.)

8. *conversational style.* The paradoxical affection of writers for speech over their own medium, writing, is reflected in modern times by an immoderate praise of the "conversational style." In earlier times, a conversational mode of writing was avoided as lacking coherence and artifice. What is nowadays

praised as conversational style is merely a different sort of artifice, a derivative of the Plain Style (see MAUGHAM, No. 7, note 4). Eliot himself has set the matter in a clear light in his essay on "Charles Whibley":

> People sometimes talk vaguely about the *conversational style* in writing. Still more often, they deplore the divorce between the language as spoken and the language as written. It is true that the spoken and the written language can drift too far apart—with the eventual consequence of forming a new written language. But what is overlooked is that an *identical* spoken and written language would be practically intolerable. If we spoke as we write we should find no one to listen; and if we wrote as we speak we should find no one to read. The spoken and the written language must not be too near together, as they must not be too far apart. Henry James's later style, for instance, is not exactly a conversational style; it is the way in which the later Henry James dictated to a secretary. The famous monologue at the end of *Ulysses* is not the way in which persons of either sex actually *think:* it is a very skilful attempt by a master of language to give the illusion of mental process by a different medium, that of written words. There is, however, an essential connexion between the written and the spoken word, though it is not to be produced by aiming at a "conversational" style in writing, or a periodic style in speech; and I have found this intimate, though indefinable, connexion between the speech and the writing of every writer whom I have known personally who was a good writer—even between the speech and the most recent writing of Mr. James Joyce. (*Selected Essays, 1917–1932* [New York, 1932], pp. 407–408) See also WOOLF (No. 10, note 7) and SAINTSBURY (No. 13, notes, conclusion).

SAINTSBURY (No. 13, p. 59)

1. *him.* Dr. Samuel JOHNSON (see No. 30).
2. *"green-goosish."* Naive: the goose is, for some reason, the animal most often associated with lack of cleverness, as opposed to the fox, for example, in Aesopian fables; green, the color of unripe fruit, has long been used to mean immature. A green-goose is literally a gosling, and by extension, a simpleton. What do Saintsbury's quotation marks around this compound signify?
3. *almost more.* Does this mean more, or less, or the same?
4. *latter.* This may refer to the quantity of wisdom in the letters, the possibility that they are often omitted, that they require supplementing by the

minor works, or that these works are not read at all. Which of these possibilities applies? Does it matter?

5. *writer.* This point is made by Macaulay (see MACAULAY, No. 22, paragraph 1).

6. *description.* See MACAULAY, paragraph 3.

7. *vulgarisation.* French term meaning "popularization" in a good sense. What is meant by the material in the parenthesis? What is the reason for its placement between the relative pronoun and the subject of a dependent clause?

8. *diction.* Is the material between dashes different in kind from that in parentheses? If Saintsbury had not used parentheses before, would he still have used dashes here?

In general, a **parenthesis** is an aside, an interruption of the flow of ideas by the interposition of grammatically unrelated words, phrases, clauses, or sentences in the body of a discourse. Strictly speaking, the parenthesis is the thing inserted; its typographic boundary markers may be round or square brackets, braces, dashes, commas or nothing at all ("This I think is the place."). Some distinction is usually made between what goes between parentheses and between dashes, but it is not clearly marked. Dashes are considered most abrupt, parentheses less so, commas still less and obviously no mark at all least. Braces and square brackets are usually reserved for editorial comments; i.e., comments made by someone other than the writer.

Because interruption of the flow of a discourse is by definition distracting, like digressions, which are merely parentheses of a sentence or more, their extensive use is considered a blemish or a vicious mannerism. Certainly an addiction to parenthesis, which Saintsbury admittedly had, leads to difficulty for the reader and to obscurity. It is likely to be characteristic of a writer with a great many ideas or a great deal of information which he is not sure he knows how to subordinate to his main argument. It is perhaps more likely to occur when the writer is not strongly pursuing a line of argument.

9. *differentia.* That which distinguishes two closely related things in a definition. Does the interrupted structure of this sentence help to emphasize Saintsbury's contention: Macaulay's claim (that Johnson's latinized diction was the main and most objectionable feature of his style) is in error? Is this in fact Macaulay's claim?

Note the extensive use of reference in the first half of this paragraph: *latter, his, him, they, them, itself, it, his, he, it, it, it, his, he, that* (first four sentences). Does this practice lead to any difficulty in sorting out referents?

10. *he did indulge.* Note the repetition of the subject and verb after the dash. Saintsbury begins the sentence with subject and verb auxiliary ("Johnson did"), follows this by a series of four possibilities in the form of phrases

("whether from . . . from . . . from . . . or from . . ."), and then arrives at what should be the main verb ("indulge"). Instead, he places a dash and restates the subject and the auxiliary ("he did") before giving the verb. The repetition, a specialized form of **anacoluthon** called **epanalepsis,** seems to help the reader to keep the subject in mind. The suspension traditionally is supposed to heighten the interest and the drama of a sentence. Does it accomplish its purpose here? Saintsbury had the option of beginning with the series of *whether* phrases, followed by "Johnson did indulge. . . ." Possibly he did not take it because it would have left in doubt, through the long series of qualifications, who the subject was. The other option ("Johnson, whether from . . . did indulge. . . .") would have separated the subject from any part of the verb by four and a half lines.

11. *diction.* Saintsbury uses this word to mean vocabulary, or lexical choice, though Johnson and earlier authorities, in reducing style to diction, included syntax as well as vocabulary. In the first example of "translation" given by Macaulay, both syntax and vocabulary are modified. To most people still, *style* means *diction* (lexical choice).

12. *"translated".* Johnson's supposed tendency to express himself in normal English and in "Johnsonese," as reported by Boswell and repeated and ridiculed by MACAULAY (paragraph 1).

13. *staple or secret.* *Staple* means bulk or substance, chief ingredient. *Secret* means chief but concealed ingredient or cause. Does each of these terms contribute something separate and necessary to the meaning of the sentence? Is the alliteration part of the attraction of the doublet? Note that it is repeated in the same form in the next sentence.

14. *rhetorical tesselation.* A *tessella* is a small *tessera,* or square of stone used in mosaic. A *tessellation* (the usual spelling) is a mosaic, or decorative picture (wall, floor) made of many small stones, or in this case, a linguistic construction made of many small units according to the principles of rhetoric. According to W. K. Wimsatt (see Wimsatt, Bibliography No. 41), Johnson's principal methods were **parallelism, antithesis, inversion,** and **chiasmus.** (See notes to JOHNSON, No. 30, note 2.)

15. *"dressed."* This term from infantry drill looks back to *military, file* and *squadron* just above.

16. *quaternions.* The context shows that this word means sets of four. Saintsbury was noted for his use of such rare words.

17. *rhythm and thought.* It is fairly evident that Saintsbury in this sentence was giving his own version of a Johnsonian sentence or was at any rate exemplifying his explanation. How much like Johnson is this sentence?

18. *Polonius.* "More matter with less art." *Hamlet,* II, i, 95. Note the indirectness of the allusion.
19. *it.* There are three *it*s in this last sentence, of which the second is expletive. What do the first and third refer to?
20. *passages.* Saintsbury's note: "There is, as every student knows, a great deal of it in *The Rambler;* some but rather less in *Rasselas;* and comparatively little in the *Lives.*" Macaulay was known for compelling agreement on disputed points by saying "as every schoolboy knows."

Many readers have commented adversely on Saintsbury's style, accusing him of obscurity, excessive complexity, pedantic allusiveness, and vagueness. There is no question, if the selection discussed is typical, that linearity of sentence structure is not a feature of Saintsbury's style. His use of pronouns has been commented on and his use of semicolons should be noted. Can any generalizations about his expectations and assumptions about his audience and his subject be made from a study of this passage? One of his friends, Oliver Elton, in the Introduction to a posthumous collection of Saintsbury's Introductions (*Prefaces and Essays,* London, 1933) has this to say:

> Saintsbury's style is something of an acquired taste; it has been known to perplex young students, and it has annoyed many a purist. One way to relish it was to know the man, to whom the style was wholly natural; but now he is gone, and it is through the style that the reader must appreciate the man. He, from the first, was inclined to let the purist go hang; and he professed small regard for the purist or the formal grammarian. . . . At first Saintsbury's English is more regular, in the good tradition of the essay . . . when he is no longer in any uniform, academic or scholastic . . . then, indeed, his style is *released.* . . . It has certainly attracted not only many a scholar but many who read simply for pleasure and who enjoy the quips, and twirls, and sallies, and parentheses, and allusions. (pp. xi–xii)

The same writer, in a memorial volume (*A Saintsbury Miscellany,* New York, 1947), talking about the three *Scrap Books,* "which are a mirror of the real, the ultimate Saintsbury," says:

> The much-abused 'style' is there, at its best and worst and freshest: whims, jests, funny ferocities, sudden far-off allusions in parenthesis ('divine Parenthesis,' I think he once called it), capitals, italics, rare or not rare quotations. Everywhere a Sterne-like oddness and twist of language—only it is not, like Sterne's, the effect of care and artifice. It is the native idiom of the speaker in his talk and letters and his thoughts. Many who had disliked

> it were reconciled, once they came to know and like the man. In his writings, he would bring in the ego, perhaps to excess; but that mattered little if the ego attracted you." (pp. 3–4)

Elton, like others of Saintsbury's friends and contemporaries, is a grudging defender. He apologizes for the style on the basis of his affection for the man. In fact, he interprets the style as an expression of the personality of the speaker. And it is not the style but the speaker that he describes.

A later and more whole-hearted defender is Edmund Wilson, who has written: "Reading *The Peace of the Augustans,* I came at last to realize that Saintsbury, besides being a great critic and scholar, was one of the best English *writers* of his time." (*Classics and Commercials* [New York, 1962], p. 366). This does not seem to have been Saintsbury's own opinion, for in one of his books, as Wilson points out, he apologizes for his own prose in this characteristic way:

> With this I may leave the present essay to its chances; only repeating my acquaintance with two quotations which I made thirty-six years ago when touching, for the first time, the subject of Prose Style generally. One was Nicholas Breton's warning to somebody "not to talk too much of it, having so little of it," and the other, Diderot's epigram on Beccaria's *ouvrage sur le style ou il n'y a point de style.* These are, of course, "palpable hits" enough. But you may criticise without being able to create, and you may love beauty, and to the possible extent understand it, without being beautiful. (Preface, *A History of English Prose Rhythm* [London, 1912], p. ix.)

But the truth to Wilson is otherwise: "He had, in fact, invented a style of much charm and a certain significance: a modern, conversational prose that carries off asides, jokes and gossip as well as all the essential data by a very strong personal rhythm, that drops its voice to interpolate footnotes without seriously retarding the current, and that, however facetious or garrulous, never fails to cover the ground and make the points." (p. 307) To Wilson, Saintsbury's is a style of great originality, comparable only to that of Ford Madox FORD (see No. 8). Both of these writers are significant because "they found out how to manage a fine and flexible English prose on the rhythms of informal speech rather than those of literary convention."

These opinions should be subjected to two discounts: Saintsbury is a neglected writer and Wilson, like any critic, likes to turn up neglected masterpieces; in this century, the highest form of praise for a writer's style consists of saying that he does not sound like a writer but a speaker. Nonetheless, does an examination of the selections by Saintsbury and Ford support Wilson's opinion? In what sense can writing be like speech? If it succeeds, is that a virtue?

WILDE (No. 15, p. 65)

1. *former . . . latter.* Former refers to *Life, latter,* to *Literature.* The object of using these substitution words is not economy, for together they are longer than the words they replace. Their use must be dictated by the intention to avoid repetition, presumably unless it is intended for emphasis. Wilde does not hesitate to repeat *principles.* It seems reasonable to infer that writers who are thus careful of repetition have regard for rhetorical construction and may be counted on to take advantage of rhetorical opportunities. The next use of *literature* does not occur for another twenty lines. Does Wilde's practice of careful use of repetition result in any greater number of pronouns than might be expected in a text of this size?
2. *metrical movements of a prose.* The careful arrangements of phrases and clauses, by length, sound and construction, taught by the ancient rhetoricians, practiced notably by Cicero, and imitated by the Elizabethan Ciceronians, such as John Lyly, the Euphuist. (See ELIOT, No. 12, notes 4 and 6.)
3. *introduction of printing.* In Wilde's time, others (such as Henry JAMES) bewailed the effect on literature of increasing literacy and education among the lower orders. In our time, there has been much interest in the consequences of perceiving through a given medium or sense organ. (See MC CLUHAN, No. 77.) Wilde for some reason, however, believes that language intended for the ear is fundamentally better than writing.
4. *Mr. Pater.* Walter PATER (see No. 16). Wilde's judgment was the prevailing one in his time, but Pater's reputation has suffered since, partly perhaps because of the fact that he was so conscious an artificer of style, partly no doubt because of his subject matter, which can be described as aesthetic and miscellaneous. No doubt, too, he suffered from once having been an ideal. When ideals become assimilated, they are derided as obsolete or commonplace, as has been the fate of HEMINGWAY (No. 88).
5. *writing a definite mode of composition.* If we find nothing startling in this comment of Wilde's, we should realize how different are the views of his time and ours. What does the sentence mean?
6. *England's great poet.* Another instance of avoidance of repetition, not far from what H. W. Fowler calls "elegant variation," the attempt to decorate by finding ornamental synonyms (*Modern English Usage,* Oxford, 1926). Wilde avoids the repetition of *Homer, Greeks, Pater* and mentions MILTON only twice in four sentences covering 17 lines.

7. *return to the voice.* Both in modern linguistics and prosody, the oral aspect of language has been acquiring momentum. Today, prosody requires some knowledge of supra-segmental phonemes and cannot be responsibly taught without the use of linguistic knowledge. The events of the present day have certainly ratified part of Wilde's beliefs on this score.

PATER (No. 16, p. 67)

To Walter Pater, Sir Thomas Browne represented a stage of English prose when it was informal and unprofessional. The author of that time, like Montaigne earlier, "likes talking to himself; and when he writes . . . he does but take the 'friendly reader' into his confidence." Such writers, according to Pater, have many faults: unevenness, lack of design, caprice. But to compensate for this lack, they (Browne, for example) have sincerity and raciness, as shown in the following paragraph:

> The whole creation is a mystery and particularly that of man. At the blast of His mouth were the rest of the creatures made, and at His bare word they started out of nothing. But in the frame of man He played the sensible operator, and seemed not so much to create as to make him. When He had separated the materials of other creatures, there consequently resulted a form and soul: but having raised the walls of man, He was driven to a second and harder creation—of a substance like Himself, an incorruptible and immortal soul.

What Pater had described in this way was later categorized more formally by Morris W. Croll, who found that the informality of the prose of Browne was an aspect of the opposition to Ciceronian style later to be known as Senecan style. Of this there were supposed to be two types: the loose style and the curt style, the latter being what Browne practiced. Both had in common, however, a seeming negligence resulting from the way in which connectives were used, which distinguished them profoundly from the highly organized means of transition and connection favored by the Ciceronian stylists (see Croll, Bibliography No. 15).

1. *exact expression of his mind.* Croll notes that the Senecans hoped to portray thought more naturally than the highly formal Ciceronians had permitted or encouraged.

2. *Johnson.* Because JOHNSON had written a Life of Sir Thomas Browne and because both were partial to a Latinate diction, it was long believed that Johnson derived his style from his study of Browne. W. K. Wimsatt, however, shows that Johnson differs considerably from Browne, that their ideals were distinct and that the influence must have been minimal (see Wimsatt, Bibliography No. 41).

The following selection from Johnson's commentary on the style of Browne suggests that he was not an uncritical admirer of it:

> His exuberance of knowledge, and plenitude of ideas, sometimes obstruct the tendency of his reasoning and the clearness of his decisions: on whatever subject he employed his mind, there started up immediately so many images before him, that he lost one by grasping another. His memory supplied him with so many illustrations, parallel or dependent notions, that he was always starting into collateral considerations: but the spirit and vigour of his pursuit always gives delight; and the reader follows him, without reluctance, through his mazes, in themselves flowery and pleasing, and ending at the point originally in view.
>
> "To have great excellences and great faults, *magnae virtutes nec minora vitia,* is the poesy," says our author, "of the best natures." This poesy may be properly applied to the style of Browne; it is vigorous, but rugged; it is learned, but pedantick; it is deep, but obscure; it strikes, but does not please; it commands, but does not allure: his tropes are harsh and his combinations uncouth. He fell into an age in which our language began to lose the stability which it had obtained in the time of Elizabeth; and was considered by every writer as a subject on which he might try his plastick skill, by moulding it according to his own fancy. Milton, in consequence of this encroaching license, began to introduce the Latin idiom: and Browne, though he gave less disturbance to our structures in phraseology, yet poured in a multitude of exotic words; many, indeed, useful and significant, which, if rejected, must be supplied by circumlocution, such as *commensality* for the state of many living at the same table; but many superfluous, as a *paralogical* for an unreasonable doubt; and some so obscure, that they conceal his meaning rather than explain it, as *arthritical analogies,* for parts that serve some animals in the place of joints.
>
> His style is, indeed, a tissue of many languages; a mixture of heterogeneous words, brought together from distant regions, with terms originally appropriated to one art, and drawn by violence into the service of another. He must however be confessed to have augmented our philosophical diction: and in defence of his uncommon words and expressions, we must consider, that he had

> uncommon sentiments, and was not content to express in many words that idea for which any language could supply a single term.
>
> But his innovations are sometimes pleasing, and his temerities happy; he has many *verba ardentia,* forcible expressions, which he would never have found, but by venturing to the utmost verge of propriety, and flights which would never have been reached, but by one who had very little fear of the shame of falling. (*Works,* ed. Arthur Murphy [London, 1816], Vol. XII, pp. 302–304)

SAINTSBURY (No. 13) also mentions the possible influence of Browne.

3. *And all is so oddly mixed.* Here Pater has fallen into the loose mode of connection characteristic of Browne. The next sentence, which begins a paragraph, also shows this construction. Compare this tendency with that of WILDE, for example, and of Browne in the paragraphs quoted above and below.
4. *the age they lived in.* A twofold version of the Reflection Theory of style, wherein the writer's mind and personality are reflected in his style and the temper of the society is reflected in the individual. This second aspect presupposes the existence of a period style (see Introduction).
5. *formal kind of literature.* It is difficult to imagine a definition of "formal" which would exclude, as Pater seems to do, the following passages from Browne:

> What Song the Syrens sang, or what name Achilles assumed when he hid himself among women, though puzling Questions are not beyond all conjecture. What time the persons of these Ossuaries entred the famous Nations of the dead, and slept with Princes and Counsellours, might admit a wide solution. But who were the proprietaries of these bones, or what bodies these ashes made up, were a question above Antiquarism. Not to be resolved by man, nor easily perhaps by spirits, except we consult the Provinciall Guardians, or tutellary Observators. Had they made as good provision for their names, as they have done for their Reliques, they had not so grosly erred in the art of perpetuation. But to subsist in bones, and be but Pyramidally extant, is a fallacy in duration. Vain ashes, which in the oblivion of names, persons, times, and sexes, have found unto themselves a fruitless continuation, and only arise unto late posterity, as Emblemes of mortall vanities; Antidotes against pride, vain-glory, and madding vices. [*Urne Buriall*]

The contrasting prose of the following selection may be nearer to Pater's idea of Browne's typical prose:

> Sect. 5. There is I thinke no man that apprehends his owne miseries lesse than my selfe, and no man that so neerely apprehends anothers. I could lose an arme without a teare, and with a few

groans, mee thinkes, be quartered into pieces; yet I can weepe most seriously at a Play, and receive with a true passion, the counterfeit griefes of those knowne and professed impostours. It is a barbarous part of inhumanity to adde unto an afflicted parties misery, or endeavour to multiply in any man, a passion, whose single nature is already above his patience; this was the greatest affliction of Job, and those oblique expostulations of his friends a deeper injury than the downeright blowes of the Devill. It is not the teares of our owne eyes onely, but of our friends also, that doe exhaust the current of our sorrowes, which, falling into many streames, runnes more peaceably within its owne bankes, and is contented with a narrower channel. [*Religio Medici*]

RUSKIN (No. 17, p. 69)

Ruskin is in the Mandarin tradition, with his contemporaries WILDE and PATER. Like Pater, he wrote about aesthetic as well as literary matters, though his wider sympathies also made him a powerful critic of his society. His most characteristic writing is highly ornamental description, of which the following is a typical example:

> Let us, for a moment, try to . . . imagine the Mediterranean lying beneath us like an irregular lake, and all its ancient promontories sleeping in the sun: here and there an angry spot of thunder, a gray stain of storm, moving upon the burning field; and here and there a fixed wreath of white volcano smoke, surrounded by its circle of ashes; but for the most part a great peacefulness of light, Syria and Greece, Italy and Spain, laid like pieces of a golden pavement into the sea-blue, chased, as we stoop nearer to them, with bossy beaten work of mountain chains, and glowing softly with terraced gardens, and flowers heavy with frankincense, mixed among masses of laurel and orange, and plumy palm, that abate with their gray-green shadows the burning of the marble rocks, and of the ledges of porphyry sloping under lucent sand. Then let us pass farther towards the north, until we see the orient colors change gradually into a vast belt of rainy green, where the pastures of Switzerland, and poplar valleys of France, and dark forests of the Danube and Carpathians stretch from the mouths of the Loire to those of the Volga, seen through clefts in gray swirls of rain cloud and flaky veils of the mist of the brooks, spreading low along the pasture lands: and then, farther north still, to see the earth heave into mighty masses of leaden rock and heathy moor, bordering with a broad waste of gloomy purple that

> belt of field and wood, and splintering into irregular and grisly islands amidst the northern seas, beaten by storm, and chilled by ice drift, and tormented by furious pulses of contending tide, until the roots of the last forests fail from among the hill ravines, and the hunger of the north wind bites their peaks into barrenness; and, at last, the wall of ice, durable like iron, sets, deathlike, its white teeth against us out of the polar twilight. And, having once traversed in thought this gradation of the zoned iris of the earth in all its material vastness, let us go down nearer to it, and watch the parallel change in the belt of animal life: the multitudes of swift and brilliant creatures that glance in the air and sea, or tread the sands of the southern zone; striped zebras and spotted leopards, glistening serpents and birds arrayed in purple and scarlet. Let us contrast their delicacy and brilliancy of color, and swiftness of motion, with the frost-cramped strength, and shaggy covering, and dusky plumage of the northern tribes; contrast the Arabian horse with the Shetland, the tiger and leopard with the wolf and bear, the antelope with the elk, the bird of paradise with the osprey: and then, submissively acknowledging the great laws by which the earth and all that it bears are ruled throughout their being, let us not condemn, but rejoice in the expression of man of his own rest in the statutes of the lands that gave him birth. [*The Stones of Venice*]

1. *model of English.* Compare JOHNSON (No. 30) and the selection from the Introduction to the King James Version (No. 47) with the present selection and estimate whether Ruskin is more like the one or the other. Take note of what criteria favor one or the other.

2. *the Idler and the Rambler.* Periodicals written by Samuel Johnson and reprinted in book form.

3. *turns and returns.* It is interesting to speculate on Ruskin's intention in playing with this pair of words, the names of the two periodicals, and the verbals *iterated* and *reiterated.* Is there any possibility of its being exemplificatory? Does the rest of the sentence offer any help?

4. *paviour's.* If a swordsman cleaves a crest, what does a paviour do to a pile?

5. *Macaulay's.* Another bad notice for MACAULAY, whose prose is here compared to a Rorschach blot, though this was not then used for diagnostic psychiatry.

6. *two horizons.* The last sentence of the Ruskin selection is longer than any other in the passage. Is this a Johnsonianism, typical Ruskin prose, or an effect of punctuation?

ARNOLD (No. 18, p. 71)

In this influential essay, Arnold propounds his "touchstone" theory of poetry. A touchstone is a great line of poetry from one of the greatest poets (Homer, Dante, Shakespeare, MILTON). The reader or critic stores a collection of these in his mind and determines by comparison whether a poem under examination is of the highest quality. Arnold has a high opinion of Chaucer but does not rank him among the very greatest because he lacks "high seriousness."

1. *if we ask.* Asking a question is a standard rhetorical means of directing the reader's interest to the matter under discussion. Even if the reader becomes aware of the artificiality of the question-and-answer device, he nonetheless responds to its slight dramatic quality. Without the use of the device, the selection would open in a heavily declarative fashion: "The immense superiority of Chaucer's poetry over the romance-poetry. . . ." Even a writer as willing to be pompous as Matthew Arnold may feel that this opening requires too much of an effort from the reader.

The effort to involve the reader by making the first statement into a question is more likely to be effective if the writer assumes that the reader is as interested as he is. "If we ask ourselves . . ." is plausible and perhaps effective; "if I ask myself" would be absurdly ineffective. It would have the flavor of a soliloquy.

2. *romance-poetry.* Long narrative poems usually written by French writers of the late Middle Ages (e.g., Chrestien de Troyes).

3. *why it is . . . world.* This appositive both translates and emphasizes the dependent clause which precedes it. It is a perfect illustration of the difference between literal and figurative statement. The literal statement is more precise: it specifies the two terms of the comparison and the relationship between them. But it is also less vivid: the words "immense superiority" do not convey with real immediacy the nature of the difference between the two kinds of poetry. Arnold's decision to supplement the literal statement with the figurative apposition reveals his awareness of the need for emphasis. The figurative statement, with its image of a different world, summons up echoes from literature, mythology, folklore and proverbial expression (e.g., "O brave new world"), but it omits the one specific attribute, the superiority of Chaucer. Things in different worlds are not necessarily in a relation of higher and lower. Arnold has

overcome this difficulty awkwardly by adding the literal and the figurative together.
4. *style.* Note the alliteration in *superiority, substance, style.* Is this accidental? The antithesis between substance and style is made more evident by the alliteration and by the repetition of the modifying phrase, "of his poetry."
5. *poetry.* In this one sentence, the word *poetry* occurs four times, and the word *superiority* twice. Arnold might have arranged his sentence in such a way as to avoid this repetition, but he did not. Repetition is an ingredient of this passage and in fact, an oft-noted characteristic of Arnold's style.

The use of pronouns and other substitution words was probably a late development in Indo-European grammar. Essentially, if a thing has a name, that can be used whenever there is need to refer to it. The tendency to use pronouns and other substitution forms may have developed from an economy principle. It is obvious that personages with long names and titles are more conveniently referred to by a simple *he.* Pronouns, of course, do more than merely provide handles for reference: they supply relational data. Thus, *this, that, these, those* give the number and nearness to the speaker of the things referred to. Once the use of pronouns had become firmly established, the avoidance of repetition became a norm and deliberate repetition became a rhetorical device. It is only in relation to normal practice that stylistic deviation could take place. In modern English (from ca. 1550 to the present), the avoidance of repetition is a regular practice of writers to such an extent that any repetition not absolutely required (to prevent confusion) is interpreted as emphasis with a rhetorical intention. The number of figures which employ repetition of sounds, words, phrases, constructions and clauses is quite extensive and constitutes a substantial part of the classical rhetorical repertory.

Closely related to the avoidance of repetition is the practice that H. W. Fowler (in his *Modern English Usage*) has called "elegant variation." It consists, not of using substitution forms, but synonyms in order to avoid repeating a necessary but colorless term. Thus, sports journalists are required by the content to make frequent reference to the ball, the inning, the base, and other baseball items. Bored by this necessity and anxious to vivify his writing, the journalist may resort to such exotic variations as *pill, sphere, leather* for "ball," *chukker, period, stanza* for "inning," *sack, bag,* and other figurative alternatives for "base." The result may be confusing to one not blooded in the sport, as when the bowler delivers the pill to the batter who slams the leather through the pitcher's box. Fastidious newspapers, like the *New York Times,* discourage their reporters from practising elegant variation. A spartan and puritanical repetitiveness marks their sports pages.

Amateur fiction writers are also proverbial users of elegant variation. In dialogue, the tag "he said" must occur frequently. The novice often feels that it can be satisfactorily replaced by such variants as *spoke, uttered, stated, asserted, chuckled, snorted, laughed, stuttered* and the like. Writers sensitive to repetition avoid the problem by leaving out the tag whenever possible. Others, like Hemingway, seem to revel in the puritan joy of repeated *saids.*

Arnold's repetitions in this passage have two components. As noted above, the repetition of the phrase *of poetry* separates and emphasizes *substance* and *style.* Thus, one component is structural. The other is more elusive and may be characterized as a willingness to suffer the non-avoidance of repetition. Subjectively, it might be described as a carelessness about the reader's feelings, if it is correct to suppose that the reader responds to repetition as to stimulation. The reader is thus stimulated by Arnold's repetition to seek for rhetorical significance, but generally it has no significance. So the reader's response is dulled, a bad outcome for any writer.

6. *is given by.* An unusual expression here, meaning perhaps "results from."

7. *large, free, simple, clear yet kindly.* An interesting series in apparently normal order. (For a discussion of **seriation,** see GRAVES, No. 1, note 1.) If the series is in normal order the conjunction *yet* connects *kindly* with the preceding four adjectives. But the possibility exists that "clear yet kindly" is a unit, which would recast the series as an irregular four-unit asyndetic one. Normally, this ambiguity could be resolved by reference to the meaning of the items. In this case, that is not possible because of the abstract and vague quality of the terms used. The very number of terms used implies a certain impressionism in the concept.

8. *view of human life.* The interpretation of this phrase, together with its modifying adjectives, is crucial to an understanding of this paragraph. Arnold seems to be claiming that Chaucer is greater than the French romance-writers because his "substance" (subject-matter?) is better and that this substance derives from a viewpoint which may be more simply termed "humane." Perhaps to Arnold, Chaucer's view of human life was more modern, more consonant with his own view, less medieval than that of the romance-writers.

9. *command of it.* The construction after the dash consists of an apposition to "superiority in substance." Since Arnold has already said that Chaucer is superior to the romance-writers in the respect of "view of human life," he adds nothing substantive by saying that these latter are lacking in this. If A is superior to B in having C, it adds nothing to say that B is lacking in C. Yet this is what Arnold does, cloaking his pleonasm in a double negative ("unlike the total want"), a remote abstraction ("want of all . . . command"), and a vague reference ("it").

10. *human point of view.* Arnold's struggle to make precise the grounds of

his preference for Chaucer and his attribution of superiority of substance to him are evidenced by the restatement, in this sentence, of the content of the previous sentence. The adjective *central,* the adverb *truly* demand from the reader an adherence to Arnold's views which he has only been able to claim, not to compel. The use of such peremptory terms frequently betrays uncertainty in the writer.

11. '. . . *good sense.*' For support, Arnold calls upon another great poet and critic, who also felt on reading Chaucer that Chaucer was of a different order from his own contemporaries. In his Preface to the *Fables* (1700), Dryden eulogizes Chaucer in the terms quoted by Arnold.

12. *large, free, sound.* The first two of this series of three adjectives are identical with the first two of the longer series used above. The third ("sound") is new. Why did Arnold begin as before and change at this point, leaving out the rest of his modifiers? The meaning of *sound*—"without defect as to truth, substantial"—is crucial to the answer. A sound representation has truth and substance. In other words, Chaucer's poetry has truth of substance, because it has truth of substance, in effect, because Arnold approves of it.

13. *truth of substance.* The rhetorical repetition after the semicolon is intended to conclude on a note of triumphant proof, despite the tautology of the argument. It should be noted that Arnold is not trying to obfuscate the reader. He is dealing with one of the most difficult problems in criticism: demonstrating that one literary artifact is greater in value than another. He is himself a victim of the problem and of his own argument.

14. *style and manner.* Like the other categories used by Arnold in his criticism, this one is not very precisely delimited except by contrast with substance. Arnold says "style" *and* "manner," though he does not intend to refer to two separate entities. This pleonastic doublet evidences only, it seems probable, the writer's uncertainty about the nature of the entity style.

15. *divine.* The purpose of this adjective is not descriptive but impressionistic. It signifies not a similarity of Chaucer's diction to other things divine but rather the height of Arnold's enthusiasm. The purpose of repeating the modifier may be to show that "liquidness of diction" and "fluidity of movement" are in some sense synonymous.

16. *diction. Diction* today means choice of word. *Good* diction is a choice of word characterized by precision. Earlier, the term included, especially in discussions of poetry, a reference to the meter of the line, which is of course determined largely by the choice of word.

Diction may also be used technically to specify a predominant characteristic or ingredient of the vocabulary, as "Latinate diction." For such a purpose, however, the word *vocabulary* is now used, the vocabulary being the total lexi-

con of a writer in terms of its components, whereas his diction is the choices he makes on particular occasions. Shorn of its modifiers, Arnold's sentence implies his high approval of Chaucer's choice of words, and perhaps also his meter.
17. *temperately.* The sentence is inverted for emphasis. A sentence of this type is often called "periodic." The inversion permits the writer to place the object or complement in initial position, followed by whatever dependent or qualifying clauses are necessary and ending with the verb. The normally ordered sentence is much less emphatic, if only because the reader is trained to respond to inversion. It would have been much less effective to have said: "It is difficult to speak temperately of his style and manner. . . ." The inversion also permits the announcement of the subject at the beginning of the paragraph. (See MACAULAY, No. 22, note 27 on **inversion.**)

The expression "it is difficult to speak temperately" is an example of **litotes,** or understatement. Instead of saying, "Of his style and manner, it is easy to speak enthusiastically," Arnold prefers to imply more by using the negative form. *Enthusiastically* is definite and specific, but the opposite of *temperately* is less clear-cut and therefore more vaguely impressive. It may be *intemperately, passionately, fanatically* or even more immoderate forms. Litotes expresses a contained or repressed excitement. This particular example of it may possibly not be anything more than a habit or mannerism.
18. *rapture.* A reference to the difficulty of speaking "temperately" (see preceding note).
19. *'gold dewdrops of speech.'* Quoted from John Lydgate, *The Life of Our Lady* (ll. 1401–11). The passage reads:

> . . . and eke my master Chaucer . . .
>
> That made first to distill and rain
> The gold dew drops of speech and eloquence
> Into our tongue through his excellence.

20. *Dryden.* In the Preface to the *Fables* (1700), DRYDEN says: "He [Boccaccio] and Chaucer, among other things had this in common, that they refined their mother-tongues; but with this difference, that Dante had begun to file their language . . . Chaucer . . . first adorned and amplified our barren tongue from the Provençal, which was then the most polished of all the modern languages."

In the Preface to his *Dictionary* (1755), JOHNSON quarrels with Dryden's view in the following terms:

> The history of our language is now brought to the point at which the history of our poetry is generally supposed to commence, the time of the illustrious Geoffry Chaucer, who may perhaps, with

> great justice, be styled the first of our versifiers who wrote poetically. He does not however appear to have deserved all the praise which he has received, or all the censure that he has suffered. Dryden, who mistakes genius for learning, and, in confidence of his abilities, ventured to write of what he had not examined, ascribes to Chaucer the first refinement of our numbers, the first production of easy and natural rhythms, and the improvement of our language, by words borrowed from the more polished languages of the continent. Skinner contrarily blames him in harsh terms for having vitiated his native speech by whole cartloads of foreign words. But he that reads the works of Gower will find smooth numbers and easy rhymes, of which Chaucer is supposed to have been the inventor, and the French words, whether good or bad, of which Chaucer is charged as the importer. Some innovations he might probably make, like others, in the infancy of our poetry, which the paucity of books does not allow us to discover with particular exactness; but the works of Gower and Lydgate sufficiently evince that his diction was in general like that of his contemporaries: and some improvements he undoubtedly made by the various dispositions of his rhymes, and by the mixture of different numbers, in which he seems to have been happy and judicious.

Although Dryden called Chaucer "the father of English poetry," he conceded that "the verse of Chaucer . . . is not harmonious to us. . . . They who lived with him, and some time after him, thought it musical; and it continues so even in our judgment, if compared to the numbers of Lydgate and Gower his contemporaries. There is the rude sweetness of a Scotch tune in it, which is natural and pleasing, though not perfect."

21. *numbers.* Metrical harmony, scansion. Dryden and his contemporaries found the verse of Chaucer defective because they no longer pronounced the final *e* at the end of lines, which made most lines too short by one syllable.

22. *rhymes.* "Smooth numbers" refers to regular iambic pentameter couplets; "easy rhymes" are full or perfect rhymes, in which the rhyme-syllables are identical.

23. *father . . .* An expansion of Dryden's phrase, quoted above.

24. *"well of English undefiled."* Edmund Spenser, in *The Faerie Queene,* IV, ii, 32: "Dan Chaucer, well of English undefiled,/On Fame's eternal beadroll worthy to be filed."

25. *lovely charm.* A variant of the *liquid/fluid* attribute and another instance of Arnold's tendency to reiteration.

26. *tradition.* The logical structure of this sentence is that Chaucer is the father of English poetry "because he founds a tradition," a tautology or circular argument only slightly disguised by the intervening construction "makes

an epoch." In this sentence the three elements (Chaucer as father of English poetry, as well of English, and as founder of a tradition) are actually parallel items. Arnold attempts to give to his argument a semblance of logical structure by subordinating one predication to another. The weakness of the argument is revealed by the fact that the sentence is as plausible if the evidence is made the conclusion and vice versa: "Chaucer makes an epoch and founds a tradition because by the lovely charm of his diction, the lovely charm of his movement, he is the father of our splendid English poetry, our 'well of English undefiled.'" To be sure, rhetorically this version may not be as effective as the other.

27. *virtue.* Strength, power.

These two paragraphs well illustrate the rhetorical effectiveness of relentless repetition and assertion. After submitting to the reiteration of *liquid, fluid, divine, lovely charm, diction* and *movement,* the reader is induced to believe in the reality of the entities that Arnold speaks about. Both propaganda and advertising operate on the same principle.

Though Arnold's manner of proceeding was effectual in persuading his readers, it nonetheless was not found wholly admirable by all critics. Lewis E. Gates, in the Introduction to a book of selections from Arnold's prose (New York, 1897), calls his most characteristic style "colloquial in its rhythms and idioms." Such a description must be taken at a heavy discount, for it is the favorite way to speak of styles one approves of. (See SAINTSBURY, note 21.) Even Ruskin has been credited with this particular effect. Gates is more informative, however, and notes Arnold's penchant for repetition:

> Often Arnold ends a sentence and begins the next with the same word or phrase; this trick is better suited to talk than to formal discourse. . . . Arnold is never afraid of repeating a word or a phrase, hardly enough afraid of this. . . . At times, his repetitions seem due to his attempt to write down to his public; he will not confuse them by making them grasp the same idea twice through two different forms of speech. Often his repetitions come palpably from sheer fondness for his own happy phraseology. . . . indeed iteration and reiteration of single phrases or forms of words is a mannerism with Arnold, and at times proves one of his most effective means both for stamping his own ideas on the mind of the public and for ridiculing his opponents.

Elsewhere, he partly retracts the imputation of Colloquialism: "In the choice of words, however, Arnold is not noticeably colloquial. . . . His style, though idiomatic, stops short of the vocabulary of every day. . . . Certain words are favorites with him, and moreover, as is so often the case with the literary temperament, these words reveal some of his special preoccupations. Such words are *lucidity, urbanity, amenity, fluid* (as an epithet for style), *vital, puissant. . . .**

Propositional Reduction

¶ 1. Chaucer's poetry is superior to romance poetry both in content and style.
2. Chaucer's superiority of content over the romance poets results from his view of life.
3. Unlike the romance poets, Chaucer is able to see the world from a human point of view.
4. Chaucer's view of life is illustrated by the Prologue to *The Canterbury Tales.*
5. Dryden's comment about Chaucer is correct: "It is sufficient to say, according to the proverb, that *here is God's plenty.*"
6. Dryden's comment about Chaucer is correct: "He is a perpetual fountain of good sense."
7. Chaucer's poetry is true if poetry achieves truth by its representation of life.

¶ 8. The diction and meter of Chaucer's poetry are superior to the romance poets.
9. Chaucer's qualities justify the praise that his successors have given him.
10. Johnson is incorrect when he says that Dryden is incorrect in crediting Chaucer with first improving the scansion of English poetry and when he says that Gower also used good meter and rhymes.
11. Improvement of scansion is more than regular meter and rhymes.
12. Versifiers may produce regular meter and rhymes without writing poetry.
13. Chaucer's diction and meter originated the tradition of English poetry.
14. Chaucer's diction and meter are traceable in the poems of Spenser, Shakespeare, Milton, and Keats.
15. Chaucer's diction and meter impress all readers.[?]

Logical Diagram

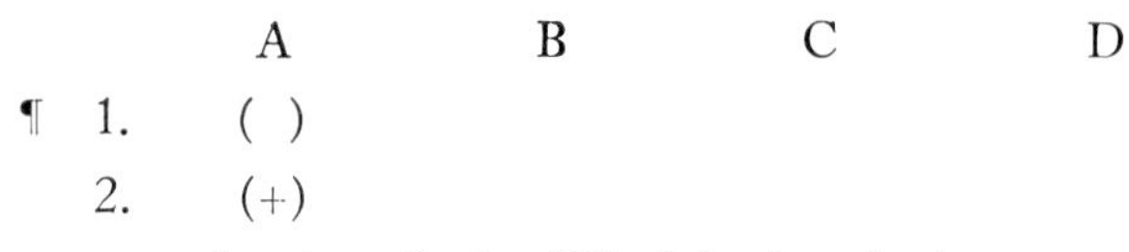

	A	B	C	D
¶ 1.	( )			
2.	(+)			

* These passages are taken from Section VII of the Introduction, pages lix-lxxvi.

3.		(=)		
4.			(×)	
5.	(+)			
6.	(+)			
7.				(:)
¶ 8.	( )			
9.	(+)			
10.	(−)			
11.		(=)		
12.			(×)	
13.	(−)			
14.	(+)			
15.				(:)

TROLLOPE (No. 19, p. 73)

Trollope's *Autobiography* is a mine of information for anyone interested in an unsentimental account of a writer's life. After reading how he rose at 5:30 a.m. every day to write for three hours before going to his work at the post office, his watch on the table, his quota one thousand words per hour, it is difficult to think of a writer as needing the goad of inspiration. Where the image of the inspired writer arose in modern times, one cannot be sure—doubtless from the Romantics, perhaps Byron or Coleridge. Trollope turned out the equivalent of ten printed pages every morning on his schedule, or three novels of three volumes each every ten months. Much of the credit he gave to his groom, whose duty it was to bring him coffee and wake him and who never failed at his duty. Since Trollope, writers have talked honestly about their professional habits and their habits have been remarkably alike: work in the morning, work every day (see the *Paris Review* interviews: Bibliography, Nos. 2 and 12). Trollope was able to write at this pace because he had trained himself to write without nibbling at the pen or gazing at the wall. Like the other descendants of the novelist Stendhal, whose main quest was for clarity and who said he read French law before beginning to write, he is a Plain Stylist, a Puritan. In the selection, he defends his practise of rapid composition.

1. *good and lucid style.* Trollope equates good style with writing that anyone may understand. This is the halmark of the Plain Stylist. But note the dash, and the parenthetical "in other words" and "I may say." This should not be considered the result of carelessness because Trollope reread everything several times, as he notes below. If he left this in, it was because the tentative, fumbling quality of the parentheses either achieved an effect he wanted or because it was clearer than any more compressed formulation.
2. *ear of the telegraphist.* The series of similes in this sentence is not merely ornamental figuration. The activities listed had a conceptual similarity to the process Trollope is describing. Writing, that is, must be second nature, like musical performance, public speaking, type setting, or interpreting Morse code. Are these four illustrations equally apt? Are they parallel? Would any single one have been preferable, if more dramatically handled? Is this an instance of Trollope's being seduced away from his ideals of plainness?
3. *smells of oil.* An old phrase, referring to oil used in lamps, presumably because scholars (not "natural" writers) were more likely to write at night.
4. *Rapid writing . . . commenced.* In what sense is Trollope using *ear?* Is syntactical accuracy more likely in writing or in speech? What is the remedy for the inaccuracy of rapid writing?
5. *plural tendencies.* He is referring to disagreement in number such as is likely in the following construction: "A total of fifteen cases *were* found" (instead of *was*).
6. *Tautologies.* Repetition as an error due to inattention rather than as a means of emphasis. The term is used loosely to include repetition of senses ("The modern world of today") and of words, either in the same or different senses ("a good example, for example").
7. *long sentences of Gibbon.* The average sentence-length for Gibbon's *Decline* is 38 words; the average for all of Macaulay's prose is 24 words per sentence (see Milic, Bibliography No. 49, p. 247). For MACAULAY, see below (No. 22). The following example of Gibbon's prose is the last paragraph of the famous fifteenth chapter of the *Decline and Fall of the Roman Empire:*

> But how shall we excuse the supine inattention of the Pagan and philosophic world to those evidences which were presented by the hand of Omnipotence, not to their reason, but to their senses? During the age of Christ, of his apostles, and of their first disciples, the doctrine which they preached was confirmed by innumerable prodigies. The lame walked, the blind saw, the sick were healed, the dead were raised, dæmons were expelled, and the laws of Nature were frequently suspended for the benefit of the church. But the sages of Greece and Rome turned aside from the awful spectacle, and, pursuing the ordinary occupations of life

> and study, appeared unconscious of any alterations in the moral or physical government of the world. Under the reign of Tiberius, the whole earth, or at least a celebrated province of the Roman empire, was involved in a præternatural darkness of three hours. Even this miraculous event, which ought to have excited the wonder, the curiosity, and the devotion of mankind, passed without notice in an age of science and history. It happened during the lifetime of Seneca and the elder Pliny, who must have experienced the immediate effects, or received the earliest intelligence, of the prodigy. Each of these philosophers, in a laborious work, has recorded all the great phenomena of Nature, earthquakes, meteors, comets, and eclipses, which his indefatigable curiosity could collect. Both the one and the other have omitted to mention the greatest phenomenon to which the mortal eye has been witness since the creation of the globe. A distinct chapter of Pliny is designed for eclipses of an extraordinary nature and unusual duration; but he contents himself with describing the singular defect of light which followed the murder of Cæsar, when, during the greatest part of the year, the orb of the sun appeared pale and without splendour. This season of obscurity, which cannot surely be compared with the præternatural darkness of the Passion, had been already celebrated by most of the poets and historians of that memorable age.

The average sentence-length is probably consistent with the quoted average. How does it compare with Macaulay's? With Trollope's?

8. *multiplicity of divisions.* Short sentences or frequent separable clauses.

BAGEHOT (No. 21, p. 79)

Few today are aware that the style of MACAULAY, throughout the nineteenth century and well into the twentieth, was the kind of wonder that Hemingway's became after the First World War. As such it excited a great deal of comment, much of which was disapproving (see HEMINGWAY, No. 88, notes). Bagehot here takes up an issue of considerable interest: the impression of dishonesty and insincerity conveyed by Macaulay's writing. Since much of the criticism implies that what Macaulay says is untrue, one is tempted to conclude that readers have compared his words with the reality and found they did not match. But in fact, this is not the case. Readers form the same impression of Macaulay's falseness whether they know the facts or not and even when what he asserts is undoubtedly true. The inescapable conclusion is that Macaulay's lack of honesty is—in the broadest sense—a stylistic feature. As Bagehot suggests, the reader feels that reality cannot be as simple or as clear-cut as Macaulay makes it; he must therefore be deceiving us.

1. *likely to deny.* The first three clauses of this paragraph each have inverted structure: the first sentence has the direct object first; the second sentence has a prepositional phrase, modifying the predicate noun, in initial position; the second clause begins with the object of the infinitive which ends the sentence.
2. *Yet it has a defect.* This interspersing of short sentences after long ones is one of Macaulay's most characteristic maneuvers. Is this imitation or parody of Macaulay, or influence by Macaulay?
3. *nothing is doubtful.* Here the effect mentioned in the previous note is achieved on a greater scale. Four successive clauses, which are almost synonyms of each other, sound like so many blows of a fist on a table to emphasize the message. This may well be an unconscious habit of Bagehot's.
4. *uncommon phenomenon.* Note this appositive, which repeats the nominal cluster that immediately precedes it. Bagehot seems to be devoted to this construction.
5. *No one can tell . . . them.* Observe the antithetic repetition in the two sets of noun clauses which serve as objects to the verb *tell.* What possible reason distracted Bagehot from saying plainly, "No one can tell where they lie or what they contain"?
6. *vestige of vestiges.* Bagehot has apparently been smitten by the effect of this combination. See also "fragment of fragments," "little of that little."
7. *witness of their occurrence.* This phrase is in apposition to "trace of themselves" just before. It is another example of a habit of Bagehot's of antiphonal repetition. See also "confusion of life, tumult of change" below and other examples in paragraph two.
8. *very confused materials.* A sentence with complicated architecture, which may be schematized thus:

> It would have been a relief to the readers of Macaulay if he had shown a little the outside of uncertainties, which there must be—the gradations of doubt, which there ought to be—the singular accumulation of difficulties, which must beset the extraction of a very easy narrative from very confused materials.

Parallels one and two are truly antithetic and match very exactly in form. The third branch is more distant and serves to round out the paragraph. Bagehot contrasts the uncertainties which must exist as part of the events with doubt which ought to be in the chronicler. Does the structure of the sentence serve to convey this distinction?
9. *flour perfect.* An attempt to maintain the consistency of the image of the mill. One may guess that the mill could be set to grind coarse or fine flour. Or

that the reference is to the grain (the input) rather than the output. The appositive after the dash tries to clarify this. What is the use of an image which must be explained in literal terms?

10. *A man like Macaulay . . . sensation.* After the long-winded explanation of the uncertainty of events, Bagehot winds up with a dramatic series of declarative clauses of almost identical construction.

MACAULAY (No. 22, p. 81)

This selection is taken from a long essay which was nominally a review of J. W. Croker's five-volume edition of James Boswell's *Life of Samuel Johnson* and which appeared in the *Edinburgh Review* in September 1831. Like most review-articles of the time, this one was a treatise on the subject of the book rather than a review of the book itself.

1. *Burke.* Edmund Burke, orator and statesman, friend of Dr. Johnson, was reputed to have said that Boswell's *Life* would do more for Johnson's reputation than all of Johnson's own books together.

2. *justly observed.* A device which performs two functions: it appeals to an external authority upon which great prestige is thereby conferred; it allies the writer with that prestige by his approval of the authority ("justly"). Clearly, Macaulay would not have cited authorities of whom he disapproved.

This remark may be related to Macaulay's best-known rhetorical device which consisted of adding the clause "as every schoolboy knows" to assertions of which he was not certain or which he felt might be doubted.

3. *books.* The plural is hardly justified here, for Johnson appears, apart from the *Life,* only in Boswell's earlier *Journal of a Voyage to the Hebrides,* which served as a trial balloon for the greater work. The plural form is needed, however, to contrast with Johnson's books ("his own"), which is the first of a set of antitheses that dominate the structure of this selection.

4. *manner.* In this sentence, three antitheses are set in motion: *conversation/writing, quite equal/far superior, matter/manner.*

5. *clothed.* An unconscious reference to the notion of style as "the dress of thoughts," as the Earl of Chesterfield put it. Benedetto Croce calls this the theory of "ornate form." (*Aesthetics,* 1905.)

6. *his wit and his sense.* A pleonastic doublet, perhaps intended to balance "forcible and natural."

7. *forcible.* The modern term is *forceful.*

8. *systematically vicious.* "Vicious" is weaker in Macaulay than it would be in a modern writer, in whose hands the term would have a moral implication. Macaulay means *bad* or *defective,* but according to a system whose principles he will set forth below.
9. *in a language . . . thinks.* The repetition of a word or construction at the beginning of parallel phrases or clauses is called **anaphora.** The three phrases which begin with "in a language" are all in apposition with "in a learned language" and are intended negatively to explain it. The purpose is, however, not informative but polemical, for the phrase *learned language* is clear enough. By adding emphasis with three appositive anaphoric parallel clauses, Macaulay tries to insure that the reader will follow his intention of divorcing Johnson's written style from all normal human activity. Note within the second segment the climax achieved by the polysyndetic triplet ("quarrels . . . drives bargains . . . makes love").
10. *clear.* Having accumulated all the emphasis at his command, Macaulay feels justified in believing that his point has been proved. The initial "it is clear," however, is yet another claim made to buttress the earlier one.
11. *tongue.* If Johnson thinks in language, the expressions should first reach his mind, not his tongue. Macaulay uses *tongue* here because of its added concreteness.
12. *simple, energetic, and picturesque.* Is this a generalization based on evidence or merely an assertion framed to support Macaulay's argument here?
13. *for publication.* Although Johnson's conversation is what is contrasted with his writing, Macaulay also intends to draw on Johnson's letters. Therefore, he must distinguish between writing letters and writing "for publication."
14. *Johnsonese.* The *-ese* ending is derogatory when applied to the name of an author accused of writing in a language of his own creation (cf. *Carlylese, Hemingwayese;* vs. *Miltonic, Shakespearean*). So far this language has not been defined, except as a learned language and negatively. The adding of a derogatory label at this point guarantees that the reader will side with Johnson's detractors, who include Macaulay.
15. *Hebrides.* Properly titled, *A Journey to the Western Islands of Scotland* (1775).
16. *letters.* In a letter dated 15/21 September 1773, sent from "Dunvegan in Skye" to Mrs. Thrale in Southwark, Johnson wrote what Macaulay cites, except that Johnson had written "bed in which." The event took place in an inn at Glenelg on September 1 of that year.

Boswell, in his account of the trip which he published a decade after Johnson's book in the year after Johnson's death, put it this way: ". . . from a wretched bed started a fellow from his sleep like Edgar in *King Lear:* 'Poor Tom's a-cold'."

17. *putrefaction.* The passage in Boswell's *Life* from which this is taken shows that Johnson was aware of this tendency and that he was practising a form of self-parody in making such "translations." Macaulay's point must be taken as deliberately misleading in its suggestion that Johnson was incapable of regularly using the language of every day. The passage follows:

> He seemed to take pleasure in speaking in his own style; for when he had carelessly missed it, he would repeat the thought translated into it. Talking of the Comedy of 'The Rehearsal,' he said, 'It has not wit enough to keep it sweet.' This was easy—he therefore caught himself, and pronounced a more rounded sentence; 'It has not vitality enough to preserve it from putrefaction.' (entry date June 1784).

18. *Mannerism.* Macaulay here uses *mannerism* and *manner* as if they were synonymous. "Mannerism" means the habitual use of some pronounced deviation from the norm. "Manner" is any way of doing things. A mannerism may be vicious or agreeable but it can hardly be natural. Macaulay sets up this false dichotomy in order to excuse writers he approves of (Milton and Burke) and to condemn Johnson.

19. *readers.* An indirect way of excepting these writers from the disapproval of the previous sentence. Note that nothing is said to show that Milton's and Burke's mannerism is different from Johnson's. The difference is merely implied here, asserted later.

20. *offensive.* The three parts of this parallel triplet define Macaulay's notion of Johnson's mannerism or style. What kind of evidence is available for any of the three contentions it makes? By what process did Macaulay arrive at this formulation?

21. *such.* Does this pronoun refer to "offensive," to the three *which*-clauses, to any one of them, or to some combination of adjective and clause? Note the potential for ambiguity in the word *such.*

22. *point them out.* Why does Macaulay introduce his description of Johnson's style (or rather its "characteristic faults") by a denial of the need to do so? This traditional mode of emphasis in classical rhetoric is called **paraleipsis** or **praeteritio.** The most famous example in English is in Antony's speech to the crowd (*Julius Caesar,* III, ii, 134ff.), in which he refers to Caesar's will, and says: " 'Tis good you know not that you are his heirs;/For if you should, O, what would come of it?" Cicero, in his attack on Catiline in the Senate, makes use of the same device: "I pass over in silence the ruin of your fortune which will take place on the next Ides. . . ." (First Oration, vi, 14). Generally,

paraleipsis is a means of making an attack while seeming not to and preserving for the attacker an appearance of objectivity. Macaulay obviously dislikes Johnson's style but seems to believe that his attack will be more effective if it is indirect.

Moreover, like the earlier reference to "Mr. Burke," the mention here of the public ("all our readers") is an appeal to authority. Although Macaulay's claim—that what he proposes as Johnson's faults is well-known—may be true, his rhetorical procedure is nonetheless intended to lead the reader into agreement with him rather than into a dispassionate examination of the facts.

23. *king's English.* Macaulay is here repeating the most common accusation against Johnson: that he was addicted to long, polysyllabic words. Note that he emphasizes the accusation by making it twice, saying that Johnson "made less use" of the short Anglo-Saxon words and "felt a vicious partiality" for long Graeco-Latin borrowings. Either would have been sufficient. Actually, according to later and closer students of Johnson's style, his diction is not the distinguishing mark of his style (see SAINTSBURY, No. 13, above). W. K. Wimsatt, in two books (*The Prose Style of Samuel Johnson* and *Philosophic Words* [New Haven, 1941 and 1948]), gives a detailed account of Johnson's vocabulary and of his rhetorical and syntactic practice. Wimsatt agrees with Saintsbury that the distinguishing mark of Johnson's style is the ordering of his sentences: the balance, the parallelism, the antithesis, rather than his choice of word. Macaulay notices these things too but accords them only secondary importance.

24. *epithets.* This refers to Johnson's supposed use of adjectives before the noun, which Macaulay finds verbose.

25. *exquisite.* A dandy of the early nineteenth century whose chest was made more prominent by the insertion and application of starched cloth under and over his shirt.

26. *expressed.* Even Wimsatt admits that Johnson carried this tendency on occasion to excessive lengths: ". . . we may call this a fault of *style* . . . because it arises from a habit of meaning. It may be called an exploitation of medium. It is cultivating expressive forms for their own sake." (See Wimsatt, Bibliography. No. 41, p. 49).

27. *inversions.* An **inversion** is any disturbance of the regular order of constructions in an English sentence, whose usual pattern places the subject first, the verb second, and objects and complements last. The most typical form of inversion puts the direct object or complement first, followed by the subject and verb. Thus, "I have read this book," when inverted, becomes "This book I have read." Other forms of inversion are possible, but sometimes adjustments of the syntax are required to preserve the idiom of English. Like all devices,

this one loses force if it is practiced often. Johnson's "harsh" inversions, it seems probable, are only so because they are too frequent or because they are Johnson's. (For examples of Johnson's inversions, see JOHNSON, No. 30 and for a comment on inversion, see CAMPBELL, No. 32.)

28. *all these peculiarities.* An instance of **epanalepsis,** in which the long subject consisting of four more or less parallel constructions, each introduced by *his* followed by an adjective and a noun, each representing one of the "characteristic faults" of Johnson's style

(his constant practice
his antithetical forms
his big words
his harsh inversions)

is so far from the verb and so scattered geographically that a summarizing subject ("all these peculiarities") is introduced to serve as the immediate subject of the verb. Technically, this new subject is in apposition to the four-part one but the net effect is of **anacoluthon,** a device in which a certain syntactic intention is abandoned in mid-sentence in favor of a new one. Among the ancients, this was supposed to reflect emotion. Here in Macaulay's hands it may show impatience, a desire to abandon the inordinate complexity that the necessity to describe Johnson's style has led him into, and an anxiety to finish the discussion abruptly. This is very effectively done in that Macaulay manages to imply that Johnson is to blame for the very awkwardness of Macaulay's own style in this long sentence and in that his epanaleptic turn at the end fits the abruptness and apparent candor of the last clause. Macaulay seems to lose patience with the whole question, becomes as sick of it as he says the public has become. Of course, it must be remembered that Macaulay attributes to the public his own beliefs and that the whole of this passage is very deliberately and subtly managed. Macaulay's emotions have not really gotten out of hand.

Macaulay's style has often been criticized as insincere and glib. (see BAGEHOT, No. 21.) But it has also been praised for its vividness and ease. A recent critic, G. S. Fraser (see Bibliography, No. 43), believes that it has had much influence on the prose of modern historians and essayists, even on such a writer as Bertrand RUSSELL (see No. 2), in his nontechnical works. Fraser describes the style as dependent "on point, balance, an abundance of not too recondite literary and historical allusion, periodic order, sharp antithesis. . . ." In his opinion, it is the typical style of the *Edinburgh Review,* as exemplified by Sidney SMITH (see No. 27), but without Smith's good humor, "handled with a new breadth, a new, sometimes harsh vividness, perhaps a new coarseness . . .

never slovenly or straggly . . . no obscurities and no fine shades." Though it gives the impression of haste and rush, it is never too difficult for even the simple reader. "In its use of diverse exemplification and concealed repetition—many concrete instances of even the most obvious generalisation, and the generalisation itself clothed in a succession of different phrases—it is very much the style of an orator. It hammers its points home, it illustrates them to a degree . . . almost of tedium . . . it perhaps rises too often, to a peroration. . . ." (Fraser, pp. 9–11.)

Like many another writer whose style is dominated by a rhetorical device (see JOHNSON, notes), Macaulay was sometimes prevented from telling the plain truth by the necessity of organizing meaning into forms which not only had no necessary relation to the content but were actively opposed to it. As Fraser notes, on Macaulay's summary of Boswell,* Macaulay must have known that he was exaggerating and distorting the psychological facts but "the rhetorical machine carried him away, he could not resist a coarsely effective antithesis." (p. 14)

Macaulay's lack of honesty is a recurrent accusation among all his critics. But this criticism is not the result of comparing his statements with reality and finding that the words did not match the things. Rather it is the consequence of a discomfort arising from his rhetoric, in which everything is clearer, simpler and better organized than it could ever possibly be in the real world.

Some of this quality is present in the present selection. Fraser's analysis and Matthew Arnold's repeated attacks on Macaulay's rhetoric (conveniently summarized by Fraser) leave unsettled the question whether Macaulay knew one truth and expressed another as a result of the rhetorical dominance of his style or whether the truth he knew was the one that he expressed because he perceived it by means of his rhetoric. In other words, was his rhetoric merely a device or the expression of a way of perceiving?

Propositional Reduction of Paragraphs 2 and 3

¶ 1. Natural mannerism is acceptable.
2. The mannerism of Milton or Burke is acceptable.
3. Unsuitable, deliberate or strained mannerism is offensive.
4. The mannerism of Johnson is offensive.

¶ 5. Johnson's style is faulty.
6. Johnson's vocabulary contains more Greek and Latin borrowings than is usual.
7. Johnson's style contains these peculiarities: padding, false antithesis, use of big words, and inversion.

* "If he had not been a great fool, he would never have been a great writer. Without all the qualities which made him the jest and torment of those among whom he lived,

Logical Diagram

	A	B	C	D
¶ 1.	( )			
2.			(×)	
3.	(–)			
4.				(:)
¶ 5.	( )			
6.			(×)	
7.			(+)	

CARLYLE (No. 23, p. 83)

The subject of Carlyle's writing in the selection, Johann Paul Friedrich Richter (1763–1825), adopted the French pseudonym "Jean-Paul" out of admiration for Rousseau. As a writer, Richter is a Romantic but his work escapes classification and calls forth from critics the most varied descriptions: irregular, imaginative, digressive, chaotic, incoherent, grotesque, extravagant, baroque. Richter supposedly imitated Laurence Sterne; Thoreau thought that Carlyle was himself impelled to follow Richter in his own highly individual style. This is seen at its most typical in *Sartor Resartus* (1836):

> 'Men are properly said to be clothed with Authority, clothed with Beauty, with Curses, and the like. Nay, if you consider it, what is Man himself, and his whole terrestrial Life, but an Emblem; a Clothing or visible Garment for that divine ME of his, cast hither, like a light-particle, down from Heaven? Thus is he said also to be clothed with a Body.
>
> 'Language is called the Garment of Thought: however, it should rather be, Language is the Flesh-Garment, the Body, of Thought. I said that imagination wove this Flesh-Garment; and does not she? Metaphors are her stuff: examine Language; what, if you except some few primitive elements (of natural sound), what is it all but Metaphors, recognised as such, or no longer recognised; still fluid and florid, or now solid-grown and colourless? If those same primitive elements are the osseous fixtures in the Flesh-Garment, Language,—then are Metaphors its muscles and tissues and living integuments. An unmetaphorical style you

without the officiousness, the inquisitiveness, the effrontery, the toad-eating, the insensitivity to all reproof, he would never have produced so excellent a book."

shall in vain seek for: is it not your very *Attention* a *Stretching-to?* The difference lies here: some styles are lean, adust, wiry, the muscle itself seems osseous; some are even quite pallid, hunger-bitten and dead-looking; while others again glow in the flush of health and vigorous self-growth, sometimes (as in my own case) not without an apoplectic tendency. Moreover, there are sham Metaphors, which overhanging that same Thought's-Body (best naked), and deceptively bedizening, or bolstering it out, may be called its false stuffings, superfluous show-cloaks (*Putz-Mäntel*), and tawdry woollen rags: whereof he that runs and reads may gather whole hampers,—and burn them.'

Than which paragraph on Metaphors did the reader ever chance to see a more surprisingly metaphorical? However, that is not our chief grievance; the Professor continues:

'Why multiply instances? It is written, the Heavens and the Earth shall fade away like a Vesture; which indeed they are: the Time-vesture of the Eternal. Whatsoever sensibly exists, whatsoever represents Spirit to Spirit, is properly a Clothing, a suit of Raiment, put on for a season, and to be laid off. Thus in this one pregnant subject of CLOTHES, rightly understood, is included all that men have thought, dreamed, done, and been: the whole External Universe and what it holds is but Clothing, and the essence of all Science lies in the PHILOSOPHY OF CLOTHES.'

Sutherland (Bibliography No. 22) says that Carlyle's prose exemplifies the nineteenth century tendency to be oneself at all costs in the most violent and intractable form. Arguing that there is always a touch of the charlatan about his work, he contends that it is not Carlyle's sincerity but that of his prose style that is in question (pp. 95–96). In another view, its highly rhetorical character is made up of a number of stock devices such as "the pluralizing of proper nouns, the repeated coordination of words and phrases, the use of exclamations and apostrophes and interrogations, the hyphenating of words, the employment of alliteration and rhyme and assonance" but also of striking departures in rhythm, diction, and imagery (Charles F. Harrold, Introduction, *Sartor Resartus* [New York, 1937], p. lix). The same scholar attributes Carlyle's style to the influence of the great divines of the Age of Milton, to Hudibras, Swift and Sterne, not to mention Richter.

But these descriptions are applied to Carlyle's most individual work. The present selection seems, on a cursory reading, to be cast in a plainer mode. Yet if there is anything which is essentially Carlyle in the elaborate style, it must be present in some form in any of his writings, including the present selection. A comparison of the excerpted passage from *Sartor* with the selection should provide some data. It is interesting that Carlyle criticizes Richter for faults of which others have accused him.

1. *no one can deny.* The first three sentences all begin with a syntactic inversion.

2. *thinking and existing.* Carlyle here assumes the truth of the ancient belief that the true personality is reflected in the style. Plato maintained that only the good man could have a good style, against the Sophists' contention that they could teach anyone to win in argument. Seneca later implied that a writer's weaknesses of character would be reflected in defects of style. Montaigne claimed that he wrote as he was, both vices and virtues being honestly represented in the unique amalgam of his style. Later ages believed, with Chesterfield, that style was "the dress of thoughts," whereas against that dichotomy Croce proposed the inviolable unity of form and content. The Romantic view, like Montaigne's, still persists in seeing an organic connection between the unarguable uniqueness—genetic and environmental—of the individual and the demonstrable uniqueness of his style. This Reflection Theory has been widely applied in more metaphorical ways. Thus, the characteristics of the language of 1600 are said to reflect the quality of uncertainty of that society.

Actually there is no evidence to support the interrelation of personality and style claimed by the reflection theorists. A personality may be unique without necessarily giving rise to a certain style. Both personality and style may be unique—indeed, both are by definition unique—but independent, without one being the reflection of the other. Reflection theorists tend to find what they are looking for. Thus, it is fair to suppose that something had to be known about England in 1600 before it could be perceived that social characteristics were reflected in the style of the time. How can Carlyle's question be answered, about Richter or about himself?

3. *Slawkenbergius.* A character with a very large nose in Laurence Sterne's *Tristram Shandy.*

4. *grave language.* What function does this phrase fulfill in the sentence and in the paragraph?

5. *Lessing.* Gotthold Ephraim Lessing (1729–1781), according to Macaulay, "the first critic in Europe."

6. *in every fashion.* Carlyle espouses, regardless of the consequences, the belief that the best way to write is that which is "natural" to the writer. In all its confusion of theory, this is a very modern view and related to plain style views.

7. *Tried by this test.* Observe the frequency with which Carlyle begins sentences with something other than the subject: an inverted construction or a front adverbial modifier. Note also his tendency to compile elaborate sets of formal parallels.

8. *safeliest.* A coinage, a nonce-word, an archaism or standard form? What alternatives are there?

HAZLITT (No. 24, p. 85)

Although Hazlitt sounds like a proponent of the Plain Style, especially in his condemnation of Dr. JOHNSON (No. 30), he is really in favor of the Middle Style, as Dr. Johnson described the prose of ADDISON (No. 37, and see also No. 30, note 10). This is an ideal also favored by the practitioners of the "Casual Style" (see WHITE, No. 78), the *New Yorker* writers (No. 76). In this selection, which is the first half of Hazlitt's essay, the stress is on the lexical aspect of style, the vocabulary or diction. To the ancient rhetoricians and to most people still today style means diction, the choice of word in the sense that a writer chooses among terms of synonymous reference on the basis of their contextual effect of connotation. Let us take Hazlitt's first sentence: "It is not easy to write a familiar style," he says. He might, without modifying the syntax, have made different word-choices. Instead of *easy,* he might have chosen *simple.* Or he might have replaced the understated *not easy* by a negative adjective, such as the neutral *hard,* the more formal *difficult* or the informal *tough.* Idioms and slang phrases would furnish other alternatives: "not child's play," "no piece of cake," "no breeze," "no joyride," "no walkover." Thus, in framing the first part of his sentence, Hazlitt had to choose, consciously or otherwise, from among the following possibilities (assuming that they were available in the idiom of his time):

	not easy simple child's play	
It is	no piece of cake breeze joyride walkover	to write a familiar style
	hard difficult tough	

For *write,* the options are less numerous, as the phenomenon is more specialized. Some alternatives are *compose, express oneself, communicate,* but none of them is really synonymous with *write.* But when it comes to the last two words of the sentence, "familiar style," the opportunities become considerable. To begin with, the concept of *style* is sufficiently vague to allow a large number of alternatives. Moreover, part of its meaning has already been expressed in the verb *write.* "To write a style" is redundant, because the idea of style is implicit in *write.* To be less redundant, the verb would have to be something like "have" or "produce" or "use." The alternatives cited above would require the transformation of the direct object into a prepositional phrase complement. Though one may say "write a familiar style" or "write in a familiar style," one cannot say "compose (or communicate) a familiar style." One must say "compose in a familiar style." Finally, what is a *familiar* style? Is it one which is *common, easy, general, habitual, known, usual, intimate, commonplace, hackneyed, current, prevalent, customary, regular, conventional, traditional?* All these senses are implied by the term *familiar,* which may be why Hazlitt chose it. The effect of these various lexical alternatives, apart from the possible change of meaning, might be considerable. What, for instance, would have been the difference if Hazlitt had begun his essay with one of the following instead of the sentence he actually used:

> It is hard to write in a common way.
> It is difficult to compose in a middle level.
> It is painful to communicate on an intimate footing.
> It's no breeze to write in a corny way.

1. *Dr. Johnson's style.* Does an examination of the JOHNSON selection (No. 30 and note 10) support Hazlitt's censure of Johnson? Compare MACAULAY's view (No. 22) and SAINTSBURY's (No. 13). What description could be applied to Hazlitt's own diction in this selection? What is the meaning of *rubric, cum grano salis, coterie, chapman?*
2. *proper force of words . . . application.* How would you explain the idea of this sentence? Is it opposed to any prevalent view?

SHELLEY (No. 25, p. 89)

Shelley's best-known essay inevitably invites comparison with its spiritual ancestor, Sir Philip Sidney's *Apology for Poetry* (1595), also known as *Defense of Poesy.* Sidney and Shelley, poets both, make claims for the poetry of prose, citing Plato as an example of the writer whose imagery made him a poet, despite the medium of prose. The following is Sidney's argument on this point:

> And truely, euen *Plato,* whosoeuer well considereth, shall find that in the body of his work, though the inside and strength were Philosophy, the skinne as it were and beautie depended most of Poetrie: for all standeth vpon Dialogues, wherein he faineth many honest Burgesses of Athens to speake of such matters, that, if they had been sette on the racke, they would neuer haue confessed them. Besides, his poetical describing the circumstances of their meetings, as the well ordering of a banquet, the delicacie of a walke, with enterlacing meere tales, as *Giges* Ring, and others, which who knoweth not to be flowers of Poetrie did neuer walke into *Apollos* Garden.

Though this paragraph is perhaps not the best possible example of Sidney's style, it illustrates adequately George Philip Krapp's contention that Sidney and LYLY (No. 12, note 4) represent the furthest elaboration of Elizabethan prose:

> —when Sidney broke down the barrier between poetry and prose, he had no intention of bringing either poetry or literary prose down to the level of everyday discourse. The high style in prose offered to him as broad a field for the exercise of rhetorical ingenuity as verse, and he agreed with his courtly contemporaries in the opinion that a prose style worthy of the scholar and of a lofty theme demanded such bravery of speech as would set it apart from the common speech of men. At the same time it is not difficult to separate the more extreme mannerisms and rhetorical ornaments of Sidney's style as mere surface display from a background of sound and genuine prose expression. (See Krapp, Bibliography No. 18, p. 381)

In the fourth paragraph of the selection, Shelley defines poetic prose as composed of two elements, figurative language and prose rhythm, or in his words: "the truth and splendour of [the poet's] imagery and the melody of his language."

1. *figure of speech.* A kind of **metonymy.**
2. *imperial faculty.* This image is an example of Shelley's more or less inevitable production of figurative language in expository contexts.
3. *former.* Refers to "conception," whose association with a mirror clearly shows Shelley's Platonic ideas. See also the last two lines of the selection.
4. *guitar and a harp.* Does the imagery of this passage, whatever its affective quality, help to clarify the meaning?

5. *Plato was essentially a poet.* Compare this with the Sidney passage previously cited.
6. *Cicero.* Cicero's philosophic writings are probably modelled on Plato's, but his elaborate rhythms seem to be his own refining of the Asiatic style of oratory.
7. *Lord Bacon was a poet.* Bacon's "new philosophy" appealed to the revolutionary in Shelley.
8. *Shakspeare, Dante, and Milton . . . power.* Shelley's opinions of great poets as philosophers no longer finds much sympathetic response.

COLERIDGE (No. 26, p. 93)

In this selection from his literary autobiography, Coleridge is commenting on WORDSWORTH's famous Preface (No. 28) to the *Lyrical Ballads,* a book of poems on which they collaborated. Wordsworth's Preface to the second edition of the book put forward his views on poetic language, with which Coleridge disagreed as he reveals here.

1. *"unelaborated expressions."* Quoted from Wordsworth's Preface.
2. *To this I reply.* The complication of this sentence, with its succession of qualifications and limitations, may be considered typical of Coleridge's expository and argumentative utterance, as this is revealed in his lectures, essays, and in this work.
3. *Hooker.* Richard Hooker (1554–1600), author of the *Laws of Ecclesiastical Polity* (1594), a work much praised for its style. The following opening paragraph of Part I may be considered typical:

> I. He that goeth about to perswade a multitude that they are not so well gouerned as they ought to be, shall neuer want attentiue and fauourable hearers; because they know the manifold defects whereunto euery kind of regiment is subiect; but the secret lets and difficulties, which in publike proceedings are innumerable and ineuitable, they haue not ordinarily the iudgment to consider. And because such as openly reproue supposed disorders of state are taken for principall friends to the common benefite of all, and for men that carry singular freedome of mind; vnder this faire and plausible coulour whatsoeuer they vtter passeth for good and currant. That which wanteth in the waight of their speech, is supplyed by the aptnes of mens minds to accept and belieue it.

> Whereas on the other side, if we maintaine thinges that are established, we have not onely to striue with a number of heauie preiudices deepely rooted in the hearts of men, who thinke that herein we serue the time, and speake in fauour of the present state, because thereby we eyther holde or seeke preferment; but also to beare such exceptions as minds so auerted beforehand vsually take against that which they are loath should be powred into them.

4. *Tom Brown or Sir Roger L'Estrange.* Both of these writers, who flourished half a century later than Bacon or Hooker, were journalists, pamphleteers, men of letters, but hardly on the same level of respectability as the foregoing. Brown, who had been a schoolmaster, was a hack satirist of great vigor who wrote in a highly idiomatic manner. The following paragraph is from his *Amusements, Serious and Comical, Calculated for the Meridian of London* (1700):

> Here a sooty chimney-sweeper takes the wall of a grave alderman, and a brook-man jostles the parson of the parish. There a fat greasy porter runs a trunk full-butt upon you, while another salutes your antlers with a basket of eggs and butter. 'Turn out there, you country putt,' says a bully with a sword two yards long jarring at his heels, and throws him into the kennel. By and by comes a christening, with the reader screwing up his mouth to deliver the service *à la mode de Paris,* and afterwards talks immoderately nice and dull with the gossips, the midwife strutting in the front with young original sin as fine as fippence; followed with the vocal music of 'Kitchen-stuff ha' you maids,' and a damned trumpeter calling in the rabble to see a calf with six legs and a top-knot. There goes a funeral with the men of rosemary after it, licking their lips after three hits of white sack and claret at the house of mourning, and the sexton walking before, as big and bluff as a beefeater at a coronation. Here a poet scampers for't as fast as his legs will carry him, and at his heels a brace of bandog bailiffs, with open mouths ready to devour him and all the nine muses; and there an informer ready to spew up his false oaths at the sight of the common executioner.

5. *universal use.* Coleridge here states the view that a writer's language contains the characteristics of 1) his individual style, 2) his social dialect, and 3) the language as a whole. The linguist is interested in the last, the sociolinguist or dialectologist in the second, and the student of style—what shall we call him: "stylistician"?—in the first of these.

6. *unmeaning repetitions.* Coleridge's description of the *real* language of men—something that would sound like a tape recording of a conversation—touches an issue that Wordsworth avoided: that real or natural language is discon-

nected, rambling, repetitious, and hardly poetic in arrangement or intensity. Artistic language must be artificial. Some modern novelists and dramatists have made much of the realistic effects resulting from the use of accurate transcriptions of speech.

7. *song of Deborah.* Judges 5:27. The form of repetition exemplified here is called **anaphora** and consists of the recurrence of the same structural element at the beginning of successive larger units. Here the primary repeated element is "at her feet":

> *At her feet* he bowed, he fell, he lay down;
> *at her feet* he bowed, he fell;
> *where* he bowed, there he fell down dead.

The third anaphoric recurrence is implied rather than stated, but the passage gains emphasis from the subordinate anaphoric *he*'s preceding each verb. Thus the quotation consists of anaphora on two different structural levels.

WORDSWORTH (No. 28, p. 105)

The work from which this selection is taken is properly considered one of the most influential critical statements ever made, not because it describes Wordsworth's procedure accurately—COLERIDGE showed that it did not—but because it brought forward a new kind of ideal of style and broke with eighteenth century practices. This ideal of "real language" was specifically designed for poetry but ultimately affected prose as well, leading to another justification of the Plain Style. It has obviously not affected Wordsworth's prose, which is not any more *natural* or *real* than Dr. JOHNSON's. Whatever may be Wordsworth's claim for the realism of his work, his poetry did not realize it. At least, much poetry of the earlier eighteenth century had a more genuine colloquial sound than anything that Wordsworth wrote. The following couplet which opens Pope's *Epistle to Dr. Arbuthnot* shows this clearly:

> Shut, shut the door, good John! (fatigued, I said),
> Tie up the knocker, say I'm sick, I'm dead.

The later poets of the century were doubtless some of them guilty of the artifices that Wordsworth accuses them of, but for their artifice he has merely substituted his own highly marked idiosyncrasy, as is shown by the very large number of parodies his work has inspired.

1. *personifications of abstract ideas.* The rhetorical figure of **personification** consists of giving human attributes to an idea, concept, notion, quality, attitude, or other abstraction. Strictly speaking, personification occurs whenever we place a non-human (or inanimate) entity into the position of a grammatical subject with an active verb. Thus, "His novel shows great vividness" is technically a personification. But since this is a consequence of the formal characteristics of the English language, it is not treated as a figure but as a normal use. The sort of personification that Wordsworth disapproves of consists of transforming an attribute into an entity. In Pope's couplet "The hungry judges soon the sentence sign/And wretches hang that jurymen may dine," the adjective *hungry* is an attribute or modifier of *judges.* In Johnson's time, Pope might have personified *hunger* and attributed to it the quality of *judge*-ness, thus achieving the result that Wordsworth complained of, perhaps in this way: "Judicial Hunger soon the sentence signs. . . ." The poetry of the later eighteenth century is crowded with personified abstractions. There are five in the first stanza of the Epitaph of Thomas Gray's "Elegy Written in a Country Church-Yard":

> Here rests his head upon the lap of earth
> A Youth to Fortune and to Fame Unknown,
> Fair Science frown'd not on his humble birth,
> And Melancholy mark'd him for her own. [1751]

Generally speaking, personification (until it becomes routine) is a way of "marking" or "foregrounding" a statement. By the unusual device of endowing the inanimate with life, the poet gives the statement additional emphasis. When personification becomes conventional, of course, it may be a means of signalling that the communication in which it is found is on a particular level or in a particular dialect or genre, that it is poetry in short, as the presence of obscene words in a book today means that the book is a modern novel.

2. *poetic diction.* Generally, a choice of word or phrase characteristic of poetry as distinguished from prose and perhaps best typified by archaisms like *ere* (for *before*). The question of poetic diction implies the question whether poetry is different from prose. If it is—as it must be—the difference lies in the words and those words constitute poetic diction. Wordsworth's argument is that the difference lies not in the use of a specified class of words marked as "poetic" but in the poetic use of the common vocabulary. The kind of language he was attacking was indeed prevalent in the eighteenth century but the elements of this stock diction have been shown to date from much earlier (see John Arthos, *The Language of Natural Description in Eighteenth-Century Poetry,* Ann Arbor, 1949). The main components of this diction can be specified as certain favored words and periphrastic epithets.

Among the favored words were those that had a technical application

drawn from ancient science, such as *aether, exhalation, infuse, orb,* and *vapor.* The second category **(periphrasis)** is more than a simple lexical choice; it involves a figure of rhetoric. Periphrasis is an indirect way of naming something, either by improving it **(euphemism)** or by stressing one of its features. Generally, both tend to give the referent added importance through the elevation of the language. It nearly always takes the form of an epithet (often ending in *-y*) followed by a noun, e.g. "the downy kind" (birds). In the poetry before Wordsworth, thus, the humble sheep were dignified by being called "bleating flocks," "woolly breed," or "fleecy care"; the sea was romanticized as "watery plain," "liquid empire," "glassy deep," and "fluid reign." Even plain things described periphrastically do not remain commonplace. Everything develops a different flavor, which the age of Gray was willing to consider poetic but the age of Wordsworth rejected as affected and unnatural.
3. *good sense.* Note the inversion at the beginning of this sentence and what looks like a personification in the *practice* which is *friendly* to a *property* (of poetry). "Good sense," like "Nature" is a quality claimed by critics for poetry they approve of and denied to poems they condemn.
4. *when prose is well written.* With this qualification, Wordsworth insures the safety of his argument.
5. *short composition of Gray.* Wordsworth here reprints Gray's "Sonnet on the Death of Richard West" (written in 1742 and only published posthumously), with the sixth, seventh and eighth, as well as the thirteenth and fourteenth lines in italics:

> In vain to me the smileing Mornings shine,
> And redning Phoebus lifts his golden Fire:
> The Birds in vain their amorous Descant joyn;
> Or chearful Fields resume their green Attire:
> These Ears, alas! for other Notes repine,
> *A different Object do these Eyes require.*
> *My lonely Anguish melts no Heart, but mine;*
> *And in my Breast the imperfect Joys expire.*
> Yet Morning smiles the busy Race to chear,
> And new-born Pleasure brings to happier Men:
> The Fields to all their wonted Tribute bear:
> To warm their little Loves the Birds complain:
> *I fruitless mourn to him, that cannot hear,*
> *And weep the more because I weep in vain.*

Wordsworth then comments: "It will be easily perceived, that the only part of this Sonnet which is of any value is the lines printed in Italics; it is equally obvious, that, except in the rhyme . . . the language of these lines does in no respect differ from that of prose."

PIOZZI (No. 29, p. 107)

In this Preface to her dictionary of synonyms, Mrs. Piozzi (earlier Mrs. Thrale and the friend of Dr. JOHNSON) attempts to explain her intentions. Her book was probably the second such work of reference in English and contributed a method of discriminating synonyms still used in our general dictionaries. Though the distinction between synonyms is a stylistic matter much of the time, Mrs. Piozzi was interested in maintaining proper idiomatic usage in the social rather than the literary sphere.

1. *modestly.* The feminine subservience implied by this word and various phrases throughout the selection was more apparent than real. Mrs. Thrale had no reluctance about disagreeing with Dr. Johnson, the lexicographer, on matters of lexicography.
2. *Ars recte loquendi.* The art of speaking correctly. Sanctius is probably Francisco Sanchez, a Spanish scholar who wrote with great energy and authority on grammar and rhetoric.
3. *Ars recte scribendi.* The art of writing correctly. This phrase and its corollary were of common use among rhetoricians and scarcely required attribution.
4. *Ammonius.* Of the 24 classical persons by that name who are known to us, the present Ammonius may be a grammarian of the second century B.C. who wrote commentaries on Homer, Pindar and Aristophanes. Or he may be the much later author of a dictionary of synonyms in Greek. The work mentioned is not identifiable.
5. *here he is at a stand.* This distinction between generative and analytic grammar plays a part in modern linguistic theory.
6. *Selden.* John Selden (1584–1654), man of law and scholar, whose *Table Talk* collected by his secretary became a very popular miscellany. According to that book, what Selden actually said was: "Though some make slight of libels [lampoons and other popular writings], yet you may see by them how the wind sits: as, take a straw and throw it up into the air, you shall see by that which way the wind is, which you shall not do by casting up a stone. Solid things do not show the complexion of the times so well as ballads and libels."
7. *levior cortice.* "Lighter than a cork," proverbial phrase from Horace, *Odes* (Bk. III, ix, 22). Considering the claims of modesty and humility made by Mrs. Piozzi in this short excerpt from her Preface, is there anything inconsistent in the fact that there are seven allusions or citations requiring annotation?

JOHNSON (No. 30, p. 109)

Samuel Johnson's *Prefaces, Biographical and Critical, to the Works of the English Poets* (usually called *The Lives of the English Poets*) was his last important work. Each Life is the Preface to the works of an English poet and this consideration dictates its structure. The first part is usually a chronological account of the poet's life and works, the second an assessment of his achievement and character. The present selection comes from near the beginning of the critical part of the *Life of Swift;* it is strongly flavored with Johnson's disapproval of SWIFT and with his efforts to do him justice despite this feeling.

1. *expression.* An indirect way of saying: "he has written on various subjects in various manners."
2. *Tale of a Tub.* Swift's *A Tale of a Tub* was published anonymously, as were all his other works with a single exception, his *Proposal for Correcting, Improving and Ascertaining the English Tongue* (1712). Because of its apparent attack on religion combined with unusual vulgarity, the *Tale* attracted a great deal of criticism and was never really acknowledged by Swift.
3. *little resemblance.* Outwardly, this may appear to be true to the reader. But, in the internal workings of the syntax, the details of the grammar, it corresponds to the style of Swift in his other works. This sense of *style,* which means the consistent verbal habits of an author, does not (and perhaps cannot) vary a great deal in a mature writer from one work to another. This is as true for Johnson as it is for Swift. (See Milic, Bibliography No. 49, where extensive support will be found for this point of view.)
4. *exerted.* Notice the formal structure of this sentence, which consists of an almost regular arrangement of parallelism and antithesis:

It exhibits	a vehemence and rapidity of mind,
	a copiousness of images
and	vivacity of diction,
such as he afterwards	never possessed,
or	never exerted.

The parallel series of direct objects of the verb *exhibits* is balanced by a parallel pair of verbs. The direct objects represent the attributes of the work but they are parallel in form only, if we ignore the slight irregularity of the first element. The attributes in substance are not really parallel, since *mind* is not the same kind of thing as *images* or *diction*. The latter two are characteristics (however vague) of the writing itself, whereas *mind* is not so much in the writing as behind it. It is what controls all the characteristics of the writing, including imagery and word-choice. This may be an example of what W. K. Wimsatt calls "cultivating expressive forms for their own sake" (see Wimsatt, Bibliography No. 41, p. 49). That is, it may be that Johnson's habitual tendency to frame sentences in parallel forms expresses itself even when the parallelism of thought is not there or at the expense of the meaning, which is to some extent distorted by the forced parallel. The same is not true of the parallel verbs in the second clause which are truly parallel both in meaning and form.

The concept of **parallelism** is of enormous importance in nearly all forms of expression. It is closely connected with **repetition,** of which it seems to be a variant. Primitive poetic expression depends heavily on the repetition of key phrases, some of which may be considered to have ritualistic power. The refrain in the popular ballads is probably an instance of this, with the special circumstance that the words are meaningless, mere patterns of sounds drawn from the phonemic system of the language; e.g., "With a hey and a ho and a hey nonny no." Parallelism is a more sophisticated variation of this process in that not the words themselves but some abstracted feature, such as the grammatical form or a category of meaning, is repeated, though the parallel is supported by the repetition of certain function words to enforce the resemblance. In the example from Johnson, note the repetition of the article and preposition (*a, of*) in the first clause and the adverb *never* in the second.

Principally, parallelism is a means of emphasis, as repeated structures call attention to themselves by their very nature. The emphasis may be logical, in the sense that the several items of the parallel are shown to have a structural or functional relation. Or it may be affective, in that the repetition of structures produces an increase in the emotional power of the whole construction. When these two aspects are combined, the resulting utterance is rhetorically effective, as in President Kennedy's "Ask not what your country can do for you; ask what you can do for your country," where, however, the parallelism of thought and structure is supported in addition by **antithesis** and inversion of word order.

5. *easy language.* The phrase "equable tenour of easy language" is not readily interpreted by a speaker of present-day English. *Equable* in a literary context is defined by the Oxford English Dictionary as "maintaining a constant level, uniform." *Tenour* (or *tenor*) is simply "character, quality, nature." *Easy,* in the same context, means "showing no trace of effort, smooth, flowing" (OED). A more modern restatement would read: "a uniform quality of effort-

less language." Why did Johnson not say "uniform and effortless language"? *Quality* (or *tenor*) is here merely a dummy word whose function is to support the extra adjective. The phrase is an example of the rhetorical figure **hendiadys,** in which one predication is given the form of two. An everyday example is "nice and warm," which actually signifies only "warm in a nice way" or "nicely warm." Johnson seems to be saying that Swift's writing appears effortless and is uniformly so, but this is more than he wants to say, so he adds the next clause, "which rather trickles than flows," in effect wiping out the adjective *easy,* whose meaning is "flowing." The whole framework affords, after subtractions, merely the information that Swift's language is uniform. The contortions of this sentence may possibly reflect the struggle between Johnson's intention to be fair to Swift and his temperamental unwillingness to say anything good about him.

6. *simplicity.* This is a nominal option of the proposition "He liked to write simply." Observe that the ideas rendered by the verb and the adverb in the propositional version are abstract nouns in Johnson's sentence. This should not be taken to imply that Johnson favored the nominal style: the evidence points the other way (see Milic, Bibliography No. 49, pp. 195 ff.). But his tendency was definitely to the abstract and non-sensory (see Wimsatt, Bibliography No. 41, pp. 54 ff.).

7. *choice.* Though Swift is hardly noted for his figurative language, except possibly in *A Tale of a Tub* and in some of his poetry, Johnson's dictum is obviously impressionistic and subjective. The reader is invited to equip himself with a definition of *metaphor* and to scan the SWIFT selection (No. 36, pp. 123–125) in order to verify Johnson's assertion.

8. *He studied purity.* An archaic way of saying "He tried to achieve correctness."

9. *safe.* The key words in this passage are *purity, exact, solecisms, authority, safe,* which symbolize and summarize the eighteenth-century ideal described as "correctness." (See Sterling A. Leonard, *The Doctrine of Correctness in English Usage, 1700–1800,* [New York, 1962, orig. 1929].) This ideal differs a great deal from our notion of what is suitable language. We are greatly influenced—even the most reactionary among us—by usage and the nature of the audience addressed. Writers of the eighteenth century, however, believed in an ideal of correctness expressed in grammatical and rhetorical rules, from which not even the greatest writers dared to deviate. Johnson himself severely castigated Shakespeare for his indulgence in low diction (words like "knife" and "blanket" in tragic or elevated situations). The best writers were those whom it was safe to imitate, who could serve as authoritative models to those desirous of improving their style.

10. *transitions.* Another sentence illustrating Johnson's devotion to architecture in his sentence structure. (Compare the opinion of SAINTSBURY on this point: last sentence of No. 13 and note.) The semicolon after the first clause may be disregarded; in Johnson's time it had not much more weight than a comma. Thus the sentence consists of two elements which may be displayed as follows:

His sentences are never too much dilated
or contracted;
and it will not be easy to find any embarrassment in the complication of his clauses,
any inconsequence in his connections,
or abruptness in his transitions.

The first part of the sentence deals with the size of Swift's sentences; the second with their structure. Thus the two parts are balanced in idea. A **dilated sentence** is one in which a number of extra modifiers, dependent clauses, and other constructions have been inserted. It is generally associated with a concern for rhythm, such as is characteristic of **Ciceronian** style. A **contracted sentence** is one from which connectives and adverbial modifiers have been omitted. This mode is associated with **Senecan** (i.e., anti-Ciceronian) style. Though each of these types has a characteristic form, the defining limits are impossible to state precisely. (For an account of these styles, see Croll, Bibliography No. 15.)

The three items in the second part of the sentence deal, as has been noted, with sentence structure. The awkward phrase "embarrassment in the complication of his clauses" means little more than that Swift did not lose track of his syntax in framing complex sentences: hardly a compliment to a writer of his stature. The two other items in the triplet refer respectively to "connections" and "transitions," matters which it is difficult to keep entirely separate. Although *connection* seems to suggest *connective* (a kind of word used to join parts of a discourse), it is probable, from its association here with *inconsequence,* that Johnson is talking about logical sequence, the organization of the train of ideas. And *transitions* refers to the devices used to signal relations such as consequence (e.g., *therefore, consequently*) as well as to the necessity for these devices. Thus, an abrupt transition might be an unmarked one (such as was favored by the Senecan stylists) or one inadequately marked or a sudden change of course resulting from logical incoherence. The demarcation line between connection and transition is difficult to draw with any exactness. Why then did Johnson divide what might have been conveniently treated as two items into three? Another question: Why does Johnson's approval of Swift's style in this sentence avail itself of the following terms: "never too much," "not be easy," "embarrassment," "inconsequence," "abruptness"? How else might this have been stated?

To provide a basis of comparison, here is Johnson's judgment on the prose of ADDISON, consisting of the last two paragraphs of his *Life of Addison:*

> His prose is the model of the middle style; on grave subjects not formal, on light occasions not groveling; pure without scrupulosity, and exact without apparent elaboration; always equable, and always easy, without glowing words or pointed sentences. Addison never deviates from his track to snatch a grace; he seeks no ambitious ornaments, and tries no hazardous innovations. His page is always luminous, but never blazes in unexpected splendour. It was apparently his principal endeavour to avoid all harshness and severity of diction; he is therefore sometimes verbose in his transitions and connections, and sometimes descends too much to the language of conversation: yet if his language had been less idiomatical it might have lost somewhat of its genuine Anglicism. What he attempted, he performed; he is never feeble, and he did not wish to be energetick; he is never rapid, and he never stagnates. His sentences have neither studied amplitude, nor affected brevity; his periods, though not diligently rounded, are voluble and easy. Whoever wishes to attain an English style, familiar but not coarse, and elegant but not ostentatious, must give his days and nights to the volumes of Addison.

11. *thoughts.* It may be asked: how does one tell when a writer's style is *not* suited to his thoughts?

12. *learning.* In this elaborate parallel structure, Johnson has undertaken the task of characterizing Swift's thoughts, an undertaking fraught with risk, in view of the tenuousness of the available facts. The sentence may be visually set forth as follows:

His style was well suited to his thoughts,
which are never subtilised by nice disquisitions,
decorated by sparkling conceits,
elevated by ambitious sentences,
or variegated by far-sought learning.

Compared with several previous examples examined above, this set of parallels is remarkably accurate in form, four main-verb structures with attached modifying prepositional phrases. The verbs are similar (even parisyllabic), the prepositions identical, each noun preceded by an adjective, the nouns all plural but the last.

If the substance of the parallel is examined, however, it will be noticed that the items are not really of the same class. In comparing Swift's style to his thoughts, Johnson proposes to describe his thoughts, presumably to enable the reader to verify this claim by making the comparison himself. The four parallel structures may therefore be taken as descriptions of Swift's thoughts, stated negatively. Thus when Johnson states that Swift's thoughts are "never subtilised by nice disquisitions," he implies that some thoughts do have this characteristic. But a *disquisition* is an investigation or a treatise (*nice* in this eighteenth-century meaning being equivalent to *precise*), ideas more properly applied to the expression of thoughts than to the thoughts themselves. Similarly, a *sentence* may be either an opinion or an aphorism; in the former case it is applicable though redundant, in the latter inapplicable, like *disquisition*. Conceits are ideas—the word is derived from *concept*—and may be related to thoughts. Learning, however, is not thought but the content of memory on which thought is probably dependent. Despite the strict formal parallelism, therefore, the substance of the four items is not parallel. Possibly, the formal aspect is intended to buttress the weakness of the substance. Or this may be another example of the devotion to the form dominating and shaping the content.

13. *He pays no court to the passions.* A decorated way of saying that Swift is not passionate, but emotionless, imperturbable or perhaps even stolid. (Note the different effect as we move from the negatived adjective to the derived negative forms—containing privative affixes—finally to the positive form.) *Stolid* is not synonymous with *not passionate* but one is implied by the other. *Pays no court* is not more vivid but negative and faintly disapproving.

14. *understands him.* Another parallel series of clauses, rising to a climax in the third element. For convenience in analysis, it may be proper to treat the colon as a full stop and the three elements separated by semi-colons as a unit. Displayed in parallel, they look as follows:

> He pays no court to the passions;
> he excites neither surprise nor admiration;
> he always understands himself, and his reader always understands him:

The principle of organization in this sentence is both parallelism and antithesis. Formally, the parallel is weak, marked mainly by punctuation and the basically regular (subject-verb-complement/object) syntax. The first two elements, describing as they do negative aspects of Swift's performance, are antithetic to the third, which stresses positive aspects. The antithesis is substantively reinforced by the consideration that the negative aspects deal with the emotions and contrast with the positive, which deal with the intellect. The extra length, provided by repetition, of the last element helps to balance the first two against the third, quantitatively.

The student may wish to consider the significance of the doublet "neither surprise nor admiration" in what is supposed to be an approving context. He may also try to determine how the third element might have been given a more economical form and what the rhetorical consequences of such a change would be.

15. *peruser.* A synonym for *reader,* used to avoid unintended (unemphatic) repetition. A pronoun would have been ambiguous, since it could refer to the reader or Swift.

16. *wants.* *Needs* or *requires.*

17. *common words and common things.* Why not "common words and things"?

18. *neither.* Note the position, technically faulty, of this conjunction.

19. *profundities.* Another example of Johnson's insatiable lust for balanced antithesis: *elevations* are indeed *mounted* but their opposite (*depths* or *profundities*) should in that case be *descended into* rather than *explored.* Unfortunately, Johnson could not think of a transitive verb parallel to *mount,* meaning to go down into a depth, so he settled for the neutral *explore,* which could as easily have applied to *elevations.* There seems to be some reference here to the awe-struck feelings of eighteenth-century travellers who crossed mountains, specifically the Alps on their way from France to Italy.

20. *solid ground.* This clause merely restates the content of the previous one, the appositive modifier ("along solid ground") also being redundant. Even for Johnson, to whom **pleonasm** was meat and drink, this passage seems unusually decorated with superfluity.

21. *obstruction.* This pair of prepositional phrases is also pleonastic, as not only are *asperities* and *obstruction* synonymous in this context, but together they repeat *solid ground* and *level* and the whole clause is merely a corollary of the previous one.

22. *attain.* This is a typical instance of a characteristic device of Johnson's, the inversion of the object, which is here placed first. Because the whole of the previous paragraph consists of clauses (nine at least, not counting relative clauses) in regular order, the use of inversion at this climactic point in Johnson's discussion of Swift's style achieves a desirable emphasis. The inversion places the important consideration first: Swift's "easy and safe conveyance of meaning." How does Johnson know that Swift desired this? Does Johnson himself subordinate the conveyance of meaning to some other expressive purpose?

23. *having attained.* We would say and most of Johnson's contemporaries would have said "for having attained *it.*"

24. *praise.* Johnson is determined to do justice to Swift's style but equally de-

termined not to give him too much. The contrast between *certainly* and *perhaps* reflects this struggle.

25. *didactick.* Again Johnson inverts the sentence, though not as much as the previous one. There the object was placed first, here it is merely a qualifying prepositional phrase.

26. *known before.* The clause in apposition presumably explains the word *didactick*, which means "instructional" (in Johnson's own dictionary it is defined as "perceptive").

27. *proper.* If this word here means "suitable," it is an absolute rather than a comparative and the qualification Johnson gives it ("in the highest degree") is merely decorative.

28. *but against.* The opposition of *against* to the initial *for* may also help to explain the inversion of the sentence.

29. *makes no provision.* In this incidental phrase lies concealed the rationale of Johnson's own ideals (and perhaps practice) of style and the explanation of his devaluation of Swift.

30. *persuade.* This conclusion summarizes, both by the contrast of structures and by its brevity, the complex first-clause system of the sentence. *Instructs* connects with *didactick* but *persuade* is only implied by *lie neglected.*

The reader is again invited to observe the extensive use of negative expression in this selection but especially in the last paragraph.

Propositional Reduction

¶ 1. Swift's works are of many kinds.
2. *A Tale of a Tub* is unlike Swift's other works.
3. *A Tale of a Tub* has more images and a different diction from Swift's later works.
4. *A Tale of a Tub* is totally different from Swift's other works.

¶ 5. Swift's works aside from *A Tale of a Tub* are written in an effortless simple language.
6. Swift liked to write simply.
7. Swift used metaphors very little.
8. Swift tried to be correct in his syntax.
9. In his sentences, Swift never makes the following errors: excessive expansion or deletion; confusion resulting from too much complexity; incoherent or abrupt transitions.

¶ 10. Swift's style suited his thinking, which is plain, unpedantic, and without digressions.
11. Swift's writing is dispassionate, intelligible, and makes no demands on the reader.

¶ 12. Swift succeeded in writing intelligibly and deserves moderate praise for this.
13. Swift's style is informative but not persuasive.

Logical Diagram

	A	B	C	D
¶ 1.	( )			
2.	(–)			
3.			(×)	
4.		(=)		
¶ 5.	( )			
6.		(=)		
7.			(×)	
8.			(+)	
9.		(=)		
¶ 10.	( )			
11.		(=)		
¶ 12.	( )			
13.		(=)		

MONBODDO (No. 31, p. 111)

1. *style.* Monboddo's definition is the one that may be called absolute: style is a good quality which may or may not be possessed by a composition. Thus a discourse which is laudable is said to have style, whereas a commonplace one does not. This definition has yielded to the more modern one in which every writer is thought to have idiosyncrasies, the sum of which is his style.
2. *two parts.* Diction and syntax, though rhetoric is involved in arrangement. For most people style has been identical with diction. Monboddo, however, insists that it is arrangement, which he calls *composition,* which is synonymous with style. Doubtless his preference is closer to the truth.
3. *proper or tropical.* Choice of word may be literal or figurative. *Tropical* is from *trope.*
4. *second part of style.* In his explanation, Monboddo makes clear that the rhetorical figures dealing with sound, such as alliteration, assonance and the like, are included in his concerns. The second subdivision must refer to the syn-

tactical variations which will nevertheless be synonymous in the different versions. The last deals with metaphor and other figurative, rather than formal, aspects.

5. *colours of style.* Ornaments or embellishments. Monboddo's view is what has been censured by Benedetto Croce, as the theory of ornate form in which the plain stuff of discourse is decorated until it is beautiful enough for the purpose. The Earl of Chesterfield's remark has the same tenor: "Style is the dress of thoughts."

CAMPBELL (No. 32, p. 113)

1. *the third place.* Though the grammatical terminology has changed in two centuries, the facts of the language have not. It is still true, as Campbell avers, that English word order puts the subject (nominative) first, the verb second and the object (accusative) next if the verb is transitive (active). If the verb is copulative or linking (substantive, esp. *be*), the subjective complement (participle, adjective or predicate) takes the place of the object.

2. *Alter the arrangement.* In the original Greek, the reading is "Megale e Artemis Ephesion." The Latin Vulgate has "Magna (est) Diana Ephesiorum." French word order is not sufficiently flexible to permit the inversion. (Summarized from a footnote by Campbell.)

3. *consonant to nature.* What is customary, it cannot be denied, comes to be thought natural. Thus what violates custom calls attention to itself and is therefore emphatic. When the violation of custom becomes sufficiently regular to become custom itself, the emphasis diminishes and only irregularity is left. Campbell is arguing against confusing the natural with the customary.

4. *second nature.* This saying is found in Cicero (*De Finibus,* Bk. V, Ch. 25, Sec. 74) and Galen (*De Tuenda Valetudine,* Ch. I) and is proverbially ascribed to Hippocrates.

5. *unnatural in another.* Campbell here argues against the doctrine of universals of language, which was popular in his time. Word order, being an aspect of syntax, is most likely to differ among languages, although this is seldom realized by native speakers. The most common error among learners of another language is to maintain the word order of the native language.

6. *oblique cases.* The inflectional forms other than the subjective.

7. *notwithstanding.* Here this seems to mean *except* rather than *despite the fact that.*

8. *regimen is a substantive.* When the agreement involves the verb *to be.* The English sentence "we see them," in French is rendered "nous les voyons," with the oblique pronoun placed immediately before the verb. It is not perfectly clear what Campbell is thinking of in speaking of the substantive regimen with pronouns. It appears from a later footnote, however, that he is resisting the claims of a French writer that French is a language with natural word order. Campbell finds French word order both inconsistent and more rigid than that of English.

9. *Is it not most natural.* Having shown the force of custom in these matters and the fallacy of equating nature with custom, Campbell falls into his own trap and claims that the subject-predicate arrangement is the more logical (most natural) one.

10. *Hebrew.* Campbell here invokes the simple-language fallacy characteristic of those who are not really familiar with the complexities of a linguistic system. Modern linguistic science has shown the futility of such descriptions as "simple" and "difficult," since all languages to non-speakers are equally difficult and since all are equally well able to express complexities of thought.

11. *something musty.* In *Hamlet* (III, ii, 366), Hamlet reveals his dissatisfaction to Rosencrantz as being caused by his lack of power ("advancement"). Rosencrantz replies that Hamlet has been made the King's heir. At this point, Hamlet says, "Ay, sir, but 'while the grass grows'—the proverb is something musty." The proverb is known from the thirteenth century: "Dum herba crescit, equus moritur" ("While the grass is growing, the horse starves.") *Something* is colloquial for *somewhat.*

12. *"Nearest the heart, nearest the mouth."* A proverbial way of accounting for slips of the tongue, such as giving the name of someone in one's thoughts for the name which should be given, errors nowadays known as "Freudian slips." Campbell's implication is that the first thing to be spoken will be that which is most on our minds regardless of the formal restraints of the language. This is a highly dubious doctrine. If such a principle were followed as Campbell here describes, it would merely make the utterance of the speaker incomprehensible.

GOLDSMITH (No. 33, p. 117)

1. *pedantry.* The inversion of normal word order in this first sentence is worth examining, partly because it is a common device of the period, partly

because it implies a more significant principle of arrangement, the **periodic sentence.** Here the order of the constructions is the following:

Complement

From a desire in the critic of grafting the spirit of ancient languages upon the English/

Verb **Adverb** **Subject**

have proceeded/of late/several disagreeable instances of pedantry.

To account for **inversion,** it is usual to point to changes in emphasis which the practice permits, in the sense that normal order emphasizes the subject whereas this particular reordering emphasizes the complement and minimizes the subject. If the normal order had been followed, the sentence would have read, "Several disagreeable instances of pedantry have of late proceeded from a desire in the critic of grafting the spirit of ancient languages upon the English." The original sentence presents a proposition—that some critics have tried to impose a foreign idiom upon English—but this datum is not located where it might be looked for, in its usual place at the beginning of the sentence, which could be accomplished by a very slight modification of the original structure, thus: "A desire in the critic of grafting the spirit of ancient languages upon the English has of late resulted in (or has of late produced/engendered) several disagreeable instances of pedantry." Since it seems to be the cause and not the consequence that Goldsmith is interested in, then either the inverted "From a desire" construction or the normal "A desire" would accomplish his purpose. His selection of the inversion may be explained by his probable intention of giving major attention to the cause. There is also the possibility that such a construction appealed to Goldsmith, seemed elegant at the time, was thought to improve readability. . . .

Inverted sentences have a certain kinship with **periodic sentences,** which by some rhetoricians (see Croll, Bibliography No. 15) are contrasted with curt and loose sentences. The periodic sentence cannot be defined very strictly but any sentence in which the basic elements are postponed until the end, with or without subject-verb-object inversion, can be safely considered periodic. It may be added that very short sentences cannot be periodic because there is nothing with which to postpone resolution. The following famous lines from Gibbon's *Memoirs* provide a good example of an eighteenth-century periodic sentence: "It was at Rome, on the 15th of October, 1764, as I sat musing amidst the ruins of the Capitol, while the bare-footed fryars were singing vespers in the Temple of Jupiter, that the idea of writing the decline and fall of the city first started to my mind." Gibbon defers the real proposition of the sentence four times, until he has provided the adverbial data of place, time when and during which, and manner. The effect of shifting all the normally post-verb adverbial complements forward is to create suspense and to prepare the reader for something momentous. The effect would be ludicrously anticlimactic if nothing of consequence were revealed. It is notable that Gibbon altered the syntax of his prototypic sentence to the form of an impersonal with postponed subject filled by a noun clause to facilitate the periodic structure.

Another well-known example, by an exponent of the loose style, Sir Thomas Browne, is the following: "What song the sirens sang, or what name Achilles assumed when he hid himself among women, though puzzling questions, are not beyond all conjecture." Here there is no inversion and yet the deferment of the predicate, by reason of the parallel noun clauses and the parenthetic phrase, causes the sentence to have the feeling of a "period."

2. *deservedly famous.* The final clause is so placed as to seem to modify *disrepute,* which is the nearest noun. It actually modifies "species of composition."

3. *blank verse.* This really means only that in English there is no alternation of stressed and unstressed syllables.

4. *novels, romances.* At this period, writers of fiction were not highly regarded, partly because their audience was thought to consist mainly of women of the servant class. Goldsmith himself was soon to become a member of this despised group of writers by producing the very popular *Vicar of Wakefield* (1766).

5. *monkish stupidity.* Goldsmith refers to the fact that classical Latin poetry used no rhymes but that rhymes arose after the decay of inflections and lexical change had transformed that language into Low or Vulgar Latin, a change associated with monks because the main texts in this language were written and preserved in religious houses.

6. *Celtic . . . island.* In this factually dubious set of assertions, Goldsmith is reflecting the interest in their ancestral past which had already begun to grip the English. This rejection of the ordered classic past was leading to a new interest in Gothic structures, in spurious Gaelic poetry ("Ossian"), and in fake ruins.

7. *deceives us into instruction.* A reference to the Horatian principle of instructing while pleasing, which was implicitly believed in the eighteenth century. It is obviously contrary to the somber Gothic quality of the new "Celtic" poetry, and Goldsmith feels the contradiction. To him, the light Horatian quality which permitted instruction without solemnity was indispensable.

8. *his we and his us.* Goldsmith seems to be resenting especially the editorial *we* and the tendency of contemporary critics to enumerate, presumably points of objection, with "firstly" and the like.

HUME (No. 34, p. 119)

This selection, consisting of the preliminary portion of the essay from which it is drawn, reveals that Hume proceeded like a philosopher even when the target of his investigation was literary rather than epistemological. He begins by citing a definition of his subject, fine writing. According to ADDISON, fine writing equals naturalness plus non-obviousness. To show the truth of this formula, Hume considers examples of writing which have only one of these qualities and finds that merely natural writing does not please. On the other side, Hume shows the inadequacy of writings which are merely surprising (non-obvious). He concludes by restating Addison's recipe for writing as a just mixture of simplicity and refinement, terms he prefers to those with which he began.

1. *fine writing.* Compare the different use made of this term by L. P. SMITH (No. 9).
2. *affect not.* We would say "do not affect." Is this Hume's personal archaism or do his contemporaries use the same form? When does the unemphatic *do* form first appear in these selections?
3. *waterman.* In earlier times, London, like Venice, depended on water transportation for intra-urban traffic. Watermen rowed boats.
4. *tea-table.* SWIFT compiled such a book, now usually known as *Polite Conversation,* originally titled *A Complete Collection of Genteel and Ingenious Conversation* (1738). Hume here does not seem aware of its existence.
5. *Gothic building.* Until the later eighteenth century, Gothic architecture was considered by Englishmen with very few exceptions as so much waste. *Gothic* was a term of abuse, meaning "old-fashioned," "ugly," "over-decorated."

BERKELEY (No. 35, p. 121)

Like SWIFT, Berkeley was educated at Kilkenny School and Trinity College, Dublin. In 1713, Swift presented him at court. Berkeley was a writer and a university lecturer on philosophy at Trinity, but also earned appointments as chaplain to an ambassador, as Dean of Derry, and finally as Bishop of Cloyne.

1. *Words are signs . . . significant.* The placing of this clause before a colon and a number of other features of pronoun use and word order emphasize the difference between our English and Berkeley's. Two possible rewordings which better fulfill modern requirements are the following:

a. "Words are signs which do or should stand for ideas, and so far as they suggest any they are significant."

b. "Words are signs: They do or should stand for ideas, which make them significant."

which. The use of this relative word is quite different from modern practice, especially when it fills an object position.
2. *annexeth.* An archaic termination nearly obsolete in Berkeley's time.
3. *whereof.* Another archaic usage perhaps traceable, like the previous one, to Berkeley's religious training and duties.

SWIFT (No. 36, p. 123)

The selection is taken from one of a number of Swift's writings in which he shows an interest in how the language should be used. In his most famous work on this subject, *A Proposal for Correcting, Improving and Ascertaining the English Tongue* (1712), he suggested the formation of an academy to prevent the language from deterioriating further. In his theoretical views about language, Swift is conservative, but his practice shows that he could not (or would not) act on his own beliefs (see Milic, Bibliography No. 49, Ch. I, for a discussion of this question).

In the work from which this selection is taken, Swift gives advice on preparing sermons to a young clergyman. Although it is not altogether a "straight" work and contains satirical touches, it is largely "free of that subtle and disturbing irony that mars so much of his work," as one recent cleric noted. Nonetheless, it is typical Swift, in content and style. In reading this, it might be well to remember JOHNSON's remarks about the clarity of Swift's writing (see above, No. 30).

1. *And.* Swift often begins a sentence with a coordinating conjunction (*and, or, for, nor, yet, so*) or with a word like *however, moreover, therefore* (sen-

tence adverb or sentence-connector). If we examine the twenty-five sentences in this passage, we shall find that six begin with coordinating conjunctions, three with subordinating conjunctions and three with sentence adverbs. In almost half, Swift avoids beginning with the subject in a traditional manner. Compared with the rest of his writing, this is rather a high percentage. In 2000 sentences, Swift averaged an initial connective in one-third of his sentences (see Milic, Bibliography No. 49, p. 125).

The significance of such a method of connection is difficult to assess. We cannot, of course, tell what motivates the writer. Writing being to some degree an unconscious process, a writer's own opinions about *why* he does anything are just as inaccurate as his ideas about *what* he does. Swift, for example, disliked monosyllabic words, but he used as many as any of his contemporaries. He scorned the words *mob* and *banter,* yet they appear in his writings. Evidently, the motivation of a writer in selecting the details of his syntax is also a mystery. What is perhaps less mysterious is the effect on the reader, since every reader (including the writer himself) is involved in this process.

To determine the effect on readers of initial connectives, we must first know what the norm is. One of the traditional school rules forbids the use of *and* and other coordinating conjunctions at the beginning of the sentence, on the ground that such words should coordinate equal constructions, a rule violated if *and* or *but* is placed at the head. Sentence-connectors are not subject to this prohibition, though preferred placement for them is usually after the initial construction. The rule about *and* is of course generally disregarded, but its influence continues: it is still unusual to see *and* at the beginning of a sentence. The violation of the norm here as elsewhere tends to produce emphasis (see Introduction p. 14). We notice the initial connective because we do not expect to find it there. If a writer uses this device all the time, however, then we adapt to this variability and the device loses all power to be emphatic. But if the whole writing population should one day start its sentences with conjunctions, emphasis would then be achieved by returning to the old norm, beginning with the subject.

Aside from the possible emphasis of such a use of the conjunction as Swift makes here, another effect may be observed. Inasmuch as we are subject to the norm which places coordinating conjunctions within sentences, the presence of such a word as *and* or *but* may mislead us into thinking that we are in mid-sentence rather than between sentences. This is all the more likely in such a text as Swift's which is riddled with capitals, italics, colons and semicolons. The net effect appears that continuity is intensified: the argument seems to hold together better. Naturally, this effect is more probable if the sentences are long and complicated as they are here.

2. *hard Words.* Throughout the history of English, "hard words" (those drawn from Greek or Latin) have been made the target of contempt and ridicule by traditionalists. The current attention to jargon (highly technical or specialized language) is merely an extension of this tendency. This has a good deal to do with the fact that English is a Germanic language infused with a very large number of borrowed Greek, Latin and French words. Linguistic conservatives like Swift feared that the acquisition of more such words would eventually change the character of English.

3. *it is not.* This ramshackle sentence contains eight clauses with, at the beginning, a good deal of inversion. Here are the first two clauses in their present order and in a more standardized order (typical of our day):

And *upon this account* it is that *among hard Words* I number likewise those which. . . .

And it is *upon this account* that I number *among hard Words* likewise those. . . .

Rhetorically these inversions are not very significant, especially since they may reflect the linguistic practices of the period more than the style of the writer. Grammatically, the main process is the shifting of modifying prepositional phrases forward, ahead of the verbs they complement.

The remainder of the sentence is a string of dependent clauses introduced by *which, as, because, which, as if* and *which.*

The peculiarity of this linear system of sentence construction, which is mainly additive, is that the sense of the sentence seems to be completed several times before the sentence actually ends. This kind of syntax is considered faulty by many critics: see, for instance, Herbert Read, *English Prose Style* (Bibliography No. 7, p. 44), who compares the jerky rhythm of such a sentence to that of a car in distress. There is no doubt that there is something disconcerting about reading a sentence which seems to be ending but does not end, as if a series of afterthoughts had occurred to the writer and been tacked on at the end. The sentence might be properly ended after *Science,* after *Writers,* and after *understand them.* This method of sentence construction, whether good or bad, was doubtless a regular feature of Swift's style. Read suggests that such sentences should be broken up into smaller ones. What would the effect be of such a change and what syntactic adjustments would be required by it?

4. *Beatifick Vision.* The "hard words" cited by Swift were likely to occur in theological and philosophical discussions in his time. His opposition to them is based not only on his linguistic views but on his lack of sympathy with the theological doctrine their use implied. Swift shared the widespread belief of his time that God's light must be plain to any human being without the prerequisite of

training in theological disputation or classical learning. The words listed here have in common that they are mostly compounds derived from Greek and Latin sources, and that they seem to have entered the language around the beginning of the seventeenth century. The *Oxford English Dictionary*'s earliest citations for each word are given in parentheses after it: *omniscience* (1612), *omnipresence* (1601), *ubiquity* (1579), *attribute* (1589), *beatifick vision* (1639), *excentrick* (1551), *idiosyncrasy* (1604), *entity* (1596). These dates may be taken as fairly accurate in the sense that they represent a minimum. A word on this list may have been in use longer but not less long. Thus the words Swift objects to had been in the language for over a century by the time he was writing, though their use was specialized and perhaps fairly rare. It is possible that Swift found the members of this particular list in a book at his elbow while he wrote.

5. *the like.* Swift's tendency to make lists or catalogues has been observed by several critics (see Milic, Bibliography No. 49, Ch. IV). Several features of **seriation** are clearly manifested in the list of "hard words" just presented. There are eight items presented which are given in two sublists more or less as follows (shown algebraically):

A, B, C, D, E, etc.
\+ F, G, H, etc.

Lists may differ from each other in the matter of quantity, of order, and of conclusion. All three of these deserve commentary in this case. Generally speaking, a list is such only if it contains four or more items, structures of fewer than four being conventionally described as rhetorical devices (doublet, tricolon). Lists of four and more have a different sort of effect and need special arrangement not to seem impenetrable. The normal order of any list or series in English is usually serial with a conjunction (*and* or *or* and sometimes *but*) inserted between the last two items, thus: A, B, C, and D. Variations from this order take two regular forms: **asyndeton** and **polysyndeton** (see GRAVES, No. 1, note 1). Asyndetic order involves the omission of the conjunction; polysyndetic order its repetition. Thus asyndeton: A, B, C, D. polysyndeton: A and B and C and D. In neither case is the reader able to predict where the series will end unless he has read the last item. Thus these variations function as superadditions of emphasis to a series, which is already emphatic.

Aside from these traditional departures from normal seriation, any number of variations are possible, especially if the items listed are not from the same class. Most series consist of nouns or adjectives, sometimes verbs or adverbs, but prepositional phrases and even clauses may be strung in sequence on the same regular principles. If, however, there is a mixture of different kinds of units, different both in type and in size, the nature of the series is concealed, though the serial effect is still perceived through the formal chaos. The following is an example of a mixed series from Swift's *Polite Conversation:*

> . . . how can she acquire, those hundreds of Graces and Motions, and Airs, the whole military Management of the Fan, the Contorsions of every muscular Motion in the Face; the risings and fallings; the quickness, and slackness of the Voice, with the several Tones and Cadences; the proper Junctures of smiling and frowning; how often, and how loud to laugh; when to jibe and when to flout; with all the other Branches of Doctrine and Discipline above recited.

Another device that promotes irregularity is the medial placement of the connective, as in the example in the selection, which is really one series with two connectives or endings. These take a form peculiar to Swift, which might be described as variations on *etc.,* something I have called a "continuator." Here the two variations are "with a thousand others . . ." and "and the like." The effect is to imply that the number of the terms Swift objects to is enormous. He actually cites eight such terms, but after the first five he hints that he might have named a thousand more, and to still our doubts at his **hyperbole** (exaggeration) he easily produces an additional three and hints at yet more with his "and the like." The intention is probably—the effect is surely—to suggest copiousness.

Sometimes Swift uses the continuator ironically to comment on the nature of the list he has provided. A classic example from *Gulliver's Travels* is the following:

> These unhappy People were proposing Schemes for persuading Monarchs to chuse Favourites upon the Score of their Wisdom, Capacity and Virtue; of teaching Ministers to consult the publick Good; of rewarding Merit, great Abilities and eminent Services; of instructing Princes to know their true Interest, by placing it on the same Foundation with that of their People: Of chusing for Employments Persons qualified to exercise them; with many other wild impossible Chimaeras. . . .

6. *justest in the World.* Placing the modifier in a separate construction (instead of saying "a general and just complaint") has the effect of providing it with special emphasis and allowing it to be itself intensified.
7. *meanest.* Humblest, lowest in the social or educational scale.
8. *nineteen in twenty.* Swift cited only eight but the implication of endless resources is here strengthened by these figures.
9. *Things sacred.* Even in Swift's time this French inversion of noun and adjective was uncommon and occurred only in certain set phrases.
10. *Justice enough.* Another such inversion.

11. *Families.* In the eighteenth century, the word meant "household" and included servants.
12. *Dr. Tillotson.* John Tillotson (1630–1694), Archbishop of Canterbury, was famous for the clarity and simplicity of his sermons. A paragraph from one of the best known, "The Advantages of Religion to Societies," is quoted below.

> And this will most evidently appear by putting this supposition. Suppose the reverse of all that which we now call virtue were solemnly enacted, and the practice of fraud and rapine, and perjury, and falseness to a man's word, and all manner of vice and wickedness were established by a Law: I ask now, if the case between virtue and vice were thus alter'd, would that which we now call vice in process of time gain the reputation of virtue, and that which we now call virtue grow odious and contemptible to human nature? If it would not, then there is something in the nature of good and evil, of virtue and vice, which does not depend upon the pleasure of authority, nor is subject to any arbitrary Constitution. But that it would not be thus I am very certain, because no Government could subsist upon these terms. For the very injoining of fraud and rapine and perjury and breach of trust doth apparently destroy the greatest end of Government, which is to preserve men in their rights against the incroachments of fraud and violence. And this end being destroyed human societies would presently fly in pieces, and men would necessarily fall into a state of war. Which plainly shews that virtue and vice are not arbitrary things, but that there is a natural and immutable and eternal reason for that which we call goodness and virtue, and against that which we call vice and wickedness.

The relationship between Tillotson's style and Swift's should be noted, in view of Swift's admiration for his sermons, and perhaps because one of Swift's best ironical pamphlets is entitled "An Argument Against the Abolishing of Christianity."
13. *he be any where.* The use of the base form *be* rather than an inflected form (here *is*) after *if* was at this time construed as a "subjunctive." It has now gone out of use except for special purposes.
14. *Pedants.* Originally this word merely meant a schoolteacher. The word, directly borrowed from Italian, is obviously related to *pedagogue, pediatrician, encyclopedia.* In that sense, it is obsolete. The contemptuous sense of a person concerned with trifling details, a doctrinaire, probably arose in the seventeenth century. Swift's friend ADDISON defined it this way in the *Spectator* No. 105: "A man who has been brought up among books, and is able to talk of nothing else, is a very indifferent companion, and what we call a pedant. But, methinks,

we should enlarge the title, and give it everyone that does not know how to think out of his profession, and particular way of life."

15. *Polite Conversation.* This phrase and the two following were slang or fashionable terms in this period to justify social rather than professional activity on the part of clergymen. To Swift, polite conversation was the meaningless and hackneyed chatter of ladies and gentlemen of fashion. He immortalized it in his *Complete Collection of Genteel and Ingenious Conversation,* generally called *Polite Conversation* (1738).

16. *appear by.* It is the impression of some who have read much Swift that he used the preposition *by* in a way peculiar to himself. This may be an instance of such a use.

17. *quaint, terse, florid Style.* These terms do not say much more than that the preachers Swift alludes to tried to achieve some kind of stylistic effect and that he disapproved of it. *Terse* means "economical" but *florid* implies abundance—a contradiction.

18. *Periods and Cadencies.* These are arrangements intended to be rhythmic, usually with the aid of inversion, sometimes at the expense of clarity.

19. *gaming Ordinary.* A game in a room of a tavern where cheap meals were available at fixed prices.

20. *White Friars.* This place was once the Carmelite convent near Fleet Street. Because it was considered a sanctuary, it attracted debtors anxious to avoid arrest and low characters of all sorts. Swift may be exaggerating the versatility of even eighteenth-century clergymen, whom social censure not moral concern would have kept out of such places.

21. *Palming, Shuffling, Biting, Bamboozling.* Shoplifting, cheating at cards, hoaxing, and deceiving others in order to cheat them. The bite was also a practical joke much practised at the Court of Queen Anne. It consisted of making the hearer believe some outrageous or extravagant lie and then confronting him with his credulity. The same has at various times been called a "sell," a "rag," a "leg-pull," a "fetch," and a "con," among others. The current term is "put-on."

22. *It would be endless.* Another instance of Swift's tendency to copiousness.

23. *I shall therefore say nothing.* If Swift had gone on to say something about the styles he mentions, this would have been an example of **paraleipsis,** in which the speaker introduces a matter by pretending he will not mention it.

24. *slovenly or indecent.* These five terms (*mean, paltry, fustian, slovenly, indecent*) share the same general vagueness as afflicts all impressionistic adjectival descriptions of style. The writer may feel that his impression is adequately conveyed by the adjective, for he has after all some sense of what it refers to, but the reader has nothing but the adjective and he cannot build understanding

on so slim a foundation. *Mean* and *Paltry* imply writing which contains few ideas, or ideas couched in humble language. *Fustian* refers to inappropriately elevated language, sometimes called *bombast. Slovenly* and *indecent* suggest vulgar or obscene terms or improper ideas. Because of the fuzzy terminology, Swift has not told us anything even if he intended to.

25. *flat, unnecessary Epithets.* The advice is redundant, since no one would deliberately use unnecessary words.

26. *old, thread-bare Phrases.* The same is true of this recommendation. It may be noticed that the two ideas are not really parallel. He warns against:

> the Frequency of flat, unnecessary Epithets and
> the Folly of using old, thread-bare Phrases

Neither in form nor in substance are these items parallel. Does an inspection of the rest of this selection suggest that Swift is careful of parallelism?

27. *natural words.* The contrast is between clichés and the writer's own words. Some speakers believe that the clichés they use are their own words. For them, the advice is wasted.

28. *too little cultivated in this Kingdom.* The language is used but not sufficiently regarded or thought about. Swift's proposal to found an English academy to regulate the language (on the model of the Académie Française) was intended to set things right.

29. *Affection.* False elegance, excessive show, pedantry, bombast—all sins of pride. There is a moral basis to Swift's strictures.

30. *When a Man's Thoughts are clear . . . best understood.* This belief is an item of faith with Swift, as it has been with many who advocate the Plain Style. Swift's assertion that sins against clarity are deliberate goes against much that we know about the mechanism of writing.

31. *Simplicity . . . Perfection.* Two great ideals often found yoked in antiquity, especially in the works of rhetoricians. The poignant striving after naturalness and simplicity seems often to be a baffled response to the complexity of human life.

Propositional Reduction of the first three paragraphs

¶ 1. Some clergymen unnecessarily use the jargon of theology in their sermons.
2. No clergymen can justify the need for words like "Omniscience."
3. Some terms in the Bible (esp. St. Paul) might be simplified.

¶ 4. The use of hard words in sermons has caused much justified complaint.
5. A clergyman's sermon should be understood by his most ignorant listener.

6. God does not require learning.
7. Most literary men would agree that most hard words in sermons could be easily simplified.

¶ 8. Common people cannot be expected to understand theology.
9. In sending a servant with a message, it is usual to make certain that he can understand it.

Logical Diagram

		A	B	C	D
¶	1.	( )			
	2.			(×)	
	3.			(+)	
¶	4.	( )			
	5.		(=)		
	6.		(!)		
	7.		(+)		
¶	8.	( )			
	9.			(×)	

ADDISON (No. 37, p. 127)

1. *tho'*. A common clipped spelling of the period, intended to give a conversational flavor to eighteenth-century writing, according to some critics. SWIFT, in a paper he wrote for Steele's *Tatler* (No. 230), complained of a number of such innovations. Apart from contractions (especially terminal "em" or "um" for *them*), he noted such words as *Phizz, Hipps, Mobb, Pozz, and Rep* (for *Physiognomy, hypochondria, positively, reputation*), only one of which (*Mob*) has survived. He also took exception to such technical terms, imported by military and diplomatic usage, as *speculation, operation, preliminary, ambassador, pallisadoe, communication, circumvallation,* and *battalion,* most of which are perfectly reputable today. Another class of word that upset Swift was vulgar slang, as typified by such words as *banter, bamboozle, country put, kidney* (as in the phrase, "of that kidney"). Swift's concern about the state of the language, which he also expressed in an essay entitled *A Proposal for Correcting, Improving and Ascertaining the English Tongue* (1712), was most probably galvanized by his feeling that the language was changing rapidly, something that others had also observed. The most readily observable change perhaps oc-

curred during the Restoration (1660–1700). Before that time the Renaissance accents of MILTON, Donne and Browne dominated English prose; after, the prose of DRYDEN, DEFOE, Addison and Steele prevailed. The self-evident difference between these two schools has been variously described and variously accounted for. The later prose has been called clear, modern, polite, flat, middle-class. It has been explained by reference to the rise of the middle class, the conversation of gentlemen, the aristocratic emphasis on lack of pedantry, the rise of science, and the demise of religious fanaticism. The fact is that there was a change in the state of the language and the way it was used, and that the change can be described fairly accurately. But reasons for the change we do not have.

2. *Reason, Reflection and good Sense.* Lannering (see Bibliography, No. 24) has called attention to Addison's reliance on pleonastic doublets and series to diffuse his meaning over a larger number of words. Here we have an irregular triplet whose separate members do not individually add much to the meaning, which might be adequately conveyed by a single one of them. Another series is found in the next sentence ("Poetry, Painting, Musick . . ."). There are also, still in this first paragraph, two doublets: "broken and cultivated," and "Punns and Quibbles." How many more are to be found in the selection and are they also pleonastic?

3. *Bishop Andrews.* Lancelot Andrewes (1555–1626) was the favorite preacher of King James the First, who made him Bishop of Chichester, of Ely and of Winchester, a Privy-Councillor and Dean of the King's Chapel. He was first on the list of those appointed to make the Authorized Version of the Bible. In a famous essay ("For Lancelot Andrewes"), T. S. ELIOT calls him the greatest of English sermon-writers, consistently greater than John Donne, whose sermons are however better known. Both were learned and 'witty' preachers and qualified for Addison's disapproval as arrant punsters. The following contrasted quotations show what two such virtuosi could do with the idea of seeing:

> And yet (to end this point,) Both these, the *starr,* and the *Prophecie,* they are but *circumfusa Lux:* [light surrounding] Without, both. Besides these, there must be a *Light Within,* in the eye: Els, (we know) for all them, nothing will be seen. And, that must come from Him, and the enlightening of *His Spirit.* Take this for a *Rule:* No knowing of *Ejus, absque Eo, of His,* without *Him,* whose it is. Neither, of the *starr,* without Him, that *created* it; Nor of the *Prophecie,* without Him, that *inspired* it. But, this third comming too; He sending the light of His *Spirit,* within, into their minds; they then saw cleerly. This, the *starr;* Now, the Time; He the Child, that this day was *borne.*

(Lancelot Andrewes, "Sermon Preached before the King . . . December 25, 1622")

> When Christ tooke the blinde man by the hand, though he had then begun his cure upon him, yet hee asked him, if hee saw ought: Something he was sure he saw; but it was a question whether it were to be called a sight, for he saw men but as trees. The naturall man sees Beauty, and Riches, and Honour, but yet it is a question whether he sees them or no, because he sees them, but as a snare. But he that sees God in them, sees them to be beames and evidences of that Beauty, that Wealth, that Honour, that is in God, that is God himselfe. (John Donne, "Sermon XXII, preached on Easter-Day, 1628")

4. *hard Names.* Addison defines a pun as "a jingle of words" and uses the following various names for the thing: *quibble, clinch, conundrum, paragram, paronomasia, ploce, antanaclasis.* All of these have in common some similarity of sound between words differing in meaning. *Quibble, clinch* and *conundrum* are general terms covering almost any kind of word-play involving likeness of sound, but carry the connotation of low or vulgar wit. The other terms, derived from the classics and associated with the rhetorical tradition of schemes, figures and tropes, are here used to imply bombast or pedantry: "hard Names" for trivial things. A **paragram** is a play on words, sometimes limited to the change in the initial letter of a name, usually for derogatory reasons, as *Sheats* for *Keats.* **Paronomasia** is the general term for word-play among the Greek rhetoricians, though often applied to instances of assonance for antithetic effect: "a little more than kin and less than kind." In **ploce,** the same word is repeated in an emphatic or expressive sense, as in Lear's "O let me not be mad, not mad, sweet Heaven!" **Antanaclasis** is the repetition of the same word in contrasted meanings, as "in a fraternity, there is no fraternity."

DEFOE (No. 38, p. 129)

Daniel Defoe, the journalist, hack-writer, novelist and author of one of the world's most popular stories, here presents a proposal for an academy to regulate the English language, as the French, Italian and German academies were then purifying their languages. Defoe was not the first to make this suggestion, nor was SWIFT in his *Proposal,* dated 1712 (No. 36, note 28), to be the last. The notion of regulating, purifying, censoring the language is one which seems to have perennial interest. The furor which greeted the publication of the third unabridged edition of the Merriam-Webster dictionary in 1961 is witness to this. The purists believed that the editors of the dictionary had refused to draw the line at lexical items that failed to meet a certain standard of purity. The editor and compilers, who prided themselves on linguistic science, would have incurred Defoe's wrath too, presumably as learned men. There is no easy selection of party to make in this dispute. The purists are needed to keep every new wrinkle from becoming part of the fabric and the innovators are necessary to prevent the fabric from becoming musty and from decaying.

1. *foster upon.* This seems to be an error for *foist on* or *upon,* though it might possibly be justified by analogy with an extended sense of *foster,* meaning to induce a ewe to suckle a lamb not her own.
2. *be esteem'd.* A patriotic sentiment more characteristic of the middle class than of the aristocracy, to whom such notions as nationalism and patriotism were alien. The aristocracy of all the nations of Europe felt, until the French Revolution, more closely connected than the several classes of any given nation.
3. *Vulgar.* Popular (belonging to the *vulgus*) rather than learnèd. We would say *vernacular.*
4. *hard Words.* A dislike of technical terms and long words borrowed from Greek and Latin was widespread at this time. BERKELEY, SWIFT and ADDISON, among others, all use the phrase (No. 35, last line, No. 36, first line, and No. 37, last paragraph), or its equivalent *hard Names.* This feeling about the language has at its core the sense that English is at its best the language spoken in England before the Norman Conquest (Old English or Anglo-Saxon) and that the borrowings which transformed English after that time really adulterated it. MACAULAY (No. 31, last paragraph) censures Dr. JOHNSON for his "vicious partiality" for Greek and Latin borrowings at the expense of the "strong, plain words" which are the basis of the English language.

It is a fact that English was gradually and systematically enriched by additions from the ancient languages and as well from French, Italian, Spanish and other tongues. Part of its expressiveness and flexibility is often attributed to this richness of its vocabulary. For reasons which are to be sought in the rapidly changing economic and intellectual development of England at this time, the process of word-coining and borrowing reached a peak in the middle of the sixteenth century. The resulting controversy was associated with *inkhorn* (or *inkpot*) terms, as the undesirable newcomers were called by their opponents. WILSON (No. 52) is the author of one frequently-cited complaint against this trend. In his book, he includes a letter he has concocted to illustrate the vice of inkhornism. The following extract italicizes the objectionable words:

> Pondering, *expending,* and *revoluting* with my selfe, your *ingent affabilitie,* and *ingenious capacity* for *mundane* affaires: I cannot but *celebrate,* & *extol* your *magnifical dexteritie* above all other. For how could you have *adepted* such *illustrate* prerogative, and *dominicall superioritie,* if the fecunditie of your *ingenie* had not been so *fertile* and wonderfull pregnant. Now therefore being *accersited* to such *splendente* renoume and dignitie *splendidious:* I doubt not but you will *adjuvate* such poore *adnichilate* orphanes, as whilome ware *condisciples* with you, and of *antique* familiaritie in Lincolneshire.

Of the twenty-four inkhorn words, ten are now standard English; the others never achieved currency.

Purists of all times have pilloried certain words in an effort to keep English from contamination, but the language has a way of absorbing such impurities and assimilating them. Swift, in his paper for the *Tatler* (No. 230) of 1710, also publishes a supposed letter proscribing the following words: *pozz* (*positive*), *plenipo* (*plenipotentiary*), *bamboozle, speculations, phizz* (for *physiognomy*), *hipps* (related to *hypochondria*), *rep* (*reputation*), *incog* (*incognito*), *mobb* (*mob*), *banter.* Half of these are now current. The others were probably not defeated by Swift's objections. More recently, objections were loudly voiced to the third edition of Merriam-Webster's unabridged dictionary (1961), though not technical terms but grammatical improprieties and slang exercise the purists of today.

The necessity of an appropriate vocabulary for technical subjects has been well defined by Dr. Johnson:

> Few faults of style, whether real or imaginary, excite the malignity of a more numerous class of readers, than the use of hard words . . .
>
> But words are only hard to those who do not understand them, and the critick ought always to enquire, whether he is incommoded by the fault of the writer, or by his own.
>
> Every author does not write for every reader; many questions are such as the illiterate part of mankind can have neither interest nor pleasure in discussing, and which therefore it would be an useless endeavour to level with common minds, by tiresome circumlocutions or laborious explanations; and many subjects of general use may be treated in a different manner, as the book is intended for the learned or the ignorant . . .
>
> He that reads and grows no wiser, seldom suspects his own deficiency; but complains of hard words and obscure sentences, and asks why books are written which cannot be understood.

Among the hard words which are no longer to be used, it has been long the custom to number terms of art. "Every man (says Swift) is more able to explain the subject of an art than its professors; a farmer will tell you, in two words, that he has broken his leg; but a surgeon, after a long discourse, shall leave you as ignorant as you were before." This could only have been said by such an exact observer of life, in gratification of malignity, or in ostentation of acuteness. Every hour produces instances of the necessity of terms of art. Mankind could never conspire in uniform affectation; it is not but by necessity that every science and every trade has its peculiar language. They that content themselves with general ideas may rest in general terms; but those whose studies or employments force them upon closer inspection, must have names for particular parts, and words by which they may express various modes of combination, such as none but themselves have occasion to consider. . . .

That the vulgar express their thoughts clearly is far from true; and what perspicuity can be found among them proceeds not from the easiness of their language, but the shallowness of their thoughts. (*The Idler,* No. 70. August 18, 1759).

LOCKE (No. 39, p. 131)

1. *ideas or propositions.* This is a perfect example of an ambiguity implicit in one of the standard usages of English. The reader of this sentence cannot tell for certain whether the word *propositions* is synonymous with *ideas* or alternative to it. The effort that has been sporadically made to use typographic means (e.g., punctuation, such as commas or round brackets) to distinguish the two, has not found universal acceptance to this day. In Locke's day of irregular pointing, the ambiguity would be all the more likely. The commas around *propositions* actually tell us nothing. By careful study of the context or from a knowledge of philosophical terminology, we might conclude that propositions are not another name for ideas. But Locke might have made the opposition more positive if he had used certain devices for contrasting that are among the standard resources of the language. Thus he might have used one of the following formulations "to signify the connection that the mind gives":

1. *to ideas, or to propositions, one with another.*
2. *either to ideas, or to propositions, one with another.*
3. *to ideas, or to their formal counterparts, propositions, one with another.*

Any of these versions would preclude the confusion, assuming that alternation was what Locke intended. An inspection of the remainder of the paragraph shows that he uses *ideas* interchangeably with *thoughts* and *sentiments,* whereas *propositions* is reserved for a context in which *sentence* and *discourse,* which are formal things, are discussed.

2. *does not only need.* This may be a late instance of unemphatic *do* used as an auxiliary before a verb, though the presence of a following *not* might give it the appearance of a modern use. We would say "not only needs" or more precisely "needs not only signs. . . ."

3. *shew.* This archaic spelling of *show* persisted into the present century and may still be found in the writings of George Bernard SHAW, despite his keen interest in reforming spelling.

4. *shew or intimate.* This doublet, in a philosophical writer like Locke, should not be mistaken for a rhetorical device. He is intent on conveying two different notions not, on achieving rhythmic balance or serving some other formal end.

5. *several ways.* This phrase is used here as if it were an adverb, like *diversely,* for example. The same purpose would be served in present-day English by converting the cluster into a prepositional phrase ("in several ways"), which would still be an adverbial modifier.

6. *as is.* Modern practice has found ways of differentiating between words used as examples and those that are part of the discourse itself. Thus a modern Locke might have written: "This it does in several ways: as, *is* and *is not* are the general signs of the mind affirming or denying."

7. *in words.* To the ear of a present-day speaker of English, the placement of this phrase sounds slightly unidiomatic or archaic. A more modern word order might be: "without which there is no truth or falsehood in words." Actually a modern speaker would have avoided the use of the verb *be* to mean *exist.* It seems unlikely that Hamlet's "To be or not to be" and Pope's "Whatever is, is right" could occur in present-day speech because of what seems to be a general agreement to limit the forms of *be* to copulative or auxiliary uses. Archibald MacLeish's "A Poem Should Not Mean But Be" is generally recognized as an unusual (therefore emphatic) use. (See Introduction, p. 14)

8. *the mind does.* Another instance of the unemphatic *do.*

9. *affirmations and negations.* As propositions must be either positive or negative, Locke uses this formulation instead of the term "proposition."

10. *reasoning, or narration.* An alternative doublet (meaning, either an expository or narrative discourse) as opposed to a pleonastic one, in which two names are given for the same thing, as for example "persuasive or argumentative."

11. *beauty of a good stile.* A typical rather than emphatic word order inversion of the period. The modern ordering would be "that the clearness and beauty of a good style more particularly consists." Locke was doubtless conscious of the advantage of having the phrase "good stile" at an emphatic place at the end of the sentence and may have deliberately chosen this word order, but it was far less deviant in his time than it would be today. *Clearness* (for *clarity*), *right use* and *more particularly* all smack of an older vocabulary.

stile. This spelling reflects an awareness that *style* comes ultimately from the Latin *stilus,* pointed implement for writing on wax, rather than from the Greek *stylos,* column. The metaphorical steps from instrument to the marks made by the instrument, then to the abstract governing character of the marks themselves took a very long time to achieve. *Stilus* meaning *style* in our sense does not occur in Latin until the third century of the Christian era, and in English until the fourteenth century.

12. *ideas clear and distinct in his thoughts.* This phrase provides another example of the inversion of noun and modifying adjective, which has already been noted, and a distinction between *ideas* and *thoughts* inconsistent with Locke's previous use of these words. Above, he uses the terms interchangeably; here, he considers ideas as constituents of thoughts.

13. *think in train.* Pay attention to the sequence and connection of his ideas.

14. *and therefore it is.* In this old-fashioned use of *therefore,* its origin as something equivalent to "for that" may be glimpsed. In later use, of course, the term becomes free-standing, requiring no integration into the structure of the sentence, a true adverbial.

15. *well expressing themselves.* To illustrate concisely the difference between Locke's language and ours, here is the second paragraph of the selection as it might be turned into present-day American English, including the changes in punctuation that we would consider appropriate:

> The words used to connect the affirmations and negations that make up an argument or a narrative are called "particles." Clarity and beauty of style depend on the proper use of these particles. Coherent thought requires not merely clarity in one's ideas, nor their consistency, but their proper connection and sequence. To express one's ideas coherently, words are needed to signal their relation: e.g., connection, limitation, discrimination, opposition, emphasis. . . . Carelessness in this aspect of writing can only confuse the reader. Thus, these particles, though not themselves names of ideas, are yet indispensable and contribute a great deal to effective expression. (N.B. This version is not presented as superior to Locke's.)

16. *one after another.* Although ambiguously placed, this modifier applies to *men,* rather than to "cases and genders," . . . and implies that the grammarians referred to borrowed liberally from each other, a doubtless well-founded charge.
17. *gerunds and supines.* This series shows a certain attention to arrangement, three parallel doublets. The first one pertains to nouns, the second to verbs, and the third to certain forms of verbs. The gerund is the verbal noun in *-ing* (e.g., "his *going*") ; the supine is a form of the infinitive in Latin grammar, though it was once used to refer to the English infinitive with *to.*
18. *ranked.* Locke uses this word in successive sentences in almost identical phrases, varied only for elegance, not for meaning.

(Particles) *ranked into their several orders.*
" *ranked into their distinct subdivisions.*

19. *significancy.* Significance, meaning. Many words now ending in *-ce* once had the *-y* ending of this word. Some still have both: *militance, militancy.*
20. *nicely.* Carefully, precisely. A *nice* person was one who was particular, careful, precise. A *nice* distinction is still occasionally one which requires mental subtlety to appreciate. Today, by a process of generalization, the word has come to mean little more than vague approval. Originally, it meant ignorant (from Lat. *nescius*) or foolish, then effeminate and delicate, then dainty and fastidious, then refined, careful, precise, and now hardly anything definite.
21. *postures of his mind.* This metaphor reveals only that Locke suggests introspection as an aid to proper expression. He actually cannot provide any guidance, for the mind cannot be observed, even by itself.
22. *usual in dictionaries.* In Locke's time, dictionaries were little more than lists of difficult or unusual words, with very short definitions, often little better than synonyms, and no examples. The first wordbook called a dictionary was Henry Cockeram's *The English Dictionarie* (1623), though the first English wordbook (Robert Cawdrey's *A Table Alphabeticall*) had been published in 1604. The first good dictionary of English was Nathan Bailey's *An Universal Etymological English Dictionary* (1721), which was used as a basis by Samuel JOHNSON in compiling his great *Dictionary of the English Language* (1755), superseded only by Noah WEBSTER'S *American Dictionary of the English Language* (1828) and the *Oxford English Dictionary* (1888).
23. *intimation.* Communication or expression.
24. *views, postures, stands, turns.* The use of these words denoting physical behavior to express figuratively the action of the mind suggests the difficulty that Locke had in conveying his sense of what mental activity is. The length of the series also conveys the struggle.

25. *opposite significations.* Locke is here really referring to the fact that these logical particles are used rhetorically rather than logically in writing. The notional aspect of connectives is no certain guide to the structure of the argument in which they are found. *And* is sometimes used to bring in a conclusion, whereas *therefore* may introduce a proposition that does not legitimately follow from what has come before (see Introduction).

26. *First, but.* This *but* is purely pleonastic and emphatic and can be omitted.

27. *Secondly . . . but.* This *but* is equivalent to the adjective *only.*

28. *Fourthly, but.* These two *buts* are really the same, notionally "adversative."

29. *Fifthly . . . but.* This *but* is equivalent to *and.*

30. *syllogism.* The conclusion of the syllogism would be, "Therefore, this dog has sense."

31. *whole sentence.* Function words are notoriously difficult to define.

Propositional Reduction of Paragraphs 1–4

¶ 1. Words may symbolize ideas or connections between ideas or propositions.
2. Symbols for ideas and mental action on ideas are necessary for communication.
3. *Is* and *is not* are symbols for affirmation and negation.
4. Connection is needed between parts of propositions and between sentences.

¶ 5. The proper use of particles (words that express the connection between affirmations and negations) is necessary for clear and attractive writing.
6. Proper thinking requires clear and consistent ideas, coherently arranged in sequence.
7. Effective expression requires the use of words to show the relation among the parts of the composition.
8. Particles are indispensable for effective expression.

¶ 9. Particles are the most neglected part of grammar.
10. Much has been written about the standard grammatical concepts.
11. Grammatical concepts (including particles) have been classified.
12. To understand particles, it is necessary to observe one's mind at work.

¶ 13. Particles cannot be understood if they are merely translated.
14. The elusive actions of the mind, which the particles reflect, must be studied.

15. Because there are more actions of the mind than particles, some have more than one meaning and some have contradictory meanings.
16. Hebrew has a one-letter particle with many meanings.

Logical Diagram

		A	B	C	D
¶	1.	( )			
	2.		(=)		
	3.			(×)	
	4.		(+)		
¶	5.	( )			
	6.		(=)		
	7.		(+)		
	8.				(:)
¶	9.	( )			
	10.		(=)		
	11.		(+)		
	12.		(−)		
¶	13.	( )			
	14.	(−)			
	15.		(=)		
	16.			(×)	

DRYDEN (No. 40, p. 135)

John Dryden (1631–1700) is (with Pope) considered one of the two greatest poets of the Neo-Classical period. He was also one of the foremost dramatists of the Restoration and even matched himself against Shakespeare: his best play (*All for Love,* a blank verse tragedy) is a re-doing of *Antony and Cleopatra* according to the French classical rules of unity. For the modern reader, his prose is the most rewarding part of his work, for Dryden was the best critic of his time and a great stylist. Though Dryden's style is markedly his own, it bears some traces of the aristocratic casualness that was one of the linguistic habits of the time. The use of *'tis,* the colloquial idioms ("make Pindar speak English"), the use of homely analogies ("when a Painter copies from the Life"), the parenthetical apologies for using a learned word ("distinguish and *as it were* individuate him") and disarming introductory verbs ("I confess," "I dare say")—all these stem from the Restoration desire to be above pedantry, to be 'cool.'

1. *Wits.* At this time, the word meant something akin to what we mean by "genius."
2. *Sir John Denham.* A poet (1615–1669), whose "Cooper's Hill" is the earliest instance of descriptive poetry in English.
3. *Mr. Cowley.* Abraham Cowley (1618–1667), poet, activist in the royalist cause and Fellow of the Royal Society, was in his time compared to MILTON.
4. *libertine.* Extremely free. Dryden here quotes Cowley, whose Preface to his *Pindarick Odes* (1656) contains the sentence: "The Grammarians will perhaps not suffer this libertine way of rendring foreign Authours to be called Translation."
5. *unequal parts to him.* Without his poetical ability.
6. *Genius.* The intellectual power of a person, not the person himself.
7. *Caput Mortuum.* A death's head, a skeletal skull.
8. *verbal Version.* Literal translation.
9. *Characters that distinguish.* His individual style.
10. *to vary but the dress.* Like most of his contemporaries, and perhaps like most translators, Dryden was a firm believer in the separateness of content and form. The Earl of Chesterfield's later (1749) formulation, "Style is the dress of thoughts," perhaps states it most exactly.
11. *compass.* Range.

SPRAT (No. 41, p. 139)

This selection from Bishop Sprat's *History of the Royal Society* is undoubtedly the most often quoted. It is also one of the standard documents in the history of the Plain Style. The traditional plaints against the false allurements of rhetoric are hardly novel, but the formula for scientific writing that Sprat presents in the last paragraph does represent something new. In a sense, his formulation of the practice of the members of the Royal Society has been influential, for scientific writing today differs markedly from literary writing, notably in an adherence to an austerely impersonal manner which eschews figurative language.

Most readers find it tedious and it is often charged with a predilection for jargon, in the sense of a specialized vocabulary and certain monotony of syntax (passives, attributive noun chains, etc.). Needless to say, Sprat does not himself, at least in this selection, practice the "close, naked, natural way of speaking."

1. *spirit and vigour.* One of a number of pleonastic doublets that Sprat indulges in.
2. *naked Innocence.* An abstract personification, balancing "armed Malice."
3. *Ornaments of speaking.* Sprat refers here to rhetoric in general, that is, to careful attention to the manner of one's presentation, and to the devices of rhetoric, the tropes, schemes, figures which were the staple of rhetorical instruction. A few lines before, he called it "eloquence."
4. *keep up . . . in any request.* That is, to defend the good against evil is the main reason why there is any longer a use for rhetoric.
5. *larger, fairer and more moving images.* Rhetoric originally enlivened virtue and made it palatable by imaginative figurative description. It gave truth an appearance of reality ("cloth'd with Bodies"). And it made such matters perceptible by the senses rather than merely by the intellect. This is a form of Horace's "dulce et utile" formula.
6. *disgust.* Reject with distaste. That is, the habit of ornament has caused men to reject truth unless it is sugarcoated with imagery.
7. *Passions.* Rhetoric appeals to the senses, not to the mind, in Bishop Sprat's opinion.
8. *bewitching.* Probably an error. Sprat intends that the mind is too easily seduced or bewitched.
9. *right practice.* Proper conduct, ethical behavior.
10. *Tropes and Figures.* The devices of rhetoric: metaphor, personification, synecdoche, anaphora, etc.
11. *vanity.* Trifle.
12. *vicious abundance of phrase.* Sprat is railing here against one of the classical ideals, copiousness, according to which sentences should be filled with matter and with words, perhaps as the sign of a mind richly furnished. The fulfillment of this ideal to excess led to repetition for its own sake, to pleonasm and other vices of style.
13. *deceipt.* A learned respelling intended to show the Latin origin of the term (cf. *deception*). Many of these inserted letters have dropped away, but we still have a number of such words in common use: *debt, comptroller, doubt, receipt, victuals.*
14. *common places of complaint.* Regular topics of comment about evils that

cannot be remedied, e.g., the weather. The *place* in *commonplace* is etymologically related to *topic,* which derives from *topos,* place.

15. *Royal Society.* A group of scholars and scientists who met under the protection of King Charles II to study, perform experiments, and express opinions. Unlike the French Academy, which was its spiritual ancestor, the Royal Society was oriented toward science. Some of its more imaginative experiments earned its members undeserved ridicule. To the group of Augustan wits (Pope, SWIFT, Gay, *et al.*), the word *projector* (deviser of scientific experiments or projects) or the name "Gresham College" (where the Society met) was tinged with absurdity.

16. *Natural Philosophy.* Science, natural and physical.

17. *primitive purity and shortness.* Underlying this statement is a belief in the origin of language as names for things, later expanded into constructions. Gulliver learns the language of Lilliput by pointing to objects and remembering their names. There is no evidence that this view has any validity.

18. *things . . . words.* A reference to a controversy about *res et verba,* one side of which argued that an excess of words over things in speech was a sign of decadent superfluity. There is no question that this view is sentimental and naive.

19. *Mathematical plainness.* One of the members of the Society, John Wilkins, had sketched plans for a language consisting of symbolic notation, which would do away with the confusion and obscurity of natural language.

20. *Artizans.* Wordsworth later spoke of preferring the common speech of farmers and even later writers have implied a preference for the speech of the people as against that of intellectuals (LAWRENCE, HEMINGWAY).

HOBBES (No. 43, p. 145)

1. *generall use.* Contrasted with "speciall uses" halfway down the paragraph.

2. *commodities.* Purposes, results.

3. *whereof.* An old form, equivalent to "of which, " now found only in legal language.

4. *passion.* In this context, this word means no more than *wish.*

5. *Arts.* Knowledge.

6. *pleasure or ornament.* Hobbes in this obscure way is referring to literature (poetry, drama, fiction).

7. *metaphorically*. Hobbes's scorn for metaphor is akin to SPRAT's (No. 41). Metaphors, to the person intent on truth, are literally lies. In this depreciation of figurative language, there lies a deep suspicion of rhetoric and the arts of language.

To illustrate the difference between Hobbes's English and ours, here is a modernized version of the selection:

> Language is used to turn thoughts into words so that our thoughts may be recorded and that we may communicate them to each other. There are four subsidiary uses: acquiring knowledge; exchanging knowledge; communicating intentions; enjoying literature.
> There are four corresponding defects or abuses of language:
> changeability of the meaning of words; deceptive imagery; lying; invective.

The above is a reduced version as well as a modernized one, a consequence of Hobbes's tendency to reiterate and expand and perhaps of the involuted nature of the syntax of the seventeenth century. Part of the unnecessary extent of Hobbes's original is the structural framework: the contrast between general and special uses and between uses and abuses. These contrasts bind the writer to an attempt at parallelism which the substance does not readily provide. The evidence of the struggle is in the inflation.

MILTON (No. 44, p. 147)

This selection is taken from the Introduction to the second part of Milton's treatise of ecclesiastical disputation.

1. *this manner of writing*. Theological disputation in "the cool element of prose."
2. *another task*. Poetry. Milton believed that he had been designated to be England's epic poet.
3. *no Empyreall conceit*. Pedestrian taste, lack of imagination.
4. *envy*. This word is difficult to interpret in this context. The adjective *envious,* in the old sense of "bearing ill-will," would make sense. Or the noun *enemy* (occasionally printed for *envy* in texts of the period) could be made to fit. Possibly, if the form *envy* occurred as an adjective, the obscurity could be

dealt with. As it is, if the antecedent of *it* is "the gentler sort," the present reading is not English idiom.

5. *exercis'd to the tongues.* Educated in foreign and classical languages.

6. *suffer.* Permit.

7. *the stile . . . was likely to live.* This sentence well illustrates Milton's addiction (at least in this selection) to grammatical parenthesis. The basic sentence structure is "I must say that it was found the stile was likely to live." All the rest is inserted at convenient places. The following is a list of the inserts, some of them bearing further inserts (shown by parenthesis marks):

> therefore
>
> after I had from my first years (by the ceaseless diligence and care of my father [whom God recompense]) been exercis'd to the tongues, and some sciences (as my age would suffer) by sundry masters (both at home and at the schools)
>
> whether ought was impos'd me by them that had the overlooking, or betaken to of mine own choice (in English or other tongue [prosing or versing, but chiefly this latter])
>
> by certain vital signs it had.

The length of Milton's sentences is proverbial and it possibly contributes to the difficulty they give the reader. But it is not the length but the grammatical complexity—frequency and depth of embedding of inserted constructions—which is perceived by the reader as difficulty. Compare the linear additive syntax of SWIFT (No. 36, note 3).

8. *latelier.* More recently.

9. *manner.* Custom.

10. *other things.* Presumably translations or imitations.

11. *shifted.* Managed.

12. *in scarsity.* Despite the scarcity.

13. *men buy Leases.* English leases were often for the term of ninety-nine years.

14. *there ought no regard be sooner had, then to God's glory.* No concern should precede God's glory.

15. *my country.* Milton, as a citizen, a politician, a religious polemist and a poet, was equally a patriot. He felt that the poetical honor of his country depended on him and he was moved to accept this responsibility at whatever sacrifice.

16. *second rank among the Latines.* Milton could not hope to achieve the first poetical rank if he wrote in Latin.

17. *Ariosto.* Italian epic poet who wrote in the Italian vernacular.

18. *mother dialect.* English. Milton obviously believed that the modern lan-

guages and particularly English were not as fit to be used for epic poetry as the classical languages, partly because of their own character and partly because of the restricted distribution.

19. *not caring to be once nam'd abroad.* The major sacrifice that Milton sees in his decision to write in English is that his fame will not extend to the learned in Europe.

20. *monks and mechanicks.* A reference to the writers of the chronicles which passed for history in the Middle Ages and up to Shakespeare's time: chiefly Bede, Geoffrey of Monmouth, Holinshed.

JONSON (No. 46, p. 151)

The full title of this posthumously published work is *Timber, or Discoveries Made upon Men and Matter, as they have flow'd out of his daily Readings, or had their refluxe to his peculiar Notion of the Times.* Like many men of his time, Jonson kept a commonplace book (often no more than a collection of loose sheets) in which were gathered the words of writers he wished to preserve or remember. Since Jonson had no control over the publication of *Timber,* his editor having merely turned over the collection of papers to the printer, it is possible that he had planned to do more in the way of organizing and original thinking than presently appears. As they stand, the contents of *Timber* are largely translations from foreign rhetoricians or quotations from English ones. The date of composition of the whole book is conjectural but parts can be fairly exactly dated. The best guess is between 1623 and 1635. The present selection is mainly a free rendering of part of the rhetorical treatise by Juan Luis Vives (1492–1540), *De Ratione Dicendi.* It is an interesting realization of the possibility that a translation can achieve a fame denied to the original. Jonson's peculiar and individual style may be credited with this success. The matter is commonplace (in the literal sense) but the words are not. They are, in Pope's phrase, "Nature to advantage dress'd."

BACON (No. 48, p. 155)

1. *three vanities in Studies.* Three types of useless or foolish activity in scholarship. Bacon, when he divides anything for the purpose of discussion, tends to

find things divided into three. The mystic numerology behind this preference is impossible to explain but the fact is there. Some ascribe it to rhetorical tradition, others to the triune god. The beginning of Bacon's Essay "Of Studies" (1625 ed.) shows another set of threes and other comments on the same subject:

> *Studies* serve for Delight, for Ornament, and for Ability. Their Chiefe Use for Delight, is in Privatenesse and Retiring; For Ornament, is in Discourse; And for Ability, is in the Judgement and Disposition of Businesse. For Expert Men can Execute, and perhaps Judge of particulars, one by one; But the general Counsels, and the Plots, and Marshalling of Affaires, come best from those that are *Learned*. To spend too much Time in *Studies,* is Sloth; To use them too much for Ornament, is Affectation; To make Judgement wholly by their Rules is the Humour of a Scholler.

2. *distempers.* Diseases, stronger than frivolities (*vanities*) mentioned first.

3. *begin.* It is worth observing that Bacon's punctuation (or his printer's) in this selection, especially the beginning, is nothing short of chaotic. At least it does little to help the reader follow Bacon's thought. The formal structure of the sentences does lead to Bacon's meaning, provided it is properly interpreted. With the confusing punctuation omitted and the material re-arranged for better visibility, the "sentence" (construed as ending with "begin") looks like this:

There be therefore chiefly **three vanities in studies**
(whereby learning hath been most traduced)

For those THINGS we do esteem vain, which are either *false*
or *frivolous*
those which either have no *truth*
or *use*
and those PERSONS we esteem vain, which are either *credulous*
or *curious*
(and curiosity is either in *matter*
or *words*)

So that in *reason*
as well as in *experience*

There fall out to be these **three distempers of learning**
(as I may term them)

1. The first, *fantastical learning*
2. The second, *contentious learning*

3. and the third, *delicate learning: vain imaginations*
vain altercations
vain affectations.

(and with the last I will begin).

4. *Prouince.* Duty, business, function.
5. *exquisite trauaile.* Precise study, accurate scholarship.
6. *manner of Stile and Phrase.* An expression that illustrates Bacon's own tendency toward copiousness, which he decries below as a sin of the Ciceronians. Throughout this selection, as can be seen in the frequent doublets ("pressing and applying," "coyne and frame," "embleme or portraiture"), triplets and longer series, parallel and antithetic, Bacon is fully in the middle of the copious rhetorical tradition he is contending against. The sentence displayed in note 3, above, shows schematically how much more than is strictly necessary Bacon puts into his sentences. He would claim that it was rather weight than "copie" but this is doubtful.
7. *kinde of Writing.* Bacon attributes the Revival of Learning in the Renaissance, with the consequent renewal of study in the philology and rhetoric of the classical authors, to the activity of Martin Luther in his struggle against the Pope. This view may easily be dismissed as partisan and biased, perhaps in the nature of an official propaganda line.
8. *Schoole-men.* Scholastic philosophers, formalists whose principles were based on the authority of Aristotle and the Church Fathers.
9. *Stile and fourme.* Somehow, even in modern use, the word *style* is usually joined to another, in order to support its vagueness or emptiness. Bacon does this more for reasons of copiousness than uncertainty. Note "Stile and Phrase" above.
10. *coyne and frame new tearms of Art.* Make up new words to refer to technical aspects of their philosophy.
11. *lawfulnesse.* Propriety, consonance with idiom. New words, in this sense, should be like old words, formed on an analogous basis, not imported crude and unmodified from a foreign language. Thus, *paraphrasis* is objectionable, but *paraphrase* is naturalized.
12. *Pharisees.* the quotation is from the Vulgate (John 7:49). Literally, it means "This cursed crowd which does not know the law." The King James version has "But this people who knoweth not the law are cursed."
13. *wordes than matter.* Bacon here expresses a principle which has been idealized in all times even when no effort has been made to practise it. It is at the basis of the Plain Style (see MAUGHAM, No. 7, notes) and the reform of English proposed by the Royal Society (see SPRAT, No. 41). Even a writer as elaborately rhetorical as Bacon has no hesitation in posing as a Plain Stylist. The expression *words and matter* clearly enough suggests what Bacon is saying

but he will not let it rest there. He copiously augments by listing the ingredients of a care for words: choiceness of phrase, composition of the sentence, arrangement of clauses, use of figures of speech. The first three of these are roughly synonymous, so that even this expansion could have been held down. Having, however, committed himself to this augmentation of "words," he is obligated to do likewise with "matter" and to produce another four or five items to augment it. This procedure adds six lines to his text without supplying anything substantial. It is all decorative.

14. *Then grew . . . price.* Then the style of Osorius began to be appreciated. "Flowing and watery vein," it must be admitted, is a wonderfully censorious characterization of a style, even though it is not descriptive.

15. *Sturmius.* The editor of the *Select Letters of Cicero* recommended by ASCHAM (No. 51).

16. *Car of Cambridge.* Nicholas Carr (1524–1568), Regius Professor of Greek at Cambridge, published a Latin version of Demosthenes.

17. *Cicero.* A reference to the Ciceronian-Senecan struggle then taking place but whose origins go back to early antiquity. The Greek orators were followers of either the Asiatic or Attic schools, basically differentiated by their use or rejection of rhetorical ornament, amplification and symmetry. The same division existed in Rome, among both orators and historians. The name of Cicero was linked with the Asiatic style, which much later became known as the Ciceronian. Cicero was the foremost orator of his time, an important man of affairs, a writer of philosophical essays and of several books on rhetoric. His influence on later ages, owing in part to the survival of most of his works, was enormous. His works became, for the medieval and Renaissance writer, a text book of vocabulary, syntax and rhetoric. A famous example of his style, from his oration "Pro Milone," selected and quoted by himself in his *Orator,* will reveal the nature of the form that the writers of the Renaissance emulated, whether writing in Latin, French or English:

> Est enim, iudices, haec non scripta sed nata lex, quam non didicimus, accepimus, legimus, verum ex natura ipsa arripuimus, hausimus, expressimus, ad quam non docti sed facti, non instituti sed imbuti sumus. (For this law, gentlemen of the jury, is not written but born; we did not learn, receive and read it, but we seized, plucked and wrested it from Nature herself; for this we were not taught, but made; we know it not by training, but by instinct.)

Among the symmetrical arrangements and formal patterns (called "Gorgian schemes" or figures after Gorgias, the supposed originator of this elaborate kind of rhetorical ornament) discernible in the Latin original are the following: **antithesis,** or opposition of meanings ("non scripta sed nata," "not written but born"; "non docti sed facti," "not taught but made,"; "non instituti sed imbuti," "not by training but by instinct); **parison,** or matching of structure in consecutive clauses, both in length and class of word (e.g. "didicimus, accepimus, legimus . . . arripuimus, hausimus, expressimus," "learn, receive and read . . . seized, plucked and wrested"); **homoioteleuton,** or like endings of words (*-imus, -ti*). Other figures associated with the Ciceronian style, but not illustrated in this passage, include **isocolon,** clauses of the same length, **antimetabole,** corresponding structures but with inversion (A,B,C; C,B,A), **paromoion,** or internal rhyme, **anaphora,** beginning successive clauses with the same word, **epistrophe,** ending successive clauses with the same word, and **symploce,** a combination of anaphora and epistrophe. It does not take much imagination to see that a system of such artificiality applied to a vernacular language like English would produce a prose very formal and mannered.

Some extracts from sixteenth-century prose will show the degree of Ciceronian influence:

A. Neither to the achieving of temperance in prosperity, nor to the purchasing of patience in adversity, nor to the despising of worldly vanity, nor to the desiring of heavenly felicity (Sir Thomas More.)

B. No, I will never so return thither again, to spend my age there in need and care, where I led my youth in plenty and hope, but will follow rather Isocrates's counsel, to get me thither where I am less known, there to live, though not with less care, at least with less shame (Roger Ascham).

C. Now it is done only for you, only to you; if you keep it to yourself, or commend it to such friends who will weigh errors in the balance of good will, I hope, for the father's sake, it will be pardoned, perchance made much of, though in itself it have deformities (Sir Philip Sidney).

D. I seek not the condemnation of the dead, or the disgrace of the living, but the good amendment of the one by the naughty example of the other (Gabriel Harvey).

The balances, parallelisms and antitheses in these extracts are easily observed. Example A contains two sets of matched and rhyming structures (*-ing, -ance, -ity; -ing, -ly, -ty*). The whole "sentence" is built on perfectly symmetrical principles. The figures involved are parison, homoioteleuton, isocolon and anaphora. The others, though less perfectly formal, display the same qualities. These are best revealed when the sentences are read aloud or written out as poetry is. Sidney's sentence (C) in addition shows metrical scansion: "if you *keep* it to your*self* or com*mend* it to such f*riends*" (where italics represent heavy stress). There is an alternation of anapestic and iambic rhythm. Such rhythmic prose was uncommon in English but the occasional instances show how far the imitation of classical models could go. The ultimate caricature of the Ciceronian style was the Euphuism of John LYLY (See ELIOT, No. 12, note 4).

It was to be expected that a reaction to such a fashion should take place, and it did. In England, the reaction occurred late in the sixteenth and early in the seventeenth century. At first, the movement was merely anti-Ciceronian. Afterwards, its proponents found their ideals in Attic prose and in the works of Seneca. Thus anti-Ciceronianism became Atticism and Senecanism. The counter-movement favored a deliberate lack of symmetry, thus avoiding the schemes of arrangement defined above, and a carelessness with connectives, which led to a certain obscurity. Actually, there were several counter-movements, with differing ideals (see Croll, Bibliography No. 15). Eventually, as with Bacon, the controversy turned into the struggle between matter and words, or substance against style, which is merely another name for the plain versus the elaborate way of writing. The battle is still raging.

Bacon affected the Senecan mode in the first version of his *Essays*. The 1597 version of the excerpt from "Of Studies" quoted above (note 1) in its 1625 revision shows the abruptness of the Senecan style:

> Studies serve for pastimes, for ornaments and for abilities. Their chiefe use for pastime is in privatenes and retiring; for ornamente is in discourse, and for abilitie is in judgment. For expert men can execute, but learned men are fittest to judge or censure.
>
> To spend too much time in them is slouth, to use them too much for ornament is affectation: to make judgement wholly by their rules, is the humour of a Scholler.

For other aspects of the Ciceronian-Senecan conflict, see MAUGHAM (No. 7, note 4) and PATER (No. 16, notes).

18. *Erasmus.* Desiderius Erasmus (1466–1536), Dutch scholar and humanist, wrote a lampoon on Ciceronianism.

19. *Decem . . . Cicerone.* "Ten years have I spent in reading Cicero."

20. *One, (Asine).* The echo replied with the ending of Cicero(ne)'s name (*donkey* in Greek) and *asine* (*donkey* in Latin).

21. *Secundum maius & minus.* More or less.

22. *Letter.* Bacon refers to the elaborately embossed or illuminated initial capital of a state document or ancient book.

23. *Pigmalions frenzie.* Pygmalion made a statue of Galatea and fell in love with it.

ASCHAM (No. 51, p. 167)

Roger Ascham was an educator—an unusual man who had an unusual career. He studied classics at St. John's College, Cambridge, and became the first Regius Professor of Greek. He was very interested in archery, believing in its importance in education, and wrote his first book, *Toxophilus* (1543), on that subject. The book was written in English, in the form of a Platonic dialogue, and it is most interesting because of Ascham's reminiscences, anecdotes and charming prejudices. Ascham became tutor to Princess Elizabeth and Latin secretary to Queen Mary. He held enlightened views on education, being against flogging and in favor of patience and gentleness, and made these known in the *Scholemaster,* which remained unfinished at his death. Its main purpose is to explain a method for teaching children Latin, the method being the "double translation" of Cicero's letters. The method is neither new nor especially valuable, but the book has been valued for its humanity, its incidental good criticisms and its championship of English as a literary vehicle.

1. *both learned and mother tonges.* Both the classical and the vernacular languages.
2. *ye onelie learne.* A pretty example of three parallel antitheses.
3. *rude . . . rudelie . . . rudest . . . rudenes.* Uneducated, ignorant. Ascham is aware of and partial to the effect of reiteration for emphasis.
4. *asonder.* Apart or separate. Ascham means that "good matter and good utterance" are in the classical languages never separate. This is a point he will develop in the next paragraph.
5. *most proper in wordes.* The sequence of parallel phrases which begins here is an example of **anaphora,** a series introduced by the same word or words. The parallel construction does not make it anaphoric; it is the use of the identical words (here *most*).
6. *found fonde. Fond* here means foolish or wrong. That is, any classic writer on religion or philosophy whose ideas are incorrect or illogical has expressed himself in bad style ("rude in uttering their mind"). Foolish ideas, according to the Platonic notion, go with perverted language.
7. *Stoickes . . . Monkes.* The Stoic and Epicurean philosophers were held to be irreligious. Monks and Friars, during the Tudor era, were synonymous with corrupt life. Libertines were free thinkers and loose livers. Anabaptists

were members of a sect that arose in Germany, but the name was contemptuously applied to any group of Protestants considered heretical. Note how Ascham arrays these six names in two parallel series of three:

Stoickes, Anabaptistes and Friers
with Epicures, Libertines and Monkes.

To have arranged them serially would have been more chaotic, less orderly to a mind trained in classical rhetoric.

8. *They be not wise.* Ascham seems here to be proposing a version of Croce's organic binding of style and substance: substance cannot be good without good style. Actually, his notion seems more closely related to Plato's view—that good substance and good style come from the same source, the good man.

9. *apte and good wordes began to be neglected.* This is the theory of the reflection of the state of society in the state of the language (cf. CARLYLE, No. 23). If society degenerates, the language will reflect this degeneration. The view is easily extended to the moral estimate of a writer by the quality of his language. Such moral evaluations are quite distinct from stylistic analysis, which does not concern itself mainly with moral but with other sorts of evaluation.

10. *contemned.* Scorned, treated with contempt.

11. *Academici and Peripatetici.* The Academic and Peripatetic philosophers: Plato and Aristotle, respectively.

12. *both learned, wise, and also an honest man. Both* has often been applied to more than two objects. The Oxford English Dictionary cites examples of this illogical use from Chaucer to De Quincey.

SHERRY (No. 53, p. 173)

1. *peradventure.* Perhaps. *Peradventure, perchance* and *perhaps* developed in that order. All three have about the same meaning. *Perhaps,* when it arose, displaced the other two. *Peradventure* derives from French *par aventure,* with an adjustment in the first vowel to make it conform to the English prefix *per-* and an inserted *d* to conform to the English word *adventure. Perhaps* was formed by the linking of *per-* and the English word *hap,* which meant chance or accident (cf. "by hap," "mayhap," "haply").

2. *newe fangle.* As a noun, meaning novelty, new fashion. The adjectival *newfangled* is still in common use. Both are depreciatory.

3. *tale of Robynhoode.* A tall or unlikely story, from the many false accounts circulating about the exploits of Robin Hood.

4. *scheme and trope.* Sherry's is probably the first use of *scheme* in English. *Trope* came into French around this time and there is record of earlier use in English. He is right, however, in supposing that his readers would not know the meanings of these words. Four centuries later, to most readers they are still foreign. The two words are roughly synonymous and mean "figure of speech," a way of saying something which is out of the ordinary.
5. *paraphrasis, homelies, usurped, abolyshed.* If it is Sherry's claim that these words are as new as the ones he proposes, this is merely another instance of the fallibility of native speakers as observers of their own language. Two of these words (*homily* and *usurp*) were known to Chaucer, and *abolish* was used by CAXTON. Only *paraphrase* was of recent date (first recorded use dated 1547). If he means that they are borrowings and not of the native word-stock, then he is right.
6. *enrychynge our tongue.* Sherry, like many of his contemporaries, had a sense of the inadequacy of the English language, of its lack of suitable words for the new things that were being discussed. This lack he attempted to repair by the creation of neologisms, such as *scheme* and *trope.* Others, whom he is here obliquely praising, were doing the same with such enthusiasm that a literary battle over "inkhorn terms" subsequently developed (see Richard Foster Jones, *The Triumph of the English Language,* Stanford, 1953, Chapters III and IV, esp. pp. 89–91; and DEFOE, No. 38, note 4).
7. *slacknes.* Slackness.
8. *set lyght.* To account of small value, to despise.
9. *Gower, Chawcer and Lydgate.* John Gower (1325?–1408), English poet who also wrote in French and Latin; Geoffrey Chaucer (1340?–1400), one of the greatest English poets; John Lydgate (1370?–1451?), priest and court poet.
10. *Thomas Eliot.* Sherry was much influenced by the example of Sir Thomas ELYOT (No. 55) in adding to the English vocabulary. His Latin-English dictionary appeared in 1538.
11. *copye.* Copiousness, richness. *Copia verborum* ("plenty of words") was by many of the ancient rhetoricians held to be an ideal of style.

ELYOT (No. 55, p. 177)

1. *tongues, whiche be fiue in numbre.* The "three tongues" were Greek, Latin and Hebrew. The other two necessary for a poet to know may be French and Italian.

2. *uneth.* Hardly.
3. *rules and figures.* French grammarians and rhetoricians were active in the Renaissance giving their language respectability and a status nearly equal to the classics.
4. *fatigate.* Fatigued, tired.
5. *exquisite.* Exact, abstruse.

COX (No. 56, p. 179)

Not much is known about Leonard Cox except that he took a Cambridge B.A. and in 1530 applied for the M.A. at Oxford. He taught school and published several books including the one on rhetoric from which the selection is taken. This is probably the earliest rhetoric text in English. It is mainly a paraphrase of the standard works on the subject.

1. *any maner thynge.* Any kind of thing. *Manner* in this construction with ellipsis of *of* is derived from the use of *kin* (later *kind*), e.g., "what kin tidings" (nowadays "what kind of tidings"). *Manner* took the place of *kin* and, according to the Oxford English Dictionary, "succeeded to its syntax."
2. *hym behoueth.* An old construction, literally "it behoves him," with the objective pronoun first and the impersonal subject deleted.
3. *the carte afore the horse.* Cox's use of this proverb is among the earliest recorded, and yet he refers to it as common and presumably ancient.
4. *eloquence.* Cox's list (Invention, Judgment, Disposition, Eloquence) differs from the standard division of rhetoric into five parts, which are usually Invention, Disposition, Style, Delivery and Memory. Nowadays, only the second and third are considered proper to rhetoric.
5. *difficile.* A French counterpart of the word *difficult. Propriete* is not used to mean *propriety* but *property* or *ability.* At this time, a good many words still had French spellings.
6. *Inuencyon . . . placys.* Invention (or what to say) was regularized in a set of topics (*topic* means *place* in Greek, wherefore Cox's *placys;* cf. *commonplace*). The Topics of Invention were a set of ready-made formulas suitable to various occasions: the beginning of a speech, the length, the speaker's reference to himself and every imaginable contingency. Writers of letters are still great users of topics: receipt of letter, apology for not writing, references to weather and health, types of closings are all topics.

CAXTON (No. 57, p. 181)

William Caxton was the first English printer and was therefore in an ideal position to bring his own efforts before the public. His own writing is mainly confined to forewords and prefaces to the works he brought out (about eighty books), most of which he translated from French. The language in which Caxton writes is in a stage between Late Middle English and Early Modern English. Of the texts of this period, his are probably the most securely dated, for as a printer he did not need to write until he was ready to go to press. As he observes in this selection, English was undergoing great changes in his time. Typographical conventions had not yet become conventional, so his practice may seem a little odd to the modern reader. He uses a period where we would expect a comma and a long space (or nothing but a following capital) where we expect a full stop. He uses *and* and an ampersand indifferently, though the ampersand most often joins pleonastic doublets (*penne* & *ynke, fayr* & *straunge*). Except for *I,* he capitalizes only the first letter of a "sentence" and his spelling is highly variable.

1. *y^t^*. Scribal contraction of *that.*
2. *rude and brood.* Primitive and coarse.
3. *ded do shewe.* Double auxiliary, one of which may be intensive.
4. *vnderstonden.* The variability of English inflections at this period is shown by the alternate forms of *understood: understonden* here, *understande* above. Other variations on the past and present tenses of the verb appear below.
5. *tamyse.* The river Thames.
6. *zelande.* Holland.
7. *atte forlond.* On a cape or headland.
8. *mete.* Any food, here eggs.
9. *eggys.* The form now spelled *eggs,* by Caxton spelled either *eggys* or *egges,* came in in the fourteenth century. The old form, *eyren,* was going out of use by the end of the fifteenth century.
10. *clerkes.* Literate men, writers or scholars.
11. *vplondyssh.* Rustic, living in the backwaters of civilization.
12. *faytes.* Deeds.
13. *entermete.* Concern himself.
14. *vyrgyll or the pystles of ouyde.* Virgil or the epistles of Ovid.

15. *redar & enformer.* Teacher or adviser.
16. *vnconnynge.* Uneducated, ignorant.
17. *gentylnes and scyence.* Courtesy and knowledge.

BUTLER (No. 58, p. 183)

See BRADLEY (No. 62)

RALEIGH (No. 59, p. 185)

See BRADLEY (No. 62)

HARRISON (No. 60, p. 189)

See BRADLEY (No. 62)

SHAW (No. 61, p. 191)

See BRADLEY (No. 62)

BRADLEY (No. 62, p. 195)

1. This annotation takes up the group of five writers—Samuel BUTLER (No. 58), Walter RALEIGH (No. 59), Frederic HARRISON (No. 60), George Bernard SHAW (No. 61) and Henry BRADLEY—whose works have been drawn on to illustrate the manner of writing characteristic of the year 1900. Writers differ from each other in style, but the language changes enough from one era to another to obliterate the differences in style between writers of different eras. A comparison of the individual styles of non-contemporary writers must first discount the changes in the language and in rhetorical fashions. That is, such a comparison must rest upon a knowledge of the *diachronic* differences so they will not be mistaken for individual *stylistic* ones.

In order to make this principle evident, the student is invited to examine a group of writers who put pen to paper at the same moment, within half-a-dozen years at any rate. These five selections illustrate the state of British English around the year 1900 (two other sets do the same for 1800 and 1700).

The state of the language being a constant, any differences must be the result of individual style. This is all the more true inasmuch as the subject matter is similar in all the selections. The only factor which militates against the linguistic and rhetorical uniformity of the texts is the varying age of the writers. In 1900, Butler was 65, Raleigh 39, Harrison 69, Shaw 44 and Bradley 55. The significance of this factor is that there is a generation's gap between the youngest and the oldest and that to some extent writers of different generations write differently, though they may write at the same moment. It is not so much the change in the language that is reflected in such a case (though some lexical items may come and go), but fashions in rhetoric, inculcated in these writers' schooling at different epochs. This variable may be tested by comparing Raleigh and Harrison and noting whether one is more noticeably old-fashioned than the other. The comparison can be extended to include writers of the same age as Harrison in 1900 regardless when their works were written.

An examination of these five texts is not likely to reveal a great deal about the state of the language in 1900. Essentially, these five pieces will seem as different to us as their authors. Bradley was a lexicographer, Butler a novelist, Harrison a writer on history, Raleigh a critic and academic, Shaw a playwright. According to this sorting, Butler and Shaw might be expected to have something in common, regardless of age, and the same for the other three. Moreover, the type of piece they were writing might produce another set of categories. Harrison's is an essay, Butler's a journal, Shaw's a preface to a play, Raleigh's a treatise on a rather specialized topic and Bradley's a popularization of a rather technical matter. The individual value of each of these various aspects of the texts' subject matter, (date of composition, age of the author, his profession, the type of composition) cannot be easily assessed. The main fact about this group of writings of 1900 is that they are on the whole still quite modern despite the seven decades that separate us from them. From this, we can infer that the language of this period was not much different from ours. As a consequence, these writers do not give us the feeling that linguistically or rhetorically they have very much in common with each other.

If the reader goes through each of these pieces in the manner suggested by Leo Spitzer (see Introduction, p. 17) and notes the various items which strike his eye or ear, he will doubtless gather a certain harvest. The most obvious items are lexical and among them the most visible are the allusions and references to proper names that we are expected to recognize. Butler writes of WORDSWORTH, Newman and Stevenson, who are hardly obscure, though the former two are not very often read outside of schools today. Raleigh only mentions Montaigne. Harrison alludes to a collection of historians, some of them quite obscure. In addition to Gibbon, whom he is writing about, he names CAR-

LYLE, Voltaire, HUME, ADDISON and Burke. Shaw alludes to Bradlaugh, Bunyan, Darwin, Job, Handel, Luther, Giotto, Palestrina, Cherubini and refers to the Ancient Mariner, rather a wide range (music, painting, literature, religion and science). Bradley mentions no proper names, but he is writing for the uneducated public. Thus, it might be concluded that the writers of this time had certain expectations about the education of their readers, Shaw and Harrison the most, Bradley naturally the least.

If the vocabulary is examined in the same way, the reader will turn up some slang now out of date (Butler's *shies,* Raleigh's *hackney*), several terms now out of use (Harrison's *rehearse*—in the sense of *repeat*—Shaw's *aforetime,* Raleigh's *interdict*) and a few words that were in vogue then but have been replaced by others (Shaw's *belletrist,* Bradley's *phraseological*). A search for syntactic structures and inflections now obsolete will prove fruitless. The language of 1900, barring the differences noted, is the language of our time and the individuality we observe in these styles is the individuality of the authors.

D'ISRAELI (No. 63, p. 199)

[This note covers also GODWIN (No. 64), WOODHOUSELEE (No. 65), TOOKE (No. 66), and DRAKE (No. 67). The reader should also consult note 1 under BRADLEY (No. 62)].

1. The modern reader who examines these five texts of 1800 is likely to feel in stranger territory than he did reading those of 1900. The appearance of the page is different, mostly because of the capitalized nouns. The punctuation too differs: there are more commas, colons and semicolons, and they are used differently. The range of allusion is greater; there are more Latin tags and references to ideas and objects unfamiliar today. The main aspect of strangeness is in the vocabulary. The words are for the most part those that we use, though there are exceptions (*enervate, massy, defalcation, phlegmatic, poesy, mediately, forcible*), but they are not used in the same way. There are subtle alterations of meaning which give us the sense of a language spoken differently, in a manner no longer current. Such expressions as "enter upon examples" (for "cite examples"), "just composition" (for "good writing"), "the style is not yet castigated" (for "the style is not yet purified"), "works of the same species" (for "works in the same genre"), "transfusion from one language to another" (for "translation . . .") are merely a few which show words familiar

to us used in a different idiom. The words *just, enter, species* are in our vocabulary but we use them in a different sense, in different contexts, as part of different collocations. There is also, to add to the unfamiliar aspect of these writings, some use of inflections no longer actively employed. We recognize "if it introduce," "though it claim," "were prejudice set aside" as constructions having to do with what used to be called "the subjunctive." We recognize them, as they are rather minor inflectional changes, and they do not interfere with understanding, but they add to unfamiliarity. Finally, there are a number of rhetorical practices that were more common in 1800 than they are now, though we still find them today. Word-order inversion was fashionable then (see JOHNSON, No. 30), but it is not now. We may expect therefore to meet a good deal of it: "Of this latter encomium, part is true"; "Of his wit, I entertain the highest opinion"; "Among such authors, we may place Tillotson . . . ;" "Elevated emotions these writers rarely awaken." Personification of abstractions is common too: "the charms of amenity," "the fetters of versification." There is much more balance, parallelism, antithesis than we are willing to accept. The writing of Tooke, however, appears more modern than the others and Godwin seems to have tried to follow his own prescription for a good style, at least in the respect that he avoids inversion.

GODWIN (No. 64, p. 201)

See D'ISRAELI (No. 63)

WOODHOUSELEE (No. 65, p. 205)

See D'ISRAELI (No. 63)

TOOKE (No. 66, p. 207)

See D'ISRAELI (No. 63)

DRAKE (No. 67, p. 211)

See D'ISRAELI (No. 63)

WOTTON (No. 68, p. 213)

See BENTLEY (No. 70)

HUGHES (No. 69, p. 217)

See BENTLEY (No. 70)

BENTLEY (No. 70, p. 221)

[This note covers also WOTTON (No. 68), HUGHES (No. 69), DENNIS (No. 71), and WATTS (No. 72). The reader should also consult note 1 under BRADLEY (No. 62)].

1. The prose of 1700 is, overall, not much more unfamiliar than that of 1800. Nearly three centuries have not altered the language as much as one might expect. According to some scholars, modern English prose began during the Restoration, a time just previous to 1700. The prose of 1700 does not differ so much from that of 1800, 1900 or our own day, as that of 1600 does from that of 1700; this can be observed by a look at the writing of JONSON (No. 46), BACON (No. 48), or PUTTENHAM (No. 49). Historians of English include the 1600 stage of the language in the period known as "Early Modern English." Therefore, we must not expect these five writers to be strikingly unfamiliar to us. But there are differences from our own day.

Among the most obvious are certain spellings and contractions. Familiar words are unfamiliarly spelled: *subtilty, busie, ingages.* Words ending in *-ic* have a *k* on the end (*critick, musick, rhetorick*). Past forms in *-ed* are commonly written with an apostrophe before the terminal consonant (*form'd, call'd, learn'd, acquir'd, reform'd, employ'd, conceal'd*). Contractions like *'tis, o'er, tho'* are frequent and apparently not considered informal. A number of obsolete forms may also be found: *thereby, wherein, methinks,* easily recognizable but no longer in use. Some items of vocabulary may be completely unknown to the modern reader: *idiotism, novity, flagitious, capacitated.* Others are used in markedly different senses: *analogy, numbers, moles.* The use of the article varies too, e.g., *the Latin, the French, the English* (referring to the language, not the people). Comparative inflection is less bound by rule than ours. Dennis says "more full," "more strong," "more easy," where we would insist on the *-er* inflection (*stronger, easier, fuller*). Old uses of verbal forms, showing the gerund at a stage closer to its origin as a verb, may be noted in the constructions "the diffusing their language," "a disposing of the words." Our tendency would be to convert the gerunds into nouns and to insert *of:* "the diffusion of their language," "a disposition of the words." As the punctuation suggests, the writer of 1700 has a notion of a sentence not quite so rigid as developed later and is still current. Wotton, for instance, begins a sentence with *so that,* a sentence that is really only a subordinate clause. As Wotton uses this construction three times, it may well be his own particular quirk. These observations by no means exhaust the list of differences between the language of 1700 and that of the present day, but they may serve both as guide and starting point.

DENNIS (No. 71, p. 223)

See BENTLEY (No. 70)

WATTS (No. 72, p. 227)

See BENTLEY (No. 70)

WOLFE (No. 73, p. 229)

Tom Wolfe (as he signs himself) was first noticed as a writer in the pages of *Esquire* and later in *New York,* the Sunday magazine section of the New York *Herald Tribune.* The essay which later became the book *The Kandy-Kolored Tangerine Flake Streamline Baby* first appeared in *Esquire.* As Wolfe tells it, his assignment had been to cover a stock-car race in California for *Esquire*—the title is the name of one of the cars in the race—but he found the account difficult to write in the traditional manner:

> . . . at first I couldn't even write the story. I came back to New York and just sat around worrying over the thing. I had a lot of trouble analyzing exactly what I had on my hands. Finally, I told Byron Dobell, the managing editor at *Esquire,* that I couldn't pull the thing together. O.K., he tells me, just type out my notes and send them over and he will get somebody else to write it. So about 8 o'clock that night I started typing the notes out in the form of a memorandum that began, "Dear Byron." I started typing away, starting right with the first time I saw any custom cars in California. I just started recording it all, and inside of a couple of hours, typing along like a madman, I could tell that something was beginning to happen. By midnight this memoran-

> dum to Byron was twenty pages long and I was still typing like a maniac. About 2 a.m. or something like that I turned on WABC, a radio station that plays rock and roll music all night long, and got a little more manic. I wrapped up the memorandum about 6:15 a.m. and by this time it was 49 pages long.

Part of the reason why Wolfe wrote this essay (the second of two parts) and why *New York* published it doubtless was based on the fact that an attack on the hallowed *New Yorker* would attract a good deal of attention and create readership, which the failing *Herald Tribune* badly needed. A more serious reason had to do with the increasing dissatisfaction of young writers with the *New Yorker's* formulas and its "casual style." The obvious target was the cult of worship extended to former editors and writers and the self-conscious practices indulged in by the initiates and the aspirants at the magazine. Wolfe effectively ridiculed all this not only by the substance of his satiric attack but by the new style in which he conveyed it. If a descriptive adjective could adequately account for a style, Wolfe's might be called *impressionistic.* But his style is too complicated to fit under that label, or the label *conversational* which has also been applied to it. Its main feature is a callous disregard for certain conventions. Exclamation points, italics, ellipses and dashes are used frequently for emphasis; one-word and incomplete sentences abound. There is a good deal of syntactical looseness and a systematic avoidance of the well-formed sentence. Rhetorical questions are placed at points of emphasis, often with the impersonal *one* as subject. The vocabulary is perhaps the most striking aspect, with coinages, hyphenated collocations, and many other informal and slangy items unashamedly in view. The whole makes an impact which is both powerful and overemphatic.

MACDONALD (No. 75, p. 237)

Dwight MacDonald is known as a reviewer and writer of articles for the *New Yorker, Commentary* and the *New York Review of Books.* Thus he qualifies as both an insider of the literary establishment and an intellectual. As such he is usually outspokenly critical of nearly anything he reviews, apparently seeing himself as the defender of some set of virtues or values under attack by the mass culture. He has variously disapproved of the New English Bible, the Great Books, modern linguistics, HEMINGWAY, and Webster's Third. His criticism often extends not only to the works under discussion but to the critics who have approved of them or disapproved for the wrong reasons.

Although he is a critic of culture, including literary culture, his criterion is a moral one, even in the matter of language, where he is a militant purist.

1. *Cozzens.* James Gould Cozzens (b. 1903), American novelist, whose *By Love Possessed* appeared in 1957.
2. *straightforward if commonplace style.* This labelling is an evasion designed to allow the emphatic contrast with the style of the book under review, which is presented later.
3. *awkward contestant.* This verbless sentence, together with such phrases as "fuzzing it up" and the informal contraction "there's" imply a viewpoint at least outwardly at odds with MacDonald's overt linguistic purism. The reason for this discrepancy is contained in a passage from the same review: "the long, patient struggle of the last fifty years to bring the diction and rhythms of the prose closer to those of the spoken language. . . ."
4. *Messrs. Gill, Fischer, and Balliett.* Reviewers for the *New Yorker, Harper's* and the *Saturday Review,* respectively.
5. *cooniness.* Cageyness, canniness, astuteness.
6. *Zeitgeist.* Spirit of the times.
7. *praise with faint damns.* Play on Pope's characterization of ADDISON:

> Damn with faint praise, assent with civil leer,
> And, without sneering, teach the rest to sneer.
> [*Epistle to Dr. Arbuthnot,* ll. 201–2].

8. *dictionary.* MacDonald's test for whether a word is properly used. Later in the review, MacDonald lists Cozzens' defects of style as: (1) "Melodramatics" (stilted use of language), (2) "Confucius Say" (pompous sententiousness), (3) "Pointless Inversion," (4) "Toujours le Mot Injuste" (polysyllabic and pedantic word-choice). The following is a paragraph from the novel, quoted by MacDonald to illustrate some of these defects and characterized as a typical sample from the novel:

> Recollected with detachment, these self-contrived quandaries, these piffling dilemmas that young love could invent for itself were comic—too much ado about nothing much! Arthur Winner Junior was entangled laughably in his still-juvenile illogicalities and inconsistencies. Absurdly set on working contradictories and incompatibles, he showed how the world was indeed a comedy for those who think. By his unripe, all-or-nothing-at-all views, he was bound to be self-confounded. By the ridiculous impracticalness of his aspirations, he was inescapably that figure of fun whose lofty professions go with quite other performances. The high endeavor's very moments of true-predominance guaranteed the little joke-on-them to follow.

The New Yorker (No. 76, p. 241)

Despite the attacks that have been levelled against it (see WOLFE, No. 73), *The New Yorker* has held a high position in the esteem of American readers, especially among educated Easterners, as well as academics and city-dwellers throughout the country. This dominance has resulted from the scrupulous editorial work insisted on by Harold Ross, its editor for several decades, and from the presence on its staff and in its pages of some of the best writers in American letters: Updike, Salinger, Thurber, Benchley, Perelman. The term *writer* here means "craftsman with words" rather than the more elevated implication of the term. *The New Yorker* writer is exemplified by E. B. WHITE (No. 78), who is primarily a craftsman, a stylist exercising his talent on essentially minor matters, "a minor-league Thoreau" one non-admirer has called him. The "Notes and Comment," the lead section of "The Talk of the Town," has always been anonymous and (though only part of it was written by E. B. White) has had considerable outward uniformity of style. The present piece (author unknown) shows the magazine's typical concern with literary craftsmanship, in this case the rhetorical effectiveness of the Inaugural Address of President John F. Kennedy. The Address, delivered on January 20, 1961, is given in its entirety below.

INAUGURAL ADDRESS OF PRESIDENT
JOHN FITZGERALD KENNEDY
ON
FRIDAY, JANUARY 20, 1961

Mr. Chief Justice, President Eisenhower, Vice President Nixon, President Truman, reverend clergy, fellow citizens, we observe today not a victory of party, but a celebration of freedom—symbolizing an end, as well as a beginning—signifying renewal, as well as change. For I have sworn before you and Almighty God the same solemn oath our forebears prescribed nearly a century and three quarters ago.

The world is very different now. For man holds in his mortal hands the power to abolish all forms of human poverty and all forms of human life. And yet the same revolutionary beliefs for which our forebears fought are still at issue around the globe—the belief that the rights of man come not from the generosity of the state, but from the hand of God.

We dare not forget today that we are the heirs of that first revolution. Let the word go forth from this time and place, to friend and foe alike, that the torch has been passed to a new generation of Americans—born in this century, tempered by war, disciplined by a hard and bitter peace, proud of our ancient heritage—and unwilling to witness or permit the slow undoing of those human rights to which this Nation has always been committed, and to which we are committed today at home and around the world.

Let every nation know, whether it wishes us well or ill, that we shall pay any price, bear any burden, meet any hardship, support any friend, oppose any foe, in order to assure the survival and the success of liberty.

This much we pledge—and more.

To those old allies whose cultural and spiritual origins we share, we pledge the loyalty of faithful friends. United, there is little we cannot do in a host of cooperative ventures. Divided, there is little we can do—for we dare not meet a powerful challenge at odds and split asunder.

To those new States whom we welcome to the ranks of the free, we pledge our words that one form of colonial control shall not have passed away merely to be replaced by a far greater iron tyranny. We shall not always expect to find them supporting our view. But we shall always hope to find them strongly supporting their own freedom—and to remember that, in the past, those who foolishly sought power by riding the back of the tiger ended up inside.

To those peoples in the huts and villages across the globe struggling to break the bonds of mass misery, we pledge our best efforts to help them help themselves, for whatever period is required—not because the Communists may be doing it, not because we seek their votes, but because it is right. If a free society cannot help the many who are poor, it cannot save the few who are rich.

To our sister republics south of our border, we offer a special pledge—to convert our good words into good deeds, in a new alliance for progress, to assist free men and free governments in casting off the chains of poverty. But this peaceful revolution of hope cannot become the prey of hostile powers. Let all our neighbors know that we shall join with them to oppose aggression or subversion anywhere in the Americas. And let every other power know that this hemisphere intends to remain the master of its own house.

To that world assembly of sovereign states, the United Nations, our last best hope in an age where the instruments of war have far outpaced the instruments of peace, we renew our pledge of support—to prevent it from becoming merely a forum for invective—to strengthen its shield of the new and the weak—and to enlarge the area in which its writ may run.

Finally, to those nations who would make themselves our

adversary, we offer not a pledge but a request: that both sides begin anew the quest for peace, before the dark powers of destruction unleashed by science engulf all humanity in planned or accidental self-destruction.

We dare not tempt them with weakness. For only when our arms are sufficient beyond doubt can we be certain beyond doubt that they will never be employed.

But neither can two great and powerful groups of nations take comfort from our present course—both sides overburdened by the cost of modern weapons, both rightly alarmed by the steady spread of the deadly atom, yet both racing to alter that uncertain balance of terror that stays the hand of mankind's final war.

So let us begin anew—remembering on both sides that civility is not a sign of weakness, and sincerity is always subject to proof. **Let us never negotiate out of fear. But let us never fear to negotiate.**

Let both sides explore what problems unite us instead of laboring those problems which divide us.

Let both sides, for the first time, formulate serious and precise proposals for the inspection and control of arms—and bring the absolute power to destroy other nations under the absolute control of all nations.

Let both sides seek to invoke the wonders of science instead of its terrors. Together let us explore the stars, conquer the deserts, eradicate disease, tap the ocean depths, and encourage the arts and commerce.

Let both sides unite to heed in all corners of the earth the command of Isaiah—to "undo the heavy burdens and to let the oppressed go free."

And if a beachhead of cooperation may push back the jungle of suspicion, let both sides join in creating a new endeavor, not a new balance of power, but a new world of law, where the strong are just and the weak secure and the peace preserved.

All this will not be finished in the first 100 days. Nor will it be finished in the first 1,000 days, nor in the life of this administration, nor even perhaps in our lifetime on this planet. But let us begin.

In your hands, my fellow citizens, more than in mine, will rest the final success or failure of our course. Since this country was founded, each generation of Americans has been summoned to give testimony to its national loyalty. The graves of young Americans who answered the call to service are found around the globe.

Now the trumpet summons us again—not as a call to bear arms, though arms we need; not as a call to battle, though embattled we are; but a call to bear the burden of a long twilight struggle, year in, and year out, "rejoicing in hope, patient in tribulation"—a struggle against the common enemies of man: tyranny, poverty, disease, and war itself.

Can we forge against these enemies a grand and global alliance, North and South, East and West, that can assure a more fruitful life for all mankind? Will you join in that historic effort?

In the long history of the world, only a few generations have been granted the role of defending freedom in its hour of maximum danger. I do not shrink from this responsibility—I welcome it. I do not believe that any of us would exchange places with any other people or any other generation. The energy, the faith, the devotion which we bring to this endeavor will light our country and all who serve it—and the glow from that fire can truly light the world.

And so, my fellow Americans, ask not what your country can do for you: Ask what you can do for your country.

My fellow citizens of the world: Ask not what America will do for you, but what together we can do for the freedom of man.

Finally, whether you are citizens of America or citizens of the world, ask of us the same high standards of strength and sacrifice which we ask of you. With a good conscience our only sure reward, with history the final judge of our deeds, let us go forth to lead the land we love, asking His blessing and His help, but knowing that here on earth God's work must truly be our own.

1. *figures of speech.* As *The New Yorker* writer says, the Address is rich in rhetorical figures, such as **antithesis, personification, anaphora, paronomasia** as well as more complex and more obscure ones. In fact, it has been questioned whether the substance has not been diminished by the excessive stress on the form. Where there is so much emphasis, the effect of any given device may be decreased. In any case, it is unquestionably good training in rhetorical analysis to examine closely the fabric and structure of this Address.
2. *ourself.* The extension of the editorial *we* (which is singular) to the reflexive form. *The New Yorker* seems to be the only periodical to use this form.

McLUHAN (No. 77, p. 245)

Marshall McLuhan is the apostle of a new belief in the power of the media of communications. In *The Gutenberg Galaxy* (1962) and *Understanding Media* (1964), he has set out a view summarized in the dictum "The medium is the message." The wide and perhaps uncritical acceptance of his often inconsistent opinions has had an enormous effect in certain areas of American life: public relations, advertising, the popular arts, communications media and perhaps even literature, not to mention teaching and the theories applying to the foregoing. For a few years, there was a "McLuhan craze," but it seems to have abated, so that his views can be examined in a rational context. In the present selection, which predates the wide interest in his views, he is concerned with one of his typical questions, the influence of typography on Western thought and culture, specifically on language.

1. *stylistic revolution.* McLuhan here seems to be proposing yet another explanation for the change in prose style which seems to have taken place during the Restoration in England (1660–1700). The scientific revolution, the aristocratic influence, the conversational tendency, the change in ways of preaching have all been put forward as explanations of the revolution in style. McLuhan's view is not consistent with any of these.
2. *rodeo.* The larding of his prose with items from popular culture (Burma Shave, Miss Rheingold) and with informal images ("purr of his sentences," "macadamized regularity") does not alter its essentially academic character. The most interesting stylistic feature of McLuhan's writing is its dogmatic tone, its assuredness, an effect achieved by avoiding the use of modifiers, qualifiers, concessives, or other signs of uncertainty usual with academic writers. For example, McLuhan says "Individual writers throughout the sixteenth century varied tone sentence by sentence, even phrase by phrase, with all the oral freedom and flexibility of pre-print days." The average respectable scholar would not dare to commit himself to what he would consider to be an unverifiable statement and an oversimplification. He could not be sure it was true because he had not examined all the writers of the period. Moreover, he would hesitate to say the tone shifted so frequently because one exception would defeat him. He would not say *tone* without defining it, nor would he so certainly liken this effect to oral freedom without including a cautionary word or two about such comparisons. The following might be a more typical scholarly version of McLuhan's sentence: "Owing possibly to their still-active relation to the oral tradition preceding the invention of printing, many writers in the sixteenth century felt less constrained to maintain a uniformity of tone than their successors in the seventeenth century. The tone (meaning level of diction, variety of syntax) shifted frequently and irregularly, from sentence to sentence at times and even within sentences." This admitted caricature of scholarship is not far from reality and it would be supported by most scholars with an illustrative quotation showing the effect at work. The later quotation from Nashe does not specifically illustrate anything.

WHITE (No. 78, p. 249)

(No. 78, p. 249)

This selection is taken from the last chapter of a book with an interesting genesis. In 1957 E. B. White wrote an article for *The New Yorker* about a textbook that he had used as a student at Cornell University. The book was *The Elements of Style* by William Strunk, Jr. (Ithaca, N.Y., 1918). The book's original publishers invited White to take part in a new edition to appear under the joint names of Strunk and White (with the same title), to consist of *The New Yorker* article as an Introduction, the four chapters of the original book, and a fifth chapter ("An Approach to Style") to be contributed by White.

The entire book is only eighty-five pages long and is essentially a rulebook. Strunk's first two chapters offer a total of eighteen rules of usage and principles of composition, dicta like "Do not break sentences in two," "Use the active voice." The last two chapters give specific instructions on how to handle margins, quotations and references and treat particular instances of usage problems ("alright," "can't hardly". . .). White's chapter consists of a discursive section (from which the selection is taken) and a list of eighteen "reminders" ("Write . . . naturally," "Revise and rewrite," "Use orthodox spelling"). This book despite its outmoded aspect has had a fantastic sale for a textbook of English. Part of it may be due to the American desire to reduce all really difficult things to a few simple rules. But most of it comes simply from White's reputation as a writer of the first order: not a great writer, but a craftsman and handler of the language, the master and perhaps inventor of the "casual style."

White's writing dominated and shaped *The New Yorker* for a long time and his influence is doubtless still considerable, though recently he has come to be treated as a classic, which is a danger to a living writer. It usually means that he begins to look to his laurels, to write self-consciously. As White's writing is in the highest degree self-conscious, this status may not affect him untowardly.

Apart from his position at *The New Yorker* (No. 76), White is known as a writer of a number of books, containing sketches, essays, parodies, poems and pieces defying classification. Many of them contain items reprinted from *The New Yorker* and from other periodicals (*Harper's, Holiday*). His best-known books are *One Man's Meat* (1942), *Stuart Little* (1945), *Here Is New York* (1949), and *The Second Tree from the Corner* (1953). Though he has received many honors (degrees, medals, prizes, citations) and his style has been praised extravagantly, his writing has not been closely examined or described. The nearest thing to an analysis of White's style is a witty piece by William H. Whyte, Jr., "You, Too, Can Write the Casual Style" (*Harper's,* Oct. 1953, pp. 87–89). Whyte specifically exempts Thurber and White from his criticism but it is applicable all the same. He lists a dozen devices used by the casual stylist to achieve the characteristic effect. The more important ones are: "heightened understatement," "the multiple hedge," "narcissizing your prose," and "the planned colloquialism." An examination of the present selection will show that Whyte was right on the target.

1. *something of a mystery.* White likes to think of human activities, skills, talents, and nature as mysterious, as things it is better not to examine for fear of destroying them, for the attempt is doomed in any case. Humor, style, personality—these are beyond the touch of science. The *something* is an example of Whyte's "heightened understatement," as are also "let him try" and "see what happens." A non-casual writer might say more directly: "Style is a mystery; anyone who tries to rewrite a familiar sentence will fail."
2. *simple declarative sentence.* The sentence is declarative but not simple. It contains a dependent clause, of the kind called a restrictive adjectival, which makes the sentence complex. A simple declarative version would have been "These times try men's souls." The myth of the simple, declarative sentence is perplexing. Why a careful writer like White should call a complex sentence simple is beyond understanding. Perhaps, since he approves of the sentence, he *wants* it to be simple because simple sentences are good, in his estimation, though he does not use them any more than other writers.
3. *flashy.* Another casualism, the unexpected use of a colloquial or slangy word.
4. *ordinary.* The word *try* in the sense of "subject to an ordeal, put to a severe test" is by no means as ordinary as White implies.
5. *variations.* The simple declarative version (mentioned above) is for some reason not included among the possible variations. There is reason to suspect that White made his argument look stronger by thinking up obviously inadequate versions. In any case, the test is not a fair one because the familiar sentence always sounds "righter" than any concocted variation. It has the power of familiarity as have many quotations which, though often repeated, are literally not understood.
6. *Thomas Paine.* White wants us to know that he was quoting Thomas Paine but was unwilling to be so uncasual as to come right out and say it. It is introduced indirectly along with the information that he lived more than 150 years ago ("well along in its second century").

7. *sentiment stick.* This colloquialism, like *flashy* above, gives emphasis to White's diction. But it also robs his writing of clarity right here. In what sense did Paine make his "sentiment stick"? Did everyone then agree that those were trying times? Or does everyone now believe that those were trying times then? Or does everyone agree that he stated it correctly? There may be other possibilities covered by White's vague phrase, which mainly seems to mean that the sentence was remembered.
8. *couched.* A rather fancy item of vocabulary, which contrasts well with the previous colloquialism. Without it, it would seem elaborate. In the context, it effects an impressive mixture of levels.
9. *put our finger on.* A casual colloquialism, meaning "determine," that helps to set up the more elevated phrase to follow.
10. *marked for oblivion.* A perversion of the phrase "marked for greatness."
11. *"rhythm" and "cadence."* Two of the favorite terms in impressionistic criticism of style. White is unwilling to explain the mystery of style, or even to try, at least in this sentence. He puts up a series of straw men, of which rhythm and cadence are the first, and then distracts us with *"soulwise,"* before passing on to another sentence.
12. *main question.* White does not tell us what the "main question" is.
13. *"soulwise."* White has created the outrageous neologism *soulwise,* used it in a sentence, called it silly and inappropriate, and then argued the question whether it is inappropriate by analogy with *otherwise.* The whole procedure is irrelevant and has many of the features of what Whyte calls "the multiple hedge." The main function, I believe, of all this evasive action is to conceal the fact that White has nothing to say about the advantage of Paine's sentence over the concocted alternatives. The *soulwise* matter offers a vivid way out of the paragraph.

Propositional Reduction

¶ 1. It is impossible to rewrite a familiar sentence.
2. Any familiar quotation can be used.
3. An example of a familiar quotation is "These are the times that try men's souls."
4. "These are the times . . ." is a simple declarative sentence containing eight short words.
5. "These are the times . . ." contains no unusual lexical items.
6. "These are the times . . ." has been quoted for almost two centuries.
7. Several variations of "These are the times . . ." are possible.
8. Thomas Paine's sentiment is less effective in any alternative version.
9. The reasons why Thomas Paine's sentiment is less effective in any alternative version are difficult to discover.

10. The alternative versions of "These are the times . . ." are grammatical and clear.
11. The alternative versions of "These are the times . . ." are correct but not as impressive as the original.
12. The alternative versions of "These are the times . . ." are unimpressive not because of "rhythm" or "cadence."
13. The neologism *soulwise* in one of the alternative versions of "These are the times . . ." is not adequate reason for the inferiority of that version.
14. The neologism *soulwise* is not necessarily inappropriate.
15. *Soulwise* is as serviceable as *otherwise.*

Logical Diagram

	A	B	C	D
¶ 1.	( )			
2.		(=)		
3.			(×)	
4.		(=)		
5.		(+)		
6.		(+)		
7.	(–)			
8.	(–)			
9.	(–)			
10.		(=)		
11.		(+)		
12.		(+)		
13.		(+)		
14.		(–)		
15.		(+)		

KEROUAC (No. 79, p. 251)

Jack Kerouac became a spokesman for the "Beat Generation," with the publication of his novel *On the Road* (1957). The writing of this group was notable for its disregard for matters of form. Kerouac especially was attacked for this tendency by reviewers in the more conservative and puristic journals, such as *The New Yorker*. The present selection illustrates as well as expounds Kerouac's philosophy of writing. See GRAVES's reference to Beat poets (No. 1).

1. *Timing.* The syntax of this paragraph is elliptical, what has been called "telegraphic style." That is, words like *the, its,* and certain verbs and auxiliaries are omitted. The effect is to produce unusual collocations, such as "forever hold tongue," which is a telescoping of the phrase "hold one's tongue" and "for ever hold your peace" from the Solemnization of Matrimony in the Book of Common Prayer. The omission of a determiner makes the phrase sound less familiar. But the more important aspect of the syntax is its obscurity: the relations between the items separated by dashes and the one in parentheses are not clear. Perhaps they are not intended to be organically related but merely sequential.
2. *jewel center.* Apparently a term specially meaningful to Kerouac, signifying something like *core* or *nucleus* (used again in the next paragraph). If this is an image, it conflicts with the immediately following image of the writer as swimmer in the sea of language, which itself is abandoned to bring in the notion of release and exhaustion. If this last were part of the previous image, the swimmer/writer would drown. But Kerouac does not claim to be consistent in his imagery. As he says throughout this selection, the writer should be spontaneous and avoid craftsmanship, revision, and other efforts to conform to an ideal of form.
3. *afterthink.* A back-formation from *afterthought.*
4. *P.S. reasons.* Postscript, things forgotten and added later.
5. *defray.* An individual use of this word, which normally means *pay.*
6. *blow!* A musical image, as of a horn-player, related to "song of yourself" just before.
7. *"good"—or "bad."* A number of words are set in quotation marks in this selection. Some, like "ludicrous," "crafted," and others, seem to be references to the criticism directed against the writer and to the canons of traditional good writing. Other quotations are conventional uses of the words of other writers, attributed to Yeats, Reich and Williams. Like his use of other traditional devices, Kerouac's use of quotations is deviant, almost wilful.
8. *outfanning.* Like *afterthink, mindflow, jewel center, time-race,* this word is a kind of neologism of a certain type (either attributive noun + noun or preposition + verb) that Kerouac seems prone to. It can be best understood in the light of his rejection of traditional ideas of proper language and his desire to find new ways of expression. Actually, the forms of these neologisms are

quite standard word-creation patterns in English (e.g., *output, jet-age*). It is difficult to think of anything in language-modification which has not been tried (and accepted) before. The omission of articles is hardly new, having been practiced in headlines, telegrams and poetry for some time. WOLFE (No. 73) has perhaps been most successful in this sort of innovation.

9. *false colons.* Though Kerouac uses no colons in this selection (either full or semi-), he does have recourse to a certain number of "timid usually needless commas." He makes extensive use of the dash, as he advocates, but he also uses the traditional round brackets (parentheses), hyphens, periods and quotation marks, which are by some considered signs of timidity or caution, because they signalize the quoter's unwillingness to take responsibility for another's words. Kerouac also likes italics and extra capital letters. His typographical means of emphasis are reminiscent of Laurence Sterne's.

10. *fish.* Apart from the "blowing" of the horn-player, the main image in this selection is the one concerned with water ("seas of thought," "swimming in sea of English," "fish . . . down," in addition to those mentioned above). The two may be connected in some sexual way by the references to rhythm, breath, exhalation, release.

McCARTHY (No. 80, p. 253)

Mary McCarthy began her writing career as a reviewer and went on to become the theater critic of the *Partisan Review*. These pieces and her other essays and short stories have been collected in several volumes. She has also written several novels, of which *The Group* (1963) is the best-known. One critic has noted that Mary McCarthy's prose is the product of her discovery of Latin literature and language in school and college. This sort of statement is not easily verified, for such an influence, if it existed, need not manifest itself in Latinate constructions. Whether or not the remark is true or verifiable, it is plain that Mary McCarthy's sentences are not short or simple in syntax. They tend to complexity, with extensive use of apposition and parenthesis, but they are not obscure. One has the feeling, subjective to be sure, that the prose is under control and that the huge amounts of data with which her sentences bulge cannot distract her from her argument. It could be said that the main feature of Mary McCarthy's sentences is copiousness, fullness, an accumulation of fact, explanation, illustration, restatement. The principle behind the copiousness is the expansion of the basic sentence.

There are several modes of this expansion, the most frequent being the appositive or parenthetical insertion. The insertions may occur between commas, dashes, or round brackets. The very first sentence well shows this procedure: "The notion that life is senseless, a tale told by an idiot—the undertheme of twentieth-century literature—is affirmed again by FAULKNER in *The Sound and the Fury*." The first construction is explained by the appositive between the comma and the dash (itself an unmarked quotation from Macbeth's famous soliloquy, like the title of Faulkner's book). Then both items together are defined by the appositive between dashes, before the sentence reaches the predicate. Another example comes in the middle of the first paragraph: "The sign of this kind of writing, the mark of its affiliation with the pure impressionist or stream-of-consciousness novel, is that when you start the book you do not know where you are." In this sentence also it is the subject that is expanded with the appositive explaining and augmenting it. Actually, the appositive does not merely restate or define the subject: it offers an alternative subject in some kind of relation with the first one, though the relation is not that of synonymy.

Related to the appositive expansion is the serial mode, in which a series of items is presented either formally (after a colon) or informally, sneaked, as it were, in a place where the reader did not count on such expansion. The former type occurs in the second sentence: "Yet, here as in *Ulysses,* characters appear from the mists of their own reveries and sensations: the idiot Benjy, Jason, Dilsey, the Negro cook." It is worth noting that the series is **asyndetic,** a procedure which gives an effect of endless continuity. The informal mode is illustrated by the following sentence, where everything after *professor* is **serial augmentation:** "It is exhilarating but not altogether honest to make believe I am a devious red-haired man professor with bad breath and bits of toilet paper on his face, to talk under my breath his sibilant, vindictive thought-language and draw his pale lips tightly across my teeth."

Yet another type of rhetorical expansion is what looks like an afterthought. A concessive or a relative clause or an appositive is tacked on at the end of a sentence, additions which both qualify and explain what has gone before. The following sentence combines both types: "Once you know where you are, you can relax and study your surroundings, though you must watch out for sudden, disorienting jolts and jerks—an indication that the character is in movement, colliding or interacting with objective reality." In this sentence, the basic statement (up to *though*) is practically negated by the succeeding concessive clause. The following appositive, which might as well have taken the form of a *which*-clause, itself contains a compound appositive, after the comma.

There are variations, in this selection, of these basic patterns, as well as other types of augmentation (pleonastic doublets, extensive similes), but the principle is ever-present. Other features of style are visibly important in this prose (e.g., the variable level of lexical choice), but the rich copiousness and the various means by which it is realized are surely the most significant. Like another satirist (Jonathan SWIFT), whose sentences showed the same tendency, Mary McCarthy has a fertile and lively mind, whose contents struggle for expression. It may not be entirely impressionistic to relate this estimate to the fullness of her sentences.

FAULKNER (No. 81, p. 257)

On one thing most critics of Faulkner are agreed: his sentences are very long and complicated. The 28 sentences of the present selection have an average length of 38 words. This is significantly longer than the comparable prose of some of the other modern American authors in this book:

	Average number of words per sentence
ANDERSON (No. 89)	27.52
MACDONALD (No. 75)	25.25
POUND (No. 87)	18.74
TRILLING (No. 82)	24.88
WHITE (No. 78)	15.85

These figures suggest that Faulkner's sentences are indeed at least ten words longer on the average than the run of serious writers, in expository prose, at any rate. It is probable, however, that he would be challenged by WOLFE (No. 85) and MILLER (No. 83). As for the complexity, though it is easily perceptible to the reader, it has been illustrated in an article by Richard Ohmann (see Bibliography No. 37) which shows that the number of grammatical transformations required to construct one of Faulkner's sentences is much greater than those few used by HEMINGWAY. The intuitive response of the reader and critic, then, concerning the length and complexity of Faulkner's sentences would seem to be justified, something which is by no means always true.

1. *a dream.* The use of a colon before and after this word is very unusual. From the evidence in this selection, it would be reasonable to conclude that

Faulkner was a great appreciator of colons. He uses perhaps a dozen in the selection, including another double and even a triple. The significance of this preference is difficult to be sure about, but it has an obvious connection with long sentences. Whether Faulkner's sentences are long because he uses colons or he uses colons in order to prolong his sentences, it is difficult to say. Inasmuch as he uses also semicolons, dashes and parentheses, it seems probable that Faulkner's sense of a sentence is that it must contain a certain quantity of material and that these devices are merely ways of keeping it in order.

2. *dreamed in sleep.* The structure of this complicated sentence can be analyzed as follows. The words before the second colon are not properly part of the sentence itself. The second colon could easily have been a period. The next element, up to the dash, is really the first proposition of the sentence. The construction between the dash and the semicolon is an inserted appositive intended to clarify the participial phrase beginning with *leading.* The sentence begins again, after the adverbial phrase ("and with me to listen now"), without another subject before the verb *went on,* followed by two participle phrases, the second of which is interrupted by a parenthesis syntactically unrelated to the sentence itself, more like an aside, and concluded at *his writing.* This is followed by another adverbial phrase ("me listening . . .") which matches the earlier one, followed by a colon introducing another appositive. A schematic display of the sentence follows, showing the basic structure separate from the adverbials, appositives and parentheses:

He told me what it was at once: a dream.
He had dreamed the night before
that he was walking for miles
along country roads (leading a
horse which he was trying to
swap for a night's sleep)

not for a simple bed for the
night, but for the sleep itself

(and with me to listen now)
went on from there (elaborating it,
building it into a work of art
with the same tedious

it had the appearance of
fumbling but actually it
wasn't: it was seeking,
hunting

almost excruciating patience
and humility with which he did all

his writing [me listening and believing no word of it]) — that is, that it had been any dream dreamed in sleep.

The left-hand column contains the basic structural elements, along with their adverbial and participial modifiers (with parentheses marks around them). The right-hand column contains appositives and true parentheses. The main clause (italicized) is a very minor part of the sentence. Everything else is stuffed into syntactical openings of various kinds, of subordinate status.

3. *Because I knew better.* The contrast between this short utterance (not a complete sentence) and the long one preceding suggests that Faulkner had artistic control over his sentence structure, that his sentences were not long simply because they got away from him.

4. *invented it, made it.* The second verb supplements the first. It is an afterthought but not a revision, or it would have replaced the first verb. The afterthought, to Faulkner, is part of the structure. The same occurs a little further on: "most of it or at least some of it." There are many more such afterthoughts in this passage.

5. *patience and humility.* A perfect example of the effectiveness of the afterthought device. By correcting himself, subtracting humor from the list of Anderson's qualities in the event he is narrating, Faulkner immeasurably emphasizes the humorlessness of Anderson's soul-searching. To have said "with patience and humility but little humor" would hardly have been as effective as giving the tribute and then withdrawing it. This is really a comic device, occasionally used by Mark TWAIN (see No. 91).

6. *purity and integrity and hard and unremitting work and accomplishment.* Faulkner leans to **polysyndeton** when he reels off a string of items like this one. The superfluous connectives blur the relation between the items, making it appear that the sequence is A + B + C + D + E, whereas it is actually (A + B) + ([C + D] [E + F]), with C and D both modifying E and F.

7. *Winesburg, Ohio* and *The Triumph of the Egg.* According to most critics, Sherwood Anderson's best works (published in 1919 and 1921, respectively).

8. *Melville, Twain, Dreiser.* This is Faulkner's elaborate way of suggesting that these writers influenced Anderson.

9. *just style.* It seems to be Faulkner's belief that Anderson worked hard to keep his style consistent and uniform, regardless of the substance. He disregards the possibility that the style remained what it was, despite Anderson, but that he had written himself out at a certain point in his career.

10. *bound girl.* A European immigrant who was given passage to the United States against a promise of working for a given number of years as a servant.

11. *The Torrents of Spring.* Hemingway's first "novel," published in 1926. It was written in a burlesque of Sherwood Anderson's manner.
12. *primer-like style.* See the notes to ANDERSON (No. 89).

MILLER (No. 83, p. 263)

Henry Miller was for a long time known only because of two books, *Tropic of Cancer* (1931) and *Tropic of Capricorn* (1939), that were considered too obscene to be printed in (or even imported into) the United States. In today's freer climate, Miller's books are available everywhere and inevitably his appeal has diminished. Karl Shapiro has called him "the greatest living author." Others have called him a bohemian, a disciple of LAWRENCE, a descendant of WHITMAN and a number of less complimentary names. Unquestionably, for a long period he was America's most controversial writer.

1. *the mood seizes me.* Miller's most characteristic feature of style is the list, in this case of verbs: "I invent, distort, deform, lie, inflate, exaggerate, confound and confuse. . . ." He makes no effort to find the word which will exactly convey the idea he has in mind; he simply strings together all the words he can think of which approximate the idea. As he says himself, he has no faith in words, or presumably in the possibility of choosing the right word, and no respect for the conventions of proper writing, though he does not go out of his way as does KEROUAC (No. 79) to show his disrespect.
2. *clear as a bell.* The use of this hackneyed simile is another indication of Miller's unwillingness to make the effort to be a skillful writer. He uses the first available form, even if it is a cliché, careless of the opinions of critics, some of whom have severely commented on this aspect of his style.
3. *a living blissfully with it.* Even prepositions stimulate Miller to seriation, as in the string that follows "living blissfully": *with it, in it, through* and *by it.* None of the individual units of the series conveys particular components of meaning of any importance. After all, what is the difference between living *with* or *in* a mystery? It is the concatenation that is effective, as it conveys to the reader the writer's attempt to include all the aspects of living in relation to the mystery.
4. *incalculable dimensions.* Like many of the series that Miller uses (often at or near the end of sentences), this one contains an alliterative pair (*climates, conditions*).

5. *unknown center.* Compare this expression and idea with KEROUAC's (No. 79) *jewel-center.*
6. *illusive.* A rare variant of *illusory.*
7. *metamorphic.* *Changing,* from *metamorphosis.*
8. *accouchement.* French word meaning delivery of a baby. Writers have frequently compared the creation of their works to childbirth.
9. *completely vanished.* This fourteen-line sentence is a series of series, whose progress well matches the continuous but erratic process that Miller is trying to describe. Consciously or not, he has here matched the effect to the substance skillfully, like a good rhetorician, which he denies that he is.
10. *cold eye of the critic.* Like nearly every writer, Miller has only loathing for critics. It is a natural enmity, that of the synthesizer for the analyzer.
11. *Or I could produce.* Miller's serial tendency extends to parallel strings of sentences.
12. *in the form of deed . . . of a spider's web.* The last seven sentences of this selection contain five different series, of which the present is the longest, containing eleven items: "deed, event, fact, thought, emotion, desire, evasion, frustration, dream, revery, vagary. . . ." Two sets of the items (*evasion, frustration; revery, vagary*) are linked by terminal assonance. The movement of this series is an interesting study in free association. It moves from the concrete ("deed, event, fact") to the internal activity of the mind ("thought, emotion"), then to a specific emotion ("desire") and to two consequences of it ("evasion, frustration"), finally to the domain of escape from frustration ("dream, revery"). *Vagary* is probably just the result of phonetic association with *revery,* especially if it is mispronounced, with the accent on the first syllable.

The nature of this series, as described, and the frequency with which series occur in Miller's work, which this selection typifies, provide an interesting demonstration of the unconscious character of certain features of style. If Miller were a self-conscious writer, he would hardly use such a device so often because he would be aware of its fusion into the context. Each repeated use diminishes the emphasis. For him to use it so often, it must fulfill some unconscious expressive need that makes him unaware of how often he uses it.

WOLFE (No. 85, p. 273)

Most readers are familiar with the outline story of the genesis of Thomas Wolfe's first novel, *Look Homeward, Angel* (1929): how Wolfe wrote an endless amount, stuffed the papers into a trunk, brought them to Maxwell Perkins, the editor at Scribners, who for eight months pruned, polished, excised, amended, revised—in a word, edited—the manuscript to make a book out of it. For this Wolfe was, as he should have been, grateful, and he dedicated his second novel, *Of Time and the River* (1935), to Perkins. *The Story of a Novel* (1936), from which the selection is taken, is a humble, candid account of the partnership between Wolfe and Perkins. It was seized on by the critic Bernard DeVoto in an article in the *Saturday Review of Literature* (April 25, 1936), entitled "Genius Is Not Enough," as the basis of an attack on Wolfe. DeVoto claimed that Wolfe had relied too heavily on the editorial aids of his publisher, that he lacked the maturity and discipline to be an artist and was in a sense not the sole author of his own book. Wolfe took this so much to heart that he left Scribners for another publisher and another editor.

Wolfe's style has been called *rhetorical,* sometimes *bombastic, hysterical* and *noisy,* sometimes *poetic.* It has nearly always been noticed and awarded a significant share in the unusual quality of Wolfe's work. Although the selection describes the process which produced the characteristic Wolfe output, it is itself written more soberly than his fiction. Still, it is typical of Wolfe's style, and its virtues and defects are those of the author. Wolfe is obviously not a Plain Stylist, nor a Mandarin (see No. 6), but what I have called an Expressive writer (see No. 7, notes). Like KEROUAC (No. 79) and MILLER (No. 83), Wolfe pours himself out, hardly caring how he does it, or so it seems. This trio, at any rate, though for different reasons, are not wordsmiths in the way that writers like WHITE (No. 78) and SMITH (No. 9) are, for example. The images that Wolfe uses to describe his writing support this view: "frenzied labor," "burning lava from a volcano," "white heat." Revision is described by the words "cutting," "coldly surgical."

A writer viewing himself as in the grip of uncontrollable forces is not likely to produce exquisite, well-shaped sentences. He is likely to write long, rambling sentences, swelling with appositives, afterthoughts, lists, and other forms of augmentation. The average length of the thirty-seven sentences in the selection is around 35 words, almost as high as FAULKNER (No. 81, notes).

1. *bloody execution.* This, along with *carnage,* in the next sentence may be set beside *cutting* and *surgical,* which have been cited.
2. *The first chapter.* This sentence may be examined as a typical instance of Wolfe's method of progression within the sentence. He begins with the subject ("The first chapter in the original manuscript"), follows it with an appositive ("a chapter which the editor, himself, admitted was as good a single piece of writing as I had ever done") and proceeds to the predicate ("was relentlessly kicked out"). Having reached the point at which he wishes to give the reason

for the event stated in the predicate (something that might have been handled with a clause beginning with *because*), he launches into the second half of a compound sentence ("and the reason it was kicked out was that it was"), which involves him in a repetition of the verb-cluster (*kicked out*), the awkward "the reason was" construction and a string of inelegant *was*'s: "*was* kicked out *was* that it *was*." The predicate of the last *was* is a compound *not . . . but . . .* construction in which he first says what the chapter was not ("not a true beginning for the book") before revealing what it was ("but merely something which led up to the true beginning"), with another repetition of a nominal. He concludes with a third stage of his compound sentence ("therefore, it had to go"), information which has already been given, more than once. The last clause is a kind of abstract of the previous parts, perhaps resulting from an awareness of its indirectness. A Plainer Stylist required to compress this sentence might have done it thus: "The first chapter in the original manuscript, which the editor said was my best work, was deleted because it merely led up to the beginning of the book." This is not better than Wolfe; it is merely plainer, intended to contrast with his Expressive method.

3. *flood and fabric.* *Flood* fits in with Wolfe's running water imagery, but *fabric* comes from another realm of matter (the warp and woof of experience?). Together they do not mix well.

4. *talk.* In this passage is shown another tendency of Wolfe's expressive side, the unnecessary repetition of words, or the failure to avoid such repetition. Five instances occur in three lines: "All were good talkers; often all talked, or tried to talk, at the same time. The talk was wonderful and living talk. . . ."

5. *torrential discourse.* Words as water. See above, *flood, poured,* and just below, *flood-tide river,* and later *flow of his creation.*

6. *a half million words.* Despite his consciousness that he writes too much, Wolfe is in some way fond of his enormous productivity. He displays the figures as a rich man might proclaim his riches. "100,000 words," "50,000 words," "80,000 words," "200 pages," "thousands of words," "well over a half-million words," "a dozen additional chapters" are repeatedly paraded before us, to compel our admiration at so much creativity. It is not hard to believe the anguish that cutting must have caused to such a writer.

STEIN (No. 86, p. 277)

Historians of literature have had a field day with Gertrude Stein. With James Joyce, she has been credited with initiating "the revolution of the word." To others, she is a disciple either of Mark TWAIN or of Henry JAMES, but in any case an important landmark in the progress of the "colloquial style" in American literature. According to herself and her friends, she and Sherwood ANDERSON provided Ernest HEMINGWAY with the model he needed. Hemingway himself disputed this claim. In any case, Gertrude Stein was certainly, but for other reasons, as controversial a writer as Henry MILLER. For her style, she received more censure than praise and a good deal of ridicule from the uninformed. Critics have been divided about the value of her books: see, for example Alfred KAZIN (No. 74) for the prevailing negative view and Sherwood ANDERSON (No. 89) for what now sounds like old-fashioned approval. Despite their differences, most readers have agreed that Gertrude Stein's style is characterized by long sentences, a great use of the connective *and,* unusual punctuation, and repetition. The average sentence-length of the present selection is 30.3 words, though in a similar passage of her *Autobiography of Alice B. Toklas* it is only 19.7. Her use of *and* is high by comparison with other British and American writers, though not as high as that of Dwight MACDONALD (No. 75) or of HEMINGWAY (No. 88). The figures for the two works by Gertrude Stein are 3.86 (the present selection), and 4.23 (*Autobiography*), and for MacDonald and Hemingway, 4.70 and 4.66 respectively, representing *and* as a percentage of the total words in the selection. About the repetition, there is hardly any question. In fact, it is the subject of the selection itself.

1. *with anything.* It can be seen from this example that one reason for Gertrude Stein's long sentences is her punctuation. Any other writer would have ended the sentence here and begun the next element as a new sentence. The remainder consists of three parallel clause-systems stitched together with *ands.* The omission of one *and* would make it much more conventional. Repunctuating the sentence as follows would reduce much of its Steinian flavor: "In short, this generation has conceived an intensity of movement so great that it has not to be seen against something else to be known, and therefore this generation does not connect itself with anything; that is what makes this generation what it is and that is why it is American; this is very important in connection with portraits of anything." It would be even more conventional if the semicolons were replaced by periods. The main purpose of this demonstration, however, is to show that typography (e.g., punctuation) rather than syntax is responsible for some of the irregular effect of Gertrude Stein's prose.

2. *is there insistence.* The same typographical idiosyncrasy makes Gertrude Stein punctuate her questions without question marks.

3. *the same emphasis.* This long sentence (19 lines) really consists of a dozen sentences (depending on how one punctuates) concatenated into one single ut-

terance. The utterance is a sentence not by grammatical criteria but by typographical ones: that it begins with a capital letter and ends with a period.
4. *that have been on this earth.* This parenthetical insert is relatively uncommon in Gertrude Stein's practise. She does not so much insert or embed constructions into her sentences as string constructions one after the other. Thus one might call her syntax linear rather than nested (cf. MILTON, No. 44). A linear syntax can proceed well with a minimum of punctuation. It usually consists of clauses tied with simple connectives like *and* or *but* or of successive subordinate clauses, generally relative. A nested syntax operates by means of embedded clauses, one construction being interrupted before its conclusion to allow the insertion of another, or by means of inserted appositives between constructions, themselves perhaps interrupted by other insertions. Either type of nesting depends greatly on the devices of typography to keep the relations distinct and the sense clear. Hemingway and FAULKNER are practitioners of extreme forms of linear and nested syntax, respectively.

POUND (No. 87, p. 281)

1. *estimator.* Note the dogmatic force of the utterances in this paragraph. There are no connectives between sentences and hardly anything is modified or restricted. Everything has the finality of the Mosaic Law. This absoluteness is supported by such words as *not, exactly, all other, only,* which reveal no doubt about anything. This manner is somehow doubtless related to Pound's personality, which found the ideas of Fascism attractive and led him to prison, the insane asylum, and exile for treason.
2. *questions of viewpoint.* Despite the linguistic purism to which Pound seems to be leaning in this selection, he is not in the camp of those who want to maintain propriety. Efficiency, rather than decorum, is the ideal he professes. His paragraphing, it can be seen, is anything but conventional and his syntax is irregular: the second paragraph consists of two sentences joined by a comma (before "they may").
3. *atrophies and decays.* It may be supposed that Pound is not an expert on the animal nervous system, yet he has no reluctance to expound this aphorism as a fact and by analogy to draw a completely unjustified conclusion from it in another realm. If a nation's literature declines, a great many possibilities exist. Some literature has probably declined in our time: what do we make of that?
4. *Your populace.* The use of *you* and *your* for *the* and *a* is often used in a

conversation to generate intimacy and rapport. It is a man-of-the-people gesture with Pound, who doesn't have great sympathy for the people but not much for intellectual pretension either.

5. *'representatives.'* The force of these quotation marks is to cast doubt on the genuine representativeness of democracy.

6. *swindling classes.* The intemperate language of the propagandist does not trouble to identify the objects of his dislike.

7. *Ubicunque lingua romana, ibi Roma.* Wherever Latin is, there is Rome. Probably either a misquotation from Horace or a pseudo-Horatian line concocted by Pound. It is perhaps worth wondering whether Pound consciously used *in re* and four *via*'s in the previous paragraph to prepare for the Latin quotation.

8. [*'Insults o'er dull and speechless tribes'*] Line 12 of Shakespeare's Sonnet No. 107. The previous lines reveal that Shakespeare was here using the well-known poetic contrast between the poem, which is immortal, and the body, which is mortal. It is not clear what relevancy this point has except that it shows the power of the word:

> My love looks fresh, and death to me subscribes
> Since spight of him Ile live in this poore rime,
> While he insults ore dull and speachlesse tribes.

9. *Horace and Shakespeare.* A covert reference to the two preceding quotations.

10. *monumental and mnemonic.* Horace's reference is to Latin as a monument of Rome; Shakespeare's to English as a record of things said.

11. *'language to conceal thought'.* The phrase has been attributed to Voltaire ("Ils . . . n'emploient les paroles que pour deguiser leurs pensées.") *Dialogue XIV* (1766) and by his biographers to Talleyrand ("La parole a été donnée à l'homme pour déguiser sa pensée."). Voltaire was being critical of the practice; Talleyrand, as a diplomat, was justifying it.

12. *and so forth.* An informal conclusion to a sentence by a writer who does not care to take the trouble to conclude more properly. In some cases the use of a "continuator" (See SWIFT, No. 36, note 5) is a rhetorical device. Here it seems to be primarily heedlessness, both of propriety and of the reader. There is another example two paragraphs further: "something of that sort."

13. *'embittered'.* There is no doubt that those who foretell the decline of civilization, Pound included, are called 'embittered' and other things.

14. *'statesman cannot govern . . . without language.'* Research has failed to turn up the source of this quotation, which may be from one of the Oriental writers in which Pound has dabbled or of his own making. The expression "participate his discoveries" has been obsolete since the middle of the eighteenth

century, but the word *scientist* was first used around 1840. Earlier the scientist was called a "natural philosopher." Consequently, on the basis of internal evidence, this quotation appears fraudulent.

15. *abrupt and disordered syntax.* Pound calls such syntax "scandalous." It is not clear whether he includes under syntax the relations between sentences, that is, the use of connectives and transitions to bridge the gaps between propositions. His practice in these matters would certainly qualify as "abrupt." In the next paragraph, he justifies his practice: "Abrupt and disordered syntax can at times be very honest." There is a degree of self-consciousness in this self-justification: the contrast between the hesitant *at times* and the unnecessary intensifier *very. Honest,* like *unique,* does not benefit from intensification.

16. *different constructions of throat.* All the evidence suggests that human throats (the human sound-producing organs) are identical, though individuals may have defects. Any human being can learn to make any sound in any language. This is obviously not a matter that Pound has investigated. Like a propagandist, he invents the facts he needs to support his views.

HEMINGWAY (No. 88, p. 285)

To most readers, whether in English or in translation, Hemingway means *style.* The Nobel Prize citation referred to his "style-forming mastery." There is no question that Hemingway's has been the most influential, the most imitated, and the most parodied style in American letters. As early as 1932, Wolcott Gibbs of the *New Yorker* wrote "Death in the Rumble Seat," a clever parody of Hemingway's bullfight pieces. E. B. WHITE's "Across the Street and Into the Grill" closely followed the publication of *Across the River and Into the Trees* (1950), a book which attracted a good deal of other unfavorable notice. Lillian Ross and Dwight MACDONALD, both of the *New Yorker,* wrote semiparodic biographical pieces about the later Hemingway. About his style, Hemingway himself said "what amateurs call a style is only the unavoidable awkwardnesses in first trying to make something that has not heretofore been made. Almost no new classics resemble other previous classics. At first people can see only the awkwardness. Then they are not so perceptible. When they show so very awkwardly people think these awkwardnesses are the style and many copy them. This is regrettable." (See Bibliography No. 12, pp. 230–1.) The reading public has equated Hemingway's style with short sentences and with simplicity. The critics have not been so naive. Although they have not succeeded in providing us with a complete description of it, they have noted some of the obvious features. Mark Schorer in 1941 mentioned that Hemingway's style was characterized by "ascetic suppression of ornament and figure," by understatement and by "directness and brevity of its syntactical constructions . . . sharpness of its staccato and repetitive effects." ("The Background of a Style," *Kenyon Review,* III [1941], 101–105) Harry Levin's 1951 article (see Levin, Bibliography No. 38) goes into more detail. Levin calls attention to the attenuated vocabulary (rich in short words and foreign words), the informal syntax, with its reduction of inflections and faulty pronoun reference, the restricted use of adjectives (except for a few often repeated ones such as *nice* and *fine*) and of verbs (mostly *be* forms), extensive use of nouns, continuous forms of verbs and participles. Richard Ohmann has observed that Hemingway's sentences are closer to kernel sentences than FAULKNER's (see Steinmann, Bibliography No. 37). In sum, Hemingway's style is revealed as not merely a way of writing simply but a complicated set of affectations many of which leave the normal English idiom behind. If his style were perfectly idiomatic, the parodies would not be recognizable.

One aspect of Hemingway's philosophy which has some bearing on the style must be mentioned. It is perhaps best summarized by the following lines from *A Farewell to Arms:*

> I was always embarrassed by the words sacred, glorious, and sacrifice and the expression in vain. We had heard them, sometimes standing in the rain almost out of earshot, so that only the shouted words came through, and had read them on proclamations that were slapped up by billposters over other proclamations, now for a long time, and I had seen nothing sacred, and the things that were glorious had no glory and the sacrifices were like the stockyards at Chicago if nothing was done with the meat except to bury it. There were many words that you could not stand to hear and finally only the names of places had dignity. Certain numbers were the same way and certain dates and these with the names of the places were all you could say and have them mean anything. Abstract words such as glory, honor, courage, or hallow were obscene beside the concrete names of villages, the numbers of roads, the names of rivers, the numbers of regiments and the dates.

The paradoxical significance of this passage is that it reveals a writer who has lost faith in words. To Hemingway, important things must not be spoken about directly. Everything must be avoided, circumvented, implied—handled by indirection. That is why there is so much detail in Hemingway's fiction: description of guns, places, animals, fishing tackle, cafés. It is an avoidance of the theme of his work. At one time every new writer was influenced by this approach to reality, but now the style appears so mannered and dated that it can hardly serve as a model. But its philosophical basis, the verbal skepticism, has if anything increased in scope. Some of the more recent British playwrights (e.g., Harold Pinter) use conversations utterly without point or relevance and include long silences between speeches. The trend in many phases of literature seems to be in the direction of a suspicion about the misleading malevolence of language.

To speak of Hemingway's style is to think of it as an unchanging entity. To some extent this view is sound for most writers and it seems especially applicable to Hemingway himself. His earliest work bears an obvious kinship to his last book (*A Moveable Feast,* 1964). Yet a close chronological examination of the texts suggests that a curious process took place which hindered the writer's natural development. In his earliest stories and in *The Sun Also Rises,* Hemingway is not tied to any stereotype of his style. There is a certain range in his idiolect and he uses a greater variety of syntax and vocabulary, though the verbal skepticism is there from the first. After a time, perhaps by the time of the publication of *For Whom the Bell Tolls* (1940), it seemed as if Hemingway's style had become a parody of itself. The mannerisms, especially the Spanish flavor, stood out more grossly and called attention to themselves. It might be said that Hemingway's style was originally the consequence of the interaction of his personality, his idiolect, and the literary problems that he applied himself to. Later it seemed as if he had been reading his critics—something he warned writers against in *The Green Hills of Africa* (1935) and elsewhere—had learned from them what his style was really like and had then set out to imitate it. The end product is most readily visible in *Across the River and Into the Trees.* What happened to Hemingway has happened to a great many writers who continue to write after they have stopped learning. Faulkner said it about Sherwood ANDERSON: "when he had reached the point where he should have stopped writing, he had to defend that style at all costs because he too must have known by then in his heart that there was nothing else left." (No. 81). It seems applicable to Hemingway.

1. *Old Lady.* A dummy character used by the author to permit him to put some of his discursive remarks about bullfighting into dialogue form.
2. *"Foreheads Villainous Low."* The essay "Foreheads Villainous Low" is included in *Music at Night and Other Essays* (1931). The book Huxley refers to is Hemingway's *A Farewell to Arms.* The deleted compliment is a parenthesis reading "for Mr. Hemingway is a most subtle and sensitive writer." In the rest of the essay Huxley attributes the anti-intellectualism that he feels is implicit in Hemingway to universal education.

3. *Mantegna's.* Andrea Mantegna (1431?–1506) painted altar pieces and Crucifixions.
4. *Mrs. Gaskell.* Elizabeth Cleghorn Gaskell (1810–1865), daughter of a clergyman and married to another, wrote novels about the influence of industry and a *Life of Charlotte Brontë.* She is being cited by Huxley as a typical Victorian lady, proper and strait-laced.
5. *truly.* One of Hemingway's favorite words. Hemingway prefers this form over the available alternatives: "Let me give a true answer," "let me tell the truth". . . . The unusualness of the construction provides an emphasis which the alternatives lack. Note that "let me truly answer" has a different meaning.
6. *On reading that.* The vague *that* is a typical example of Hemingway's carelessness with pronoun reference.
7. *nothing to be done.* Presumably, since nothing could be done about amending the passage. More informal syntax.
8. *appearance of culture.* This sentence perfectly displays Hemingway's preference for nominal constructions. The sentence is hardly more than a string of nouns after the introductory verb framework: "I believe it is more than. . . ." The main propositional segment is the nominal string "a question of the simulation or avoidance of the appearance of culture." Hemingway makes no effort to avoid the awkwardness of three *of*'s separated only by *or*. He could have easily converted the nominals into verbals thus: "a question of simulating or avoiding the appearance of culture." Putting aside the unconscious component which makes a writer express himself in the way that is habitual to him whether he approves of it or not, it is evident that Hemingway, even if he could have, would have made no effort to avoid the awkwardness of such a construction. As he himself remarked, it was the awkwardness which was called his style. The awkwardness is emphatic, because most writers avoid it; it is individual, for the same reason; but above all it is sincere and impressive because it reveals a man writing truly at whatever cost to propriety. He will not modify the form if that interferes in the slightest with his aim to write the truth. The recurrence of such awkwardnesses is both a reminder and a guarantee of his constant concern with telling it "the way it was." It is another aspect of verbal skepticism, a distrust of the elegant phrase because it must have been achieved at the cost of truth.
9. *the writer is making.* Note the old-fashioned feeling of the word *make* in this context. Most writers do not talk of *making* characters, but of *inventing, constructing* or *thinking* them up.
10. *talks.* The repetition of this word here (five in five lines) is a sign of Hemingway's unwillingness to stoop to elegant variation. He would rather deafen the reader with the same word than let him believe that he was more

concerned about euphony than truth. Nonetheless, there is evidence that Hemingway was unwilling to push this tendency too far. He had an ear and he used it to space the repetitions so they did not become unendurable. The series of prepositional phrases ("of old masters; of music . . .") is an obvious effort to avoid using *talk* even more often.

11. *a phrase or a simile.* Hemingway cannot reveal that he knows any more highfalutin terms about the technical side of writing than these simple ones.

12. *absolutely necessary and irreplaceable.* What is impressive about this statement is the utter confidence of the writer that he is a good enough critic of his own work to detect when a simile is ideally placed.

13. *Baroque.* A period of artistic work (around the sixteenth and seventeenth centuries) characterized by a great deal of ornamentation. Baroque prose took a great many forms, some of which might properly incur Hemingway's censure (see Croll, Bibliography No. 15).

14. *time . . . for their acquiring.* Another awkwardness. In saying "time . . . must be paid heavily for their acquiring," Hemingway seems to be saying that the price must be paid *to* time rather than *in* time. It is probable that he intended the latter and was distracted from the more idiomatic phrasing ("and we must pay heavily in time for their acquiring" or "for acquiring them") by the necessity of inserting the parenthetical phrase, "which is all we have." Again Hemingway prefers the awkward form to the idiomatic one.

15. *truly written.* Here, unlike the earlier *truly* (note 5), Hemingway has placed the adverb in the pre-verb position and has really said something he did not intend. The adverb emphasizes *written,* as opposed, say, to *dictated, spoken, plagiarized,* whereas the intended contrast is between *truly* and *falsely.*

16. *And this too remember.* This pseudo-Biblical injunction, oracular in tone, is at odds with Hemingway's constant effort to be restrained about what he knows, to avoid "shooting his mouth off."

17. *popinjay.* A fop, a trifler.

18. *bloody owl.* Hemingway has here borrowed the British improper adjective *bloody* for emphasis without significance for American readers. The contrast between the serious writer, whom he approves of, and the solemn writer, whom he disapproves of, is underlined by the contrast between the avian specimens used to characterize them. But it does not make clear why an owl is less good than a buzzard. The owl, as the bird sacred to Athena, the goddess of wisdom, has always had a good reputation in the analogical bestiary.

Additional comments on vocabulary and syntax. On the whole, those critics are right who have spoken of the restricted extent of Hemingway's vocabulary, though to say that it is limited to a few short words is plainly absurd. He prefers the short familiar word but he does not always select it. His ear is alert to the possibility of novelty available from the collocation of familiar words. Thus, he will say "making talk about" when *discussing* would have been more familiar; "in a quicker ratio to the passage of time" instead of *faster*; "every novel which is truly written" instead of "every good (or true) novel"; "makes hollow places" instead of "leaves holes." If these examples are representative, it seems as if Hemingway does not so much prefer the familiar word as exploit it in the service of the kind of individual use of language his ear hankers after. The awkward collocation is merely one example of this tendency. Another may be described as laying the contextual foundation for a departure from the familiar. He uses slang (*scores, faker, showing off*), but he follows it with words like *irreplaceable, architecture, musings, remunerative, assimilated, nominal percentage.* The contrast is thus more effective. The general level is one of inarticulate and awkward selection of common words but the actual lexicon is varied and far from idiomatic. When Hemingway uses a common idiom, it stands out. In addition, of course, his vocabulary is extensively supplied with the technical terms proper to war, bullfighting, big-game hunting, deep-sea and freshwater fishing and other manly activities, to say nothing of the borrowed items from French, Italian, Spanish and Swahili.

Hemingway's syntax, as inspection of the present selection will easily reveal, does not lend itself to easy characterization. The average sentence-length of this sample is about 26 words, which is the average for American writers of this time on this sort of subject. The use of *and,* which is supposed to be Hemingway's favorite conjunction is 2.72 percent of the total number of words. This is low compared to Anderson (3.65), MacDonald (4.70), POUND (5.19), STEIN (3.88). Only White (1.66) is significantly lower. Nonetheless, it is true that in Hemingway's prose, the conjunction *and* plays a significant part. He says, for example, "Prose is architecture, not interior decoration, and the Baroque is over." The conjunction *and* in that sentence fails to convey the sense of relationship among the three parts. A piece of information has been left out which the *and* is supposed to bridge, i.e., that interior decoration was the ideal of the Baroque. Someone more intent on explicit logic than Hemingway might have said "*for* the Baroque is over." Again, he says earlier "On reading that in Mr. Huxley's book I obtained a copy of the volume he refers to and looked through it and could not find the quotation he mentions." The first *and* is conventional, but the second should be an adversative like *but.* That he could not find the quotation in his own book is hardly an expected result. The *but* would signalize a departure from expectation. Several other longish sentences show this kind of linking, one which deliberately avoids giving the reader the guidance he expects as to the interrelations of the propositions presented by the writer. Hemingway does not wish to commit himself to a particular reading of experience, at least insofar as the logic of relations between ideas reflects it.

ANDERSON (No. 89, p. 289)

Sherwood Anderson is known today solely for his *Winesburg, Ohio* (1919), a sort of novel consisting of a number of character sketches notable for their absorption with the instinctual drives, particularly sex. Though Anderson's reputation has suffered recently, and hardly anything is now said about his style (which Faulkner characterized as "primer-like"), in his prime he was taken seriously enough to inspire parodies by two powerful figures. FAULKNER (see No. 81) wrote a sketch (Foreword to *Sherwood Anderson and Other Famous Creoles*) and HEMINGWAY a novel, *The Torrents of Spring,* both published in 1926, mocking the simplicity of Anderson's attitudes, the self-conscious simplicity of his characters and the simplicity of his style. Here is Hemingway's parody of Anderson:

> Yogi Johnson looked out of the window. Soon it would be time to shut the pump-factory for the night. He opened the window carefully, just a crack. Just a crack, but that was enough. Outside in the yard the snow had begun to melt. A warm breeze was blowing. A chinook wind the pump fellows called it. The warm chinook wind came in through the window into the pump-factory. All the workmen laid down their tools. Many of them were Indians.

Now here is Faulkner (first paragraph of the Foreword):

> First, let me tell you something about our Quarter, the Vieux Carré. Do you know our quarter, with its narrow streets, its old wrought-iron balconies and its southern European atmosphere? An atmosphere of richness and soft laughter, you know. It has a kind of ease, a kind of awareness of the unimportance of things that outlanders like myself—I am not a native—were taught to believe important. So it is no wonder that as one walks about the quarter one sees artists here and there on the shady side of the street corners, sketching houses and balconies. I have counted as many as forty in a single afternoon, and though I did not know their names nor the value of their paintings, they were my brothers. And in this fellowship where no badges are worn and no sign of greeting is required, I passed them as they bent over their canvasses, and as I walked onward I mused on the richness

> of our American life that permits forty people to spend day after day painting pictures in a single area comprised in six city blocks.

The curious thing about these parodies (really burlesques) is that they are more substantive than stylistic. That is, it sounds like Anderson because it is the sort of thing Anderson says rather than because it is the way that Anderson writes. Hemingway parodies Anderson in a version of Hemingway's own style and so does Faulkner. Note, for example, the length of the sentences. As an astute critic observed of Marcel Proust's parodies of Balzac, Flaubert and other French novelists, Proust's hand was discernible in all of them, and Proust was a master of parody. The point is, of course, that the style is limited by a writer's own idiolect, whether he is engaged in parody or writing in his own name.

1. *most sweet and gracious aroma.* Anderson has a partiality for the unassuming adjective, a characteristic he shares with Hemingway. Note in this paragraph, the "*fragrant* cooky," "*great* kitchen," "*strong* fingers." Adjectives like *great, clean, strong, sweet,* tend to predominate, in this selection at least. These are the simple and basic absolutes, the primary colors, so to speak. Anderson does not search for the exotic and subtle adjective. It would alter the character of his substance.
2. *worker in words.* The slow pace of the analogy between a woman in a kitchen and Gertrude STEIN the word-cook, as it seems to be typical of Anderson, doubtless troubled more readers than those who parodied him.
3. *most of us have forgotten.* Under color of attributing a concern with language to Gertrude Stein, Anderson is really claiming to be one of the few who care about it. Since most writers are by trade and profession word-men, it is not surprising that this kind of remark may have irritated them. It is especially patronizing because Anderson says *us* but means *you.*
4. *rhythm of the individual word.* Carried away by the analogy, Anderson overlooks the fact that rhythm comes about when words are strung together, not looked at individually. A word has a stress pattern but hardly any rhythm.
5. *have always.* Middle modifiers of the type *always, now, often* (mostly time-referential) are usually placed between the subject and the verb or between the auxiliary and the verb, thus "I often recall" or "I have often recalled." Placing such modifiers after the verb, as Anderson does here and later in the paragraph ("wore often") gives them additional emphasis, reinforces the time element of the modifier. There is reason for so doing in the case of the first one, less or none for the second.
6. *sweet and healthy.* Like Gertrude Stein and Hemingway, Anderson likes to repeat words and word groups: "Great kitchen," "sweet."

7. *something the matter.* This characteristic maneuver of Anderson's consists of introducing an item vaguely into a sentence and specifying it in the next. The word *something* is twice used in this way in this selection, here and in the first paragraph, where it is repeated in the specifying sentence. Faulkner caught this trick in his parody.

8. *And I always see. . . .* Compare this paragraph opening with that of the third paragraph: "And I have always. . . ." Two sentences further down in this final paragraph also begin with *and.* On the whole, Anderson's sentence openings are restricted to a narrow range of possibilities: of the thirty-three sentences in the selection, thirteen begin with a pronoun (including *something*), five with a preposition, and five with a coordinating conjunction (*and, for*) The remaining ten include three subordinating conjunctions, two articles, a proper name and four adverbs and expletives. An examination of other writers of his time would show, I believe, that this distribution is unusual.

JAMES (No. 90, p. 293)

This selection is taken from an address given before the graduating class at Bryn Mawr, Pennsylvania, June 8, 1905. It reflects James's great interest in and concern for the proper use of English. Normally, a speech shows certain differences of syntax, vocabulary, and logical development from a writer's normal output. With Henry James, the case is different: his later work was to some extent oral, as much of it was dictated. Consequently, the form of this address is consonant with his late manner. Despite the remarkable complexity of James's syntax, HEMINGWAY claimed to have been influenced in the direction of a conversational style by him as by Mark TWAIN. What this shows is that the notion of the rhythms and forms of speech as suitable models for writing constitutes a laudable ideal but has nothing to do with the reality. Neither James nor Hemingway writes conversationally.

1. *Of the degree.* Word-order inversion to emphasize the complement in the prepositional phrase. The subject, with its several modifications and appositions, is, however, buried by this procedure. A simplified version of this sentence in normal word order would read: "The vocal tone has always been held to give a direct reflection of the degree in which a society is civilized." The reversion to normal order leaves the subject nakedly unmodified. A better rendition would move *society* forward in the sentence, thus: "The vocal tone of a

society has always. . . ." The precision of thought associated with this author and realized in his frequent qualifications, modifications, his avoidance of simplistic directness, can also be observed here. The expression "has always been held to give a direct reflection" might easily have been "has always reflected" with no loss of real meaning since James is not really citing any authority. The loss would be in apparent precision—the difference between James stating that something had always been *believed* and his saying that it was so. His choice of a verbal construction ("the degree in which a society is civilized") over the simpler nominal ("a society's civilization") is partly to avoid the awkwardness of the latter construction and even more its imprecision. A modern writer, without James's passion for accuracy, might have written: "The vocal tone of a society has always reflected its civilization." This version is at some distance from James's stylistically, but the substantive difference is slight.

2. *achieved civilization.* Note the hesitancy in the statement of the subject, with its repetitions and restatements ("the note, the representative note—representative of . . ."). James is, as it were, thinking aloud, modifying, limiting, shaping as he goes along, the outlines of his thought. The notion of tone, to which he is devoting this part of the address, is in any case so indefinable that his hesitations and tentatives are not unexpected.

3. *in very fact.* This use of *very* is archaic, looking back to the time when *very* meant *true* (from Middle English *verray,* akin to French *vrai*). The use of this assertive phrase here in conjunction with such a sign of uncertainty as "it would very much appear" actually undermines any sense the reader may have of James's confidence in the certainty of what he is saying.

4. *At one or two reasons.* This inverted phrase, placed at the beginning, is momentarily distracting (because unidiomatic) until we see that it is the complement of the verb *glance.*

5. *handed on the torch.* Another inversion, whose purpose rhetorically is not evident. It is probably the result of an idiosyncratic tendency on James's part toward inversion, a dislike possibly of beginning sentences or clauses with the subject. (Compare JOHNSON, No. 30).

6. *You don't speak . . . taken for you.* This sentence which begins here is a good example of three aspects of James's style: repetition, expansion and interruption. He repeats the key word (here it is *speak,* above it was *tone* and *a care for tone*) often enough to remind us of the subject he is treating. He repeats the form in a series of clauses ("you don't speak," "how you speak," "unless you have"). The purpose of the formal repetition is probably to make certain that the reader understands that the repeated items are expansive restatements, not new substance. Thus, "unless you have noticed differences" is merely a restatement of "unless you have discriminated," but it is a restatement with an-

other element which expands the synonymous idea. The same phenomenon occurs after the semicolon: "and you have not this positive consciousness, you are incapable of any reaction of taste or sensibility worth mentioning. . . ." These two pairs of statements are similar too in that the first item is abstract ("discriminated," "positive consciousness"), whereas the second is a concrete illustration. The effect of such expansions is to break the line of the sentence, to interrupt its flow with constant pauses. Even when James is not inserting reiterations and expansions, however, he tends to interrupt his sentence structure, with adverbs, prepositional phrases, sentence modifiers and other constructions. Like repetition and expansion, interruption is a habitual mode with him. There are only two sentences without interruption in this selection. They come together toward the end of the next-to-last paragraph: "Oh, I don't mean to say that you will find in the least a clear field and nothing but favor! The difficulty of your case is exactly the ground of my venturing thus to appeal to you." Their rarity is doubtless responsible for their visibility. They are truly emphatic.

7. *slangily.* Not merely the formal occasion but James's own sense of propriety require him to use quotation marks when he is using a slang word, after announcing that he is about to do so and apologizing for so doing. The advantage of such a hedged-around use of slang is questionable. No doubt James thought it was a daring emphasis.

8. *"negation" of tone.* It is characteristic of James that he should wonder at this stage whether his audience is aware of what he has been so subtly and carefully embroidering. It is this tendency to obscurity that has made James's style vulnerable to parody. The parodist and the reader who appreciates the parody together seem to be casting a vote against James, a vote that seems to be saying "Tell us what you are up to before you begin to analyze, ornament, qualify and subtilize it." This destructive judgment has been shared by many readers to whom James's later style is the embodiment of rhetorical vice, an undue emphasis on the form with a total disregard of the substance. A fair estimate must discover that it is James's care for the substance that leads to the contortions of the form. Nonetheless, there is in James's expression a systematic unwillingness to commit himself to a given formulation, so that even the most sympathetic reader may wonder why this writer had so little faith in his ability to choose the right words on first try. Max Beerbohm's parody "The Guerdon" well expresses this impatience. The following is the second paragraph:

> "Anything" was, after all, only another name for *the* thing. But he was to ask himself what earthly good it was, anyhow, to have kept in its confinement the furred and clawed, the bristling and now all but audibly scratching domestic pet, if he himself,

> defenseless Lord Chamberlain that he was, had to be figured as bearing it company inside the bag. There wasn't, he felt himself blindly protesting, room in there for the two of them; and the imminent addition of a Personage fairly caused our friend to bristle in the manner of the imagined captive that had till now symbolized well enough for him his whole dim bland ignorance of the matter in hand. Hadn't he all the time been reckoning precisely *without* that Personage—*without* the greater dimness that was to be expected of *him*—without, above all, that dreadful lesser blandness in virtue of which such Personages tend to come down on you, as it were, straight, with demands for side-lights? There wasn't a "bally" glimmer of a side-light, heaven help him, that he could throw. He hadn't the beginning of a notion—since it had been a point of pride with him, as well as of urbanity, not to ask—who the fellow, the so presumably illustrious and deserving chap in question *was*. This omission so loomed for him that he was to be conscious, as he came to the end of the great moist avenue, of a felt doubt as to whether he could, in his bemusement, now "place" anybody at all; to which condition of his may have been due the impulse that, at the reached gates of the palace, caused him to pause and all vaguely, all peeringly inquire of one of the sentries: "To whom do you beautifully belong?"

If the subject seems obscure, that should not be surprising, for James's obscurity is one of the targets. In any case, the reader of the parody will doubtless understand no less than did the young ladies of Bryn Mawr whom Henry James addressed.

TWAIN (No. 91, p. 297)

This selection is taken from Mark Twain's most famous piece of literary criticism: "Fenimore Cooper's Literary offenses," which originally appeared in the *North American Review* in 1895. In it Mark Twain laughs at the claims that have been made for COOPER as an expert in the subject matter of his Indian tales and as a careful stylist. It is surely one of the funniest critiques ever written. Apparently, the piece was originally longer but the *Review* printed only a part. The remainder was discovered later and printed (as edited by Bernard De Voto) in the *New England Quarterly* in 1946. The present selection is taken from the second part. The original praise of Cooper which fired Twain to this task was in the form of three quotations placed at the head of the original article:

> *The Pathfinder* and *The Deerslayer* stand at the head of Cooper's novels as artistic creations. There are others of his works which contain parts as perfect as are to be found in these, and scenes even more thrilling. Not one can be compared with either of them as a finished whole.
>
> The defects in both of these tales are comparatively slight. They were pure works of art.—*Prof. Lounsbury.*
>
> The five tales reveal an extraordinary fullness of invention. . . . One of the very greatest characters in fiction, Natty Bumppo. . . . The craft of the woodsman, the tricks of the trapper, all the delicate art of the forest, were familiar to Cooper from his youth up.—*Prof. Brander Matthews.*
>
> Cooper is the greatest artist in the domain of romantic fiction yet produced by America.—*Wilkie Collins.*

James Fenimore Cooper (1789–1851) was for some time the leading American author. His "Leather-Stocking Tales," with their romantic backgrounds and lively plotting, were popular everywhere. Mark Twain's hostility is probably the typical impatience of a writer of a new generation for a classic of a previous one.

The second essay begins with a quotation from Chapter XI of Cooper's *The Last of the Mohicans* (1826):

> Notwithstanding the swiftness of their flight, one of the Indians had found an opportunity to strike a straggling fawn with an arrow, and had borne the more preferable fragments of the victim, patiently on his shoulders, to the stopping-place. Without any aid from the science of cookery, he was immediately employed, in common with his fellows, in gorging himself with this digestible sustenance. Magua alone sat apart, without participating in the revolting meal, and apparently buried in the deepest thought.

The selection is entirely devoted to a discussion of this paragraph. It represents thus Mark Twain's demonstration of how applied stylistic analysis should be carried out.

1. *fragments patiently.* Mark Twain is exploiting the comic effect to be derived from a long series of unfavorable comments but he takes care not to dwell too long on any particular form. There are eleven elements (separated by semicolons) within this first sentence and they are of approximately the same form, but with a subtle variation to save the sentence from monotony. After the initial "No, the remark . . . was not necessary," there are five beginning with "neither was the one. . . ." The next two take the form "nor the remark . . . ," followed by "nor the explanation . . . ," which is followed by the expanded "nor the over-particular explanation . . . ," conclud-

ing with "nor the statement. . . ." The climax is reached with the next sentence: "None of these details has any value." As a practicing lecturer, Twain knew the value of the sustained laugh, which he cultivates both with the form of this long series and its substance, particularly the play with the "more preferable fragments."

2. *all his affairs.* Having succeeded in demolishing Cooper the first time with a list of all the unnecessary parts of the first sentence of the paragraph, Twain proceeds to realize this initial preparation by now listing all the contents which the reader may be expected not to care about. Instead of merely listing the items, however, Twain proceeds to embroider them with sarcastic cruelty. The "more preferable fragments" are given extensive treatment and the Indian's behavior is explicitly burlesqued. The concluding sentence loftily summarizes the entire paragraph: "We are indifferent to that Indian and all his affairs."

3. *one fact.* In rewriting Cooper's sentence, Twain has in effect made it into a Proposition. It might be further improved by the omission of the subject of the second verb (*he*).

4. *You will notice.* In the two sentences in this third paragraph, Twain makes brilliant satiric use of quotation. He quotes his own version and contrasts it with Cooper's, which he quotes in full, noting that his is more "straightforward and business-like," "less mincing and smirky." Not satisfied, he proceeds to quote both again, confident that the reiteration of the now-discredited sentence will affect the reader precisely as he wishes. He emphasizes this certainty by the scornful description he gives of Cooper's version and the unexpected "transportation of raw meat," surely not a literary point.

5. *to the stopping-place.* Once more, Twain takes advantage of our familiarity with Cooper's words to make them ridiculous. It is an unfair tactic, for nearly any writer could be destroyed by the incessant reiteration of his words. The reader, unless he is a Cooper partisan of a kind no longer extant, does not resent this because he is on Mark Twain's side.

6. *Veterinary College of Arizona.* The manuscript of this essay stated that this "lecture" was "prepared for last term by Mark Twain, M.A., Professor of Belles Lettres in the Veterinary College of Arizona." The spurious self-elevation to academic rank in a nonexistent institution was doubtless part of Mark Twain's way of replying in kind to Professors Lounsbury (Yale) and Brander Matthews (Columbia) who had praised Cooper too highly.

7. *first lecture.* The original published essay.

8. *simple breech-clout.* Stylistic analysis is helpless to explain why "dressed the humble statistic in a simple breech-clout" is funny, but funny it is. It is not merely a question of the incongruity of yoking a statistic with a breech-clout. Perhaps the very notion of such a garment as a breech-clout is comic.

WHITMAN (No. 92, p. 301)

As a poet, Whitman had incalculable influence on the form of later American poetry. It has been said that until recently every new poet's work was derivative Whitman, characterized generally by his defects, the rhetorical excess, formless verse, outpouring of soul, and frequent references to brotherhood. Whitman's prose, as revealed in this journalistic excerpt, is much less radical. It is not free of his tendency to "absolutize" the entities he discusses. Thus, English is the sum of *every* dialect and of *all,* it stands for language in the *largest* sense, it is the greatest of studies, it involves *so much,* it is *universal.* In this sense, Whitman is writing a prose poem, a rhapsody on the language, rather than a piece of expository prose. The attribution of a great deal of influence in forming the language to slang is equally enthusiastic and misleading. Slang is part of the metaphoric process by means of which words expand in meaning and move away from whatever literalism they are bound to by convention. The process is plainly visible in slang but present in every section of the lexicon. Even prepositions (*around, about*) have made metaphorical advances over their literal origins. Like EMERSON, from whom he borrowed ideas and examples, Whitman relates language to religion, a view which has an ancient history ("In the beginning was the word, and the word was with God, and the word was God.")

1. *United States.* The old-fashioned plural, implying a view of the country as still a confederation of separate states.
2. *eructation.* Belching.
3. *the term* right. Whitman probably borrowed part of this list from the beginning of EMERSON's Chapter IV, "Language," of his essay *Nature* (see No. 96). The following paragraph from that essay shows what Whitman borrowed and how different his use of it was:

> Words are signs of natural facts. The use of natural history is to give us aid in supernatural history: the use of the outer creation, to give us language for the beings and changes of the inward creation. Every word which is used to express a moral or intellectual fact, if traced to its root, is found to be borrowed from some material appearance. *Right* means *straight; wrong* means *twisted. Spirit* primarily means *wind; transgression,* the *crossing of a line; supercilious,* the *raising of the eyebrow.* We say the *heart* to ex-

press emotion, the *head* to denote thought; and *thought* and *emotion* are words borrowed from sensible things, and now appropriated to spiritual nature. Most of the process by which this transformation is made, is hidden from us in the remote time when language was framed; but the same tendency may be daily observed in children. Children and savages use only nouns or names of things, which they convert into verbs, and apply to analogous mental acts.

LOWELL (No. 93, p. 303)

It is worth comparing today's uncritical adulation of THOREAU (No. 95), as expressed for example by E. B. WHITE, with the opinion of a literary critic of his own time. Lowell is dealing with a flesh-and-blood writer, as susceptible to criticism as anyone, whereas we have made Thoreau into a kind of pastoral saint, a role he would probably have disdained.

1. *Was he indolent.* A construction which was effected or archaic in Lowell's time, or perhaps merely literary. The standard form would be: "If he was indolent. . . ."
2. *Apemantus.* In Shakespeare's *Timon of Athens,* Apemantus is a cynical philosopher who advises Timon, who is at first a generous and open nobleman.
3. *Ossian.* A legendary Irish poet, the subject of some poems published in 1760 by James Macpherson, who claimed they were translations of the original Gaelic. The hoax was easily discovered but a great number of readers (including Goethe) were taken in by the Romantic flavor of Macpherson's work.
4. *shaping of sentences.* Note THOREAU's own remarks about sentences in the selection from his work (No. 95).
5. *an observer.* It is interesting that Mark TWAIN made the same criticism of COOPER's powers as an observer.
6. *autochthonous.* Native to a place, aboriginal, indigenous.
7. *concetti.* Clever metaphors and paradoxes practiced by the Renaissance poets and their followers. Shakespeare's "Shall I compare thee to a summer's day?" and Donne's simile of two lovers as the legs of a compass are examples.
8. *Brazen Age.* Age of Brass, later and worse than the Ages of Gold or Silver but not as far down in the scale as the Heroic Age or the Age of Iron: Brass shines, as gold does, but it is not precious. It is thus attributed to superficial attractiveness without substance. The adjective *brazen* is now seldom used

to mean literal brass. In Hesiod's five ages, the Brazen Age is the age of war and violence.

9. *ruff.* A term from bridge and whist, meaning to take a trick by trumping.

10. *Cowley.* Abraham Cowley (1618–1667), poet and essayist, whose fame was for a time comparable to MILTON's.

11. *Seven years of service.* The complicated story of Laban, his two daughters Leah and Rachel, their husband Jacob, and the handmaids Bilhah and Zilpah in Genesis, chapters 29–30.

12. *sorry logician.* The adjective *sorry* in the sense of bad or worthless was in use in England but had become a rather common Americanism by the late nineteenth century.

13. *Sainte-Beuve.* Charles Augustin Sainte-Beuve (1804–1869), one of the greatest French critics. "Even while he rejects his era, a man is still very much of it."

14. *Stylites' pillar.* A pillar used by a group of ascetics and martyrs in the early Christian era for solitude, meditation and physical discomfort. They were called Stylists from the Greek word *stulos,* meaning "column."

15. *Hermitage of la Chevrette.* House offered to Rousseau by his friend Mme. d'Epinay, where he communed with nature.

16. *musquashes.* Muskrats, small outdoor rodents.

17. *salon.* Assembly of intellectual and fashionable ladies and gentlemen in a drawing room for the purpose of holding witty or deep conversation. Salons were regularly held at certain homes in France during the eighteenth and nineteenth centuries. Similar events, under a different name, were known in England and even in Boston in Lowell's time. (See POE, No. 94, note 4)

18. *Turgot.* Anne Robert Jacques Turgot, Baron de l'Aulne (1727–1781), Louis XVI's finance minister and writer on philosophical and economic topics.

POE (No. 94, p. 309)

1. *Boccalini.* Traiano Boccalini (1556–1613), author of *News from Parnassus* (1613), topical satire on literature, mores, and politics.

2. *Zoilus.* Zoilus of Amphipolis (fourth century B.C.) was known for the bitterness of his criticism of Isocrates, Plato, and especially Homer. He was nicknamed "Homeromastix" (scourge of Homer). He was primarily a rhetorician and became the prototype of the foolishly severe critic who cannot appreciate but can only find fault.

3. *Mr. Jones and Mr. Whipple.* William Alfred Jones (1817–1900), critic and later librarian at Columbia University. Edwin Percy Whipple (1819–1886), lecturer and critic, close friend of the poet Whittier.
4. *Miss Fuller.* Sarah Margaret Fuller (1810–1850), associate editor of the *Dial* with EMERSON, transcendentalist, friend of THOREAU, held a *salon* for ladies in Boston, married an Italian nobleman on the republican side during the Revolution of 1848, and was drowned at sea on her return from Italy.
5. *quips, quirks, and curt oracularities.* Irregular alliterative series, possibly to demonstrate some device of style of Miss Fuller's.
6. *Lyly's Euphusims.* See ELIOT (No. 12, notes 4 and 6).
7. *peculiarities of Macaulay.* Poe's description of MACAULAY's style accords pretty well with that of other commentators (see MACAULAY, No. 22, note 28, BAGEHOT, No. 21 and notes). It is unusual in that Poe admires and defends Macaulay's style, with which Poe's has very little in common.
8. *n'est pas si sage qu'il croit.* "Is not as clever as he thinks."
9. *cotemporaries.* Archaic variant of *contemporaries.*

THOREAU (No. 95, p. 313)

Walden (1854) is Thoreau's best-known work. Most of Thoreau's influence descends from it and from his essay on "Civil Disobedience" (1849). He kept extensive journals from which his two published books were in a manner extracted. E. B. WHITE (No. 78) is Thoreau's most vocal admirer. Thoreau's name frequently occurs in his works and there is as well an emulation of the style, or at least of some devices of it. In an essay entitled "A Slight Sound at Evening," written for the centenary of *Walden*'s publication, White refers to "the offbeat prose that Thoreau was master of, a prose at once strictly disciplined and wildly abandoned." Further on he says, "Thoreau tended to write in sentences, a feat not every writer is capable of, and *Walden* is, rhetorically speaking, a collection of certified sentences, some of them, it would now appear, as indestructible as they are errant." There is nothing very exact here, merely White's admiration and his fascination with long-lived sentences (see WHITE, No. 78, for a similar comment on a sentence by Thomas Paine). White, like Thoreau, is impressionistic, even metaphysical, in his discussions of style. Thoreau, in the selection, talks mainly about sentences too. His own sentences seem long but average only twenty-five words, ten more than White but one less than HEMINGWAY. Sentence-length is objectively measurable, no doubt, but the reader's sense for the length of a writer's sentences is dependent on a number of factors: complexity of the syntax, lexical choice, the pace of the argument, the nature of the substance, the reader's sympathy, and others to which we can give no name.

1. *healthy sentence.* One of Thoreau's most constant and characteristic tendencies is the selection of natural analogues to human activities, even when these activities are as artificial as the putting down of words on paper. He speaks of *healthy* sentences, of thoughts with "hue and fragrance." RALEIGH's style has an emphasis "like a man's tread" with "a breathing space between the sentences." His chapters are like parks or forest. The Elizabethan writers are like a green bough, etc.

2. *Sir Walter Raleigh.* Sir Walter Raleigh (1552–1618) was a soldier, a sailor and a courtier at the courts of Queen Elizabeth and James I. He was in and out of favor and spent a number of years in prison, during which time he did most of his writing. The following paragraph, taken from a piece generally referred to as "The Last Fight of the *Reuenge*," was written in 1591. It will give the reader some chance of testing Thoreau's claim on his own ear.

> After the *Reuenge* was intangled with this *Philip,* foure other boorded her, two on her larboord and two on her starboord. The fight thus beginning at three of the clocke in the after noone, continued verie terrible all that euening. But the great *San Philip* hauing receyued the lower tire of the *Reuenge,* discharged with crossebarshot, shifted hir selfe with all diligence from her sides, vtterly misliking hir first entertainment. Some say that the shippe foundred, but wee cannot report it for truth, vnlesse wee were assured. The Spanish ships were filled with companies of souldiers, in some two hundred besides the Marriners, in some fiue, in others eight hundreth. In ours there were none at all, beside the Marriners, but the seruants of the commanders and some few voluntarie Gentlemen only. After many enterchanged voleies of great ordinance and small shot, the Spaniards deliberated to enter the *Reuenge* and made diuers attempts, hoping to force her by the multitudes of their armed souldiers and Musketiers, but were still repulsed againe and againe, and at all times beaten back into their own shippes or into the seas.

3. *sap or roots.* Thoreau in this sentence reveals another of his stylistic habits, a liking for doublets. "Verdurous and blooming," "evergreen and flowers," "fact and experience," "false and florid," "sap or roots." This habit is constant in this selection and presumably affects his style elsewhere. At times, he leans to the triplet but not nearly so frequently.

4. *plain speech.* Men are really attracted by the *idea* of the beauty of plain

speech, for where is plain speech to be found? Certainly not in Thoreau. At any rate, defining "plain speech" is full of difficulties.

5. *Ibrahim Pasha.* Ibrahim Pasha (1789–1848) was an Egyptian general and statesman who spent most of his life fighting against Turks.

6. *net result.* The logic of this passage is not very clear. The paragraphing does not help the reader. Assuming that a new thought begins without transition at the sentence beginning "All men," it and the next five sentences seem to constitute a unit. A propositional reduction of these five sentences might read as follows:

1. Florid speech is an imitation of plain speech.
2. Writers will risk being misunderstood to be able to achieve florid speech.
3. The style of the letters of Ibrahim Pasha was praised for its difficulty.
4. A good performance derives from the effort of a man's lifetime.
5. A good performance is the net result of a man's lifetime.
6. Every sentence requires long preparation.

The difficulty begins with the paradoxical substance of the first sentence. Whatever plain speech and florid speech may be, it is not made clear how one of these poles can be an imitation of the other. The next sentence seems to make sense if we interpret *florid* as *elegant.* Writers have often placed elegance above clarity, but exuberance is not the same as elegance. The long illustration about Ibrahim does not support the second sentence in actuality but a point which is to be made in the sentence to follow, though it derives from the subject of sentence 2. Sentence 4 is obscure because of the ambiguity of two of its parts: *taxed* can mean *charged* or *censured; least* in its place before *thing* means one thing, but the drift of the passage would incline the reader to believe that "thing least well done" was intended. The possible interpretations of the sentence are the following:

A. A man's entire life is censured for the smallest thing he has done well.
B. A man's entire life is necessary for the smallest thing he has done well.
C. A man's entire life is censured for the thing he has done least well.
D. A man's entire life is charged for the thing he has done least well.

Since Thoreau has been talking about Ibrahim Pasha and his (bad) epistolary style, the interpretation which places *least* before *well done* (C and D) would seem more probable. But if, however, this sentence is merely a preparation for sentence six, then the reading "smallest thing [i.e., a sentence] done well" is more probable. Thoreau's inattention to coherence being what it is, the latter probability is more likely and version B is probably the right one. Understanding Sentence 5 is dependent on understanding sentence 4 as it contains two pronouns with obscure reference (*it, its*). If B is the right reading of sentence 4, then *it* refers to "smallest thing done well" and *its* to "a man's entire life." Sentence 6 brings together the two elements of sentence 4 in a different way: "smallest thing" is now *sentence* and "man's entire life" is now *long probation.* The question in the sentence which follows is a pun on *standard,* a sort of aphorism which has no perceptible application to what has gone before. A logical diagram of the six sentences just examined might possibly look like this:

	A	B	C	D
1.	( )			
2.				(:)
3.			(×)	
4.		(=)		
5.		(=)		
6.		(=)		

7. *masks.* Court plays.
8. *palaver.* American slang, meaning "chatter, loose talk," from the Portuguese *palavra,* "word, speech."
9. *true.* Thoreau referred to the "truest writer" above; now he speaks about "true lines." Later still he will talk about *truth.* This question seems to be a more constant concern with writers than with philosophers or moralists. (cf. HEMINGWAY, No. 88, note 5).
10. *energy of the body.* To believe this statement, Thoreau must have been as poor an observer as LOWELL (No. 93) claims.
11. *hard-working men.* A belief in the "force and precision of style" of the non-writer is a constant and disabling conviction of the professional writer—the writer by vocation—who is never free of doubts about how his trade is to be practiced. Because language is used by all, whether to call pigs or address the Muse, it seems as if the inarticulate might have a specially valuable contribution to make to its use. This absurd view is not shared by artists in other media. Michelangelo or Rodin did not seek the advice of housepainters or woodcutters and Mozart did not rhapsodize about the musicality of the tone-deaf. Thoreau's viewpoint here returns to WORDSWORTH's "language spoken by men" (No. 28, and see also COLERIDGE, No. 26), but the idea in general goes back to a primitivism which is behind the idea of the Golden Age and the Garden of Eden.
12. *Wolofs.* A people of the Sudan, said to be the blackest in Africa, here cited as the type of the primitive and uncultured.

13. *Sibyl.* A prophetic priestess, usually considered the mouthpiece of some god, most often Apollo.
14. labored *sentences.* That this is a pun is shown by the italics. But the play on words is not different in kind from the rest of Thoreau's imagery. Note, for example, the plow and furrow, the axe or sword, compared to the pen.
15. *Stonehenge.* Circle of large boulders in England dating from the Stone Age.

EMERSON (No. 96, p. 317)

1. *radical.* Having to do with the *radix,* or root. The modern term would be *basic* or *fundamental.*
2. *savages.* In Emerson's time, primitive peoples played a largely symbolic role in the thought of philosophers. Emerson's notion that primitive peoples have only the necessities and that their languages are simple is completely at variance with all the findings of anthropologists and linguists.
3. *infancy.* The infancy of language is something that not much can be known about, in view of the paucity of written records.
4. *symbols.* If Emerson means *sounds* when he says *symbols,* he might be closer to the facts than he is if he means that languages analyze reality in the same way.
5. *all languages.* It may be wondered whether languages of the Finno-Ugric, Ural-Altaic, Uto-Aztecan, Semitic or Bantu families were included in Emerson's calculations when he reached this conclusion about all languages.
6. *conversation of a strong-natured farmer or back-woodsman.* This Romantic notion, here as in WORDSWORTH, THOREAU and others, is utterly without basis (see THOREAU, No. 95, note 11).
7. *corruption of language.* This ancient view (held by Seneca and other classical writers) has had some popularity among modern pessimists (see for example the version held by ORWELL, No. 3). There is evidently no scientific evidence for the "reflection theory" (see CARLYLE, No. 23, note 2) implied by this relationship. Moreover, the corruption of language is no easier to describe than the supposedly parallel corruption of man. Man is man and does not change much. Language does change but no one knows why. Every theorist has always had a hankering to attribute language change to some cause. Moralists and purists prefer to charge it to the degeneration of morals. Emerson's naive belief is founded on a primitivism which, on the linguistic level, cannot be taken seriously.

8. *visible things.* Like Orwell, Emerson believes that the tendency of language to degenerate can be halted by determined opposition. This is the position of today's purists who become most inflamed by what they consider one of the canons of modern linguistic theory: that language change is inevitable and that attempted interference with its progress is hopeless.

9. *picturesque language.* Emerson goes further in praise of imagery than others have done since his time. Proust, like the ancients, believed that the greatness of a writer was plainly readable in the originality of his images. On this ground, he relegated Flaubert to the second rank, since there was not a single beautiful metaphor in all his work, despite his important innovations in syntax. Shakespeare's imagery has been lauded to the skies. Kenneth Burke has said that in the depths of his imagery the artist cannot lie. These opinions certainly agree in putting a high value on imagery and making it a fundamental part of creative writing. But the sum of these beliefs does not add up to Emerson's claim that the writer who uses imagery is inspired by God. Perhaps Emerson was adapting here the notion of Apollonian inspiration described by Plato in the *Ion.*

10. *material image.* Again, compare Orwell on this point (No. 3, note 5).

11. *vestment of the thought.* In treating the relation between thought and language, Emerson perforce uses imagery, since no known description of it is objectively valid. Thoughts are (or are not) "clothed in natural garments;" "discourse . . . clothes itself in images;" "a material image . . . furnishes the vestment of the thought." This hackneyed analogy (ancient when Chesterfield used it, a century earlier) does nothing to support Emerson's view that he is beholden to the Deity for truth. In discussing the relations between symbol and thing, he compares the corrupted symbol to paper currency and the departed referent to a lack of "bullion in the vaults." Picturesque language, he adds a little later, is a "certificate" of God's truth. Emerson's imagery is at best conventional and indebted more to the artifacts of his society (clothes, money) than to any divine insufflation. His theory is an attractive one for a writer intent on showing the hand of God in nature, but it cannot avoid colliding against facts of language. Language is essentially and progressively figurative, whether it proceeds by **metaphor** (calling one thing another to which it has some non-literal resemblance, e.g., "cat burglar") or by **metonymy** (calling one thing by the name of another to which it has a logical relation, e.g., "a hand" for a laborer, cowboy or worker). In the earliest etymological stage, words have a discernible literal significance. As a language develops, the words develop figurative senses by various means of extension or narrowing, by melioration or pejoration, specialization or generalization, etc. Thus, it might be said that the latest stage of a language is always the most figurative, words being

analogically or figuratively adapted to new needs, new technological developments: in the seventeenth century, a computer was a man who did calculations; in the nineteenth century, before the electronic era, to *broadcast* was to sow seed by hand, by casting it around (abroad). Because words change and manners change, and symbols are no longer linked with their traditional referents, alarmists have always been ready to suppose that language has in some sense degenerated. But there is no evidence that language changes for the worse, as long as we can use it to read the news, buy groceries, write poems, and converse with our friends and families. Much is made of the tendency of languages to accumulate clichés, hackneyed phrases, dead metaphors, and of careless writers to mix their metaphors. This process can be explained, however, without having recourse to gloomy prophecies about the future of our tongue. Although words are the basic units of meaning, when a new meaning is expressed by a combination of words rather than by the coinage, borrowing, or other creation of a word, the resulting collocation in a sense acts like a word, one with invisible hyphens. By force of familiarity, these collocations come to be used without regard to their literal sense, algebraically, so to speak. If two such are used in contiguity, the result may be a mixed metaphor, something sedulously avoided by careful or literary writers but practised by everyone at some time. Mixed metaphors may be the occasion for ridicule but they represent nothing more vicious than the constant assimilative tendency of language. Emerson himself is guilty of something like this when he refers to writers "who do not of themselves clothe one thought in its natural garment, but who feed unconsciously on the language created by the primary writers." The contrast between *clothe* and *feed* was doubtless not intentional: Emerson did not think of *feed* as metaphorical. And it was not until it was juxtaposed with *clothe* that it became something like a mixed metaphor. He might have avoided this effect by concluding with something like "but who borrow the garments (or mantles) of the primary writers. . . ." By his own criteria, Emerson's writing is not "proper creation," but we are not obligated to use his yardstick.

WEBSTER (No. 98, p. 321)

Noah Webster was one of the earliest proponents for a national American language, distinct from the mother tongue and not inclined to make obeisance before its superiority. To this end, he supported spelling reform and an accurate rendition of American pronunciation. In his *American Dictionary of the En-*

glish Language (1828), he had opportunity to act on these principles. In addition, he based his definitions on American as well as British usage and included non-literary words. In this selection, he shows himself to be a firm holder of certain eighteenth-century views, e.g., that the progress of civilization, including science, had almost reached its limit.

1. *principle of analogy.* The name given to the similarity of inflectional and derivational processes between new words and existing words. Thus, by analogy, verbs take the regular weak endings, even those that might historically have developed differently (e.g., *shave, shaved, shaved,* instead of the historical *shave, shove, shaven*).
2. *Queen Elizabeth . . . George II.* Elizabeth reigned from 1558 to 1603. George II died in 1760. The period Webster delimits includes a vast variety of writers and a considerable range of quality.
3. *Queen Ann and her successor.* Queen Anne reigned from 1702 to 1714. Her successor, George I, reigned from 1714 to 1727.
4. *Garrick.* David Garrick (1717–1779), the greatest actor of the eighteenth century, by his practise doubtless influenced pronunciation.
5. *Sidney.* Sir Philip Sidney (1554–1586), soldier, statesman and poet, wrote the prose romance *Arcadia* (1590) and an *Apology for Poetry* (1595).
6. *stile.* A variant spelling of *style* referring to its derivation from Latin *stilus,* writing implement, rather than Greek *stulos,* column. Purity of style meant correctness or propriety, freedom from grammatical error, faulty lexical choice and wrong idiom.
7. *best models.* Sir William Temple (1628–1699), SWIFT's patron, Dr. Conyers Middleton (1683–1750), clerical controversialist, and Henry St. John, Viscount Bolingbroke (1678–1751), statesman and friend of Swift, were all considerable personages in their time but minor writers.
8. *Mr. Pope.* Alexander Pope (1688–1744), greatest poet of the eighteenth century.
9. *Sir Richard Steele.* Sir Richard Steele (1672–1729), began *The Tatler,* a periodical essay-journal, in 1709 and joined ADDISON in the editing of the *Spectator,* the greatest such publication.
10. *Dr. Arbuthnot.* John Arbuthnot (1667–1735), physician and writer, member of the circle of wits that included Swift, Pope, Addison, Gay and Bolingbroke.
11. *Sir William Blackstone.* Sir William Blackstone (1723–1780) a judge, was the author of *Commentaries on the Laws of England* (1765–9), still a classic.
12. *Dr. Price and Dr. Priestley.* The former is probably Richard Price

(1723–1791), minister and writer, who was friendly to the United States; Joseph Priestley (1733–1804), theologian and chemist, left England for the United States because of his political views.

13. *Sir William Jones.* Sir William Jones (1746–1794), Orientalist who first described the relation of Sanskrit to European languages.

14. *Johnson's stile.* Compare this to MACAULAY's later judgment (No. 22).

15. *a Robertson, a Hume, a Home and a Blair.* Four Scotsmen who became known as writers in English: William Robertson (1721–1793), historian; David HUME (see No. 34); Henry Home, Lord Kames (1696–1782), playwright; Hugh Blair (1718–1800), minister and professor of rhetoric.

16. *foreign language.* The native language of the Scotsmen whom Webster names is English (not Gaelic). Therefore, his comment on foreign language is irrelevant, though the principle is valid.

17. *Gibbon's harmony of prose.* Edward Gibbon (1737–1794), the historian, is as famous for his style as for his scholarship, though his detractors have not been few. Webster objects to his emphasis on elegant style at the expense of meaning; others have found the style monotonous and therefore detracting from the meaning. The following is a typical passage from the first volume of the *Decline and Fall of the Roman Empire* (1776) (see also TROLLOPE, No. 19, note 7):

> So sensible were the Romans of the influence of language over national manners, that it was their most serious care to extend, with the progress of their arms, the use of the Latin tongue. The ancient dialects of Italy, the Sabine, the Etruscan, and the Venetian, sunk into oblivion; but in the provinces, the east was less docile than the west to the voice of its victorious preceptors. This obvious difference marked the two portions of the empire with a distinction of colours, which, though it was in some degree concealed during the meridian splendour of prosperity, became gradually more visible as the shades of night descended upon the Roman world. The western countries were civilized by the same hands which subdued them. As soon as the barbarians were reconciled to obedience, their minds were opened to any new impressions of knowledge and politeness. The language of Virgil and Cicero, though with some inevitable mixture of corruption, was so universally adopted in Africa, Spain, Gaul, Britain and Pannonia, that the faint traces of the Punic or Celtic idioms were preserved only in the mountains, or among the peasants. Education and study insensibly inspired the natives of those countries with the sentiments of Romans; and Italy gave fashions, as well as laws, to her Latin provincials. They solicited with more ardour, and obtained with more facility, the freedom and honours of the state; supported the national dignity in letters and in arms; and, at

length, in the person of Trajan, produced an emperor whom the Scipios would not have disowned for their countryman.

18. *orthography.* Spelling.

19. *endless innovation.* Americans have almost given up their admiration for the British branch of English but they are more devoted to innovation than ever.

FRANKLIN (No. 99, p. 325)

This selection is taken from what is supposed to be a manuscript version of Franklin's *Autobiography.* It probably accounts for a certain informality of diction and syntax in the prose.

1. *confuting.* Vanquishing in debate.
2. *Disgusts.* Distastes.
3. *occasion for Friendship.* This incomplete sentence, in its loose connection probably illustrates Franklin's more relaxed syntax. The shift to *you* is in the same vein.
4. *pointing.* Punctuation.
5. *Hints.* Notes.
6. *Sentiment.* Meaning, or proposition.
7. *extreamly ambitious.* Franklin's method is still one of the best ways of increasing one's skill in writing: practice in moving from one medium to another and emulation of a model.

MATHER (No. 100, p. 327)

Cotton Mather is best known for his part in the persecution of persons accused of witchcraft. He was, however, primarily a clergyman and writer interested in the promulgation of religious education. As the author of some 450 books, he had some views on writing and on prose style, as the present selection reveals. Like SWIFT's tract (No. 36), which is almost exactly contemporary with it, Mather's piece is directed at intending clergymen. The present selection is written in a manner which suggests that the author was an outspoken and controversial preacher. It has some touches of the sermon of the period.

1. *studied.* Sought after, included.
2. *Composures.* Compositions.
3. *Grapes.* The old fable (Aesop, La Fontaine) of the Fox and the Grapes.
4. *Bushy Tails.* A further reference to the fox in the fable.
5. *the more tis to be accounted of.* Mather seems to be taking sides in a dispute between two opposed rhetorical tendencies: the older one, of copiousness, erudition and greater formality; and a newer one of conversational ease, avoidance of pedantry, and clarity. Though he obviously prefers the older manner, his practice is in the newer vein: he has only one quotation and no learned references, his vocabulary is popular, and he uses the conversational *'em* inflection such as in "commissioned 'em"). The structure of this sentence, particularly the parallel series beginning with *And,* would put it in the older tradition:

> And who will think
> that the real Excellency of a Book will never ly in *saying of little;*
> That the less one has for his Money in a Book, 'tis really the more Valuable for it; and that the less one is instructed in a Book, and the more Superfluous *Margin,* and Superficial *Harangue,* and the less of *Substantial Matter* one has in it, the more tis to be accounted of.

This redundant piling up of elements which are merely variations of each other is in the tradition of copiousness and especially related to oral delivery, a version of the old sermon style, hitting the listener repeatedly over the head until he has understood or is in agreement.
6. *Massy.* Substantial, copious.
7. *disgusted.* Disliked.
8. *Gust.* Taste, appreciation.
9. *quae jam Cecidere.* A famous tag from Horace. With the full context it reads:

> Multa renascentur quae iam cecidere, cadent que
> Quae nunc sunt in honore vocabula, si volet usus,
> Quem penes arbitrium est et ius et norma loquendi
> [*Ars Poetica,* 11. 70–72]

(Many words which have fallen out of use shall revive, and those shall fall that now are held in honor, if usage wills it, which is the judge, the law and the rule of speech.)
10. *Jejune.* Barren.
11. *Flowres.* A reference to the "florid" (*flowered,* or *flowery*) style.
12. *with much what as much of Justice.* This curious expression is probablv

a slang idiom consisting of a standard part ("with much") and a non-standard part ("what as much," meaning some indistinct and vague quantity, formed on the same principle as "what d'ye call it"). Otherwise it is a typographical error.

13. *Jerom.* St. Jerome (342–420) accused himself in a dream of being fonder of literature than of religion: "Ciceronianus es, non Christianus" ("You are a Ciceronian, not a Christian").

14. *his own Style.* An interesting view for this time and place, but it is questionable how firmly Mather believed it, since he criticizes the critics for having all different styles.

15. *Gate.* Gait, step, walk. The implication is that a person's style is as individual (and as unconscious) as his way of walking.

16. *Condescensions.* Mutual forbearance.

17. *Cicero . . . Seneca.* A reference to the struggle between the Ciceronian and Senecan styles, which was no longer active in England by this time but was in Mather's earlier years and possibly had reached Boston by this time. (See PATER, No. 16, notes, JOHNSON, No. 30, note 9).

18. *your Erasmus's and your Grotius's.* Famed scholars of the Renaissance. The *your* is the ethical dative, usually expressing contempt.

19. *taxed.* Censured.

20. *Solaecisms and Barbarisms.* Errors of composition so named by the Greek rhetoricians. A solecism was originally the speech of the Greek colony at Soloi in Cilicia (Asia Minor) whose Attic Greek "degenerated" (diverged) in time. Loosely, it means any impropriety in diction or grammar. A barbarism is a foreignism, an importation of foreign constructions or words into the language, when these are disapproved of. The French have always been on their guard against barbarisms, where the English have welcomed foreign terms.

21. *Ingenious Blackwal.* Anthony Blackwall (1674–1730), classical scholar, author of *Sacred Classics Defended* (1725).

Bibliography

[Dates given are not dates of first publication but of most recent available edition.]

General:

1. Chatman, Seymour, and S. R. Levin. *Essays on the Language of Literature* (Boston, 1967).
2. Cowley, Malcolm. *Writers at Work* (New York, 1963).
3. Christensen, Francis. *Notes Toward a New Rhetoric* (New York, 1967).
4. Hildick, Wallace. *Word for Word* (London, 1965).
5. Milic, Louis T. *A Stylistics Reader* (New York, 1970).
6. Murry, J. Middleton. *The Problem of Style* (London, 1956).
7. Read, Herbert. *English Prose Style* (Boston, 1955).
8. Spencer, John. *Linguistics and Style* (London, 1964).
9. Spitzer, Leo. *Linguistics and Literary History* (Princeton, 1967).
10. Steinmann, Martin, Jr. *New Rhetorics* (New York, 1967).
11. Wimsatt, W. K., Jr. *The Verbal Icon* (New York, 1960).
12. *Writers at Work,* Second Series (New York, 1963).

Surveys:

13. Chambers, R. W. *On the Continuity of English Prose from Alfred to More and His School* (London, 1950).
14. Connolly, Cyril. *Enemies of Promise* (London, 1938).
15. Croll, Morris W. "The Baroque Style in Prose," *Style, Rhetoric and Rhythm* (Princeton, 1966), pp. 207–233 (Reprinted in Nos. 1 and 5).
16. Dobree, Bonamy. *Modern Prose Style,* 2nd. ed. (Oxford, 1964).
17. Gordon, Ian A. *The Movement of English Prose* (London, 1966).
18. Krapp, George Philip. *The Rise of English Literary Prose* (New York, 1963).
19. Levine, George and William A. Madden. *The Art of Victorian Prose* (New York, 1968).
20. Saintsbury, George. "Modern English Prose," *Collected Essays and Papers,* (London, 1923), Vol. III, pp. 62–87.
21. Sherman, Lucius A. "On Certain Facts and Principles in the Development of Form in Literature" (Reprinted in No. 5).
22. Sutherland, James R. *On English Prose* (Toronto, 1957).
23. Williamson, George. *The Senecan Amble* (London, 1951).

Individual Studies:

ADDISON:

24. Lannering, Jan. *Studies in the Prose Style of Joseph Addison* (Upsala, 1951).

ARNOLD:

25. Tillotson, Geoffrey. "Matthew Arnold's Prose: Theory and Practice" (in No. 19).

BACON:

26. Vickers, Brian. *Francis Bacon and Renaissance Prose* (Cambridge, 1968).

BERKELEY:

27. Davie, Donald A. "Berkeley's Style in *Siris,*" *Cambridge Journal,* IV, (1951), 427–433.

BIBLE:
28. Nida, Eugene A. "Principles of Translation as Exemplified by Bible Translating," *On Translation,* ed. Reuben A. Brower (Cambridge, Mass., 1959), pp. 11–31.

BUTLER:
29. Fort, Joseph-Barthélemy. *Samuel Butler l'écrivain: étude d'un style.* (Bordeaux, 1935).

CARLYLE:
30. Smith, Logan Pearsall. "Thomas Carlyle: The Rembrandt of English Prose," *Reperusals and Re-Collections* (London, 1936).

CAXTON:
31. Aurner, Robert R. "Caxton and the English Sentence," *Wisconsin Studies in Language and Literature,* XVIII (1923), 23–59.

COOPER:
32. Twain, Mark. "Fenimore Cooper's Literary Offenses," *North American Review,* CLXI (1895), 1–12.
33. ——. "Fenimore Cooper's Further Literary Offenses," ed. Bernard De Voto, *New England Quarterly,* XIX (1946), 291–301.

DEFOE:
34. Dobree, Bonamy. "Some Aspects of Defoe's Prose," *Pope and His Contemporaries,* ed. J. L. Clifford and L. A. Landa (Oxford, 1949), pp. 171–184.

DICKENS:
35. Quirk, Randolph. "Some Observations on the Language of Dickens," *Review of English Literature,* II (1961), 19–28.

FAULKNER:
36. Volpe, Edmund L. "Style," *A Reader's Guide to William Faulkner* (New York, 1964), pp. 36–45.
37. Ohmann, Richard M. "Generative Grammars and the Concept of Literary Style" (Reprinted in bibliog. No. 10).

HEMINGWAY:
38. Levin, Harry. "Observations on the Style of Hemingway." *Kenyon Review,* XIII (1951), 581–609.

JAMES:
39. Harvitt, Helene. "How Henry James revised *Roderick Hudson:* A Study in Style," *PMLA,* XXXIX (1924), 203–227.
40. Matthiessen, F. O. "The Painter's Sponge and Varnish Bottle," *Henry James: The Major Phase* (New York, 1963) pp. 152–186.

JOHNSON:
41. Wimsatt, W. K., Jr. *The Prose Style of Samuel Johnson* (New Haven, 1963). (Chapters reprinted in bibliog. 1 and 5.)

JONSON:
42. Barish, Jonas A. *Ben Jonson and the Language of Prose Comedy* (Cambridge, Mass., 1960).

MACAULAY:
43. Fraser, G. S. "Macaulay's Style as an Essayist," *Review of English Literature,* I (1960), 9–19.
44. Madden, William A. "Macaulay's Style" (In bibliog. No. 19).

MILTON:
45. Thompson, Elbert N. S. "Milton's Prose Style," *Philological Quarterly,* XIV (1935), 1–15.

PATER:
46. Fraser, G. S. "Walter Pater: His Theory of Style, His Style in Practice, His Influence" (In bibliog. No. 19).

RUSKIN:
47. Rosenberg, John. "Style and Sensibility in Ruskin's Prose" (In bibliog. No. 19).

SHAW:
48. Ohmann, Richard M. *Shaw: The Style and the Man* (Middletown, Conn., 1962).

SWIFT:
49. Milic, Louis T. *A Quantitative Approach to the Style of Jonathan Swift* (The Hague, 1967).

TROLLOPE:
50. Davies, Hugh Sykes. "Trollope and His Style," *Review of English Literature,* I (1960), 73–85.

WOLFE:
51. Natanson, Maurice. "The Privileged Moment: A Study in the Rhetoric of Thomas Wolfe," *Quarterly Journal of Speech,* XLIII (1957), 143–150.

Note: Authors whose names are not listed under Individual Studies should be looked up in the works under *Surveys*. For more detailed bibliographical help, consult my *Style and Stylistics: An Analytical Bibliography* (New York: Free Press, 1967), or Richard W. Bailey and Dolores M. Burton, *English Stylistics: A Bibliography* (Cambridge, Mass.: M.I.T., 1968).

INDEX

INDEX

[The names of the one hundred Stylists are printed in small capitals (e.g., SWIFT). Within such entries, the letters *S* and *A* in parenthesis indicate the pages on which the Selection and the Annotation, respectively, begin. Technical rhetorical terms (e.g., **anacoluthon**) are printed in bold face. Cited words and expressions are in italics (e.g., *incog*). An asterisk after a page number indicates a quotation.]